Ina Bornkessel-Schlesewsky, Andrej L. Malchukov, Marc D. Richards (Eds.)
Scales and Hierarchies

Trends in Linguistics
Studies and Monographs

Editor
Volker Gast

Editorial Board
Walter Bisang
Jan Terje Faarlund
Hans Henrich Hock
Natalia Levshina
Heiko Narrog
Matthias Schlesewsky
Amir Zeldes
Niina Ning Zhang

Editor responsible for this volume
Volker Gast
Heiko Narrog

Volume 277

Scales and Hierarchies

―

A Cross-Disciplinary Perspective

Edited by
Ina Bornkessel-Schlesewsky
Andrej L. Malchukov
Marc D. Richards

ISBN 978-3-11-055541-7
e-ISBN (PDF) 978-3-11-034413-4
e-ISBN (EPUB) 978-3-11-039500-6
ISSN 1861-4302

Library of Congress Cataloging-in-Publication Data
A CIP catalog record for this book has been applied for at the Library of Congress.

Bibliographic information published by the Deutsche Nationalbibliothek
The Deutsche Nationalbibliothek lists this publication in the Deutsche Nationalbibliografie; detailed bibliographic data are available on the Internet at http://dnb.dnb.de.

© 2017 Walter de Gruyter GmbH, Berlin/Munich/Boston
This volume is text- and page-identical with the hardback published in 2015.
Typesetting: RoyalStandard, Hong Kong
Printing and binding: CPI books GmbH, Leck
♾ Printed on acid-free paper
Printed in Germany

www.degruyter.com

Table of contents

Ina Bornkessel-Schlesewsky, Andrej L. Malchukov and Marc D. Richards
1 Introduction — 1

Balthasar Bickel, Alena Witzlack-Makarevich & Taras Zakharko
2 Typological evidence against universal effects of referential scales on case alignment — 7

Martin Haspelmath
3 Descriptive scales versus comparative scales — 45

Martin Cysouw
4 Generalizing Scales — 59

Stefan Keine and Gereon Müller
5 Differential Argument Encoding by Impoverishment — 75

Jochen Trommer
6 Ø-Agreement in Turkana — 131

Marc D. Richards
7 Defective Agree, Case Alternations, and the Prominence of Person — 173

Petr Biskup and Gerhild Zybatow
8 Prefixes, Scales and Grammatical Theory — 197

Jakob Hamann
9 Argument Encoding in Direction Systems and Specificity-Driven Agree — 227

Andrej L. Malchukov
10 Towards a typology of split ergativity: A TAM-hierarchy for alignment splits — 275

Corinna Handschuh
11 Split Marked-S Case Systems — 297

Ina Bornkessel-Schlesewsky and Matthias Schlesewsky
12 Scales in real-time language comprehension: A review — 321

Subject index — 353

Ina Bornkessel-Schlesewsky, Andrej L. Malchukov, and Marc D. Richards[1]

1 Introduction

Since the discovery of scales (or hierarchies) for grammatical categories in the 1970s, many cross-linguistic generalizations have been noted in the functional-typological literature, especially in such domains as person/number marking, argument encoding by case or agreement (Silverstein 1976, Dixon 1979), diatheses and direction marking (Comrie 1981, DeLancey 1981), as well as in other domains (Keenan & Comrie's (1977) Accessibility Hierarchy for relativization being a celebrated example). The formulation of scales as "implicational hierarchies" has enabled researchers in this area to formulate some of the most robust generalizations about language. More recently, the concept of scales has received considerable attention in grammatical theory as well. In particular, the work of Aissen (1999, 2003), framed within Optimality Theory (OT), has triggered a surge of research occupied with the question of how the effects of scales are related to general principles of morphosyntactic theory. Furthermore, recent work in psycholinguistic and neurolinguistic theorizing has argued for cross-linguistic principles of language processing which employ the notion of a scale. The idea is that scales may help to guide incremental argument interpretation by serving to shape the interpretive relations that are established between different arguments online (Bornkessel & Schlesewsky 2006).

As successful as this general approach has been, a number of empirical and theoretical issues surrounding the notion of scale or hierarchy remain unresolved and, indeed, the subject of some controversy. In particular, we might identify the following three groups of questions as they pertain to different areas of linguistic research:

(i) Typological/functional: How well-established is the cross-linguistic evidence for implicational scales? Various potential counter-examples have been discussed in the recent literature (see Filimonova 2005). This question becomes especially pressing as the availability of large databases (WALS, TDS) and recent comprehensive fieldwork studies promise a better understanding of the relevant empirical generalizations. At the same time, we might ask whether there is evidence for new scales that have so far gone unnoticed. And how are scales

---

[1] Editors listed in alphabetical order. The research reported and collected in this volume was funded by the *Deutsche Forschungsgemeinschaft* and carried out as part the Leipzig-based research group (*Forschergruppe* 742), *Grammar and Processing of Verbal Arguments*, of which the majority of the authors of the subsequent chapters were members. The opening five paragraphs of this introduction were written collaboratively by the members of this research group.

best represented? Are they, for example, organized in a meta-hierarchy with respect to each other?

(ii) Formal/theoretical: What is the status of scales in grammatical theory? Are they part of grammar itself (Noyer 1992, Aissen 1999, 2003), or are they epiphenomenal? If the latter, are they epiphenomena of (a) functionality or frequency distributions in language use (Bresnan, Dingare & Manning 2001, Newmeyer 2002, Hawkins 2004, Haspelmath 2008), or (b) other grammatical mechanisms such as feature geometries and/or syntactic movement (Harley & Ritter 2002, Bejar 2003)? In terms of phrase structure, we might seek to determine the relation between feature hierarchies and the order of functional projections in the syntax (Cinque 1999, Starke 2001).

(iii) Psycholinguistic/neurolinguistic: What role do scales play in the language processing architecture? Should they be afforded independent status or can they be viewed as epiphenomena of other information types (e.g. frequency of occurrence)? How can scales be modeled in a neurobiologically plausible manner?

This edited volume raises and addresses these questions in eleven papers by leading international scholars from a variety of disciplinary perspectives, shedding new light on the nature of referential hierarchies, their empirical foundation and validity, and the ways in which they can be incorporated into theoretical accounts of a wide range of linguistic phenomena. In so doing, the volume represents the state of the art in the linguistic study of referential scales.

On the methodological side, this volume brings together functional-typological, descriptive, quantitative/computational, formal and psycholinguistic approaches to the discussion of these important topics. From a theoretical point of view, these various approaches to the topic of scales reflect a wide range of opinions and perspectives on the material, particularly on the questions of how scales should be represented and at what level (if at all) they provide useful linguistic generalizations. Crucially, these different perspectives are presented with a coherent empirical focus. Firstly, the volume is inherently cross-linguistic in orientation, independently of the perspective adopted in the individual contributions (grammatical theory, typology, computational linguistics, processing). While the scale of the cross-linguistic comparison ranges from case studies in a small number of related languages (e.g. Russian versus Czech in the chapter by **Biskup** and **Zybatow**) to large-scale typological studies in areally stratified samples (over 460 languages in the contribution by **Bickel**, **Witzlack-Makarevich** and **Zakharko**), the contributions share a commonality of purpose in all aiming to provide cross-linguistically tenable solutions to the research questions raised above. Secondly, cross-fertilization among the individual contributions is furthered by the focus on various aspects of differential argument encoding as a key unifying phenomenon.

The volume opens with three articles that cast various degrees of caution and doubt on the ways in which scales are usually employed. **Balthasar Bickel**, **Alena Witzlack-Makarevich** and **Taras Zakharko**'s contribution reviews the typological evidence to question the empirical validity of Silverstein-type generalizations as universal scales determining the distribution of case-marking patterns. Rather, they argue that areal and historical factors may provide a better explanation for the attested systems. **Martin Haspelmath** then makes the case for distinguishing between at least two notions of scales, which, in turn, are claimed to be derivative from the distinction between descriptive (language-particular) categories, and comparative (cross-linguistic) concepts. The author argues that once this distinction is acknowledged, it can also resolve the problem of exceptions to universal scales, where particular reference is made to person-animacy scales. A computational perspective on scale representation is provided by **Michael Cysouw**, who argues that the concept of scale can be generalized to cover any restriction on form-function mapping and can be conceived, in its most general form, as a dissimilarity matrix. This naturally leads to the conclusion that one-dimensional scales have to be discarded in favor of multidimensional ones, which lend themselves to analysis by computational techniques designed for capturing similarities, such as multidimensional scaling. He illustrates this approach by way of inchoative-causative alternations, where different lexical items show different encoding similarities across languages.

The following five chapters (Chapters 5–9) focus on the theoretical status of scales from a variety of formal perspectives. **Stefan Keine** and **Gereon Müller** take issue with certain aspects of Aissen's influential optimality-theoretic account of differential case-marking, in particular its limitation to zero-nonzero alternations. They suggest a revision based on *impoverishment*, that is, the postsyntactic deletion of morphosyntactic features. Couched within the framework of Distributed Morphology, their paper thus provides a morphological solution to the effects of the animacy hierarchy on case marking. Also adopting a morphological perspective on differential argument encoding, **Jochen Trommer** then addresses a non-canonical case of direct-inverse marking ("Quirky Inverse Marking") in the agreement system of Turkana, an eastern Nilotic language, and proposes a more restrictive formalism for morphological spellout than those based on harmonic alignment (cf. Aissen 1999, 2003). In contrast to Keine and Müller's account, Trommer bases his proposal on the assumption that zero realization is the only kind of morphological hierarchy effect.

The remaining three chapters adopting a formal perspective investigate the nature of scales from a more syntactic point of view. As noted by Carnie (2005), animacy hierarchy effects are manifested not only morphologically (as in differential case-marking) but also in word-order phenomena (such as the scrambling of definite noun phrases). This point is taken up in **Marc Richards**'s chapter, which proposes a general analysis of case alternations and other phenomena associated with nominal hierarchies of the Silverstein type. The analysis is based on the agreement system of Chomsky 2000, which allows for defective probes (functional heads which are unspecified for person features) to assign a different case from non-defective probes. This not only provides a basis for capturing the core properties of the Person-Case Constraint and differential case-marking in a simple way, but also readily extends to scrambling phenomena, which frequently target nominals which rank high on the animacy/definiteness scale.

Petr Biskup and **Gerhild Zybatow** investigate the status of prominence scales in grammatical theory by looking at the interaction of theta-role and case scales in the domain of prefixation in Russian and Czech, proposing a structural, c-command-based approach to these scales that proceeds from independent minimalist principles and operations (including Full Interpretation and Agree). They argue for a kind of 'harmonic alignment' in the mapping between scales, such that unmarked mappings are those which involve no crossing associations and respect c-command relations; certain marked associations ("reciprocal crossings") can then be repaired by special morphological marking, if available. The relation between scales and primitive minimalist operations also plays a crucial role in the chapter by **Jakob Hamann**. He assumes a specificity-driven version of the dependency-forming operation Agree such that it applies to the goal with the highest number of features matching the probe. From this perspective, he argues that scale effects in grammar emerge as an epiphenomenon of specificity effects. Furthermore, by introducing the notion of specificity into the syntactic domain, his contribution provides a possible common denominator between the syntactic and morphological approaches to scale effects in the current volume.

Chapters 10 and 11 examine scales from a functional-typological perspective, using test cases from the domain of case-marking systems as a basis for investigating the mechanisms underlying scale effects. **Andrej Malchukov** addresses the typology of alignment splits, with a special focus on tense/aspect/mood (TAM)-based split ergativity. Building on earlier typological work, he proposes a comprehensive TAM-hierarchy for alignment splits which goes beyond the familiar perfectivity-based splits. He further shows how TAM-based splits can be reconstructed within Optimality Theory, a framework which has proven successful in the modeling of animacy-based splits. **Corinna Handschuh** then compares two possible explanations of Silverstein's generalization (her 'overt marking hypothesis' and 'alignment hypothesis') using typologically interesting marked nominative systems as a test case.

In the final chapter of the volume, **Bornkessel-Schlesewsky** and **Schlesewsky** tackle the phenomenon of scales from a psycholinguistic and neurolinguistic perspective. They review effects of scales on language comprehension, from Bever's early proposal of comprehension heuristics involving cues such as animacy (Bever 1970) and the cross-linguistic behavioral studies undertaken as part of Bates and McWhinney's Competition Model (e.g. MacWhinney and Bates 1989) to recent neurolinguistic investigations in typologically different languages. On the basis of these findings, they argue that (at least certain) scales can be derived from underlying cognitive principles and that these can be modeled in a neurobiologically and computationally plausible way in terms of attractor categories. Interestingly, their approach makes the opposite prediction to Cysouw's, namely that scales are inherently binary (i.e. falling into the attractor category or not), and that apparent multidimensionality within a single scale results from quantitative rather than qualitative differences.

By bringing together these different empirical and theoretical perspectives on scales, this volume hopefully achieves its aim of advancing our understanding of the role of scales and hierarchies across the linguistic sciences. Controversies regarding the status and representation or operationalization of scales are tackled head-on, thus resulting in a state-of-the-art overview with regard to the status of scales in language.

References

Aissen, Judith. 1999. Markedness and subject choice in Optimality Theory. *Natural Language and Linguistic Theory* 17: 673–711.
Aissen, Judith. 2003. Differential object marking: Iconicity vs. economy. *Natural Language and Linguistic Theory* 21: 435–483.
Bejar, Susana. 2003. Phi-Syntax: A Theory of Agreement. PhD thesis, University of Toronto.
Bever, Thomas G. 1970. The cognitive basis for linguistic structures. In J. R. Hayes (ed.) *Cognition and the development of language*, 279–362. New York: Wiley.
Bornkessel, Ina & Matthias Schlesewsky. 2006. The Extended Argument Dependency Model: A neurocognitive approach to sentence comprehension across languages. *Psychological Review* 113. 787–821.
Bresnan, Joan, Shipra Dingare & Christopher Manning. 2001. Soft Constraints Mirror Hard Constraints: Voice and Person in English and Lummi. In: *Proceedings of the LFG 01 Conference*, University of Hong Kong.
Carnie, Andrew. 2005. Some remarks on markedness hierarchies: A reply to Aissen 1999 and 2003. *Coyote Working Papers in Linguistics* 14.

Chomsky, Noam. 2000. Minimalist Inquiries: the Framework. In *Step by step*, R. Martin, D. Michaels, and J. Uriagereka (eds), 89–156. Cambridge, MA: MIT Press.
Cinque, Guglielmo. 1999. *Adverbs and Functional Heads*, Oxford University Press, Oxford.
Comrie, Bernard. 1981. *Language Universals and Linguistic Typology*. Blackwell, Oxford.
DeLancey, Scott. 1981. An interpretation of split ergativity and related patterns. *Language* 51, 626–657.
Dixon, R.M.W. 1979. Ergativity, *Language* 55: 59–138.
Filimonova, Elena. 2005. The noun phrase hierarchy and relational marking: problems and counterevidence, *Linguistic Typology* 9, 77–113.
Harley, H. and Ritter, E. 2002. A feature-geometric analysis of person and number. *Language* 78, 482–526.
Haspelmath, Martin. 2008. Frequency vs. Iconicity in Explaining Grammatical Asymmetries. *Cognitive Linguistics* 19.1.
Hawkins, John A. 2004. *Efficiency and Complexity in Grammars*. Oxford: Oxford University Press.
Keenan, Edward L. and Bernard Comrie. 1977. Noun Phrase Accessibility and Universal Grammar. *Linguistic Inquiry* 8: 63–99.
MacWhinney, Brian and Elizabeth Bates (eds.). 1989. *The crosslinguistic study of sentence processing*. New York: Cambridge University Press.
Newmeyer, Frederick. 2002. Optimality and Functionality: A Critique of Functionally-Based Optimality Theoretic Syntax, *Natural Language and Linguistic Theory*, 43–80.
Noyer, Rolf. 1992. Features, Positions and Affixes in Autonomous Morphological Structure. PhD thesis, MIT.
Silverstein, Michael. 1976. Hierarchy of Features and Ergativity. In: R. Dixon (ed.) *Grammatical Categories in Australian Languages*. Australian Institute of Aboriginal Studies, Canberra, pp. 112–171.
Starke, Michal. 2001. Move Dissolves into Merge: a Theory of Locality. PhD thesis, University of Geneva.

Balthasar Bickel, Alena Witzlack-Makarevich, and Taras Zakharko

2 Typological evidence against universal effects of referential scales on case alignment*

If a language develops differential subject or differential object marking by case or adpositions, this is widely hypothesized to result from a universal effect of referential scales. The effect can be understood as a universal correlation between the odds of overt case marking and scale ranks (a negative correlation for subjects, a positive one for objects), or as an implicational universal proposing that, if a language has a split in case marking, this split fits a universal scale. We test both claims with various versions of scale definitions by statistically estimating diachronic biases towards correlations or scale-fitting in an areally stratified sample of over 460 case systems worldwide. For most scales tested, results suggest evidence against universal preferences towards universal scale effects under either a correlational or an implicational model. For binary part-of-speech and information-structure distinction and object marking, the evidence for universal effects is inconclusive. What we do find, by contrast, is highly significant area effects: case-marking splits tend to have developed and spread in Eurasia and the New-Guinea/Australia ('Sahul') macro-areas. This suggests that any replication of scale effects across language families is a side-effect of areal diffusion rather than of universal principles in grammar or cognition.

1 Introduction

Typological generalizations are often first based on small-scale surveys or contrastive analyses of a few languages, and it is typically only later, after much additional empirical groundwork, that they can be evaluated through rigorous

---

* This research was supported by Grant No. BI 799/3-1 from the *Deutsche Forschungsgemeinschaft*. Bickel designed the study and wrote the paper, Bickel and Zakharko performed the statistical analyses, and Witzlack-Makarevich did most of the data analysis. All computations were done in R (R Development Core Team 2012), with the added packages vcd (Meyer et al. 2006), MASS (Venables & Ripley 2002), and glmperm (Werft & Potter 2010). We thank an anonymous reviewer for helpful comments.

quantitative analysis. Many initial generalizations have been corroborated in this way over time (as is the case, for example, with the bulk of Greenberg's word order correlations: Dryer 1992, Cysouw 2011, Bickel 2011b), but other initial generalizations have turned out to be spurious (as is the case, for example, with claims about a principled distinction between 'agglutinating' vs. 'fusional' morphologies: Haspelmath 2009). Some initial generalizations, however, have never been subject to systematic and large-scale quantitative analysis. One such generalization is the idea that, universally, some kind of referential scale governs the kinds of case or adposition markings we find, such that, for example, first and second person pronouns stand a higher chance for accusative as opposed to ergative case marking.[1]

The idea was developed in the late 70s (Silverstein 1976, Moravcsik 1978, Comrie 1981, DeLancey 1981, among others) and despite the lack of large-scale empirical tests, it is now widely taken to be an established finding. Aissen (1999), for example, counts the idea "among the most robust generalizations in syntactic markedness" and accepts a version of the idea as reflecting an inviolable component of "universal grammar" (also cf. Kiparsky 2008).

In this paper we subject the idea of scale effects on case marking to empirical testing against data from a large typological database with world-wide coverage. In order to do so, we first discuss various versions of the idea and reformulate them as precise and testable hypotheses (Section 2). In Section 3 we introduce a method for testing these hypotheses as typological claims on how languages are expected to develop over time and we explain our data coding procedure. The results of our tests are presented in Section 4. Section 5 discusses the findings and the concluding section (Section 6) compares the findings to earlier results and suggests directions for future research.

2 Claims and hypotheses

The idea of scale effects on case alignment does not easily translate into precise and testable hypotheses because there are many ways in which the idea can be spelled out – specifically, the hypotheses can be understood as absolute universals ('laws of grammar') or as probabilistic trends ('statistical universals'); as

---

[1] In the following we use the term 'case' as a cover term for any dependent-marking of argument roles, including adpositional marking and generalizing across the kind of morphology and phonology involved. By the same token we abstract away from the distribution of case exponents inside an NP: an NP counts as case-marked if there is some nonzero case exponence somewhere in the NP – even if this is limited to determiners, as is often the case for example in German.

affecting overt case exponence (Comrie 1981) or as affecting alignment in any kind of grammatical relation (Silverstein 1976); as predicting the type of entire alignment or marking systems or as predicting correlations of alignment or marking systems with ranks on the scale. In the following we discuss these different ways of spelling out the basic idea.

2.1 Universals, variation, and exceptions

When hypothesized universals are shown to have exceptions, there are two possible responses: one can try and 'explain away' the exceptions and thereby reduce the variation (i.e. choose a 'reductionist' approach); the hypothesized universal is then 'absolute', inviolable. Alternatively, one can measure the variation and try to explain the resulting distribution (i.e. choose a 'variationist' approach); the universal is then 'statistical' and violable to a degree that can be measured.

An example for a 'reductionist' approach is Kiparsky's (2008) tentative analysis of Arrernte: in Arrernte (e.g. Mparntwe Arrernte: Wilkins 1989), the first person singular pronoun and nouns have ergative case marking, all other pronouns show accusative alignment. Under a reductionist analysis, this unexpected distribution can be accounted for by claiming that despite its appearance, the first person pronoun is a noun in this language, i.e. that it belongs to the same part of speech as lexical nouns, while other pronouns constitute a part of speech of their own. The challenge for such an approach is of course to find independent evidence for the analysis. So far, we are not aware of any such evidence although we cannot obviously exclude the possibility of finding evidence in the future. The intrinsic risk of the reductionist approach is non-testability because there is always a non-zero chance of discovering further apparent counterexamples of the Arrernte kind, and for these, we cannot anticipate whether they can be explained away.

Under a 'variationist' approach, the Arrernte distribution counts as a real exception, and the question then is how many such exceptions there are, and whether they are less frequent than distributions that match the expectations. In this paper, we follow this variationist approach exclusively. The basic hypothesis then is that there are universal principles of referential scale effects that 'push' the development of case distributions in certain ways. As a result, case distributions that fit the principles are predicted to be more common than others. The null hypothesis against which this prediction can be statistically tested, is that case distributions are not affected by universal principles of referential scale effects, but instead follow from what looks like random diachronic fluctuation, i.e. current case distributions follow from whatever diachronies they went through. For example, if an ergative arose from an instrumental, we expect it to be limited to inanimates. This will then mimic a referential scale effect, but under the null hypothesis, it will be a mere epiphenomenon (cf. Garrett 1990). Indeed, under the null hypothesis, it will just be as likely that, for example, an ergative case system decays in lexical nouns but survives in pronouns (cf. Filimonova 2005). This will then lead to systems that do not mimic any referential scale effect and instead look like violations of such effects.

2.2 Marking, markedness, and alignment

Ever since its original formulations, the idea of scale effects has had two possible interpretations: under one interpretation (associated with Comrie 1981), referential scales affect the distribution of overt case exponence: low-ranking A arguments and high-ranking P arguments are predicted to carry overt case markers ('ergative' and 'accusative', respectively) while high-ranking A and low-ranking P arguments are predicted to carry no overt case markers (zero forms).[2] This can be extended to predictions on the phonological amount of case exponence, as proposed by Keine & Müller (2015).

An alternative interpretation (associated with Silverstein 1976), makes predictions not about overt marking patterns but about abstract markedness relations: under this interpretation, low-ranking A arguments and high-ranking P arguments are predicted to be mapped into marked grammatical relations, while high-ranking A and low-ranking P arguments are predicted to be mapped into unmarked grammatical relations. The terms 'marked' and 'unmarked' are used in a classical structuralist sense in this approach and describe which grammatical relation is structurally more constrained or specified than the other. There are many technical ways in which the relevant constraints and specifications can be spelled out, but the one that is most often associated with Silverstein's original proposal has to do with the alignment of grammatical relations, i.e. the way arguments are mapped into sets. Given this, the relevant specifications are defined by alignment sets: the sets {S,P}, {S,A} and {S,A,P} are all less specific than the sets {A} and {P}. Therefore, we expect low-ranking A arguments and high-ranking P arguments to be associated with {A} and {P} relations, respectively, while high-ranking A and low-ranking P arguments are expected to be

---

[2] We use A and P as symbols for proto-agent and proto-patient arguments of bivalent verbs in the sense of Dowty (1991). S stands for the sole argument of monovalent predicates.

associated with the more general sets that also include S, i.e. {S,A,P} or {S,A} for high-ranking A arguments, and {S,A,P} or {S,P} for low-ranking P arguments.

Silverstein's interpretation makes predictions for any kind of alignment set, i.e. any kind of grammatical relation. This includes not only alignment sets defined by case marking but also alignment sets defined by agreement systems, conjunction reduction, or whatever syntactic structures select specific arguments to the exclusion of others. Comrie's interpretation, by contrast, is limited to case marking. Bickel (2008) and Bickel et al. (in press) demonstrate that the generalization beyond case marking has no empirical support: tested against worldwide databases on alignment splits in agreement systems, there is no trend for such systems to follow the predictions. For alignments in other syntactic structures, we lack sufficiently rich databases, but a preliminary survey reveals no systematic trend either. For diathesis in particular, Bickel & Gaenszle (2007) show that there is no systematic association of scale ranks with passivization as opposed to antipassivization: first person P arguments, for example, are required to be passivized in just as many languages as they are required to be antipassivized. For grammatical relations targeted by relative clause constructions, there are both languages where higher-ranking arguments are preferred and languages where lower-ranking arguments are preferred (Bickel 2011a).

With regard to case systems, Silverstein's and Comrie's versions make the same predictions to the extent that structurally unmarked relations tend to have less phonological exponence than structurally marked relations. Our database contains one single language that systematically deviates from this in having a morphologically marked {S,A} case, and shows at the same time an alignment split based on a referential scale: this is Middle Atlas Berber where the marked nominative (in the form of a 'construct state') is restricted to low-ranking S and A arguments. This fits Comrie's prediction that low-ranking A arguments receive morphologically overt marking. In return, it violates Silverstein's version of scale effects because low-ranking P arguments are mapped into a structurally marked grammatical relation: P is mapped into the {P} set, which is structurally marked relative to the less specific {S,A} set. However, this is one language and we cannot make any statistical inferences from this.[3]

---

[3] The Australian language Mangarayi (Merlan 1982) is one further case of a language with a split and a marked 'nominative' (ŋarla- in the feminine, ṇa- elsewhere) in opposition to a (slightly) less marked 'accusative' (ŋan- in the feminine, zero elsewhere), but in this language, the referential split affects S rather than A or P: low-ranking S arguments and all P arguments are in the 'accusative', high-ranking S arguments and all A arguments are in the 'nominative'. Comrie's hypothesis makes no prediction on this. In terms of alignment, the low-ranking arguments show {S,P} alignment, while high-ranking arguments display {S,A} alignment. This fits Silverstein's predictions.

Since there is no evidence for scale effects beyond case-marking and since for all but one relevant language, structural markedness correlates with morphological markedness, we focus on case marking and use structural markedness, i.e. alignment sets, as a proxy for morphological markedness.[4]

The only problematic case for this approach is presented by double-oblique alignment {A,P} vs. {S} that contrasts with ergative or accusative alignment. An example is Vafsi, a Northwestern Iranian language. In past tense clauses of this language, nominal A arguments are in what is called the oblique case; P arguments are also in the same oblique case if they rank high in discourse status, e.g. by being definite (1a). Lower-ranking (e.g. indefinite) P arguments, by contrast, are in the 'direct' case (1b), which also covers S arguments (1c):

(1) Vafsi (ISO639.3:vaf; Northwestern Iranian; Indo-European; Stilo 2004)
    a. *luás-i*   *kærg-é=s*   *b̯ǽ-værdæ.*
       fox-OBL   chicken-OBL.F=3s   PUNCT-took
       A   P
       'The fox took the chicken.'

    b. *in*   *luti-an*   *yey xær=esan*   *æ-rúttæ.*
       DEM   wise.guys-OBL.PL   one donkey.DIR=3p   DUR-sold
       A   P
       'These wise guys were selling a donkey.'

    c. *zení-e*   *há-nešesd-end.*
       woman-PL.DIR   PVB-sat-3p
       S
       'The women sat down.'

Such a system sets up a contrast between {A,P} for high-ranking P arguments and {S,P} for low-ranking P arguments. Since the two alignments contain the same number of specifications (two each), one could argue that they are equally marked. However, closer inspection of the morphological markedness and of what we know from the history of these languages (Haig 2008) suggests that {A,P}, i.e. the oblique forms, represents the structurally marked forms, while {S,P}, i.e. the direct forms, represent the unmarked forms. In addition, a case

---

[4] We do not choose the opposite route (using morphological exponence as a proxy for markedness) because determining the markedness of morphological exponence requires substantial additional research in morphophonology, which goes beyond the scope of our current project. Also, we submit that any progress here will have to look into degrees of overt exponence, along the lines suggested by Keine & Müller (2015).

that covers argument roles of both single-argument and two-argument predicates has a larger distribution, and is therefore unmarked in the classical sense of the term, than one that is limited to arguments of two-arguments predicates. As a general principle, then, we define the markedness of an alignment set in terms of whether or not the set contains an argument outside bivalent verbs, i.e. S. In the following we define markedness as follows, generalizing over all verb types:

(2) An alignment set α is marked relative to another alignment set β iff α contains argument roles from fewer numerical valence types than β, where the numerical valence types are monovalent, bivalent, and trivalent.

In the Vafsi example, this means that high-ranking P arguments are mapped into a marked alignment set (the {A,P} set), while low-ranking P arguments are mapped into an unmarked set (the {S,P} set), in line with Silverstein's predictions.

Under these assumptions, hypotheses of scale effects are specifically about marked vs. unmarked argument sets: we expect marked sets to associate preferentially with low-ranking A and high-ranking P arguments. If there is no difference in markedness, then all ranks on the scale show the same distribution, and there is no prediction. This is the case in the Vafsi past tense example with regard to NPs in A function: all nominal A arguments, regardless of their discourse status, are mapped into a marked alignment set, either {A} or {A,P}, and therefore always surface in the oblique case. By the same token, the hypotheses make no prediction on systems where arguments appear in different kinds of marked cases depending on their referential status – such as for example in Finnish, where some P arguments appear in the accusative while others appear in the partitive case. Since both cases define a marked alignment that contrasts P with {S,A}, there is no difference in markedness under the assumptions made in (2).

The predictions occasionally differ for A and P arguments, a difference enshrined in the traditional distinction between 'differential subject marking' and 'differential object marking'. Since in Vafsi all A arguments are marked, there is no prediction for A marking; for P arguments, by contrast, Vafsi is in line with the prediction that higher-ranking P arguments have a higher chance of being marked than lower-ranking P arguments. While in this case, there is a contrast between 'no prediction' and 'expected', some systems of alignment sets lead to conflicts in expectations. Khufi, another Iranian language, restricts the double-oblique system to a subset of pronouns (first and second person singular, third person) and contrasts this with neutral alignment in all other NPs. The following data illustrate this: demonstrative (third person) pronouns are in the oblique case in A (3a) and P (3b) but not in S (3c) function; other pronouns and lexical nouns are always in the direct case (cf. the P arguments in 3a and 3d, the A argument in 3b and 3d and the S argument in 3e):

(3) Khufi (ISO639.3:sgh; Southeastern Iranian; Indo-European; Sokolova 1959)

    a. *way*   *xūðm*   *wīnt.*
        DIST.SG.OBL   dream.DIR   see.PST
        A   P
        'He saw a dream.'

    b. *mā́š=am*   *way*   *na*   *talǽpt.*
        1PL.DIR=1PL.PST   DIST.SG.OBL   NEG   look.for.PST
        A   P
        'We did not look for him.'

    c. *yaw*   *yat*   *tar*   *dum*   *yīd.*
        DIST.SG.DIR   come.PST   to   MID.SG.OBL   bridge.DIR
        S
        'He came towards that bridge.'

    d. *Tarsakbóy*   *žær*   *zůxt.*
        Tarsakboy.DIR   stone.DIR   take.PST
        A   P
        'Tarsakboy took the stone.'

    e. *Tarsakbóy*   *xu*   *jŏ́y-ti*   *xāb*   *na*   *xůvd.*
        Tarsakboy.DIR   REFL   place=on   night   NEG   sleep.PST
        S
        'Tarsakboy did not sleep at his place that night.'

Such a distribution is expected for P arguments: only high-ranking (first and second singular and all third person pronouns) P arguments are mapped into the marked {A,P} set; low-ranking P arguments are mapped into the unmarked {S,A,P} set. But for A arguments, the distribution is unexpected because high-ranking A arguments are also mapped into the marked set {A,P} while low-ranking arguments are mapped into the unmarked {S,A,P} set.

There are many possibilities of how markedness sets distribute across referential scales. Table 1 illustrates some of those with data we have in our data base. In Table 1 we simply divide the scale into 'high', 'mid' and 'low', and spell out the concrete scales in the last column. Obviously, this begs the question of how referential scales are actually defined. We take this up in the following.

Table 1: A selection of observed distributions of case alignment sets across referential scales ('none' means 'no prediction', 'many' means 'predicted to be frequent', 'rare' means 'predicted to be rare or non-existent')

High	Mid	Low	Prediction for A	Prediction for P	Example	Relevant scale (segment) in example
{S,A}:{P}		{S,A,P}	none	many	Anamuxra (Ingram 2001)	N-anim > N-inanim
{S,A}:{P}	{S,P}:{A}		many	many	Dyirbal (Dixon 1972)	1/2 > 3/N
{S,A}:{P}	{S}:{A}:{P}	{S,P}:{A}	many	many	Djapu (Morphy 1983)	Pro > N-high-anim > other N
	{S,A,P}	{S,A}:{P}	none	rare	Middle Atlas Berber (Pencheon 1973)	1/2/3 > N
{S,P}:{A}	{S}:{A}:{P}	{S,P}:{A}	none	rare	Gumbaynggir (Eades 1979)	3 > N-kin > N-other
{A,P}:{S}		{S,A,P}	rare	many	Khufi past tense (Sokolova 1959)	1s/2s/3 > 1p/2p/N
{A,P}:{S}	{S,A,P}	{A,P}:{S}	rare	rare	Vafsi past tense (Stilo 2004)	1p/1s > 2p > 2s/3p
	{A,P}:{S}	{S,P}:{A}	none	many	Vafsi past tense (Stilo 2004)	N-high > N-low
{S}:{A}:{P}	{S,A}:{P}	{S}:{A}:{P}	rare	none	Talysh past tense (Schulze 2000)	1s > 2p/2s/3p > 3s
{S}:{A}:{P}		{S,P}:{A}	none	many	Nepali tense set I (Bickel 2011a)	anim/def > inanim/indef
{S}:{A}:{P}	{S,A}:{P}	{S}:{A}:{P}	many	many	Diyari (Austin 1981)	1s/2s > 1d/1p/2d/2p > 3

2.3 Defining referential scales

A referential scale is a scale defined by referential categories, covering inherent referential categories like 'animate', discourse-based referential categories like 'speaker' or 'proximative' and part of speech notions like 'pronoun'. Obviously, all these categories are ultimately language-specific and can only be identified by language-specific criteria (Haspelmath 2015). Yet, for many such categories, we can generalize over language-specific scales, because they show sufficient semantic overlap across languages. For example, it seems plausible that a category like 'first person singular' in one language is the same as the category 'first person singular' in another language. With categories like 'proximative' or 'topical', this is much less clear.

What is needed then is a list of category types that abstracts away from language-specific details and allows comparing language-specific referential categories, i.e. what is variously called 'typological types' (Bickel & Nichols 2002), 'values of typological features' (Haspelmath et al. 2005), or 'comparative concepts' (Haspelmath 2007, 2010). Notions like 'proximative', 'topical', 'definite' etc., for example, are probably best captured by a typological type like 'high discourse rank', which is defined in opposition to 'low discourse rank', with the understanding that 'discourse rank' is a probabilistic notion determined by a series of factors whose weights may differ from language to language.

Such type lists can be declared *a priori*, or they can be derived inductively by generalizing over all and only those language-specific categories that are encountered. Most lists that have been proposed in the literature are probably developed on the basis of a mix of *a priori* expectations and experience gained through typological survey work. Generally recognized types include notions like first, second, and third person; singular vs. dual vs. plural; pronoun vs. lexical noun; definite/topical vs. indefinite/nontopical; human vs. (nonhuman) animate vs. inanimate (e.g. Comrie 1981, Dixon 1994, Croft 1990). In our own database work we develop lists using the 'autotypologizing' method of Bickel & Nichols (2002): this method seeks to inductively abstract away from language-specific categories to exactly that degree that is needed to capture all language-specific distinctions encountered in a sample of language. In many cases this level of abstraction is fairly high, for example with notions like 'singular' or 'second person', which apply to a large number of languages, but in some cases, it is impossible to abstract away from an individual language. In our database, this can be illustrated with the arbitrary gender categories of German, which condition a case split, so that a distinct accusative case is limited to third person masculine pronouns and determiners and to first and second person pronouns.

Another type of split refers to discourse factors – a well-studied example of this is the factors determining object marking in English (Bresnan et al. 2007). While the factors are complex and include both language-specific and cross-linguistic categories, there is a general sense that the net effect of the factors is a broad distinction between higher vs. lower prominence in discourse, manifested variably as specific vs. nonspecific, definite vs. indefinite, topical vs. nontopical and similar such contrasts. We label this broad distinction by the term pair 'high' vs. 'low discourse rank', while noting that this glosses over substantial cross-linguistic variation (a point to which we will return in the Discussion section).

After surveying 435 languages with this method, we find the list of types in Table 2 to be at the right level of abstraction for capturing all distinctions ever made by case marking in at least one language. Language-specific categories which do not apply to more than one language have an arbitrary language ID number in their label, such as German (e.g. '3sgPro-masc87').

Given the list in Table 2, the question is how it maps into a scale. It has often been noted that the details of scales vary from language to language – e.g. some languages rank first person above second person while others rank second person above first person – but that there still are some basic principles – e.g. that all languages rank speech act participants above third persons. There are many proposals in the literature on what exactly these basic principles are, and in the following we explore an entire series of possible principles. In Section 4.2 we also compute a best-fitting scale empirically and explore this as well.

The hypothetical scales we test in the following are summarized in Table 3. For example, the 'SAP>3/N' scale predicts that speech act participants rank higher than all other referents, but that languages can vary in the mutual ordering of first and second person and that differences in number are irrelevant, while the 'SAP>3>N' in addition predicts differential ranking between pronouns and nouns. The 'Pro>N' scale reduces this even further. The scale 'Pro/N-high > N-low' makes the cut slightly differently, capturing mainly effects from animacy, definiteness, specificity and related notions. The table lists two possible ranking of numbers. The sg>nsg ranking is based on the assumption that singular is more indexible than nonsingular and therefore ranks higher: singular items can be better pointed out than multiple items, in the same way as speech act participants can be better pointed at than other referents (Bickel & Nichols 2007). The reversed ranking 'nsg>sg' is based on the assumption that singular is structurally – and often also morphologically – unmarked relative to non-singular, and therefore ranks lower (Croft 1990).

Table 2: Referential categories referenced by case splits in the languages surveyed

Label	Definition
Pro	Pronouns. This refers to free pronouns that head NPs; it does not refer to pronominal agreement markers.
1sgPro	1st person singular pronoun
1duPro	1st person dual pronoun
1exclPro	1st person exclusive pronoun
1inclPro	1st person inclusive pronoun
1plPro	1st person plural pronoun
2sgPro	2nd person singular pronoun
2duPro	2nd person dual pronoun
2plPro	2nd person plural pronoun
3sgPro	3rd person singular pronoun
3duPro	3rd person dual pronoun
3plPro	3rd person plural pronoun
3Pro-anim	pronoun referring to an animate
3Pro-inanim	pronoun referring to inanimates
3sgPro-hum	3rd person singular pronoun with human reference
3sgPro-non-hum	3rd person singular pronoun with non-human reference
Pro-high	pronoun with a higher discourse rank than 'Pro-low' (where rank is determined by discourse factors with language-specific weights)
Pro-low	pronoun with a lower discourse rank than 'Pro-high' (where rank is determined by discourse factors with language-specific weights)
3Pro-high	3rd person pronoun (no number distinction) with a higher discourse rank than '3Pro-low' (where rank is determined by discourse factors with language-specific weights)
3Pro-low	3rd person pronoun (no number distinction) with a lower discourse rank than '3Pro-high' (where rank is determined by discourse factors with language-specific weights)
3sgPro-high	3rd person singular pronoun with a higher discourse rank than '3sgPro-low' (where rank is determined by discourse factors with language-specific weights)
3sgPro-low	3rd person plural pronoun with a lower discourse rank than '3sgPro-high' (where rank is determined by discourse factors with language-specific weights)
3plPro-high	3rd person plural pronoun with a higher discourse rank than '3plPro-low' (where rank is determined by discourse factors with language-specific weights)
3plPro-low	3rd person plural pronoun with a lower discourse rank than '3plPro-high' (where rank is determined by discourse factors with language-specific weights)
3sgPro-fem87	German 3rd person feminine pronoun
3sgPro-masc87	German 3rd person masculine pronoun
3sgPro-neut87	German 3rd person neutral pronoun

Table 2: *(continued)*

Label	Definition
N	lexical noun, nominalized verb – whether possessed or non-possessed (all)
N-anim	animate noun
N-inanim	inanimate noun
N-hum	human noun
N-non-hum-sg	non-human noun in singular
N-non-hum-du	non-human noun in dual
N-non-hum-pl	non-human noun in plural
N-proper	proper noun
N-common	common noun
N-common-sg	common (non-proper) noun in singular
N-common-pl	common (non-proper) noun in plural
N-def	definite noun
N-indef	indefinite noun
N-high	noun with a higher discourse rank than 'N-low' (where rank is determined by discourse factors with language-specific weights)
N-low	noun with a lower discourse rank than 'N-high' (where rank is determined by discourse factors with language-specific weights)
N-high-anim	noun denoting a higher animate (humans and some animals)
N-low-anim	noun denoting a lower animate (some animals)
N-spec	noun with specific reference
N-non-spec	noun without specific reference
N-kin	kin terms
N-non-kin	any noun apart from kin terms
N-non-kin-sg	any singular noun apart from kin terms
N-non-kin-pl	any plural noun apart from kin terms
N-pers	personal name (proper nouns which are personal names, but not toponyms, etc.)
N-pers-female	female personal name
N-pers-male	male personal name
N-non-pers	non-personal noun (common nouns and proper nouns which are not personal names (e.g. toponyms))
N-sg	noun in singular
N-pl	noun in plural
N-pl-anim	animate noun in plural
N-pl-inanim	inanimate noun in plural
N-masc-sg87	German masculine singular noun (case on determiner)
N-fem-sg87	German feminine singular noun
N-neut-sg87	German neutral singular noun
N1-sg-anim340	Russian animate noun of the inflectional class 1 (e.g. *student*)
N1-sg-inanim340	Russian inanimate noun of the inflectional class 1 (e.g. *zavod*, *mesto*)
N2-sg340	Russian noun of the inflectional class 2 (e.g. *komnata*, *muzhchina*, *sestra*)
N3-sg340	Russian noun of the inflectional class 3 (e.g. *doch'*, *noch'*)

2.4 Two models of scale effects

There are two models of how one can conceive of the way in which scales can determine the distribution of alignment sets. In the model that is traditionally assumed, scales predict a specific distribution of differential argument marking in grammatical systems: each grammatical system with a split either fits or does not fit the prediction, or, formulated as an implicational universal, 'if a language has a split in the case alignment of arguments, this split follows a universal scale'. We call this the 'Type Model'. The alternative, but so far largely unexplored model, is the 'Rank Model': in this model, scales are conceived of as ordered factors of categories that determine the relative probabilities of specific alignment sets for each category. In other words: the odds for case marking on a given argument correlate with the rank of that argument on a universal scale. In the following we discuss these models in more detail.

Type Models assess whether a split system of alignment sets in a given language fits vs. does not fit the predicted scale. For this, we define an alignment set as the set of argument roles selected by a case marker under a given referential condition (e.g. the set {S,A} selected by a nominative case under the referential condition 'third person')[5] and a system of alignment sets as the set of alignment sets defined by the case paradigm in a given language.

The criterion for fit is made explicit in (4) and relies on the same definition of markedness as in (2) above and the scales as defined in Section 2.3 ('higher' means to the left in the scales in Table 3 and 'position' refers to the set of categories between 'greater than' symbols in Table 3):

(4) For any given language, a system $\aleph$ of alignment sets that shows one or more splits, fits a scale Ξ iff the categories mentioned in the definition of Ξ are part of the referential categories attested in $\aleph$, and
   a. for A arguments, no position on Ξ that contains a marked set containing A is ordered higher than a position that contains an unmarked set containing A.
   b. for P arguments, no position on Ξ that contains an unmarked set containing P is ordered higher than a position that contains a marked set containing P.
   A position Ξ_k contains a (un)marked set iff there exists a (un)marked alignment set that is defined for at least one category in Ξ_k.

---

[5] Formally: given a set of roles R = {S,A,P} and a set of referential conditions C = {$C_1, \ldots, C_n$}, a case **K** in a given language (e.g. nominative case in Nepali) can be represented as $\mathbf{K} \subseteq R \times C$. The alignment set α of **K** for a given referential condition C_i is then $\alpha_{(\mathbf{K},C_i)} = \{R_i \in R \mid (R_i, C_i) \in \mathbf{K}\}$.

Table 3: *A priori* defined scales

Labels	Definition
1 > 2 > 3 > N	1sgPro/1duPro/1plPro > 2sgPro/2duPro/2plPro > 3sgPro/3plPro/3duPro/3sgPro-hum/3sgPro-non-hum/3sgPro-high/3plPro-high/3sgPro-low/ 3plPro-low/Pro-kin/3sgPro-masc87/3sgPro-fem87/3sgPro-neut87 > N/N-hum/N-proper/N-anim/N-kin/N-def/N-indef/N-high-anim/N-low-anim/N-sg/N-pl/ N-spec/N-non-spec/N-inanim/N-non-kin/N-non-kin-sg/N-non-kin-pl/N-pers/N-non-hum-sg/ N-high/N-low/N-non-pers/N-common/N-non-hum-du/N-non-hum-pl/N-common-sg/ N-common-pl/N-pers-male/N-pers-female/N-masc-sg87/N-fem-sg87/N-neut-sg87/ N1-sg-inanim340/N1-sg-anim340/N2-sg340/N3-sg340/N-pl-anim/N-pl-inanim
SAP > 3/N	1sgPro/1duPro/1plPro/2sgPro/2duPro/2plPro > 3sgPro/3plPro/3duPro/3sgPro-hum/3sgPro-non-hum/N/N-hum/N-proper/N-anim/N-kin/ N-def/N-indef/N-high-anim/N-low-anim/N-sg/N-pl/N-spec/N-non-spec/N-inanim/N-non-kin/ N-non-kin-sg/N-non-kin-pl/N-pers/Pro-kin/N-non-hum-sg/N-high/N-low/N-non-pers/ N-common/N-non-hum- du/N-non-hum-pl/3sgPro-high/3plPro-high/3sgPro-low/3plPro-low/ 3sgPro-masc87/3sgPro-fem87/3sgPro-neut87/N-common-sg/N-common-pl/N-pers-male/ N-pers-female/N-masc-sg87/N-fem-sg87/N-neut-sg87/N1-sg-inanim340/N1-sg-anim340/ N2-sg340/N3-sg340/N-pl-anim/N-pl-inanim
SAP > 3 > N	2sgPro/1plPro/1sgPro/2plPro/1duPro/2duPro > 3sgPro/3plPro/Pro-kin/3duPro/3sgPro-hum/3sgPro-non-hum/3sgPro-high/3plPro-high/ 3sgPro-low/3plPro-low/3sgPro-masc87/3sgPro-fem87/3sgPro-neut87 > N/N-hum/N-proper/N-anim/N-kin/N-def/N-indef/N-high-anim/N-low-anim/N-sg/N-pl/ N-spec/N-non-spec/N-inanim/N-non-kin/N-non-kin-sg/N-non-kin-pl/N-pers/N-non-hum-sg/ N-high/N-low/N-non-pers/N-common/N-non-hum-du/N-non-hum-pl/N-common-sg/ N-common-pl/N-pers-male/N-pers-female/N-masc-sg87/N-fem-sg87/N-neut-sg87/ N1-sg-inanim340/N1-sg-anim340/N2-sg340/N3-sg340/N-pl-anim/N-pl-inanim
SAP > 3 > N-high > N-low	1sgPro/1duPro/1plPro/2sgPro/2duPro/2plPro > 3sgPro/3plPro/3duPro/3sgPro-hum/3sgPro-non-hum/3sgPro-high/3plPro-high/3sgPro-low/ 3plPro-low/Pro-kin/3plPro-low/3sgPro-masc87/3sgPro-fem87/3sgPro-neut87 > N-hum/N-proper/N-anim/N-kin/N-def/N-high-anim/N-spec/N-pers/N-high/N-pers-male/ N-pers-female/N1-sg-anim340/N-pl-anim > N-indef/N-low-anim/N-non-spec/N-inanim/N-non-kin/N-non-kin-sg/N-non-kin-pl/ N-non-hum-sg/N-non-hum-du/N-non-hum-pl/N-low/N-non-pers/N-common/N-common-sg/ N-common-pl/N1-sg-inanim340/N-pl-inanim
Pro > N	Pro/1sgPro/1duPro/1plPro/2sgPro/2duPro/2plPro/3sgPro/3plPro/3duPro/3sgPro-hum/ 3sgPro-non- hum/3sgPro-high/3plPro-high/3sgPro-low/3plPro-low/Pro-kin/3sgPro-masc87/ 3sgPro-fem87/3sgPro-neut87/Pro-high/Pro-low > N/N-hum/N-proper/N-anim/N-kin/N-def/N-indef/N-high-anim/N-low-anim/N-sg/N-pl/ N-spec/N-non-spec/N-inanim/N-non-kin/N-non-kin-sg/N-non-kin-pl/N-pers/N-non-hum-sg/ N-high/N-low/N-non-pers/N-common/N-non-hum-du/N-non-hum-pl/N-common-sg/ N-common-pl/N-pers-male/N-pers-female/N-masc-sg87/N-fem-sg87/N-neut-sg87/ N1-sg-inanim340/N1-sg-anim340/N2-sg340/N3-sg340/N-pl-anim/N-pl-inanim

Table 3: *(continued)*

Labels	Definition
Pro/ N-high > N-low	Pro/1sgPro/1duPro/1plPro/2sgPro/2duPro/2plPro/3sgPro/3plPro/3duPro/3sgPro-hum/ 3sgPro-non-hum/3sgPro-high/3plPro-high/3sgPro-masc87/3sgPro-fem87/3sgPro-neut87/ Pro-high/Pro-low/Pro-kin/N-hum/N-proper/N-anim/N-kin/N-def/N-high-anim/N-spec/ N-pers/N-high/N-pers-male/N-pers-female/N1-sg-anim340/N-pl-anim > N-indef/N-low-anim/N-non-spec/N-inanim/N-non-kin/N-non-kin-sg/N-non-kin-pl/ N-non-kin-sg/N-non-kin-pl/N-non-hum-sg/N-non-hum-du/N-non-hum-pl/N-low/N-non-pers/ N-common/3sgPro-low/3plPro-low/N-common-sg/N-common-pl/N-pl-inanim/ N1-sg-inanim340
nsg > sg	1duPro/2duPro/3duPro/1plPro/N-pl/2plPro/3plPro/3plPro-high/3plPro-low/N-non-hum-du/ N-non-hum-pl/N-common-pl/N-pl-anim/N-pl-inanim/N-non-kin-pl > N-sg/2sgPro/3sgPro/1sgPro/N-non-hum-sg/3sgPro-hum/3sgPro-non-hum/3sgPro-high/ 3sgPro-low/3sgPro-masc87/3sgPro-fem87/3sgPro-neut87/N-common-sg/N-masc-sg87/ N-fem-sg87/N-neut-sg87/N1-sg-inanim340/N1-sg-anim340/N2-sg340/N3-sg340/ N-non-kin-sg
sg > nsg	N-sg/2sgPro/3sgPro/1sgPro/N-non-hum-sg/3sgPro-hum/3sgPro-non-hum/3sgPro-high/ 3sgPro-low/N-non-hum-du/N-non-hum-pl/3sgPro-masc87/3sgPro-fem87/3sgPro-neut87/ N-common-sg/N-masc-sg87/N-fem-sg87/N-neut-sg87/N1-sg-inanim340/N1-sg-anim340/ N2-sg340/N3-sg340 > 1duPro/2duPro/3duPro/1plPro/N-pl/2plPro/3plPro/3plPro-high/3plPro-low/N-common-pl/ N-pl-anim/N-pl-inanim

Obviously, if a language does not reference any of the category types defined by a universal scale, e.g. if a language does not mark number as defined by the sg > nsg scale, the fit cannot be evaluated. In general, a language can be evaluated with regard to a scale Ξ only if each position of Ξ (as defined in Table 3), has a non-empty intersection with the category types referenced by the language.

Some of the possibilities defined by (4) can be illustrated by the patterns in Table 1 above. For example, Anamuxra case marking fits the N-anim > N-inanim scale for P arguments, but there is no prediction for the case marking of A arguments. Dyirbal fits the 1/2 > 3/N scale for both arguments. The past tense systems of Khufi, Vafsi or Talysh do not fit the respective scales in Table 1 with regard to the A argument, whereas Middle Atlas Berber, Gumbaynggir and the Vafsi past tense system do not fit with regard to the P argument. However, the scales in Table 1 are tailored to each language. The hypothesis that we aim to test is that there exists one or more universal scale(s) on which all systems fit, and the definition of fits in (4) targets these universal scales. For example, differential A marking in Diyari fits a number-related scale ranking nonsingular above singular referents. It also fits a SAP > 3 scale insofar as unmarked sets only occur among speech-act participants, and so there is no case in which a marked set would ever outrank an unmarked set. But Diyari does not fit a person scale ranking first above second person because there are cases where a marked set (first person singular) outranks an unmarked set (second person plural). One could of course adjust the definition of the scale and condition – but then the scale is no longer universal.

The Rank Model is a standard logistic regression model: a scale is an ordered factor that is hypothesized to affect the probabilities of marked alignment sets. Specifically, the hypotheses to be tested are, for a given scale Ξ:

(5) a. For A: $\log\left(\dfrac{\pi(\text{marked})}{\pi(\text{unmarked})}\right) = \alpha - \beta\Xi$

b. For P: $\log\left(\dfrac{\pi(\text{marked})}{\pi(\text{unmarked})}\right) = \alpha + \beta\Xi$

That is, we hypothesize for A arguments, that the odds for marked alignment sets correlate negatively and significantly with Ξ, and for P arguments, that the odds for marked alignment sets correlates positively and significantly with Ξ.[6] This can be illustrated by the alignment systems in the Khufi participle-based tense (cf. (3) above): the difference between singular and plural speech act participants enters the analysis by different rank codings: for the sg > nsg scale, all singular pronouns are assigned rank 1, all dual and plural pronouns rank 2. The fact that all third person pronouns are (structurally) marked regardless of number is registered by the fact that they are all coded as having marked P arguments. For the regression model, speech act participants will increase the correlation between rank and markedness because only rank 1 is associated with marked P arguments; by contrast, third person P arguments will lower the correlation because they are marked on both rank 1 (singular) and rank 2 (non-singular). If a language does not reference the categories of the relevant scale (e.g. makes no number distinction) or does not reference any category of the scale (because it has no split), it is irrelevant for the model.

The chief difference between the Type and the Rank Model is that the Rank Model is much less sensitive to individual exceptions. A scale may be a significant predictor overall even if, say, a specific pronoun, does not match the prediction. What counts is the overall trend. Under the Type Model, every single exception counts as evidence against a scale effect.

---

6 In the regression model we internally code 1 as the top (e.g. first person) and 1 + n (e.g. third person) as lower on the scale, in order to match standard (Western) linguistic parlance.

3 Testing universal effects: methods and data coding

3.1 Methods

As suggested by the preceding, Type Models can be evaluated by testing frequencies of fits against non-fits and Rank Models by logistic regression tests. However, simply applying such tests to raw data does not do justice to the hypothesis: all synchronic observations about language are the result of history, and therefore, any evaluation needs to target trends in diachrony rather than current distributions. If a scale is a genuine universal, we expect that each case system has a higher probability of developing in such a way as to conform to the scale than to contradict the scale. If the proto-language already fit the scale, we expect daughter languages, and therefore the whole family descending from the proto-language, to maintain the fit. If the proto-language did not fit the scale, we expect daughter languages to change their case systems so that they fit better. In either case, families will tend to be biased towards fitting the scale (i.e. for all families, there will be more members that fit than members that do not fit). By contrast, if the hypothesis of universal scale effects is wrong, we expect case systems to develop without regard to scales, subject to no or other principles. For example, languages could preserve case systems in pronouns and not in nouns (as they often do), regardless of whether this matches scales. As a result, families will be biased for or against a given scale at random.

In addition, it is well known (and has been emphasized since at least Dryer 1989) that typological distributions are not only affected by possible structural or cognitive principles – here, scales –, but also by areal diffusion resulting from language contact. In other words, the chances of finding a specific alignment set on a specific pronoun in a specific language may just as well be determined by the fact that the case distribution assimilated to neighboring languages, e.g. by calquing patterns of information structure. Therefore, any statistical test applied to typological data needs to control for the confounding factors of linguistic areas.

In the following we adopt Bickel's (2011b, 2013) Family Bias method of testing diachronic biases under area control. For each family we determine whether it is biased towards fitting a scale as opposed to not fitting the scale, using either the Type Model or the Rank Model. If the number of families with a bias towards the fit is significantly higher than the number of families not fitting the scale, and this is independent of area (as can be tested through loglinear modeling), the hypothesis is supported. Families can also be diverse (mixed), with no significant bias towards or against a given scale. As this can arise from both imperfect developments towards a fit or away from a fit, diverse families provide no evidence on the hypothesis.

Family biases can be directly determined if families contain a sufficient number of members (in practice, at least $N = 5$). If there are fewer members or if we are dealing with isolates, we use the extrapolation strategies described in Bickel (2011b, 2013): if, say, 60% of large families are biased towards some specific structure (e.g. biased towards fitting a particular scale) rather than balanced between structures (i.e. with conflicting evidence), we estimate a .6 probability (as a 'prior' probability) that the members of small families come from larger unknown families with a bias as well (in whatever direction). Some of the known members will be representative of the bias in the unknown larger family, and so we can take their choice (e.g. towards fitting or towards not-fitting the scale) to reflect the bias. (For families with 2–4 members, we take the majority choice as reflecting the bias; if there is a tie, we pick one value at random.)

However, some known members will happen to be deviates, e.g. the odd guy(s) out that developed a non-fitting case system although the family as a whole is biased towards fitting the scale. The probability of being representative can be estimated from the strength of the bias in large families: e.g. if among biased large families, biases tend to be very strong (e.g. on average covering over 90% of members), we can estimate a high probability that the known members of small biased families are representative of the larger unknown family from which they derive; then, the probability of being the odd guy(s) out is much lower (though arguably never zero).

In summary, using the probabilities of bias and of representativity based on large families, we can estimate how many of the small families come from larger biased as opposed to unbiased families, and if they come from biased families, we can estimate whether the known members reflect the respective biases of their families or deviate from them. These extrapolation estimates introduce random error but do so along a normal distribution. Therefore, we get a fairly reliable estimate of family biases if we extrapolate many times (say one thousand times) and compute the average of this. All estimates of family biases in this paper are based on this procedure. For the taxonomy of families we rely on Nichols & Bickel (2009).

Note that none of the datasets we use is a random sample. Therefore, the principles of random-sampling theory are not applicable, and this makes it impossible to use statistical tests based on this theory. Following the suggestions by Janssen et al. (2006), we therefore employ exact and randomization tests, which test the probability of finding the observed distribution under reshuffling of the data (as provided by the R Development Core Team (2012) for binomial tests and by Werft & Potter (2010) for logistic regressions).[7]

3.2 Data and data coding

Our database contains 435 languages. Most of these were surveyed by us, but about 20% of entries was taken from earlier work in the AUTOTYP project on typological databases (Nichols 1992, Bickel & Nichols 2009a,b). Since area and family factors can be best controlled if they are sampled densely, we specifically searched for areas and families with scale-based splits, collecting as many datapoints within these groups as we could.[8]

The database does not track alignment sets per se but instead codes each case in each language for the argument roles it covers, and if this coverage depends on the referential category of the argument role, the argument role is also specified for that category. For example, the database contains entries like 'Chantyal: ergative on A in all category types; nominative on S in all category types and on P in 'N-low'; accusative on P in 'N-high' and 'Pro'. From this, we compute the alignment sets for each referential category referenced by a language (via the set-theoretical derivation in footnote 5). In the Chantyal example, the alignment sets are {S,P} and {A} under the condition 'N-low', but {S}, {A}, {P} under all other referential conditions.

Apart from referential conditions, the set of arguments covered by a case marker is also sometimes conditioned by other factors, e.g. the distinction between inflectional forms (e.g. participle-based periphrastic forms vs. synthetic forms), between categories of verbs (e.g. realis vs. irrealis sets of forms) or between clause types (e.g. main vs. dependent or finite vs. nonfinite clauses). 27 languages in the database show one or more of these splits. For the sake of hypothesis testing, we enter these systems as independent datapoints into our computations in the same way as we enter two systems of genealogically related languages as independent datapoints. This raises the number of alignment systems to 462. Whether or not there are dependencies between subsystems within a language or between systems within related languages can then be statistically

---

[7] An R function implementing the method is available at http://www.uzh.ch/spw/software. We use the function with its default parameter settings: most importantly, the threshold for taking a family to be biased is set at a significance level of $p < .1$ under an exact binomial or a permutation regression test and families count as 'large' if they contain at least 5 members. These choices are justified in Bickel (2013).
[8] The database is available as an electronic appendix at http://www.spw.uzh.ch/autotyp/available.html

assessed by looking at family-internal distributions, i.e. by looking at developmental biases in the sense discussed before.

Another factor that can condition alignment sets is whether or not a particular argument is derived by diathesis, e.g. the German nominative case covers not only S and A, but also P arguments in passive constructions. We excluded all such derived roles because they are not relevant for the hypotheses as formulated above. By the same token, we exclude languages in which cases do not cover all referential categories because under some referential conditions, diathesis is obligatory and there is no possibility of expressing a given role without derivation (as is the case for instance in Yup'ik Eskimo where indefinite P arguments must be demoted to allative case via antipassivization; Reed et al. 1977, Mithun 1999). These cases evidence effects of referential categories, and possibly scales, but of a different kind than the ones under review in the present study (but see Bickel & Gaenszle 2007).

Yet another conditioning factor is lexical classes. Apart from the alignment patterns found with the majority of verbs (majority in the sense of lexical types and discourse tokens), many languages have minor alignment patterns limited to a subset of verbs, e.g. experiencer verbs, or verbs of excretion, or verbs of obligation and similar sets. An example is German, where some experiential predicates assign accusative to S arguments (e.g. *mich friert* 'I am cold'). For current purposes we leave such classes out of the picture and limit our attention to default (majority) classes because referential scale effects do not seem to interact with lexical classes so that scale structures vary across classes; all we observe is that effects get entirely blocked by specific non-default classes.

4 Results

In the following we first give an overview of the genealogical and geographical distribution of different A and P marking (Section 4.1). We then use our database to compute a scale of cross-linguistically recurrent referential categories based on their treatment by case markers (Section 4.2). Finally, we submit the resulting scales together with the hypothetical scales from Section 2.3 to tests under the assumption of a Type Model (Section 4.3) and of a Rank Model (Section 4.4).

4.1 Genealogical and geographical distribution

Of the 462 systems in the database, 59 have splits on A, i.e. differential A marking of any kind (fitting or not fitting scales), and 149 have splits on P, i.e. differential P marking of any kind; 41 systems have both splits at the same time. The

Table 4: A splits by family

stock	N
Pama-Nyungan	29
Indo-European	15
Sino-Tibetan	8
Nakh-Daghestanian	3
Mangarayan	1
Pano-Tacanan	1
Tangkic	1
Tsimshianic	1

Table 5: P splits by family

stock	N	stock	N	stock	N
Indo-European	38	Cushitic	2	Madang	1
Pama-Nyungan	26	Omotic	2	Mangarayan	1
Sino-Tibetan	13	Semitic	2	Mirndi	1
Dravidian	7	Adamawa-Ubangi	1	Nadahup	1
Turkic	7	Arawakan	1	Nakh-Daghestanian	1
Mongolian	4	Austroasiatic	1	Oksapmin	1
Tucánoan	4	Austronesian	1	Pano-Tacanan	1
Timor-Alor-Pantar	3	Awyu-Dumut	1	Pomoan	1
Uralic	3	Haida	1	Siouan	1
Uto-Aztecan	3	Kalam	1	South Atlantic	1
Barbacoan	2	Kusunda	1	Tarascan	1
Benue-Congo	2	Kwa	1	Tungusic	1
Chadic	2	Macro-Ge	1	Zuni	1

distribution of the splits across families, shown in Tables 4 and 5, is heavily skewed, restricted to 5.5% (8 out of 144) families in the database in the case of A splits and to 27% (39 out of 144) in the case of P marking. The top five families in the tables comprise 95% of all A splits and over 63% of all P splits.

The areal distribution of languages with splits is shown in Maps 1 and 2. In both types of splits, but especially in the case of differential P marking, there are frequency peaks in Eurasia (centered on Indo-Iranian languages, but deeply extending beyond this in the case of differential P marking; Bossong 1998) and in the New-Guinea/Australia – or 'Sahul' – macroarea (centered on Pama-Nyungan languages but extending to Tangkic and Southern New Guinea).

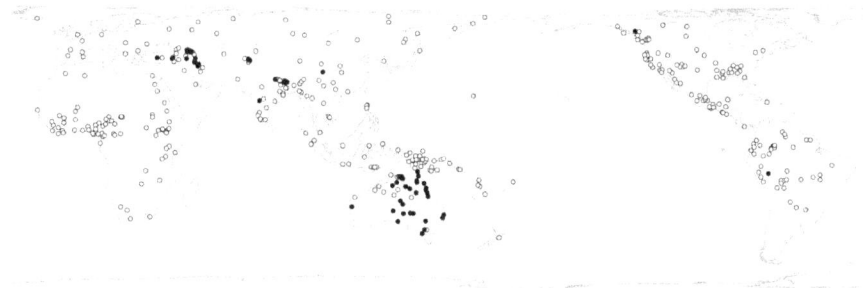

Map 1: Geographical distribution of languages with differential A marking of any kind (black dots) and languages without differential A marking (white dots)

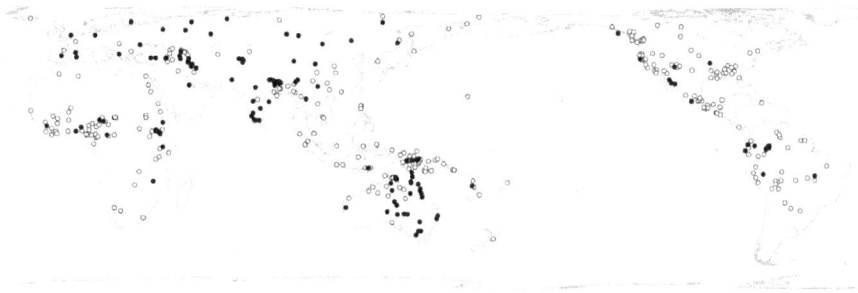

Map 2: Geographical distribution of languages with differential P marking of any kind (black dots) and languages without differential P marking (white dots)

Both these macro-areas have been noted in previous work (e.g. Nichols 1992, 1993, 1997, Bickel & Nichols 2005, 2009b). We therefore tested their relative effects on the presence of splits. Like universal biases, areal biases are the result of diachronic trends. Therefore, if areas play a role, we expect them to affect the extent to which families are internally biased towards splits. In other words, if a family is located in a split-prone area, it is more likely to develop and/or maintain a split than outside the area. We test this using the Family Bias method described in Section 3.1 above.

A difficulty arises when families straddle area boundaries: Austronesian is split between languages in the larger Eurasian sphere (Southeast Asia) and the Sahul area (assuming the main boundary lying near the Wallace Line, as suggested by Nichols & Bickel 2009). Semitic is split between Eurasia (the Arabic peninsula and adjacent areas) and Africa (e.g. Amharic). In these two cases, we assess family biases within the areas separately, i.e. testing whether different

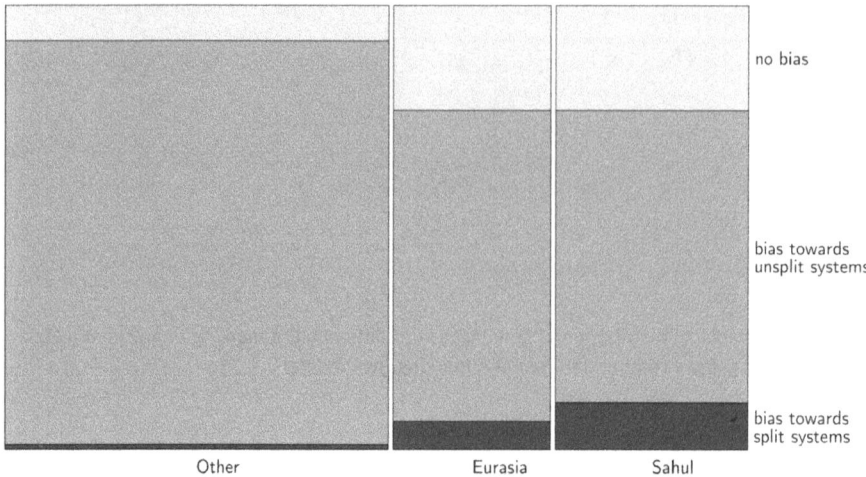

Figure 1: Estimated biases of families having split case marking for A across macro-areas. (The sizes of the individual tiles in the plot are proportional to frequencies, using the 'mosaic' plot technique provided by Meyer et al. 2006)

biases have developed depending on the area that part of the family is located in (see Bickel 2013 for general methodological discussion of this issue).

For the hypothesis of area-specific diachronic biases against or in favor of splits, diverse families are irrelevant since they can arise from imperfect biases towards *or* against splits. Thus, we tested whether the relative proportion of biases towards vs. against splits depends on area, using generalized linear modeling based on Poisson distributions (following Cysouw's (2010) suggestions; cf. Bickel 2011b). This is the case for A marking (Figure 1, likelihood ratio $\chi^2 = 6.17$, $p = .046$, $N = 135$ families). For P marking, there is no significant interaction between bias direction and areas (Figure 2, $\chi^2 = 3.95$, $p = .14$, $N = 120$ families), but this is largely due to the fact that Eurasia and the Sahul area have a similar proportions of families that are biased towards split. Taken together, the proportion in these areas is twice as high as in the rest of the world (estimated proportions: 31% split in Eurasia and Sahul vs. 14% split elsewhere, $\chi^2 = 4.62$, $p = .032$).

This suggests that splits as an abstract property are significantly affected by areal diffusion. Given this, it is imperative that any assessment of the precise nature of the splits – whether they fit a universal scale or not – control for areal diffusion.

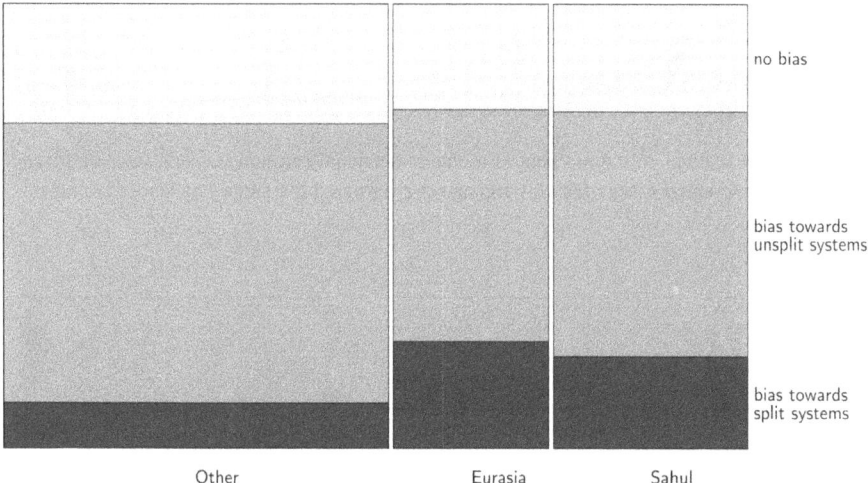

Figure 2: Estimated biases of families having split case marking for P across macro-areas (using the same mosaic plot techniques as in Figure 1)

4.2 Empirically derived scales

Scales can be thought of as summaries of similarity statements: A, B and C form a scale if both the pair of A and B and the pair of B and C are more similar to each other than A and C. As Cysouw (2015) points out, it is an empirical question to determine whether the similarity statements between such pairs of elements form a perfect one-dimensional scale, or whether they are not better represented by a multi-dimensional pattern of ordering: A, B, and C form a one-dimensional scale only to the extent that the similarity between A and C approximates the sum of the similarities between A and B and between B and C.

A general method for assessing the extent to which similarity patterns approximate a one-dimensional scale is what is called the Kruskal Stress (ϕ) in Multi-Dimensional Scaling. The key idea of Multi-Dimensional Scaling is to project a matrix of (dis)similarity statements onto a graph with k dimensions. The Kruskal Stress ϕ then measures the minimum extent to which the (dis)similarity statements have to be stretched or squeezed in order for all statements to be representable in k-dimensional space. For example, if A and C are equally similar to each other as each of the pairs {A, B} and {B, C}, projecting all three similarity statements onto a one-dimensional line incurs some amount of shrink-

Figure 3: The scale of split A marking as a one-dimensional solution to pairwise comparisons of whether referential categories of A arguments are treated the same way across languages (ϕ = 8.53%).

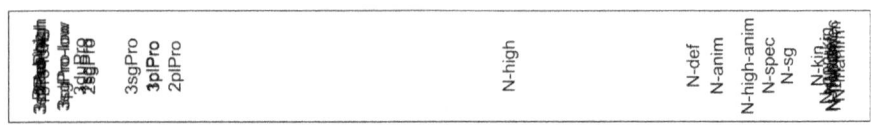

Figure 4: The scale of split P marking as a one-dimensional solution to pairwise comparisons of whether referential categories of P arguments are treated the same way across languages (ϕ = 9.79%).

ing the distances within {A, B} and within {B, C}, and stretching the distance between A and C.[9]

In order to empirically determine universal trends in the ordering patterns of referential categories, we selected those categories that are referenced by splits in at least two languages, separately for A and P. This results in 17 categories that condition A splits in 54 alignment systems, and 28 categories that condition P splits in 124 systems. From these tables, we then computed the dissimilarity between all pairs of categories by measuring the relative Hamming distance, which is the proportion of languages which split the pair of categories (so that one is in the marked the other in the unmarked set) among all languages that reference the pair of categories at all. The resulting matrix of pairwise similarity statements was then submitted to nonmetrical Multi-Dimensional Scaling (Kaufman & Rousseeuw 1990, Venables & Ripley 2002), projecting the matrix onto one dimension. The results are shown in Figures 3 and 4, together with the Kruskal Stress incurred by the projection. For both A and P splits, the Kruskal Stress is reasonably low (ϕ < 10%), and inspecting higher-dimensional

---

[9] Formally, $\phi = \sqrt{\dfrac{\Sigma_{i<j}(f(d_{i,j}) - D_{i,j})^2}{\Sigma_{i<j} D_{i,j}^2}}$, where $d_{i,j}$ are the observed and $D_{i,j}$ the projected dissimilarities, i.e. the formula basically computes the deviations of the projected from the observed distances, relative to the total of the projected distances. The function f is specific to what is called nonmetrical scaling and transforms distances so as to observe their rank order and abstracts away from their actual values. In the following we used nonmetrical scaling throughout.

solutions does not suggest further ordering patterns (nor does ϕ decrease much). Specifically and interestingly, no higher-dimensional solution points to, say, a dimension of number as opposed to a dimension of person.

For both A and P arguments, the solutions confirm what is called the Pro > N scale in Table 3, and this can be taken as an empirical confirmation of its cross-linguistic validity. In addition, the scales suggest particular rankings among persons and, for P marking only, between nouns that rank higher in discourse than other nouns:

(6) Empirically derived scales
   a. *A splits*
      1duPro > 2duPro > 1sgPro /1plPro /2sgPro > 3duPro /2plPro > 3sgPro /3plPro > N-kin/N-anim/N-high/N-def/N-indef/ N-non-kin/N-high-anim > N-low-anim/N-inanim
   b. *P splits*
      other pronouns > 1plPro/2plPro/3sgPro/3plPro > N-high > other N

The relatively low ranking of first person singular pronouns in the A scale matches our impressions: first person singular is indeed often treated differently from other persons. We briefly mentioned an example from the Australian language Arrernte above, and Bickel (2000) discusses the special status of first person singular A arguments in a number of Himalayan languages. For P splits, we have no immediate interpretation of the empirically derived scale, but we note that a high discourse status places NPs closer to pronouns than other nominal categories do (such as singular number, kinship, animacy etc.).

4.3 The Type Model

For all families containing languages with referential splits, we estimated biases towards or against fitting specific scales. As explained in Section 3.1, we performed these estimations by testing for biases in large families (via exact binomial tests) and extrapolating from this to small families and isolates. In order to control for the macro-areas (Eurasia and Sahul) that we observed to play a significant role in Section 4.1, we performed estimations separately for each macro-area.

Tables 6 and 7 show the number of families that are estimated to be biased towards ('+fit') or against ('−fit') case marking splits fitting a given scale within each macro-area.[10] Families estimated to be diverse (i.e. without evidence for a

---

10 Unlike in the geography report in Section 4.1, we display here absolute frequencies and not proportions because the absolute frequencies are much smaller.

Table 6: Estimated frequencies of families biased towards or against A-marking splits fitting a given scale, based on 144 families

Scale	Eurasia		Sahul		Other		N
	+fit	−fit	+fit	−fit	+fit	−fit	
1 > 2 > 3 > N	1.74	1.03	0	0	0	0	2.77
SAP > 3/N	1.49	0	0	0	0	0	1.49
SAP > 3 > N	1.51	0	0	0	0	0	1.51
SAP > 3 > N-high > N-low	0.32	0.01	0	0	0	0	0.33
Pro > N	1.51	0	2.29	0.1	0.52	0.47	4.89
Pro/N-high > N-low	1.56	0.1	1.62	0.05	0.02	0.5	3.86
nsg > sg	1.05	1.69	0	0	0	0	2.74
sg > nsg	0	1.48	0	1	0	0	2.48

Table 7: Estimated frequencies of families biased towards or against P-marking splits fitting a given scale, based on 144 families

Scale	Eurasia		Sahul		Other		N
	+fit	−fit	+fit	−fit	+fit	−fit	
1 > 2 > 3 > N	0.66	0.67	1.35	1.04	0.16	2.87	6.75
SAP > 3/N	0.78	0.53	1.21	1.12	1.23	2.19	7.06
SAP > 3 > N	0.66	0.69	1.32	1.04	0.35	2.58	6.63
SAP > 3 > N-high > N-low	0.34	0.01	0	0	0.03	0.49	0.87
Pro > N	12.89	1.92	5.93	0.39	8.15	2.75	32.04
Pro/N-high > N-low	8.11	0.08	2.8	0.18	4.55	0.49	16.21
nsg > sg	0	4.3	0.04	0.62	0.19	3.86	9
sg > nsg	2.38	1.98	0.66	1.7	2.23	1.78	10.73

diachronic bias) are not shown in the table since they do not give evidence for or against a hypothesized scale fit: diversity can arise through diachronic transitions both in line with and in contradiction to the hypothesis. This excludes most cases from outside Eurasia and Sahul. What is also omitted from the tables are results for the empirically derived scales in (6). These scales do not suggest any family biases at all. The reason for this is that the empirically derived scales average across the details of specific languages while the Type Model is defined with respect to language-specific ways of fitting vs. not fitting a scale. (The empirically derived scales are better testable in the Rank Model; see Section 4.4 below.)

The results suggest that there is no consistent and area-independent effect for a specific scale to match A and P marking at the same time. For A-marking splits, the number of families estimated to be biased towards fits is in the same ballpark as the number of families estimated to be biased against fits. In each case, the overall numbers are very small because only few languages and few families reference the necessary categories for evaluation under a Type Model. As a result, even when there are biases, these biases are limited to one or two families, and typically only in Eurasia: almost all evidence is limited to Sino-Tibetan and/or Indo-European. The strongest evidence in Table 6 comes from the part-of-speech scale Pro > N and the discourse-based Pro/N-high > N-low scales, but even here the total number of families estimated to be biased towards fitting the scale is below two or three and usually involves only Indo-European in Eurasia and Pama-Nyungan in Sahul.

For P-marking splits, the part-of-speech and the discourse-based scales do seem to show area-independent effects. Table 7 suggests that for these two scales, families estimated to be biased towards fitting the scales outnumber families estimated to be biased against fitting the scales, and this holds in all three macro-areas. However, the overall count is still small (estimated at $N = 32.04$ for the part-of-speech scale and at $N = 16.21$ for the discourse-based scales), and the differences in counts is appreciably strong only in Eurasia (with approximately 13:2 and 8:0 ratios). The low overall counts of families with relevant splits also makes the extrapolation procedure problematic because the procedure can rely on only very few large families – in fact only 4 in Eurasia (Indo-European, Dravidian, Sino-Tibetan and Turkic) and 1 (Pama-Nyungan) in Sahul. This leaves much guess work in the extrapolation procedure,[11] and even just a handful of further families could alter the results substantially. The small number of data and the uncertainty that comes with this precludes an overall test of whether the higher counts of families fitting the two scales is statistically significant.

4.4 The Rank Model

Estimating family biases under a Rank Model follows basically the same procedure as under a Type Model except for the way biases are tested in large families: under the rank model, a bias towards a scale means, for A-marking, that the scale is a significant predictor in a logistic regression of case-marking and that

---

[11] The prior probabilities for families to be biased (in any direction) tend to have large 95% credibility intervals in this dataset: [.48, .99] in Eurasia, [.16, .99] in Sahul and a whopping [0,1] elsewhere. (These intervals indicate the ballpark of where our estimates can be placed on the basis of the analysis of large families.)

the predictor has a negative coefficient ($-\beta\Xi$ in 5), i.e. the odds for marked alignments (such as ergative alignment) decrease when going up the scale. A bias against the scale means that the scale is again a significant predictor but that its coefficient has a reversed sign ($+\beta\Xi$). The same evaluations of biases hold for P marking, but with all signs reversed: a bias towards a given scale means that the scale is a significant predictor with a positive coefficient ($+\beta\Xi$); a bias against the scale will have a negative coefficient ($-\beta\Xi$). While the logic of these tests is straightforward, the small number of datapoints per family poses a problem for regression models. Some of these problems can be resolved by relying on permutation tests for the regressions (Werft & Potter 2010), but even then regressions can fail to converge. We interpret non-convergence and other failures in the regressions as lack of evidence for the kind of straightforward regression that we would expect if there had been a systematic diachronic bias aligning case distributions with a scale.

An additional complication arises for the extrapolation procedure of the Family Bias method. As detailed in Section 3.1, the extrapolation procedure combines statistical information from large families with observations from small families: if the distribution across large families lets us expect a small family or isolate to reflect a bias, and we estimate its member(s) to be representative of this bias, we take the direction of the bias to be given by the observed value (if there is only one member; if there are more, we take the majority value, picking one at random in the case of ties). Under a Rank Model, the analogue of observed values in small families cannot itself be a logistic regression (which is a statistical model and not a single observation). Instead, we use the observation on scale 'fits' that we used in the Type Model and take these as 'pseudo-regression' data-points when assessing the direction (positive or negative) of the regression in the small families that we estimate to be biased. Concretely: for A marking, a Type-Model fit, i.e. a fit between markedness distributions and a given scale as defined in (4a), corresponds to a negative pseudo-regression (and thus in favor of the hypothesis). Absence of a fit, i.e. a distribution that violates a given scale, counts as a positive pseudo-regression, contradicting the hypothesis. Finally, if there is conflicting evidence (e.g. because the markedness distribution does not reference all relevant categories of a given scale), but we still estimate the small families to be biased (because of the estimated prior bias probability), we choose the direction of the pseudo-correlation at random (assuming that the diachronic bias could be in any direction). The same logic applies to P marking, with all signs reversed.

Tables 8 and 9 show the results, again excluding the many families estimated to be diverse, i.e. without evidence for a diachronic bias. As noted in Section 2.4, the Rank Model is less sensitive to individual exceptions than the

Table 8: Estimated frequencies of families biased towards A-marking odds correlating negatively (−) or positively (+) with a given scale, based on 144 families

Scale	Eurasia		Sahul		Other		N
	−	+	−	+	−	+	
1 > 2 > 3 > N	4.60	3.60	7.60	6.80	1.40	1.40	25.40
SAP > 3/N	6	7	7.40	5.20	1.20	1.60	28.40
SAP > 3 > N	4.60	3.60	7.60	6.80	1.40	1.40	25.40
SAP > 3 > N-high > N-low	6.40	3	6.80	5.40	1.80	1	24.40
Pro > N	3.40	2.20	8	5.80	1.80	1.20	22.40
Pro/N-high > N-low	1	1	5.80	4.40	1.40	1.20	14.80
nsg > sg	2.80	2.60	8.80	4.40	0.80	1.20	20.60
sg > nsg	1.80	3.60	7.80	5.40	0.80	1.20	20.60
Empirical Scale (6a)	5.29	3.39	7.38	6.35	1.44	1.44	25.30

Table 9: Estimated frequencies of families biased towards P-marking odds correlating positively (+) or negatively (−) with a given scale, based on 144 families

Scale	Eurasia		Sahul		Other		N
	+	−	+	−	+	−	
1 > 2 > 3 > N	3.21	2.24	7.28	6.26	2.84	3.96	25.79
SAP > 3/N	3.21	2.24	7.28	6.26	2.84	3.96	25.79
SAP > 3 > N	5.36	3.43	7.29	6.25	2.98	3.91	29.22
SAP > 3 > N-high > N-low	9.69	5.75	10.53	10.6	5.41	5.26	47.23
Pro > N	7.63	4.36	12.6	8.31	4.17	2.8	39.87
Pro/N-high > N-low	12.13	6.52	7.74	6	6.66	4.01	43.05
nsg > sg	2.28	3.26	3.12	3.15	4.35	6.33	22.5
sg > nsg	3.28	2.26	3.12	3.15	6.35	4.33	22.5
Empirical Scale (6b)	9.60	5.66	7.30	6.35	6.28	4.34	39.53

Type Model and can therefore pick up overall trends much better. This results in much higher overall bias estimations (ranging from 14.8 to 47.23 families, with a mean of 27.37), giving more robust results.

For A marking (Table 8), the hypothesis is that families develop biases so that the odds for marked alignments (ergativity) correlate negatively with a universal scale. Our results suggest that families are in fact just as likely to develop negative or positive regressions, with differences staying below an estimated 2.4 families and mean of .56 families. Stronger differences are limited to a single macro-area: there is a slight trend of the complex SAP > 3 > N-high > N-low scale to reveal more families biased towards negative than towards positive regressions (with about a 6:3 ratio), but the effect is limited to Eurasia and therefore not universal. In the Sahul macro-area, there is a trend (with about a 9:4 ratio) for families to be biased so that alignments correlate with a nsg > sg scale, but no such effect is replicated elsewhere. Interestingly, not even the empirical scale (6a) shows a clear effect: families estimated to be biased towards this scale outnumber the opposite bias only by 1.9 in Eurasia, by 1.03 in Sahul and not at all elsewhere.

The results for P marking (Table 9) reveal a similar picture, with most differences staying below 2 families and averaging at .25. The empirically derived scale (6b) fares slightly better but the difference falls short of statistical significance (under a Poisson model controlling for area effects: $\chi^2 = 1.26$, $p = .26$). Similar to what we observe under the Type Model, more remarkable trends emerge for the part-of-speech (Pro > N) and the discourse-based scale (Pro/N-high > N-low). However, the differences are again relatively small and not statistically significant ($\chi^2 = 2.53$, $p = .12$). The discourse-based scale shows a strong difference only in Eurasia (with about a 12:7 ratio). The same is true for the more complex scale SAP > 3 > N-high > N-low (ca. 10:6 ratio) that also has – as noted above – an appreciable effect on A marking in Eurasia only.

In the preceding we observed several cases where scale effects show up only in specific macro-areas. However, none of the relevant differences reach statistical significance – except for the Pro > N scale and P marking, where the difference between Sahul and the rest of the world is significant ($\chi^2 = 6.20$, $p = .013$).

5 Discussion

Regardless of how one spells out the hypothesis of universal scale effects on case marking, our results show that there tend to be just as many families with diachronic biases in support of the hypothesis as there are families with diachronic biases against the hypothesis. If there are appreciable differences in frequencies they are limited to just one macro-area. These results are direct evidence against universal scale effects.

A possible exception from this is constituted by the part-of-speech (Pro > N) and the discourse-based (Pro/N-high > N-low) scales, which reveal area-independent effects under the Type Model for P marking. However, as noted in the Results section, under the Type Model, the evidence for this is based on very small numbers of families and is therefore not conclusive. Under the Rank Model, the evidence for the part-of-speech scale falls short of statistical significance, and it is limited to Eurasia in the case of the discourse-based scale.

This means that for these two scales we lack evidence against a universal effect although we also lack solid evidence in favor of universal effects. Interestingly, the two scales are those that fit least the spirit of the overall idea of scale effects: the part-of-speech scale could just as well be interpreted as a simple pronoun vs. noun distinction that has in fact nothing to do with any scale or hierarchy. The discourse-based scale can also be conceived of as a binary distinction of discourse-prominent vs. other referents. Moreover, as noted in Section 2.3, such a distinction lacks a reliable cross-linguistic interpretation because its constitutive categories ('high' vs. 'low') vary widely from language to language. Thus, even if we were to discover more families with diachronic biases in favor of these scales, it is doubtful whether they can be taken as support for genuinely universal and genuinely scalar effects.

We also investigated the possibility of deriving scales from the bottom up (Section 4.2). The resulting scales average over the way case marking systems are distributed over referential categories. As such they are ill-fitted for the Type Model which evaluates fits separately for each case system in each language and is highly sensitive to individual exceptions. But the empirically derived scales are suitable for the Rank Model where family biases are assessed on the basis of overall trends in regression models. Remarkably, however, the empirically derived scales did not reveal clear universal trends and the number of families that tend to violate them are not much lower than the number of families that support them (see the last rows in Tables 8 and 9).

While we find evidence against universal scale effects or, in two cases, no evidence in favor of such effects, our study reveals strong areal effects: families tend to develop referentially-conditioned alignment splits (of whatever kind, scalar or not) significantly more often in the Eurasia and Sahul macro-areas than anywhere else (cf. Section 4.1). In one case, the area difference is shown by a specific scale: for P arguments, the odds for marked alignments depend on a Pronoun > Noun scale significantly more often in the Sahul macro-area than anywhere else. Beyond this, area differences are not sensitive to specific scales but to an overall split in the abstract.

6 Conclusions

The impression of universal scale effects in the literature seems to stem from the ubiquity of such effects in Eurasia and Sahul. As soon as one controls for possible effects of areal diffusion, the numbers of families that can be statistically estimated to have developed in line with the hypothesis are in the same ballpark as the number of families that can be estimated to have developed in contradiction to the hypothesis. The only scale effects where the evidence is more ambiguous than this are effects of parts-of-speech and discourse rank in P marking. However, even if the evidence became less ambiguous, this would not necessarily speak for a universal hypothesis of scale effects on case alignments because the relevant distinction are fundamentally binary and not scalar in nature.

The present study confirms the results of Bickel & Witzlack-Makarevich (2008), which uses a smaller dataset (353 vs. 462 case systems in the present study) and a different approach to the statistical testing of linguistic universals. In the 2008 study we tested the Type Model only within sufficiently large families and assessed the Rank Model by modeling family and area membership as parameters of a single regression model. The present study relies on statistical estimates of diachronic biases. Because this can be done across all families, regardless of their size, the method is able to pick up more distributional signals in the data. As a result, we can now strengthen our claim: with the possible exceptions noted, we have now evidence for the absence of universal effects, while the 2008 study only suggested absence of evidence for universal effects.

Another finding emerging from the present study is that differential case marking on A and P is first and foremost a pattern prone to diffusion. However, what seems to diffuse is splits in the abstract and not splits tied to specific scales (with the possible exception of the pronoun vs. noun distinction in Sahul). The details of the splits seem to vary strongly across languages and are subject to idiosyncratic developments of the kind discussed by Garrett (1990) and Filimonova (2005): reanalyses of individual case markers or case attrition in nouns as opposed to pronouns. Given these findings, what becomes an urgent task now is research into the ways in which splits spread in language contact. We submit that any deeper understanding of referential scale effects in individual languages needs to explore how it arose diachronically and what role was played in this by area diffusion – especially in the Eurasia and Sahul macro-areas.

References

Aissen, Judith. 1999. Markedness and subject choice in Optimality Theory. *Natural Language and Linguistic Theory* 17. 673–711.

Austin, Peter K. 1981. *A grammar of Diyari, South Australia*. Cambridge: Cambridge University Press.

Bickel, Balthasar. 2000. Person and evidence in Himalayan languages. *Linguistics of the Tibeto-Burman Area* 23. 1–12.

Bickel, Balthasar. 2008. On the scope of the referential hierarchy in the typology of grammatical relations. In Greville G. Corbett & Michael Noonan (eds.), *Case and grammatical relations: papers in honor of Bernard Comrie*, 191–210. Amsterdam: Benjamins.

Bickel, Balthasar. 2011a. Grammatical relations typology. In Jae Jung Song (ed.), *The Oxford handbook of language typology*, 399–444. Oxford: Oxford University Press.
Bickel, Balthasar. 2011b. Statistical modeling of language universals. *Linguistic Typology* 15. 401–414.
Bickel, Balthasar. 2013. Distributional biases in language families. In Balthasar Bickel, Lenore A. Grenoble, David A. Peterson & Alan Timberlake (eds.), *Language typology and historical contingency*, 415–444. Amsterdam: Benjamins.
Bickel, Balthasar & Martin Gaenszle. 2007. Generics as first person undergoers and the political history of the Southern Kirant. Paper presented at the 7th Biannual Meeting of the Association for Linguistic Typology, Paris, September 26, 2007, http://www.uzh.ch/spw/bickel/presentations/Kiranti1U_ALT2007.pdf.
Bickel, Balthasar & Johanna Nichols. 2002. Autotypologizing databases and their use in fieldwork. In Peter Austin, Helen Dry & Peter Wittenburg (eds.), *Proceedings of the International LREC Workshop on Resources and Tools in Field Linguistics, Las Palmas, 26–27 May 2002*, Nijmegen: MPI for Psycholinguistics [http://www.uzh.ch/spw/autotyp/download/canary.pdf].
Bickel, Balthasar & Johanna Nichols. 2005. Areal patterns in the World Atlas of Language Structures. Paper presented at the 6th Biannual Conference of the Association for Linguistic Typology, Padang, July 24; available at http://www.uzh.ch/spw/autotyp/download.
Bickel, Balthasar & Johanna Nichols. 2007. Inflectional morphology. In Timothy Shopen (ed.), *Language typology and syntactic description*, 169–240. Cambridge: Cambridge University Press (Revised second edition).
Bickel, Balthasar & Johanna Nichols. 2009a. Case marking and alignment. In Andrej Malchukov & Andrew Spencer (eds.), *The Oxford handbook of case*, 304–321. Oxford: Oxford University Press.
Bickel, Balthasar & Johanna Nichols. 2009b. The geography of case. In Andrej Malchukov & Andrew Spencer (eds.), *The Oxford handbook of case*, 479–493. Oxford: Oxford University Press.
Bickel, Balthasar & Alena Witzlack-Makarevich. 2008. Referential scales and case alignment: reviewing the typological evidence. In Andrej Malchukov & Marc Richards (eds.), *Scales (Linguistische ArbeitsBerichte 86)*, 1–37. Leipzig: Institut für Linguistik [http://www.uni-leipzig.de/~asw/lab/lab86/LAB86_Bickel_Witzlack.pdf].
Bickel, Balthasar, Alena Witzlack-Makarevich, Taras Zakharko & Giorgio Iemmolo. in press. Exploring diachronic universals of agreement: alignment patterns and zero marking across person categories. In Jürg Fleischer, Elisabeth Rieken & Paul Widmer (eds.), *Agreement from a diachronic perspective*, Berlin: de Gruyter.
Bossong, Georg. 1998. Le marquage différentiel de l'objet dans les langues de l'Europe. In Jack Feuillet (ed.), *Actance et valence dans les langues de l'Europe*, 193–258. Berlin: Mouton de Gruyter.
Bresnan, Joan, Anna Cueni, Tatiana Nikitina & R. Harald Baayen. 2007. Predicting the dative alternation. In G. Bouma, I. Kraemer & J. Zwarts (eds.), *Cognitive foundations of interpretation*, 69–94. Amsterdam: Royal Netherlands Academy of Arts and Sciences.
Comrie, Bernard. 1981. *Language universals and linguistic typology*. Chicago: University of Chicago Press.
Croft, William. 1990. *Typology and universals*. Cambridge: Cambridge University Press.
Cysouw, Michael. 2010. On the probability distribution of typological frequencies. In Christian Ebert, Gerhard Jäger & Jens Michaelis (eds.), *The Mathematics of Language*, 29–35. Berlin: Springer.

Cysouw, Michael. 2011. Understanding transition probabilities. *Linguistic Typology* 15. 415–431.
Cysouw, Michael. 2015. Generalizing scales. This volume.
DeLancey, Scott. 1981. An interpretation of split ergativity and related patterns. *Language* 57. 626–657.
Dixon, R. M. W. 1972. *The Dyirbal language of North Queensland*. Cambridge: Cambridge University Press.
Dixon, R. M. W. 1994. *Ergativity*. Cambridge: Cambridge University Press.
Dowty, David R. 1991. Thematic proto-roles and argument selection. *Language* 67. 547–619.
Dryer, Matthew S. 1989. Large linguistic areas and language sampling. *Studies in Language* 13. 257–292.
Dryer, Matthew S. 1992. The Greenbergian word order correlations. *Language* 68. 81–138.
Eades, Diana. 1979. Gumbainggir. In R. M. W. Dixon & Barry J. Blake (eds.), *Handbook of Australian Languages 1*, 244–361. Amsterdam: Benjamins.
Filimonova, Elena. 2005. The noun phrase hierarchy and relational marking: problems and counterevidence. *Linguistic Typology* 9. 77–113.
Garrett, Andrew. 1990. The origin of NP split ergativity. *Language* 66. 261–296.
Haig, Geoffrey L. J. 2008. *Alignment change in Iranian languages: a construction grammar approach*. New York: Mouton de Gruyter.
Haspelmath, Martin. 2007. Pre-established categories don't exist: consequences for language description and typology. *Linguistic Typology* 11. 119–132.
Haspelmath, Martin. 2009. An empirical test of the Agglutination Hypothesis. In Sergio Scalise, Elisabetta Magni & Antonietta Bisetto (eds.), *Universals of language today*, 13–29. Berlin: Springer.
Haspelmath, Martin. 2010. Comparative concepts and descriptive categories: consequences for language description and typology. *Language* 86. 663–687.
Haspelmath, Martin. 2015. Descriptive scales versus comparative scales. This volume.
Haspelmath, Martin, Matthew S. Dryer, David Gil & Bernard Comrie (eds.). 2005. *The world atlas of language structures*. Oxford: Oxford University Press.
Ingram, Andrew. 2001. *A grammar of Anamuxra: a Language of Madang Province, Papua New Guinea*: University of Sydney dissertation.
Janssen, Dirk, Balthasar Bickel & Fernando Zúñiga. 2006. Randomization tests in language typology. *Linguistic Typology* 10. 419–440.
Kaufman, Leonard & Peter J. Rousseeuw. 1990. *Finding groups in data: an introduction to cluster analysis*. New York: Wiley.
Keine, Stefan & Gereon Müller. 2015. Differential argument encoding by impoverishment. This volume.
Kiparsky, Paul. 2008. Universals constrain change; change results in typological generalizations. In Jeff Good (ed.), *Linguistic universals and language change*, 23–53. Oxford: Oxford University Press.
Merlan, Francesca. 1982. *Mangarayi*. Amsterdam: North-Holland.
Meyer, David, Achim Zeileis & Kurt Hornik. 2006. The strucplot framework: visualizing multiway contingency tables with vcd. *Journal of Statistical Software* 17. 1–48.
Mithun, Marianne. 1999. *The languages of Native North America*. Cambridge: Cambridge University Press.
Moravcsik, Edith. 1978. On the distribution of ergative and accusative patterns. *Lingua* 45. 233–279.

Morphy, Frances. 1983. Djapu, a Yolngu dialect. In Robert M.W. Dixon & Barry J. Blake (eds.), *Handbook of Australian Languages* 3, 1–188. Amsterdam: Benjamins.
Nichols, Johanna. 1992. *Linguistic diversity in space and time*. Chicago: The University of Chicago Press.
Nichols, Johanna. 1993. Ergativity and linguistic geography. *Australian Journal of Linguistics* 13. 39–89.
Nichols, Johanna. 1997. Sprung from two common sources: Sahul as a linguistic area. In Patrick McConvell (ed.), *Archeology and linguistics: global perspectives on Ancient Australia*, Melbourne.
Nichols, Johanna & Balthasar Bickel. 2009. The AUTOTYP genealogy and geography database: 2009 release. Electronic database, http://www.uzh.ch/spw/autotyp.
Pencheon, Thomas G. 1973. *Tamazight of the Ayt Ndhir*. Los Angeles: Undena.
R Development Core Team. 2012. *R: a language and environment for statistical computing*. Vienna: R Foundation for Statistical Computing, http://www.r-project.org.
Reed, Irene, Osakito Miyako, Steven Jacobsen, Paschal Afcan & Michael Krauss. 1977. *Yup'ik Eskimo grammar*. Fairbanks: Alaska Native Language Center, University of Alaska.
Schulze, Wolfgang. 2000. *Northern Talysh*. Munich: Lincom Europa.
Silverstein, Michael. 1976. Hierarchy of features and ergativity. In R. M. W. Dixon (ed.), *Grammatical categories in Australian languages*, 112–171. New Jersey: Humanities Press.
Sokolova, Valentina Stepanovna. 1959. *Rusanskie i chufskie teksty i slovar'*. Moskva: Nauka.
Stilo, Donald. 2004. *Vafsi Folk Tales*. Wiesbaden: Reichert.
Venables, W. N. & Brian D. Ripley. 2002. *Modern applied statistics with S*. New York: Springer.
Werft, Wiebke & Douglas M. Potter. 2010. glmperm: Inference in Generalized Linear Models. R package version 1.0-3, http://CRAN.R-project.org/package=glmperm.
Wilkins, David. 1989. *Mparntwe Arrernte (Aranda): studies in the structure and semantics of grammar*: Australian National University dissertation.

Martin Haspelmath
3 Descriptive scales versus comparative scales

In this paper, I show that scales (or hierarchies) have been appealed to in various functions: They have been used to formulate descriptive generalizations (on particular languages), and to formulate cross-linguistic generalizations. They have also been used for binary relations, and for implicational relations among more than two items on the scale. This yields four uses of scales (descriptive relational, comparative relational, descriptive implicational, comparative implicational). I argue that descriptive and comparative scales must be strictly distinguished, because the descriptive categories and the comparative concepts that they are based on are quite different in nature. Description of language-specific facts in terms of scales that are also used for cross-linguistic comparison should be avoided.

1 Introduction

In this short paper, I argue that descriptive scales and comparative scales should be distinguished carefully. Failure to do so has led researchers astray in the past.

Here I distinguish between two aspects of linguistic research (descriptive and comparative linguistics), and two uses of scales (relational use and implicational use); by combining these we get four kinds of scales.

Descriptive linguistics is concerned with describing (or "analyzing") individual languages, while **comparative linguistics** (also called *typology*) compares languages (regardless of their possible genealogical relatedness) and attempts to formulate cross-linguistic generalizations.

In the **relational use of scales**, two items on a scale are compared in the formulation of a regularity. For example, in Navajo (an Athapaskan language of the southwestern United States), the rule of Subject-Object Inversion (marked by *bi*-, Hale 1973) can be formulated in terms of the scale in (1).

(1) human > animate > inanimate

Given this scale, the rule can be formulated as in (2).

(2) Subject-Object Inversion
   a. If the subject is higher than the object on the scale, inversion is blocked
   b. If the subject is lower than the object on the scale, inversion is obligatory
   c. If both have equal rank, inversion is optional

The inversion construction is marked by the prefix *bi-*, as illustrated in (3a–b), where (3a) shows the direct construction, while (3b) shows the inverse construction.

(3) Navajo
   a. *ashkii łį́į́'   yi-ztal*   (direct)
      boy   horse 3.ACC.3.NOM-kicked
      'The boy kicked the horse.'
   b. *ashkii łį́į́'   bi-ztal*   (inverse)
      boy   horse 3.ACC.3.NOM-kicked
      'The boy was kicked by the horse.'

By contrast, in the **implicational use of scales**, a statement that applies to one item on a scale also extends to all items higher on the scale. For example, if a language uses object marking for an NP type on the animacy scale, it also uses object marking for all NP types that are higher on the animacy scale.

We can thus distinguish the four kinds of scales shown in Fig. 1. The four kinds of scales are exemplified in a little more detail in the next section.

	descriptive linguistics	**comparative linguistics**
relational use	e.g. Navajo *bi-* (Hale 1973)	e.g. Ditransitive Person-Role Constraint (Haspelmath 2004a)
implicational use	e.g. differential object marking in Spanish (Aissen 2003)	e.g. universals of differential object marking (Lazard 1994)

Figure 1: Four kinds of scales

2 Four kinds of scales

Let us now look at each of the four kinds of scales in turn. I will present one example of each of the types from the literature.

2.1 Descriptive relational

A descriptive relational scale has been briefly presented above: the Navajo animacy scale for the rule of Subject-Object Inversion. Descriptive relational scales are also well-known from phonology. For example, Hooper (1976: 208) formulates a strength scale for Spanish syllable structure, shown in (4). This scale is (at least initially) formulated only for Spanish, i.e. it is a descriptive scale.

(4) w, j < r < l < m, n, ñ < s, x < β, ð, γ < ĵ, γʷ < r̃ < f, b, d, g < p, t, k < č

Given this scale, Hooper formulates the syllable structure regularity in (5) for Spanish. (Some details are omitted here because the regularity is cited here only as an example.)

(5) Syllable Structure Condition for Spanish (simplified):
    a. Spanish syllables obey a maximal template $C_1C_2C_3VC_4C_5$
    b. where $C_1 > C_2$, $C_2 > C_3$, $C_4 < C_5$ (i.e. consonantal strength first decreases and then increases monotonically)

Thus, Spanish has syllables like *voy* [boj], *tres, miel* [mjel], *prue-ba* [prweβa], *sois* [sojs], but sylables where consonantal strength increases in the onset (*rta*) or decreases in the coda (*atr*) are impossible. This is a relational use of a scale because what matters is the relation of two items on the scale to each other, not an implication.

2.2 Comparative relational

A comparative relational scale is used for formulating a cross-linguistic generalization in terms of a scale. This type of scale is exemplified by the Ditransitive Person-Role Constraint (DPRC), as discussed by Haspelmath (2004a). DPRC effects arise when the **Recipient** is not higher than the **Theme** on the person scale, i.e. when the association of the role scale (cf. 6a) and the person scale (cf. 6b) is not harmonic (cf. 7a), but disharmonic (cf. 7b).

(6) a. Role scale: Rec > Thm
    b. Person scale: 1,2 > 3

(7) a. canonical association of the scales: b. disharmonic association:

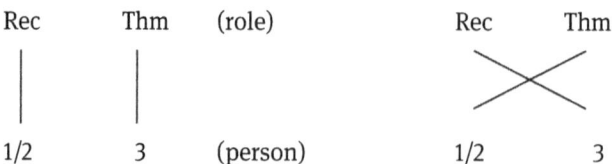

Given the two scales in (6) and their associations in (7), Haspelmath (2004a) formulates the cross-linguistic generalization in (8):

(8) DPRC generalization
All languages with bound object person forms allow (7a), and all languages that do not allow all combinations disallow (7b).

Below I give examples of DPRC effects in three languages, French (9), Modern Greek (10) and Shambala (11). In all these cases, the canonical association of the person and role scales yields acceptable combinations of bound person forms (cf. 9a, 10a, 11a), while the disharmonic association yields unacceptable combinations (cf. 9b, 10b, 11b). To express this association, some other, more elaborate construction that avoids a bound person form combination has to be used (cf. 9c, 10c, 11c).

(9) French (e.g. Grevisse 1986: §657 (b) 1°)
   a. (1>3) *Agnès   me   la   présentera.*
             Agnès 1SG.REC 3SG.F.THM present.FUT.3SG
             'Agnès will introduce her to me.'

   b. (3>1) **Agnès* *me* *lui* *présentera.*
             Agnès 1SG.THM 3SG.F.REC present.FUT.3SG
             'Agnès will introduce me to her.'

   c.   *Agnès* *me* *présentera* *à* *elle.*
             Agnès 1SG.THM present.FUT.3SG to her
             'Agnès will introduce me to her.'

(10) Modern Greek (Anagnostopoulou 2003: 252–3; cf. also Warburton 1977)
   a. (2>3) *Tha   su   ton   stílune.*
             FUT 2SG.REC 3SG.M.THM send.PF.3PL
             'They will send him to you.'

b. (3>2) *Tha   tu   se   stílune.
         FUT   3SG.M.REC   2SG.THM   send.PF.3PL
         'They will send you to him.'

c.   Tha   tu   stílune   eséna.
         FUT   3SG.M.REC   send.PF.3PL   you.OBL
         'They will send you to him.'

(11) Shambala (Bantu-G, Tanzania; Duranti 1979: 36)
 a. (1>3) *A-za-m-ni-et-ea.*
           3SG.SUBJ-PAST-3SG.THM-1SG.REC-bring-APPL
           'S/he has brought him/her to me.'

 b. (3>1) **A-za-ni-mw-et-ea.*
           3SG.SUBJ-PAST-1SG.THM-3SG.REC-bring-APPL
           'S/he has brought me to him/her.'

 c.   *A-za-ni-eta*   kwa   yeye.
           3SG.SUBJ-PAST-1SG.THM-bring   to   him/her
           'S/he has brought me to him/her.'

2.3 Descriptive implicational

The implicational use of a scale involves the statement of a regularity over an entire segment of the scale. A regularity stated about one item on the scale is automatically extended to all items that are higher (or lower) on the scale.

Implicational scales used for the description of particular languages have recently become common in optimality-theoretic approaches. Thus, according to Zec (2007), the "sonority threshold" for the syllable peak in a given language can be described through the scale in (12):

(12)   Vowel > Liquid > Nasal > Obstruent

This scale describes the likelihood that a segment type occurs as a syllable peak (most likely for vowels, least likely for obstruents). If a language allows a segment type to occur as a syllable peak, it will generally also allow all segment types that are higher on the scale. Individual languages can thus be described by specifying the cut-off point beyond which they do not allow segment types as syllable peaks. In Optimality Theory, this is generally done by turning the scale into a fixed constraint subhierarchy of markedness constraints, and by ranking a counteracting constraint among the markedness constraints to specify the cut-off point. Zec (2007) proposes the fixed constraint subhierarchy in (13) and uses the faithfulness constraint DEP ("Output depends on input") to specify the cut-off point.

(13)   *μ_h/OBSTR ≫ *μ_h/NASAL ≫ *μ_h/LIQUID ≫ *μ_h/VOWEL

Zec claims that Tashlhiyt Berber, English, Slovak and Bulgarian represent increasingly restrictive systems, and he proposes to describe them as in (14), using the fixed hierarchy and the constraint DEP (which is highlighted here). All peak types to the left of the faithfulness constraint DEP are impossible, i.e. Tashlhiyt Berber allows all four segments types in (12) as syllable peaks, while Bulgarian only allows vowels.

(14) a. Imdlawn Tashlhiyt Berber
      |DEP| ≫ *μ_h/OBSTR ≫ *μ_h/NASAL ≫ *μ_h/LIQUID ≫ *μ_h/VOWEL

   b. English
      *μ_h/OBSTR ≫ |DEP| ≫ *μ_h/NASAL ≫ *μ_h/LIQUID ≫ *μ_h/VOWEL

   c. Slovak
      *μ_h/OBSTR ≫ *μ_h/NASAL ≫ |DEP| ≫ *μ_h/LIQUID ≫ *μ_h/VOWEL

   d. Bulgarian
      *μ_h/OBSTR ≫ *μ_h/NASAL ≫ *μ_h/LIQUID ≫ |DEP| ≫ *μ_h/VOWEL

In the domain of morphosyntax, the best-known work taking this approach is Aissen (2003). According to Aissen, languages with different cut-off points of differential object marking can be described by ranking an economy constraint (*STRUC$_{case}$) at different positions within the universally fixed subhierarchy of constraints that require case-marking of objects. (This subhierarchy is derived from the universal animacy and definiteness scales as well as the grammatical relations scale by harmonic alignment.) As in (14), different kinds of languages can be described by ranking the counteracting constraint *STRUC$_{case}$ in between the constraints of the fixed subhierarchy.

(15) a. Vietnamese
      |*STRUC$_{case}$| ≫ *OJ/**HUM** & *Ø$_{CASE}$ ≫ *OJ/**ANIM** & *Ø$_{CASE}$ ≫ *OJ/**INAN** & *Ø$_{CASE}$

   b. Spanish
      *OJ/**HUM** & *Ø$_{CASE}$ ≫ |*STRUC$_{case}$| ≫ *OJ/**ANIM** & *Ø$_{CASE}$ ≫ *OJ/**INAN** & *Ø$_{CASE}$

   c. Russian
      *OJ/**HUM** & *Ø$_{CASE}$ ≫ *OJ/**ANIM** & *Ø$_{CASE}$ ≫ |*STRUC$_{case}$| ≫ *OJ/**INAN** & *Ø$_{CASE}$

   d. Hungarian
      *OJ/**HUM** & *Ø$_{CASE}$ ≫ *OJ/**ANIM** & *Ø$_{CASE}$ ≫ *OJ/**INAN** & *Ø$_{CASE}$ ≫ |*STRUC$_{case}$|

Vietnamese is an example of a language where the economy constraint is ranked very high and thus no objects are case-marked, while in Hungarian it is ranked so low that all objects are case-marked.

While the use of scales to describe particular languages is characteristic of Optimality Theory, it is not totally novel. An early representative of the descriptive relational use of scales is Cole et al. (1977).

2.4 Comparative implicational

The comparative use of implicational scales is the classical use of such scales and predates their descriptive use in optimality approaches. The two best-known examples of implicational scales are the **grammatical relations scale** (Keenan & Comrie 1977), used for the formulation of generalizations in the domain of relative clause formation, and the **animacy scale** (also called *individuation scale, empathy scale*, etc.), which is used for various cross-linguistic generalizations. An example is differential object marking, and Lazard's (1994: 229–230) discussion of it in terms of the scale in (16). (See also Lazard (1997), the English version of Lazard (1994)).

(16) échelle d'individuation ('individuation scale'):
      pronoms > humain défini > humain indéfini/non-humain défini > non-humain indéfini > indéfini non-spécifique

Lazard formulates the differential object marking generalization as in (17):[1]

(17) "On constate que, quelle que soit l'extension de l'usage de la marque, celle-ci se trouve toujours du côté du plus défini/plus humain et son absence du côté du moins défini/moins humain. Le marquage de l'objet est donc corrélatif de son individuation."

This approach was adopted by Aissen (2003), who also claims that her fixed constraint subhierarchy (which is a kind of scale) allows her to express the generalization in (17), i.e. that overt object marking generally affects the top end of the animacy scale. What Aissen adds to this is the simultaneous use of the scale as a descriptive implicational scale, as we saw in §2.3.

---

[1] "We note that whatever the extension of the use of the marker, it is always near the more definite/more human, and its absence near the less definite/less human. The marking of the object thus correlates with its individuation."

3 Conflating descriptive and comparative scales

In this paper, I argue that descriptive and comparative scales should be kept strictly apart, just as descriptive categories and comparative concepts should be kept apart in general (Haspelmath 2010, 2014).

By contrast, generative approaches generally equate descriptive categories and comparative concepts (assumed to be innate), and this is very explicit in the literature on Optimality Theory:

> McCarthy (2002: 1)
> "One of the most compelling features of OT, in my view, is the way that **it unites description of individual languages with explanation of language typology**... OT is inherently typological: the grammar of one language inevitably incorporates claims about the grammars of all languages. This joining of the individual and the universal ... is probably the most important insight of the theory."

> Aissen (2003: 437)
> "The challenge then is to **develop a theory of DOM** [= differential object marking] which expresses the generalization ..., and **at the same time** allows for the various ways in which DOM can be **implemented in particular languages**." (p. 437)

But this conflation of descriptive and comparative concepts is also the programme of Croft (2003), and his Radical Construction Grammar (2001):

> "Language-specific grammatical categories are the actual specific mappings of grammatical [forms] onto the conceptual space. Part of the representation of a speaker's knowledge, then, is a set of semantic maps onto a conceptual space whose structure is largely universal."
> (Croft 2003: 139)

As an example of this, Croft (2003: 134) mentions the role of the animacy scale in governing the occurrence of overt plural marking, as illustrated in (18):

(18) plural marking:

    Guaraní (Tupian): |1st/2nd| – 3rd – human – animate – inanimate

    Usan (New Guinea): |1st/2nd – 3rd| – human – animate – inanimate

    Tiwi (Australia): |1st/2nd – 3rd – human| – animate – inanimate

    Kharia (Munda): |1st/2nd – 3rd – human – animate| – inanimate

    English: |1st/2nd – 3rd – human – animate – inanimate|

The underlying scale is universal, and language-particular categories are expressed as mappings on this universal conceptual space.

4 Why descriptive and comparative scales should be kept separate

4.1 Descriptive categories vs. comparative concepts

I have stressed in previous work that descriptive categories (as are needed for language-specific description) are of a very different nature from comparative concepts – conflating them leads to all kinds of problems (cf. Haspelmath 2007, 2010). In particular, it is not possible to come up with a list of categories that would suffice to describe all languages – while categories in different languages tend to be broadly similar, they are never completely identical, and many languages have categories that seem to be quite unique to them. The attempt to squeeze individual languages into a straitjacket of pre-established categories does not do justice to the individual languages and often fails completely.

Descriptive scales must be based on **descriptive categories**, i.e. categories that are defined within an individual language. Comparative scales must be based on **comparative concepts**, i.e. concepts created by comparative linguists for the purpose of comparing languages.

Consider, for example, the notions of "recipient" and "theme" in the DPRC generalization in §2.2 above: These are semantic roles (defined with respect to physical transfer verbs such as 'give'), but in French the corresponding regularity actually affects all Dative Clitics, and these are only imperfectly correlated with recipients. The French Dative cannot be equated with the semantic role "recipient", so the generalization in (8) is not sufficient to predict the behaviour of French categories. On the other hand, it is clear that French is strikingly similar to Modern Greek and Shambala (and many other languages), and this similarity is captured by the generalization in (8). But the generalization is formulated in terms of comparative concepts, not in terms of categories that a particular language would have. What one needs to know about French in order to master the language thus goes beyond the cross-linguistic generalization in (8), but this additional information is not readily comparable across languages.

The situation is quite similar for Navajo Subject-Object Inversion. Frishberg (1972: 261) observes that

> "The concept of animacy with which this chapter is concerned is the native Navaho concept. Animate things in Navaho are things that are capable of self-induced motion. This definition includes horses, sheep, cars, wind, rain, and running water."

This means that what one needs to know to master Navajo goes significantly beyond knowing the general, cross-linguistic animacy scale (cf. 16) and the rules in (2). The Navajo animacy scale in (1) is specific to Navajo. Again, the Navajo situation is not unique and is broadly comparable to similar situations in many other languages, and we need comparative concepts and scales in order to express these similarities. But these comparative scales cannot be used directly to express language-specific regularities.

Let us now look at relational scales and then at implicational scales more closely.

4.2 Descriptive relational scales are different from comparative relational scales

Comparative relational scales are (by definition) universal, but descriptive relational scales may not only contain categories that do not map perfectly on the comparative concepts, but they may also include items that do not have a counterpart in a universal scale at all.

Let us consider Ditransitive Person-Role phenomena again, using the example of the well-known French contrast (9a–b), repeated here for convenience.

(9) French (e.g. Grevisse 1986: §657 (b) 1°)

    a. (1>3) *Agnès me la présentera.*
                Agnès 1SG.REC 3SG.F.THM present.FUT.3SG
                'Agnès will introduce her to me.'

    b. (3>1) **Agnès me lui présentera.*
                  Agnès 1SG.THM 3SG.F.REC present.FUT.3SG
                  'Agnès will introduce me to her.'

Universally, we can state the generalization in (19) (Haspelmath 2004a; see also (8) above):

(19) If the Recipient is higher on the person scale (1/2 > 3) than the Theme, then bound person-form combinations are possible in all languages with bound object person forms.

But for French, this is not sufficient, because the reflexive clitic behaves like the 1st/2nd person clitic:

(20) (3>1) **Agnès se lui presentera.*
              Agnès REFL.THM 3SG.F.REC present.FUT.3SG
              'Agnès will introduce herself to her.'

Apparently French has a (descriptive) scale "1/2/REFL >3", but this is a language-specific scale. In the comparative scale, "REFL" cannot be ranked because it does not behave consistently across languages.[2]

Next, let us consider the person scale in the context of monotransitive constructions. It is well known that for inverse and similar constructions, some languages have a person scale "1 > 2 > 3", but others have a scale "2 > 1 > 3" (especially Algonquian languages). Aissen (1999) solves this problem by conflating 1st and 2nd person to "local person". This is convenient for the comparative use of the person scale (because no predictions can be made for the relation between 1st and 2nd person), but for language-specific description it means that only part of the description can rely on the universal constraint subhierarchy. The other part of the description has to be done by other means, i.e. some kind of parochial stipulation. Thus, description by comparative concepts is a very odd kind of description.

4.3 Descriptive implicational scales are different from comparative implicational scales

The need to distinguish between comparative and descriptive scales is just as apparent in the case of implicational scales. There are two main reasons for this: Implications may have exceptions, and implications may be relevant only for a small part of the system, so that a description in terms of a comparative implicational scale would yield very partial descriptions.

4.3.1 Exceptions

If the language-specific situation is exclusively expressed by encoding it in the universal comparative scale, then there is no way to describe exceptional cases. But many scalar universals are in fact universal tendencies, i.e. they admit exceptions. Let us consider just two examples. These could be easily multiplied.

---

[2] Another possibility is that the ban on *me/te/se+lui* is somehow due to the fact that *me/te/se* do not distinguish accusative and dative forms, as proposed by Grimshaw (2001). In that case, this would not be a person scale effect from a French language-specific point of view at all. However, from a comparative perspective, it could still be seen as an instantiation of the generalization in (19). Basically, the language-specific analysis is irrelevant for cross-linguistic generalization and explanation (cf. Haspelmath 2004b).

Example 1: Zec (2007: 183) notes that Swahili is an exception to the universal comparative scale in (12) above. Swahili has vowels and nasals as syllable peaks, but not liquids. Zec comments: "From an OT perspective, such discontinuities may well be due to further constraint interactions." But this is not in general a viable way out: If "further constraint interactions" are invoked to explain exceptions, this opens a Pandora's box, and nothing can be excluded anymore. Such "further constraints" could always be present, and the approach would not make any predictions anymore.

Example 2: In Nganasan (Samoyedic), pronouns show no case distinctions, but nouns inflect on an accusative pattern (cf. Filimonova 2005). Aissen (2003) acts as if such exceptions did not exist, but the fact that they exist means that at least the exceptional languages cannot be described by means of the comparative scales. But if there is one language for which comparative scales cannot be used as descriptive scales, so that an alternative mechanism must be used, this means that this alternative mechanism is in principle available for all languages.

4.3.2 Partial descriptions

Descriptions that are based entirely on the scale would be very incomplete in many cases, because often the relevant patterns are deeply embedded in the grammar and cannot be described without taking other phenomena into account.

For example, in German, differential object marking in noun inflection is found only in one small subclass of singular masculine nouns (Haspelmath 2002: 245):

	MASCULINE			FEMININE		NEUTER	
NOMINATIVE	Löwe	Mann	Garten	Frau	Nase	Kind	Buch
ACCUSATIVE	Löwe-n	Mann	Garten	Frau	Nase	Kind	Buch
	'lion'	'man'	'garden'	'woman'	'nose'	'child'	'book'

This does seem to be an instantiation of the comparative scale in (16) and the generalization in (17), but it is not clear how the comparative scale would be used in the description of the German facts.

Similarly, Russian has differential object marking in noun inflection, but only in a particular (though quite large) subclass of singular masculine nouns.

	MASCULINE			FEMININE		NEUTER	
NOMINATIVE	kot	sud'j-a	nos	žen-a	ruk-a	ditja	pero
ACCUSATIVE	kot-**a**	sud'j-u	nos	žen-u	ruk-u	ditja	pero
	'cat'	'judge'	'nose'	'wife'	'hand'	'child'	'pen'

It is perhaps possible to describe these systems using Aissen's constraint sub-hierarchy, but such descriptions would be vastly more complex than alternative descriptions that do not try to describe everything with universal categories and scales.

5 Conclusion

I conclude that descriptive scales and comparative scales should be distinguished carefully. Descriptive scales are sometimes useful in that language-specific generalizations can best be formulated using a scale. Comparative scales are very often useful to formulate cross-linguistic generalizations, especially implicational generalizations. But the mere fact that a language-specific pattern instantiates a known cross-linguistic generalization does not mean that it should be described in terms of this pattern.

References

Aissen, Judith. 1999. Markedness and subject choice in Optimality Theory. *Natural Language and Linguistic Theory* 17: 673–711.
Aissen, Judith. 2003. Differential object marking: Iconicity vs. economy. *Natural Language and Linguistic Theory* 21(3). 435–83.
Anagnostopoulou, Elena. 2003. *The syntax of distransitives: evidence from clitics* (Studies in generative grammar, 54.) Berlin: Mouton de Gruyter.
Cole, Peter, Wayne Harbert, Shikaripur N. Sridhar, Sachiko Hashimoto, Cecil Nelson & Diane Smietana. 1977. Noun phrase accessibility and island constraints. In Peter Cole & Jerrold M. Sadock (eds.), *Grammatical relations*, 27–46. (Syntax and Semantics 8). New York: Academic Press.
Croft, William. 2001. *Radical Construction Grammar*. Oxford: Oxford University Press.
Croft, William. 2003. *Typology and universals*. 2nd edition. Cambridge: Cambridge University Press.
Duranti, Alessandro. 1979. Object clitic pronouns in Bantu and the topicality hierarchy. *Studies in African Linguistics* 10(1). 31–45.
Filimonova, Elena. 2005. The noun phrase hierarchy and relational marking: problems and counterevidence. *Linguistic Typology* 9(1). 77–113.

Frishberg, Nancy. 1972. Navaho object markers and the great chain of being. In: J. Kimball (ed.) *Syntax and semantics 1*. New York: Academic Press, 259–266.

Grevisse, Maurice. 1986. *Le bon usage*. 12ème édition. Paris: Duculot.

Grimshaw, Jane. 2001. Optimal clitic positions and the lexicon in Romance clitic systems. In: Legendre, Géraldine & Grimshaw, Jane & Vikner, Sten (eds.) *Optimality-theoretic syntax*. Cambridge/MA: MIT Press, 205–240.

Hale, Kenneth. 1973. A note on subject-object inversion in Navajo. In: *Issues in linguistics: papers in honour of Henry and Renée Kahane*, ed. by Braj B. Kachru. Urbana: University of Illinois, 300–309.

Haspelmath, Martin. 2002. *Understanding morphology*. London: Arnold.

Haspelmath, Martin. 2004a. Explaining the Ditransitive Person-Role Constraint: a usage-based account. *Constructions* 2/2004, 49 pp.

Haspelmath, Martin. 2004b. Does linguistic explanation presuppose linguistic description? *Studies in Language* 28(3). 554–579.

Haspelmath, Martin. 2007. Pre-established categories don't exist: consequences for language description and typology. *Linguistic Typology* 11(1). 119–132.

Haspelmath, Martin. 2010. Comparative concepts and descriptive categories in cross-linguistic studies. *Language* 86(3). 663–687.

Haspelmath, Martin. 2014. Comparative syntax. In Andrew Carnie, Yosuke Sato & Dan Siddiqi (eds.), *Routledge Handbook of Syntax*. London: Routledge, 490–508.

Hooper, Joan B. 1976. *An introduction to natural generative phonology*. New York: Academic Press.

Keenan, Edward L. & Bernard Comrie. 1977. Noun phrase accessibility and universal grammar. *Linguistic Inquiry* 8. 63–99.

Lazard, Gilbert. 1994. *L'actance*. Paris: Presses universitaires de France.

Lazard, Gilbert. 1997. *Actancy*. Berlin: Mouton de Gruyter.

McCarthy, John J. 2002. *A thematic guide to Optimality Theory*. Cambridge: Cambridge University Press.

Warburton, Irene P. 1977. Modern Greek clitic pronouns and the "surface structure constraints" hypothesis. *Journal of Linguistics* 13: 259–281.

Zec, Draga. 2007. The syllable. In: *The Cambridge Handbook of Phonology*, ed. by Paul de Lacy. Cambridge: Cambridge University Press, 161–193.

Michael Cysouw
4 Generalizing Scales

Instead of considering scales to be linearly ordered structures, this paper proposes that the linguistic notion of a scale can be fruitfully generalized as a special case of dissimilarity ('metric'). Further, to be considered a scale of typological interest, there should be a significant correlation between a meaning-scale and a form-scale. As a hands-on example of the proposals put forward in this paper, the "scale of likelihood of spontaneous occurrence" (Haspelmath 1993) is reanalyzed. This scale describes the prototypical agentivity of the subject of a predicate.

1 Scales as restrictions on form-function mapping

Scales[1] of linguistic structure are one of the more promising avenues of research into the unification of the worldwide linguistic diversity. Although our growing understanding of the diversity of the world's languages seems to throw more and more doubt on the many grandiose attempts at universally valid generalizations, the significance of scales (such as the well-known animacy scale) for human languages still appears to stand strong (for a different opinion on this specific example see Bickel et al 2015).

But what exactly is a scale? A scale seems to be mostly thought of as an asymmetrical one-dimensional arrangement (a "total order" in mathematical parlance) of certain cross-linguistic categories/functions. Put differently, a scale is a linear ordering of functions with a "high end" and a "low end". To be considered an interesting scale, the formal encoding of these functions in actual languages should be related to this linear ordering. For example, specific encodings should typically be restricted to either end of the scale, like nominative and ergative encoding on the animacy scale (Silverstein 1976).

In this paper, I will argue that this concept of a scale can be fruitfully generalized. In a very general sense, all linguistic structure consists of forms expressing particular functions. If we find restrictions across languages on the kind of forms that are used to express certain functions, then this amounts to a cross-linguistic generalization. I would like to suggest that every such restriction on

---
[1] The term "scale" is used here synonymously to what is also known as an "implicational hierarchy", "markedness hierarchy" or simply "hierarchy" in linguistics.

the form-function mapping can be considered to be a (generalized) scale. Traditional one-dimensional scales are just a special kind of such cross-linguistic restrictions on form-function mapping. When this limitation – i.e. that a scale has to be one-dimensional – is discarded, and the concept of ordering is replaced by a concept of dissimilarity, then the notion of a scale can be nicely generalized to cover many, if not all, restrictions on form-function mapping (cf. Croft 2003: 133–142).

To establish a scale in its generalized conception, it is necessary to consider three steps: first, to establish a cross-linguistic scale of functions; second, to establish a cross-linguistic scale of forms; and, third, to observe a match between the two. Strictly speaking, a cross-linguistic scale, or hierarchy, is the interpretation of any such observed match. These three topics – scales of function, scales of form, and matching them – will be discussed in turn below in Sections 4 to 6. However, first I will introduce a central tool for the generalization of scales, namely the dissimilarity matrix (Section 2), and the concrete example to be used for the discussion of the generalization, namely the "scale of likelihood of spontaneous occurrence" (Section 3).

2 Replacing ordering with distances

A scale in linguistics is normally conceived of as a linear ordering of categories or functions. However, the restriction to a linear structure is neither necessary nor advantageous. Already the perennial issue of whether first person should outrank second on the animacy scale (or vice versa) illustrates that a linear ordering is simply not powerful enough to model linguistic diversity. Probably the only reason for the existence of this focus on linear orders is that such scales are easier to handle and easier to visualize. Further, many scales currently being discussed in the literature only consist of two entities, so that the whole issue of linearity does not arise. However, to generalize the notion of a scale, it seems more fruitful to abandon the principle of a linear scale and open up the possibility for more complex topologies.

One proposal for more complex structures is implicit in the spider-web-like graphs used to display semantic maps (Croft 2003: 133–139; Haspelmath 2003). I have argued elsewhere that such semantic maps can be generalized as dissimilarity matrices (Cysouw 2007; 2010). In a dissimilarity matrix, all pairs of entities in the scale are considered separately, and evaluated individually on their similarity. A linear scale is a special case of such a general structure. For example, consider three entities A, B, and C on a linear scale. This translates to similarities by stating that the distance from A to B is the same as the distance from B to C, and both are exactly half the distance from A to C. When the distance from A to C does not exactly match the summed-up distance from A to B to C, the distances do not fit on a linear scale anymore. The principle of the generalization proposed here is that linearity might still exist, but it is not assumed *a priori*. Initially, the pairwise distances are established individually. Only afterwards might it turn out that they reduce to a nicely linear arrangement. However, most of the time they will turn out not to be that easily aligned.

Often – though not in all instances – scales are considered to be inherently directed, i.e. the have a "high end" and a "low end".[2] As I will argue in Section 5, this direction is solely caused by the scale of form (cf. Croft 2003: 140–142). Any *direction* of a scale (which I claim is based on form) is an independent insight from the discovery of the underlying configuration, or *topology*, of the scale (which I claim is based on function). How to practically proceed with the separation of these two issues is the central topic of this paper.

3 Scale of likelihood of spontaneous occurrence

As an example of the approach proposed here, I will reanalyze data from Haspelmath (1993) on the causative/inchoative alternation. In that paper, Haspelmath addresses the question of how languages mark the predicate in the alternation between an inchoative expression (i.e. an expression without an instigator of the action, like *the water boiled*), and a causative expression (i.e. an expression with an instigator, like *the man boiled the water*). He proposes a scale of the "likelihood of spontaneous occurrence" to explain why – across languages – some predicates tend to be causativized (i.e. the causative is morphologically derived from the inchoative, e.g. German inchoative *enden* vs. causative *beenden*), while others tend to be anticausativized (i.e. the inchoative is derived from the causative, e.g. English inchoative *be destroyed* vs. causative *destroy*). The idea of the scale of likelihood of spontaneous occurrence is that those predicates that are likely to occur spontaneously (i.e. without any human agent) will cross-linguistically tend to be causativized (i.e. the inchoative is the more basic expression), and *vice versa*.

Haspelmath investigated the inchoative/causative alternation of 31 meanings in 21 languages. For each of these meanings, the proportion of languages

---

[2] The combination of a linear scale with an inherent direction is mathematically equivalent to a so-called "total order". An easy way to remedy the problem of having parts of the scale that are not (clearly) ordered relative to each other (like first and second person in the animacy hierarchy) is to allow for some parallelism in the ordering (thus deviating from strict linearity). Such a model is mathematically speaking an example of a so-called "partial order".

that use a causativization strategy is shown in Table 1.[3] The order of the meanings in the table illustrates the idea of the scale of likelihood of spontaneous occurrence, with the least spontaneous meanings at the top (*split, close, break*) and the most spontaneous meaning at the bottom (*dry, freeze, boil, die/kill*).

Table 1: Cross-linguistic proportion of causativizations (adapted from Haspelmath 1993: 104).

split	0.04	develop	0.33	melt	0.68
close	0.06	roll	0.35	learn/teach	0.68
break	0.07	spread	0.35	sink	0.70
open	0.10	begin	0.38	go out/put out	0.71
gather	0.12	finish	0.38	wake up	0.75
change	0.12	fill	0.38	dry	0.77
connect	0.14	be destroyed/destroy	0.39	freeze	0.86
rock	0.25	burn	0.42	boil	0.96
improve	0.26	dissolve	0.42	die/kill	1.00
rise/raise	0.27	turn	0.48		
get lost/lose	0.28	stop	0.62		

4 Scales of functions

In most current research, scales of categories/functions are either available as hypotheses from earlier research, or established *post-hoc* as the most compelling way to interpret an observed cross-linguistic scale of form (see Section 5) and as such, they can be used as hypotheses for future research. However, scales of function can actually be established independently by using the semantic map approach, though such "scales" will normally not be nicely one-dimensional, needing more effort for their interpretation.

The basic intuition behind the semantic map approach is that cross-linguistic variation in the expression of the functions can be used as a proxy to the relation between the functions themselves. The central assumption made in this approach is that when the expressions of two functions are similar in language after language, then the two functions themselves are similar. Individual languages

---

[3] The proportion of causatives reported in Table 1 is calculated by dividing the number of languages that causativize the predicate (C) by the number of the languages that either causativize or anticausativize it (C + A), ignoring those languages that use different strategies (Haspelmath further distinguishes suppletive, labile and equipollent alternations, which will not be used here). This method of calculation is different from the proportions reported on by Haspelmath (who lists the fraction A/C). Further, this fraction is noteworthy in the case of die/kill, as most languages use a suppletive strategy for this meaning, making the proportion reported here (1.00) somewhat superficial (because A = 0 and C = 3, so C/C + A = 1).

might (and will) deviate from any general pattern, but when combining many languages, overall the cross-linguistic regularities will overshadow such aberrant cases.

Thus, the similarity between expressions ('forms') is the basic measure for establishing a semantic map. However, there are two crucially different kinds of similarity between expressions, only one of which will be used to establish the semantic map. For a semantic map, it is important whether two expressions are similar on purely language-specific grounds, i.e. they behave alike according to the grammar of the language. For example, the English verbs *walk* and *enter* behave alike as to the formation of their past forms (*walked*, *entered*). Likewise, the verbs *buy* and *fight* behave alike in choosing the same kind of past formation (*bought*, *fought*). This kind of similarity between expressions is purely language-particular and thereby crucially different from cross-linguistic coding strategies. Cross-linguistically, one might say that *walk* and *enter* both use suffixal concatenative morphology to mark past, but *buy* and *fight* use ablaut-like non-linear morphology. Such typological characteristics lead to scales of form to be discussed in the next section (see Cysouw 2010 for a more detailed exposition of this approach using linguistic behavior to establish semantic maps).

Coming back to the inchoative/causative alternation, the English expressions *open* and *close* have some similarity because they use the same inchoative/causative alternation (both verbs do not change their morphology in this alternation, i.e. they use a labile strategy in the terminology of Haspelmath 1993). Likewise, the German expressions *öffnen* and *schließen* are similar because they use the same inchoative/causative alternation, though they use a different strategy from the one found in English (in German both verbs are anticausativizing, as the inchoative form is derived from the causative form by using reflexive morphology: *sich öffnen, sich schließen*).

By combining such language-particular similarities from many languages, the similarity between functions/meanings can be approximated. So, in the above example, both English and German use the same (language-particular) construction for "to open" and "to close", so both languages argue for some similarity between these meanings. However, this is not necessary the case in all the world's languages. For example, in Hindi the inchoative/causative alternation for the verb "to open" is coded by non-linear morphology (ablaut) *khulnaa/kholnaa*, but the alternation for the verb "to close" it is coded by using the copula-like verbs *honaa* "to be" and *karnaa* "to do", viz. *band honaa/band karnaa*, lit. "be close/do close". Now, it is possible to approximate the similarity of the meanings "to open" and "to close" by (roughly speaking) taking the average of many such language-particular similarities.

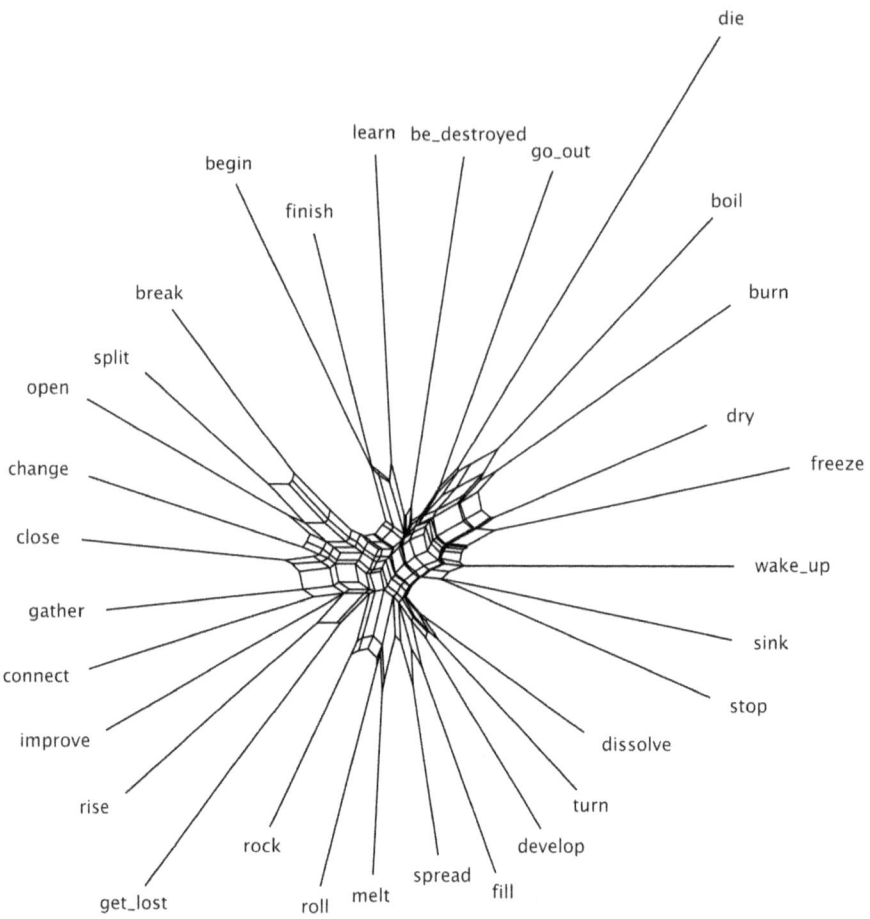

Figure 1: A scale of function of the 31 meanings in the form of a NeighborNet

When this procedure is followed for all possible pairs of meanings (see the appendix of Cysouw 2010 for the basic data), this will result in a long list of similarity measures of two meanings. For example, in the case of the meanings investigated by Haspelmath, there are 31*30/2 = 465 such pairs of meanings. Such a long list of numbers (a "dissimilarity matrix") is a generalized scale of meaning. The network in Figure 1 is an attempt to display the structure of the resulting "scale" of meanings. The figure shows a so-called "splits graph" (Bandelt & Dress 1992, Dress & Huson 2004).[4] Roughly speaking, similar functions will be

---

[4] The particular splits graph shown in Figure 1 is a NeighborNet made by the program *SplitsTree* (Huson and Bryant 2006). See Bryant et al. (2005) for an introduction to this approach with some examples from linguistics.

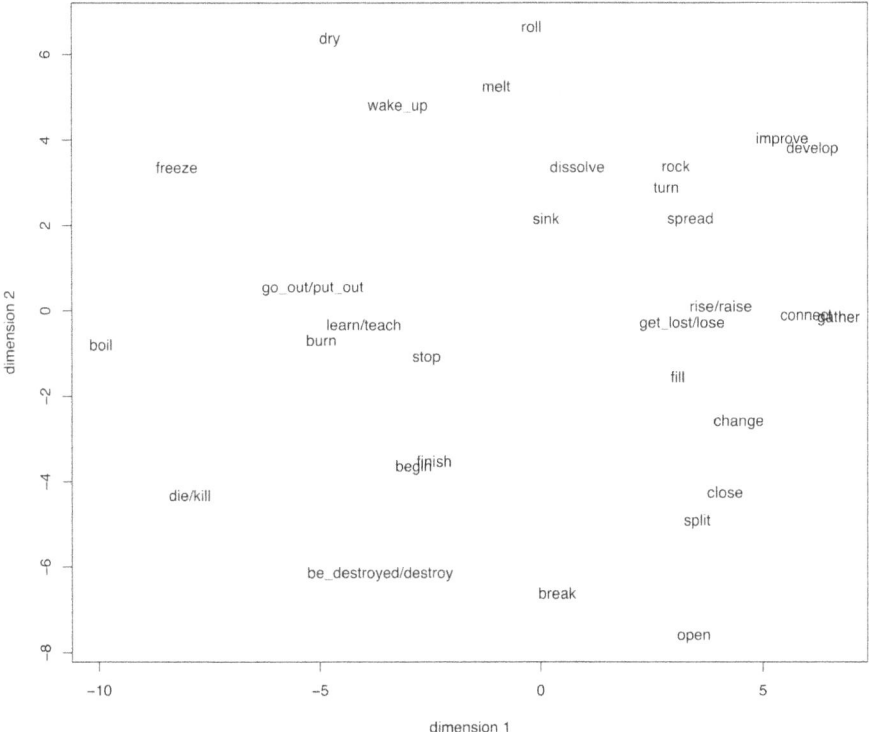

Figure 2: First two dimensions of multidimensional scaling of the 31 meanings

placed close to each other in the network-like graph. At the upper right side of the figure some of the more spontaneous meanings can be found (e.g. *freeze, dry, burn, boil,* cf. Table 1), and at the opposite site, at the left and lower left, the meanings that typically need an agent are located (e.g. *break, split, open, change*). It is already possible to discern something like the scale of likelihood of spontaneous occurrence. However, this graph also very clearly shows that the spontaneity scale is not the only thing that matters. As one might expect, meaning/function is a highly complex and multidimensional matter (cf. Wälchli & Cysouw 2011), and a multitude of other aspects of meaning are relevant for the similarity of meaning between the meanings investigated.

Another way to depict the structure in the list of pairwise similarities is to use multidimensional scaling.[5] Shown in Figure 2 are the first two dimensions of a multidimensional scaling for the same data that resulted in the network in Figure 1. Because only the first two dimensions are shown, this display might

---

[5] For all multidimensional scaling in this paper I used the function *cmdscale* from the statistical environment R (R Development Core Team, 2007).

look easier to interpret, but that is only because much of the complexity of the data is ignored to fit the display into two dimensions. The spontaneity scale can be seen ranging from the upper left to the lower right side in Figure 2 (cf. Table 1). The meanings in the upper left of the figure are highly spontaneous (*boil, freeze, dry*), while the meaning at the lower right typically need an agent (*open, split, close, break, change*).

5 Scales of form

The constructions that languages use to mark the inchoative-causative alternation are not directly comparable across languages. Take, for example, the German construction using *sich* to mark the inchoative (e.g. *sich öffnen, sich schließen*). This construction is very reminiscent of the Hebrew construction using *hit-* to mark the inchoative (e.g. *hitʕorer, hitʔasef*). Both constructions are of course different in principle – after all, they come from different languages. However, there are various characteristics that make both constructions alike to some extent. For example, they both explicitly mark the inchoative rative to the causative. Also, both constructions perform this marking by putting some extra material in front of the lexical verb (though there is of course a difference in morphological status). Further, both the German *sich* construction and the Hebrew *hit-* construction are sometimes considered to be "reflexive" constructions. These three characteristics are cross-linguistically applicable, and in this sense crucially different from the characteristics that are used to establish language-specific construction classes (Haspelmath 2010).

Such cross-linguistically applicable characteristics of expressions are called "strategies" in the typological literature. The tradition of using the term "strategy" in this way apparently originated with Keenan & Comrie's (1977: 64) classic paper on relativization strategies. There are different kinds of strategies, and these different kinds have a rather different status for the comparison of languages, but that topic will not be further developed here (see Cysouw 2010). I will here only use so-called "coding" properties that relate to the form in which the language-particular expressions are codified.[6] In this realm, one can think of

---

[6] Besides coding properties, Keenan (1976) also distinguishes behavioral properties of expressions in complex constructions as another kind of properties. Note that the German/Hebrew example discussed above included yet another kind of cross-linguistic strategy. The observation that both the German *sich* construction and the Hebrew *hit-* construction are "reflexive" constructions can be formalized by including reference to a "prototypical" element in the realm of meaning. For example, constructions from different languages are both reflexive-like when they both at least code for the meaning "rise".

characteristics like length of forms, kind of morphological process, or order of elements. The (dis)similarity of constructions with respect to such a coding property is here called a *scale of form*.

In Haspelmath's original 1993 paper on the inchoative/causative alternation, he distinguishes five different coding strategies that languages use to mark the alternation: causative, anticausative, equipollent, labile, and suppletive. Causative constructions are inchoative/causative pairs in which the causative is morphologically overtly derived from the inchoative. Anticausative constructions are the opposite: the inchoative is overtly derived from the causative. Labile constructions are alternations that do not show any overt marking on both inchoative and causative, in contrast to equipollent constructions that have some marking on both. Finally, suppletive constructions are inchoative/causative alternations where there is no (obvious) morphological relation between the two forms. The central opposition in this scale of form is the causative vs. anticausative opposition, the analysis of which led Haspelmath to the spontaneity scale (cf. Table 1).

Many such scales of form can rather easily be approximated by automatically generated measures. Such measures will never be perfect from a linguist's perspective, but they will get the job done much more quick. For example, consider simply counting the number of Unicode characters used in the written version of the inchoative and causative forms. A plot for the average (Unicode-based) wordlength of the inchoative vs. the causative is shown in Figure 3. Obviously, these two counts are strongly correlated because in most cases there is regular morphology deriving one from the other, and the counts of characters include the length of the stem. However, there appears to be an interesting cross-linguistic cline in the total length of the meanings. The expressions of "die/kill" tend to be short, while the expression of "develop" and "improve" seem to be long across languages.[7]

More relevant to the current topic is the upper left to lower right cline in Figure 3, which represents the different in length between the causative and the inchoative form. Meanings in which, across languages, the causative is longer than the inchoative should correspond to those meaning that have a preference for causativization, i.e. they should be high on the spontaneity scale shown

---

[7] This cline might be correlated to frequency of use, in that more frequently occurring meanings have shorter expressions. However, quickly checking some online corpora, the lower left to upper right cline in Figure 3 does not seem to correlate well with pure token frequency.

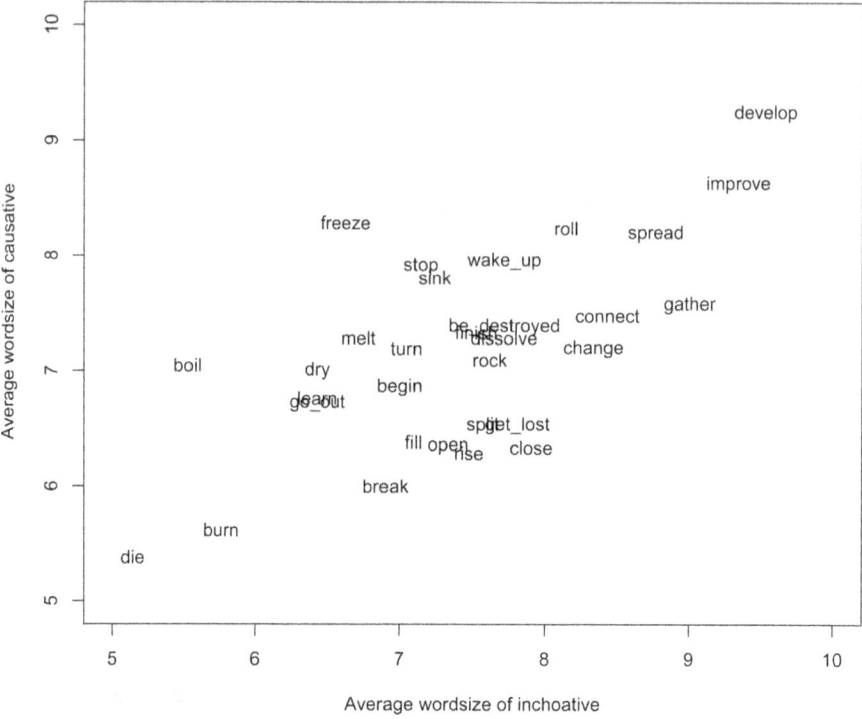

Figure 3: Average number of characters used to mark inchoative (x-axis) and causative (y-axis)

in Table 1. Unsurprisingly, as shown in Figure 4 the spontaneity scale strongly correlates with the average causative-minus-inchoative character count ($r = 0.89$). Actually, the only meaning clearly being off on this correlation is "die/kill", which is probably an effect of the imprecise estimate on the spontaneity scale (cf. note 3), and not so much an error of the approximation of counting characters. It does seem to make more sense to place "die/kill" somewhere on the higher middle of the spontaneity scale (as suggested by the counts of characters) than to place it completely on top (as suggested by the spontaneity scale in Table 1). After all, dying is indeed commonly a spontaneous activity, though it is not that uncommon to be induced by an agent.

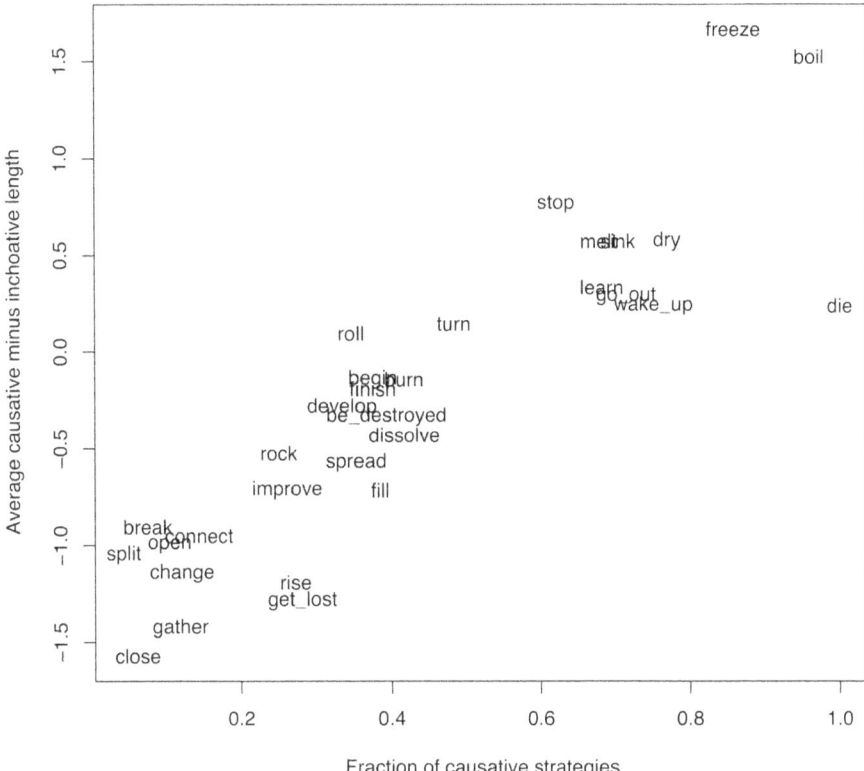

Figure 4: Spontaneity scale approximated by average length difference between the inchoative and causative forms

6 Matching form and function

Given a scale of function and a scale of form, the basic idea now is to investigate how these two scales correspond ('match'). In general, it is not immediately obvious how this should be done, but for specific cases there are many nice techniques to visualize such correlations and investigate their statistical significance. The examples discussed below illustrate some of the possibilities.

In Figure 5, the multidimensional scaling from Figure 2 is used as the basis to display the scale of function (i.e. the semantic map). The scale of form (i.e. the length difference of the actual forms) is shown as an overlay over this display. This overlay is like a geographic map using contour lines (technically called "isohypses") to indicate elevation. The level of elevation is defined by the total difference of characters between the inchoative and causative forms throughout

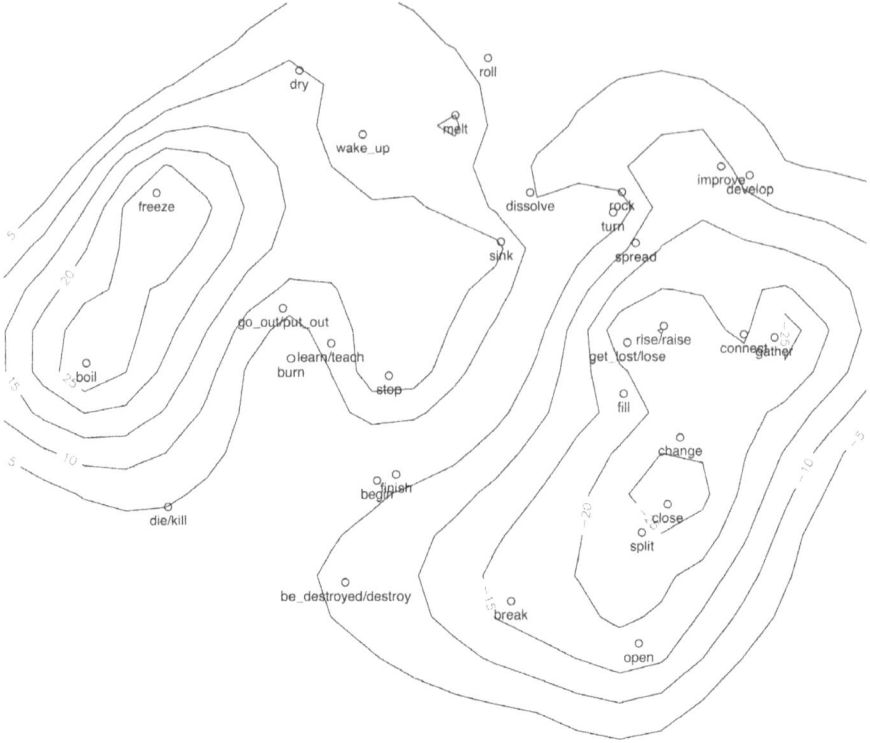

Figure 5: Summed difference in length between causative and inchoative forms throughout all languages, shown as an overlay over the scale of function

all 21 languages.[8] The scale of spontaneity can be clearly seen ranging from the highest point for "boil" and "freeze" at +25 to the lowest point for "close" at −25. This indicates that the scale of function (cf. Section 4, approximated by the location of the points in Figure 5) already includes the scale of spontaneity to some extent. This is noteworthy, because the scale of functions was made without any knowledge about the length of the forms, or about the causativization patterns.

It is also possible to give a more precise analysis of how strong the overlap between the two scales is. Statistically, the question here is to which extent the

---

[8] To make such a map, it is first necessary to make an interpolation over the measurements of elevation at the points as defined by the multidimensional scaling. It is not trivial to make such an interpolation, because the points are rather unequally distributed. To make an interpolation, I used a geostatistical technique called "kriging" as implemented by the function *krige.conv* in the R package *geoR* (Ribeiro Jr and Diggle 2001), with the parameter settings s2 = 1 and phi = 10. On this basis, the isohypses were drawn using the *contour* function.

scale of function can be explained by the scale of form. This problem is somewhat alike to a multivariate analysis of variance, if it were not for the fact that the variable to be explained (the scale of function) is of a rather unusual kind, namely a dissimilarity matrix. Recent work in bioinformatics (Zapala & Schork 2006) fortunately presents a solution for this particular problem.[9] As shown in Table 2, the length of the causative (R2 = 0.116) and the length of the inchoative (R2 = 0.249) explain about 36.5% (= 11.6 + 24.9) of the distances in the scale of function. Or, more to the point, the difference in length between inchoative and causative explains about 21% of the variation, and the sum 15% (as shown in Table 3).

Table 2: ANOVA of distance matrix by length of forms.

	Sums of Sqs	Mean Sqs	F Model	R2
Length of causative	0.022	0.022	5.449	0.116***
Length of inchoative	0.048	0.048	11.759	0.249***
Combined effect	0.012	0.012	2.962	0.063
Residuals	0.111	0.004		0.572

Table 3: ANOVA of distance matrix by length difference and length sum.

	Sums of Sqs	Mean Sqs	F Model	R2
Length difference	0.041	0.041	9.594	0.211***
Length sum	0.03	0.03	6.922	0.152***
Combined effect	0.008	0.008	1.758	0.039
Residuals	0.116	0.004		0.596

A different approach to the correlation between the scale of function and the scale of form is by using matrix correlation. Basically, the idea is to also consider the scale of form as a dissimilarity matrix and then correlate the form matrix with the function matrix. To reformulate the measurements of form (in the current case, these measurements are the average length of the inchoative and the causative expressions) into a dissimilarity matrix, all pairs of measurements have to be compared individually. As a dissimilarity, one can, for example, simply take the Euclidean distance between the measurements for each pair. This dissimilarity in effect represents the linear distance between the words as shown in the configuration of Figure 3. The length of a direct line between two words in that figure is the same as the Euclidean distance. Mathematically defined, this amounts to taking the dissimilarity as defined in (1).

(1) $\quad d(A, B) = \sqrt{(Inch_A - Inch_B)^2 + (Caus_A - Caus_B)^2}$

---

[9] The multivariate ANOVAs shown in Table 2 and Table 3 were calculated by using the function *adonis* in the R package *vegan* (Oksanen et al. 2007).

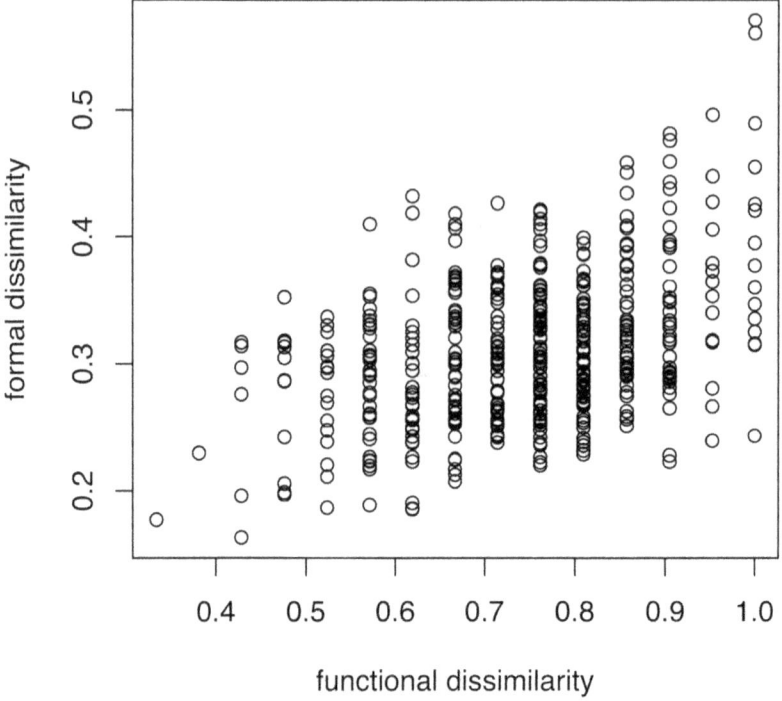

Figure 6: Correlating form and function dissimilarities

For example, "boil" has an average length of 5.52 characters for the inchoative and 7.05 for the causative. Likewise, "freeze" has an average length of 6.62 for the inchoative and 8.29 for the causative. Taking the Euclidean distance between the point (5.52, 7.05) and (6.62, 8.29) results in a dissimilarity between "boil" and "freeze" of 1.66. Doing these calculations for all pairs results in a dissimilarity matrix of form. Figure 6 shows the correlation between this scale of form and the scale of function. Each point in this figure represents one pair of meanings, plotting the dissimilarity of function against the dissimilarity of form. The figure already shows a rather nice correlation, which can also be shown to be statistically significant ($r = 0.40$, Mantel test $p < 0.0001$).[10]

---

[10] The Mantel test (Mantel 1967) was performed using the function *mantel.test* in the R package *APE* (Paradis et al. 2004).

7 Conclusions

The following points summarize the proposals put forward in this paper:
- A linguistic scale (or hierarchy) consists of three parts: a scale of functions, a scale of form, and a correspondence between the two.
- Both the scales of function and the scales of form are not necessarily linear. They can be internally structured in complex ways. Yet such complex structures are inherently interesting and still represent strong restrictions on the probabilities of linguistic variation.
- The most general description of the internal structure of these scales takes the form of dissimilarity matrices, which might boil down – under special circumstances – to a linear structure.
- Any non-random correspondence between the scale of function and a scale of form represents a generalized notion of a scale. The functional side defined the topology of the scale (the 'form' of the scale) and the the formal side defines the direction of the scale.
- The method to establish a correspondence between form and function is a kind of matrix correlation, though other methods might also be used. However, this is an area where much work has to be done to elucidate which approaches are most suitable for linguistic typology.

Acknowledgements

This paper was written while I was at the Max Planck Institute for Evolutionary Anthropology in Leipzig. A revised version was prepared while I was funded by the ERC starting grant "QuantHistLing". I thank Martin Haspelmath for in-depth discussion of the paper before the preparation of the revision.

References

Bandelt, H.J., and A.W. Dress. 1992. Split decomposition: a new and useful approach to phylogenetic analysis of distance data. *Molecular Phylogenetics and Evolution* 1(3): 242–252.

Bickel, Balthasar, Alena Witzlack, and Taras Zakharko. 2015. Referential scales and case alignment: reviewing the typological evidence. This volume.

Bryant, David, Flavia Filimon, and Russell D. Gray. 2005. Untangling our past: Languages, trees, splits and networks. *The Evolution of Cultural Diversity: A Phylogenetic Approach*, Ruth Mace, Clare J. Holden, and Stephan Shennan (eds.), 67–84. London: UCL.

Croft, William. 2003. *Typology and Universals*. (Cambridge Textbooks in Linguistics). Cambridge: Cambridge University Press.

Cysouw, Michael. 2007. Building semantic maps: the case of person marking. *New Challenges in Typology*, Bernhard Wälchli and Matti Miestamo (eds.), 225–248. Berlin: Mouton de Gruyter.

Cysouw, Michael. 2010. Semantic maps as metrics on meaning. *Linguistic Discovery* 8(1): 70–95.

Dress, Andreas W. M., and Daniel H. Huson. 2004. Constructing Splits Graphs. *IEEE Transactions on Computational Biology And Bioinformatics* 1(3): 109–115.

Haspelmath, Martin. 1993. More on the typology of inchoative/causative verb alternations. *Causatives and Transitivity*, Bernard Comrie and Maria Polinsky (eds.), 87–120. Amsterdam: Benjamins.

Haspelmath, Martin. 2003. The geometry of grammatical meaning: Semantic maps and cross-linguistic comparison. In *The New Psychology of Language: Cognitive and Functional Approaches to Language Structure*, Michael Tomasello (ed.), Volume 2, 211–242. Mahwah, NJ: Erlbaum.

Haspelmath, Martin. 2010. Comparative concepts and descriptive categories in cross-linguistic studies. *Language* 86(3). 663–687.

Huson, Daniel H., and David Bryant. 2006. Application of phylogenetic networks in evolutionary studies. *Molecular Biology and Evolution* 23(2): 254–267.

Keenan, Edward L. 1976. Towards a universal definition of 'subject'. In *Subject and Topic*, Charles N. Li (ed.), 303–333. New York, NY: Academic Press.

Keenan, Edward L., and Bernard Comrie. 1977. Noun phrase accessibility and universal grammar. *Linguistic Inquiry* 8(1): 63–99.

Mantel, Nathan. 1967. The detection of disease clustering and a generalized regression approach. *Cancer Research* 27(2): 209–220.

Oksanen, Jari, Roel Kindt, Pierre Legendre, Bob O'Hara, and M. Henry H. Stevens. 2007. vegan: Community Ecology Package. *R package*.

Paradis, E., J. Claude, and K. Strimmer. 2004. APE: analyses of phylogenetics and evolution in R language. *Bioinformatics* 20: 289–290.

R Development Core Team. 2007. *R: A Language and Environment for Statistical Computing*. Vienna, Austria: R Foundation for Statistical Computing.

Ribeiro Jr, Paulo Justiniano, and Peter J. Diggle. 2001. geoR: A package for geostatistical analysis. *R News* 1(2): 15–18.

Silverstein, Michael. 1976. Hierarchy of features and ergativity. *Grammatical Categories in Australian Languages*, R M W Dixon (ed.), 112–171. Australian Institute of Aboriginal Studies: Canberra.

Wälchli, Bernhard, and Michael Cysouw. 2012. Lexical typology through similarity semantics: Toward a semantic map of motion verbs. *Linguistics* 50(3): 671–710.

Zapala, MA, and NJ Schork. 2006. Multivariate regression analysis of distance matrices for testing associations between gene expression patterns and related variables. *Proceedings of the National Academy of Sciences of the United States of America* 103(51): 19430–19435.

Stefan Keine & Gereon Müller[1]

5 Differential Argument Encoding by Impoverishment

The present paper can be viewed as an extension of the theory of differential argument encoding developed in Aissen (1999, 2003). We maintain Aissen's hypothesis that the effects of differential argument encoding can be derived from harmonic alignment of scales, but we argue that differential encoding should best be viewed as a purely morphological phenomenon (rather than as a syntactic phenomenon, as in Aissen's approach). More specifically, we suggest that harmonic alignment of scales may bring about impoverishment operations that reduce syntactic inputs for morphological realization (see Halle and Marantz 1993). The evidence for this new approach comes from the observation that the *yes/no* alternations of case exponents as they are envisaged in Aissen's system are insufficient to capture degrees of morphological marking. As we will show based on data from a variety of languages (among them Hindi, Dyirbal, Mannheim German, Trumai, Cavineña, and Finnish), the *zero/non-zero* alternations discussed by Aissen are only part of a much broader *less/more* pattern.

1 Introduction

Implementing typologically motivated markedness hierarchies into formal accounts of grammar is the basic aim of the approach to differential argument encoding developed by Aissen (1999, 2003). Essentially, a marked (or 'unusual') object DP (e.g., an object that is animate, or that is 1. person, or that is specific) is often overtly marked for case whereas an unmarked object DP (with prototypical object properties, like being inanimate, or 3. person, or non-specific) is left without an overt marker. Similarly, marked subject DPs (e.g., 3. person subjects, or inanimate subjects) are often encoded by case marking where unmarked subjects are not. Aissen derives this phenomenon by means of two operations that are available in an optimality-theoretic approach to grammar: first, *harmonic*

---

[1] For helpful comments and discussion, we would like to thank the participants of the Leipzig workshop on scales (March 29, 2008), NELS 39 (November 7–9, 2008), and the Cologne workshop on transitivity (November 14–15, 2008), as well as written comments by Jochen Trommer and three anonymous reviewers. This work was supported by a DFG grant to the project *Argument Encoding in Morphology and Syntax*, as part of Forschergruppe 742.

alignment of scales, and second, *local conjunction* of constraints. Harmonic alignment captures complex interactions between markedness constraints for case as follows: A general constraint blocking case marking (*STRUC$_C$) may be ranked lower than a complex conflicting constraint demanding case marking for a certain (marked) type of argument (e.g., *Obj/anim & *Ø$_C$) but ranked higher than a complex conflicting constraint that requires case marking for another (unmarked) type of argument (e.g., *Obj/inan & *Ø$_C$), which results in overt marking in the former case, and zero marking in the latter.

The analysis presented here assumes that the basic mechanisms employed by Aissen – i.e., harmonic alignment, local conjunction, etc. –, provide the right tool for implementing scales in grammatical theory. However, in contrast to Aissen, we hold that this differential argument encoding is not the result of constraints that apply in the syntax; rather, these constraints belong to the morphological component (or, more precisely, the morphology-syntax interface). In essence, we argue that the theoretical means adopted by Aissen have to be combined with a a post-syntactic theory of morphology in which syntactic structures can be modified prior to morphological realization, such as Distributed Morphology (see Halle and Marantz 1993, 1994).[2]

The main empirical argument for this claim is that Aissen's analysis is not able to derive *all* cases of differential marking; it only derives a proper subpart of them. Since in her approach the case feature of canonical DPs is deleted syntactically, it can never be realized overtly. Thus, all instances of differential marking are predicted to be *zero/non-zero* alternations. This prediction is not borne out. As we will argue, there are in fact cases of marker alternations that adhere to the same scales and principles that are claimed by Aissen to regulate differential marking. Crucially, however, these alternations are between two (or possibly even more) *overt* markers. This means that there are *degrees* of morphological marking. Since the underlying factors are identical to the ones identified by Aissen, it is an undesirable state of affairs that only a proper subset of them can be accounted for. Clearly, this way a generalization is being missed.

By situating the system developed by Aissen within morphology one can overcome this shortcoming. Roughly speaking, in the approach proposed here it is not the case that the case feature of a DP can either be present or completely absent. Instead, it is possible that feature deletion only affects *parts* of case features. When the appropriate marker for a given DP is inserted, it might

---

[2] See also Bank (2008) for an analysis of German pronominal declension that rests on similar assumptions.

be the case that the best exponent is not the zero marker but a *second overt marker* (apart from the one standardly used to encode case). Hence, the system laid out here derives all cases of hierarchy-driven *less/more* alternations. Since these include the *zero/non-zero* alternation as a special case, it accommodates all instances of differential argument encoding discussed by Aissen but captures other functionally motivated alternations as well.

The article is structured as follows: Section 2 provides the background. Subsection 2.1 summarizes the analysis developed by Aissen (1999, 2003) for differential marking. In subsections 2.2 and 2.3, we briefly introduce the two theoretical concepts that we will rely on in our modification of Aissen's system, viz., *impoverishment* and *iconicity*, respectively. Section 3 sets the stage for the new analysis. In subsections 3.2 and 3.3, we informally provide some initial motivation for a new analysis by looking at differential argument encoding in Dyirbal and direct/inverse marking in Algonquian. After this, subsection 3.4 presents an overview of the grammatical architecture assumed in Distributed Morphology, and introduces the theoretical mechanisms that the analysis is based on in a more comprehensive way. Finally, section 4 forms the core of the present paper. Here we consider empirical phenomena that directly support the hypothesis that differential argument encoding is a morphological (rather than syntactic) phenomenon. First, the basic working of the theory is illustrated for Hindi. After this, we consider the cases of a colloquial variety of German spoken in the Mannheim area, the Brazilian language Trumai, and the Bolivian language Cavineña to argue that Aissen's system is insufficient. Finally, we develop a new analysis of object case marking in Finnish; in the course of doing so, we argue that what is traditionally viewed as a system comprising four different syntactic object cases should in fact be analyzed as a system based on only one object case, with a set of competing morphological exponents distributed over the various contexts according to the principles of differential argument encoding.

2 Background

2.1 Harmonic alignment of scales

The present approach follows Aissen (1999, 2003) in claiming that differential argument encoding can be derived by harmonic alignment of scales. This mechanism is illustrated below.

Consider first *Hale/Silverstein hierarchies* (Hale 1972, Silverstein 1976):[3]

(1) Scales
  a. *GF scale* (basic)
     Subject > object
  b. *θ scale*
     Agent > patient
  c. *Person scale*
     Local Pers. (1,2) > 3. Pers.
  d. *Prominence scale*
     X > x
     (discourse-prominent argument > non-discourse-prominent argument)
  e. *Animacy scale*
     Hum(an) > Anim(ate) > Inan(imate)
  f. *Definiteness scale*
     Personal pronoun (Pro) > Name (PN) > Def(inite) > Indefinite Specific (Spec) > NonSpecific (NSpec)

For instance, the definiteness scale states that pronouns are at one end of the hierarchy, that non-specific DPs are at the other end of the hierarchy, and that proper names, definite DPs, and indefinite specific DPs are in between. *Harmonic Alignment* provides a means to combine two such scales.

(2) *Harmonic Alignment* (Prince and Smolensky 1993/2004)
   Suppose given a binary dimension D_1 with a scale X > Y on its elements {X,Y}, and another dimension D_2 with a scale a > b > ... > z on its elements {a,b,...,z}. The *harmonic alignment* of D_1 and D_2 is the pair of Harmony scales H_X, H_Y:
   a. H_X: X/a ≻ X/b ≻ ... ≻ X/z
   b. H_Y: Y/z ≻ ... ≻ Y/b ≻ Y/a

   The *constraint alignment* is the pair of constraint hierarchies C_X, C_Y:
   a. C_X: *X/z ≫ ... ≫ *X/b ≫ *X/a
   b. C_Y: *Y/a ≫ *Y/b ≫ ... ≫ *Y/z

---

[3] The basic GF scale leaves open how "subject" and "object" are to be defined. Throughout this paper, we will presuppose that grammatical functions are derivative notions – essentially, positions in phrase structure representations (see Chomsky 1965). On this view, we can assume that "subject" means "specifier of vP", and object "complement of V" (see, e.g., Chomsky 2001). Still, to simplify the exposition, in what follows we will mostly use the labels "subject" and "object" (rather than, say, "Spec(v)" and "Comp(V)").

Take the binary GF scale and the animacy scale as an example. Applying harmonic alignment yields the harmony scales in (3):

(3) a. Subj/Hum > Subj/Anim > Subj/Inan
    b. Obj/Inan > Obj/Anim > Obj/Hum

These combined scales express markedness relations between combinations of features. Thus, (3a) states that the least marked kind of subject is human, followed by animate subjects. Inanimate subjects are highly atypical and therefore most marked. As for objects, the situation is the other way around (see (3b)). In an optimality-theoretic setting, these markedness hierarchies can be reinterpreted as constraint hierarchies by transforming the members of (3a), (3b) into constraints that prohibit the respective configurations, and reversing their order; see (4).

(4) a. *Subj/Inan ≫ *Subj/Anim ≫ *Subj/Hum
    b. *Obj/Hum ≫ *Obj/Anim ≫ *Obj/Inan

Take (4a) as an example. The constraint against inanimate subjects is ranked highest. This captures the generalization underlying (3a) that this kind of subject is more marked than an animate (but non-human) subject, which in turn is more marked than a human subject. Constraints are in principle violable in optimality theory; but it is of course more likely for a low-ranked constraint to be violated by an optimal candidate than it is for a high-ranked constraint. More specifically, harmonic alignment of scales captures implicational universals: If a subject argument with status X on some scale is permitted, then a subject argument with status Y on the same scale is also permitted in a language if Y outranks X; and vice versa for objects.

So far, so good. Constraints of the type in (4) may (in interaction with other constraints) lead to situations where certain kinds of arguments (as a tendency: those precluded by high-ranked constraints) cannot be realized at all; and this phenomenon is certainly well documented in the world's languages. However, differential argument encoding involves a slightly different state of affairs: The marked argument does not fail to show up completely; rather, it is morphologically marked in a way that a comparable unmarked argument is not. To derive a differential encoding of marked arguments, Aissen (1999, 2003) employs a second technique (in addition to harmonic alignment) that has been developed in optimality theory (see Smolensky 1993, 2006, Legendre, Smolensky, and Wilson 1998: among others), viz., *local constraint conjunction*. Simplifying a bit, a constraint that is the local conjunction A & B of two constraints A, B is violated if both A and B are violated (in some local domain); by definition, A & B outranks both A and B. Local conjunction is not originally envisaged as an operation that combines a single constraint A with a fixed subhierarchy of constraints $B_1 \gg B_2 \gg \ldots \gg B_n$ (as it can be derived by harmonic alignment), but Aissen assumes just this as the basic procedure underlying differential argument encoding. Furthermore, she makes the plausible assumption that iterated local conjunction of some constraint A with each of the members of a fixed subhierarchy of constraints $B_1 \gg B_2 \gg \ldots \gg B_n$ must maintain the original order of constraints within the subhierarchy, yielding A & $B_1 \gg$ A & $B_2 \gg \ldots \gg$ A & B_n. In the case at hand, Aissen stipulates that the markedness constraint $*\emptyset_C$ in (5), which acts as a general ban on absence of case marking (= A), can be locally conjoined with a subhierarchy of the type in (4) (= $B_1 \gg B_2 \gg \ldots \gg B_n$), yielding the fixed rankings in (5).

(5) $*\emptyset_C$ (Star-Zero(Case)):
"penalizes the absence of a value for the feature CASE"

(6) a. $*Subj/Inan$ & $*\emptyset_C \gg *Subj/Anim$ & $*\emptyset_C \gg *Subj/Hum$ & $*\emptyset_C$
    b. $*Obj/Hum$ & $*\emptyset_C \gg *Obj/Anim$ & $*\emptyset_C \gg *Obj/Inan$ & $*\emptyset_C$

These constraints only regard the *case marking* of certain types of DPs. For instance, $*Subj/Inan$ & $*\emptyset_C$ is violated if an inanimate subject does not bear a case feature. Therefore, all constraints in (6) penalize the *absence* of case features.

$*STRUC_C$ is a conflicting markedness constraint. This constraint is violated if a DP bears a case feature; see (7).

(7) $*STRUC_C$ (Star-Structure(Case)):
"penalizes a value for the morphological category CASE"

This constraint is not conjoined with a constraint subhierarchy but interspersed with the subhierarchy constraints derived by local conjunction. It effects a suppression of case marking for all those arguments where the respective constraint that demands case marking is ranked lower. This general procedure is illustrated in (8) for the subhierarchy derived by locally conjoining $*\emptyset_C$ (Star-Zero(Case)) with the original subhierarchy correlating object status with the definiteness scale (see Aissen 2003).[4,5]

(8) *Obj/Pro & *Ø$_C$ ≫   ← *STRUC$_C$ Kalkatungu: no objects case-marked

*Obj/PN & *Ø$_C$ ≫   ← *STRUC$_C$ Catalan: only pronominal objects case-marked

*Obj/Def & *Ø$_C$ ≫   ← *STRUC$_C$ Pitjantjatjara: only pronominal and PN objects case-marked

*Obj/Spec & *Ø$_C$ ≫   ← *STRUC$_C$ Hebrew: only pronominal, PN, and definite objects case-marked

*Obj/NSpec & *Ø$_C$ ≫   ← *STRUC$_C$ Turkish: all objects case-marked except non-specific objects

← *STRUC$_C$ Written Japanese: all objects case-marked

Taking Catalan as an example, *STRUC$_C$ outranks all constraints except *Obj/Pro & *Ø$_C$, which prohibits case features in all contexts except those involving object pronouns. As for object pronouns, the higher-ranked markedness constraint *Obj/Pro & *Ø$_C$, which requires a case feature for pronouns, renders a violation of *STRUC$_C$ non-fatal.

In what follows, we will presuppose the basic correctness of Aissen's approach to differential argument encoding in terms of local conjunction and harmonic alignment of markedness scales. However, we will deviate from Aissen's approach as far as the grammar-internal localization of these principles is concerned. In Aissen's view, the resulting constraint ranking constitutes a part of syntax: Optimization determines whether or not DP arguments bear a case feature. This yields a *yes/no* alternation: If a DPs bears a case feature, it is marked by an overt exponent; if there is no case feature, zero marking results. Hence, it is impossible to account for *degrees* of morphological marking as they arise if typical DPs are marked *less* than atypical ones, but marked nevertheless.

The present approach situates differential argument encoding within a postsyntactic morphological component where case features can be deleted postsyntactically by impoverishment. Impoverishment is triggered by markedness

---

4 Importantly, whereas *Ø$_C$ *must* be locally conjoined with subhierarchies gained from harmonic alignment of Silverstein scales in order to derive the properties of differential argument encoding in Aissen's approach, *STRUC$_C$ *must not* be so conjoined. As far as we can see, this asymmetric behaviour of the two opposed markedness constraints under consideration must be stipulated; deriving it from more basic assumptions would still seem to be a desideratum at this point.

5 As for the phenomenon of differential object marking, see de Swart (2007) for recent discussion.

constraints which interact with complex faithfulness constraints (derived from scales by harmonic alignment and local conjunction) in more or less the same way that they do in Aissen's analysis. Crucially, we also assume that traditional case features (like, e.g., *accusative*) are to be decomposed into combinations of more primitive features and thus have internal structure (e.g., [–obl(ique), +gov (erned)]; see Bierwisch 1967). Consequently, a deletion of case features may be partial, i.e., may leave some of the more primitive case features that define the syntactic case category intact, and accessible for morphological realization. Accordingly, by relocating differential argument encoding to the morphological component, we end up with a more refined and flexible system in which differential argument encoding alternations can involve various overt exponents (rather than just one overt exponent and zero exponence). Variations in differential argument encoding that go beyond zero/non-zero marking are systematically unavailable in an approach that places all the relevant operations in syntax (or does not distinguish between morphological and syntactic aspects of case – in a sense, then, we identify the lack of discrimination between abstract, syntactic and concrete, morphological case as the main problem with Aissen's approach).[6,7]

---

[6] Compare also Legate's (2008) arguments for a distinction between absolutive DPs that are inherently zero-marked and accusative DPs that may sometimes also be zero-marked morphologically but behave differently from a syntactic point of view.

[7] As noted above, throughout this paper we will assume that Aissen's approach to differential argument encoding in terms of harmonic alignment and local conjunction is basically on the right track. However, this is not a foregone conclusion; in line with this, several caveats are in order. First, various alternative (optimality-theoretic) systems have been proposed that modify or extend Aissen's approach in one way or the other; see particularly Stiebels (2000, 2002, 2008), Ortmann (2002), and Trommer (2006). We will have nothing to say about these alternative approaches in what follows (although it seems to us that most of what we have to say here could in principle also be implemented in these competing analyses, given that they share a number of properties).

Second, throughout this paper we will ignore recent attempts to derive the effects as epiphenomena of independently motivated syntactic assumptions; see Brown, Koch, and Wiltschko (2004), Harbour (2008), and Richards (2015). We take these approaches to differential argument encoding to be highly interesting and definitely worth pursuing, but as things stand, they do not yet have an empirical coverage that is similar to Aissen's original system; it remains to be seen whether what we argue for here could be maintained in its essentials if a theory is adopted according to which differential marking is an epiphenomenon.

Third, we will have very little to say about possible arguments against the whole enterprise of treating differential argument encoding in a grammar-internal way, as can be found in Carnie (2005) and Haspelmath (2007).

Fourth and finally, throughout this paper we presuppose that the phenomenon of differential argument encoding is indeed real, and not an artefact of focussing on a non-representative typological sample (see Bickel 2007 for preliminary arguments to this effect, but also Bickel et al 2015 for qualifications and further discussion of this issue).

2.2 Impoverishment

Impoverishment rules are a fundamental concept of Distributed Morphology. They are standardly taken to be deletion transformations that remove morpho-syntactic features (which need to be realized by morphological exponents in a post-syntactic morphological component) before marker (= vocabulary item) insertion takes place (see Bonet 1991, Noyer 1998, Halle and Marantz 1993, 1994, Bobaljik 2002, Frampton 2002). As a consequence of impoverishment, inflectional morphology applies to reduced feature matrices, and there can be a *retreat to the general case*: A less specific marker is inserted than would otherwise be expected. Thus, impoverishment can capture instances of syncretism; and it can do so in a way that a mere underspecification of exponents cannot: Unlike underspecification of individual markers, impoverishment can capture *system-defining* instances of syncretism, i.e., syncretism patterns that show up in more than one paradigm in a language.

A slightly different approach to impoverishment operations is put forward in Trommer (1999): On this view, there are no specific impoverishment rules that delete features. Rather, impoverishment is assumed to represent a subcase of regular vocabulary insertion: If a zero exponent is highly specific, it may have to be inserted into a functional morpheme before other (non-zero) vocabulary items (given that marker competition is resolved by choosing the most specific marker; see below). This produces the effect of impoverishment if a concept of vocabulary insertion is adopted according to which features in the functional morpheme which are not matched by the zero vocabulary item (and thereby discharged) remain accessible for further insertion (also see Noyer 1992 for this concept).

Finally, it has been suggested that impoverishment might best be viewed as being triggered by general filters blocking the co-occurrence of features (see Noyer 1992). A somewhat more flexible version of this proposal has been pursued in optimality-theoretic approaches (not necessarily by explicitly adopting the notion of "impoverishment", though): In this latter type of approach, interacting optimality-theoretic constraints may lead to optimal outputs in which morpho-syntactic features of the input have been suppressed, in violation of DEP constraints that prohibit deletion; see Grimshaw (2001), Kiparsky (2001), Trommer (2001, 2006), Wunderlich (2004), Don and Blom (2006), Lahne (2010), and Opitz (2008) for approaches along these lines.

Against this background, we would like to propose that Aissen's analyses should be reanalyzed in terms of impoverishment, by combining aspects of the various types of analyses just mentioned. First, impoverishment is a post-syntactic operation that deletes morpho-syntactic features, as is standardly assumed. And second, such deletion applies so as to satisfy complex faithfulness constraints in an optimality-theoretic setting that models the interface between syntax and (inflectional) morphology. These faithfulness constraints are created by means of harmonic alignment of markedness scales. On this view, impoverishment (at least of the type that is relevant in the present context) is functionally motivated.

2.3 Iconicity

Harmonic alignment of scales combined with impoverishment rules derives marker alternations for different kinds of DPs. However, nothing is said so far about the relation between these alternating markers. It might a priori be possible that for highly typical DPs impoverishment applies, yielding an reduced feature specification. Consequently, a less specific marker could be inserted that nevertheless could be phonologically more complex than the original marker. This would result in a typical DP being marked *more* than an atypical DP, clearly in contradiction to the intuition behind differential argument encoding. To restrict the system in such a way as to only allow for typical DPs to be marked *less* than atypical ones (and not vice versa), we adopt a meta-grammatical principle of *iconicity*, which correlates form and function of markers:

(9) *Iconicity Meta-Principle:*
 Similarity of form implies similarity of function (within a certain domain).

For iconicity to work, it has to be the case that exponents can be *underspecified* with respect to morpho-syntactic features (which may in turn be more abstract than is motivated by purely syntactic considerations – cf., for instance, [±obj], [±obl] as primitive, decomposed case features whose cross-classification yields the four cases of German, with underspecification capturing natural classes of cases). As a matter of fact, underspecification of exponents is employed as a means to capture syncretism in most contemporary morphological theories, among them Distributed Morphology (see Halle and Marantz 1993, 1994, Noyer 1992, Halle 1997, Harley and Noyer 2003: among others), Paradigm Function Morphology (see Stump 2001), Minimalist Morphology (see Wunderlich 1996, 1997b), and Network Morphology (see Corbett and Fraser 1993, Baerman, Brown, and Corbett 2005). In a typical inflectional paradigm, underspecification does not affect all exponents in the same way: Some exponents may not be underspecified at all (if there is no systematic syncretism involved); some exponents may be underspecified to varying degrees (thereby deriving syncretism domains of various sizes); and even full underspecification is often envisaged as a possibility (embodied in the concept of elsewhere, or default, markers).

Given this state of affairs, the Iconicity Meta-Principle leads us to expect that the form of an exponent correlates with the degree of its underspecification with respect to morpho-syntactic features (or, more precisely, its degree of specificity), in the sense that more underspecified markers tend to be phonologically less marked (e.g., *shorter*, or more *sonorous*) than less underspecifed markers; the fact that radically underspecified markers are often zero therefore does not come as a surprise. Something along the lines of (9) is arguably tacitly assumed (at least as a tendency) in many analyses of inflectional paradigms (also compare Halle and Marantz's 1993 discussion of highly specified zero exponents as a possible exception to the rule). To the best of our knowledge, it has first been explicitly recognized as a principle that may shape inflectional paradigms consisting of underspecified exponents in Bernd Wiese's work (see Wiese 1999, 2003, 2004).[8]

To give an example of meta-grammatical iconicity at work, consider Wiese's (1999) analysis of determiner inflection in German. To derive various kinds of syncretism in this paradigm (which spans four cases, three genders, and two numbers), Wiese (1999) proposes (10) as the set of underspecified inflectional exponents.

(10) *Exponents for determiner inflection in German*
    a. (i)   /m/ ↔ [+masc, +obl, +gov]   (DAT.MASC.SG./NEUT.SG.)
        (ii) /s/ ↔ [+masc, +obl]   (GEN.MASC.SG./NEUT.SG.)
        (iii) /s/ ↔ [+masc, +fem]   (NOM./ACC.NEUT.SG.)
    b. (i)   /n/ ↔ [+masc, +gov]   (ACC.MASC.SG.)
        (ii) /r/ ↔ [+masc]   (NOM.MASC.SG.)
        (iii) /r/ ↔ [+obl, +fem]   (DAT./GEN.FEM.SG.)
        (iv) /n/ ↔ [+obl, +gov]   (DAT.PL.)
        (v) /r/ ↔ [+obl]   (GEN.PL.)
    c. (i)   /e/ ↔ [ ]   (NOM./ACC.FEM.SG./PL.)

For present purposes, it is not necessary to go through this list of markers in detail (so as to illustrate how underspecification derives syncretism). The only property of the list in (10) that is important at this point is that specificity decreases from top to bottom in this list.[9] In the same way, the three groups of

---

8 Note that Wiese's proposal involves a radical break with traditional approaches, where iconicity is measured based on fully specified forms (see Plank 1979, Wurzel 1984).
9 Note that Wiese assumes, in accordance with much relevant literature on this topic (also see below), that specificity of (possibly underspecified) markers cannot solely be derived by comparing the sizes of the sets of features that are associated with the exponents; rather, a hierarchy of features also contributes to determining specificity. For concreteness, the hierarchy that Wiese postulates is the one in (i).
(i) [+masc] > [+obl] > [+fem] > [+gov]
Thus, e.g., /s/ in (a-ii) of (10) is more specific than, say, /r/ in (b-iii) of (10).

markers identified in (10) (viz., (a), (b), and (c)) can be ordered according to an independently motivated phonological criterion: /m/ and /s/ are heavy markers, /n/ and /r/ are less heavy markers, and /e/ (= ə) is lightest. As Wiese notes, this does not look like a coincidence; and the correlation is explained if iconicity holds in general of inflectional paradigms. Here and in what follows, we will assume that this abstract, highly theory-dependent concept of iconicity is a recurring feature of inflectional systems (see, e.g. Müller 2004, 2005, 2007b, Opitz 2006, and Georgi 2008 for additional evidence from a variety of languages).

Returning to the domain of differential argument encoding, the Iconicity Meta-Principle implies that a situation where a marker is *less* specific in terms of morpho-syntactic features but *more* marked phonologically does not arise. The working of impoverishment ensures that contexts which are affected by the operation will have to be realized by less specific (i.e., more underspecified) markers than would otherwise be possible (a retreat to the general case). Given iconicity, the less specific exponent will then also be phonologically lighter (and/or more sonorous) than its more specific competitor that is blocked as a result of impoverishment. Therefore, given that differential argument encoding can be traced back to impoverishment operations that delete features in prototypical contexts (e.g., with inanimate 3. person objects) but not in atypical contexts (e.g., with animate 1. person objects), it follows that less typical argument DPs will be phonologically more marked than more typical argument DPs (and, of course, zero marking for highly typical argument DPs is also expected as an option). Thus, the core property of differential argument encoding is captured by the interaction of impoverishment and the Iconicity Meta-Principle. In the next section, we flesh out this proposal.

3 Towards a new analysis

In this section, we will motivate the need for an extensions of Aissen's (1999, 2003) account of differential argument encoding on the basis of data from Dyirbal and Algonquian. We will then make explicit the background assumptions that the present proposal is based on.

3.1 Claim

We suggest that differential marking is not necessarily a categorial *yes/no* phenomenon; rather, it can be a gradient, *less/more* phenomenon. According to this view, alternation with zero exponence is but a special case of a more general option of differential marker realization. Differential argument encoding is brought about by impoverishment, i.e., post-syntactic deletion of morphosyntactic features. Impoverishment is triggered by faithfulness constraints which in turn are derived from a harmonic alignment of markedness scales. Impoverishment leads to the insertion of a less specific inflection marker. Consequently, it may lead to zero exponence, but it may also lead to a selection of other markers that instantiate a "retreat to the general case", and that – given the Iconicity Meta-Principle – are formally closer to zero exponence than the marker that would otherwise be expected (also see Opitz's (2008) discussion of Tlapanec for relevant discussion).

The need for an extension of the system developed in Aissen (1999, 2003) can be illustrated on the basis of differential subject and object marking in Dyirbal and inverse marking in Algonquian languages. Aissen (1999, 2003) cites both Dyirbal and inverse marking as evidence for her approach. We will argue, however, that as soon as one takes into consideration a broader array of empirical facts, it becomes clear that Aissen's approach, being confined to *yes/no* alternations, misses crucial generalizations. The upshot of the argument is that a theory that treats zero/non-zero alternations and non-zero/non-zero ones on a par is to be preferred on empirical grounds.

3.2 Differential encoding of subjects and objects in Dyirbal

Aissen (1999, 2003) uses Dyirbal as an argument in favour of her approach and argues that for both nouns and pronouns, a zero/non-zero alternation occurs that is conditioned by markedness hierarchies. In this section, based on Carnie (2005), Haspelmath (2007) and ultimately Dixon (1972, 1994), we argue that this is empirically wrong: There are alternations between two overt markers whose choice is determined by the same principles as the zero/non-zero alternation.[10]

As shown in (11), 1st and 2nd person pronouns are unmarked if used as subjects and bear the marker *-na* (accusative) if they occur in object position. The situation is reversed for nouns: Here subjects are marked overtly with *-ŋgu* (ergative) and objects show no overt exponence.

---

[10] Similar points can be made for Djapu, another Australian language (Morphy 1983, Legate 2008).

(11) a. nyura-Ø ŋana-na buṛa-n
       2PL-NOM 1PL-ACC see-NONFUT
       'You saw us.'
   b. ŋana-Ø nyura-na buṛa-n
       1PL-NOM 2PL-ACC see-NONFUT
       'We saw you.'
   c. ŋuma-Ø yabu-ŋgu buṛa-n
       father-ABS mother-ERG see-NONFUT
       'Mother saw father.'

This is consistent with the person hierarchy in (12): Local persons are canonical subjects and non-local persons are typical objects. Deviances have to be marked explicitly.

(12) *Person hierarchy*
     1,2 (local persons) > 3, other DPs (non-local persons)

As shown by Aissen, the constraint ordering in (13) yields this result.

(13) *Constraint ranking for Dyirbal*

$$\left\{ \begin{array}{l} \text{*Subj/3 \& *}\emptyset_C, \\ \text{*Obj/local \& *}\emptyset_C \end{array} \right\} \gg \text{*S\scriptsize TRUC}_C \gg \left\{ \begin{array}{l} \text{*Subj/local \& *}\emptyset_C, \\ \text{*Obj/3 \& }\emptyset_C \end{array} \right\}$$

Upon closer scrutiny, this empirical pattern turns out to be incomplete. Local subjects and non-local objects are not always unmarked morphologically. Canonical arguments do bear case.

3.2.1 Noun-class particles

In Dyirbal full DPs can take a noun-class particle, which expresses the proximity or visibility of the entity being referred to. These particles inflect for case, with nominatives/absolutives taking a different marker than -Ø.

(14) Dyirbal noun-class particles

	NOM/ABS	ERG	DAT	GEN
Class 1	bayi	baŋgul	bagul	baŋul
Class 2	balan	baŋgun	bagun	baŋun

(15) is a relevant example.

(15) bayi   ŋuma-Ø   baŋgun   yabu-ŋgu   buɾa-n
      CLASS1.ABS   father-ABS   CLASS2.ERG   mother-ERG   see-NONFUT
      'Mother saw father.'

In contrast to nouns, the nominative/absolutive form of the particle *bayi* is *not* zero marked. This cannot be derived in Aissen's system: If the case feature of the whole DP, containing noun and particle, is deleted, it is impossible to state that the particle agrees *in case* with the noun, but this is what the suffix on the particle suggests.

Within the present analysis, this state of affairs falls into place: Impoverishment applies to both the noun and the particle. Since there are different sets of markers for nouns and class particles, in the case of nouns the zero marker wins, whereas an overt marker is attached to the particles.

3.2.2 Singular pronouns

Within the pronominal system, the nominative shows zero exponence only in *most* cases, not in all cases. In 1SG and 2SG contexts, nominative is morphologically marked as well: It is not formed by taking the accusative form and simply removing the accusative ending *-na*.

(16) Dyirbal pronouns

	NOMINATIVE	ACCUSATIVE
1DUAL	ŋaldyi	ŋalidyi-na
1PL	ŋandyi	ŋandyi-na
2DUAL	ɲubaladyi	ɲubaladyi-na
2PL	ɲuradyi	ɲuradyi-na
1SG	ŋadya	nayguna
2SG	ŋinda	ninuna

Consequently, Aissen's system is capable of deriving the forms of dual and plural pronouns but is forced to regard the singular pronouns as fundamentally different in nature as they cannot constitute a case of differential argument encoding in Aissen's terms. This, however, is doubtful. Not only are the distributional patterns of nominative and accusative identical for all kinds of pronouns, indicating that the person hierarchy is active for singular pronouns as well. Moreover, it is a striking fact that the accusative forms are *more* marked phonologically than the nominative markers (i.e., they consist of more segments). Hence, hierarchical markedness correlates with morphological markedness, which strongly suggests an approach treating all kinds of pronouns alike in terms of differential argument encoding.

The present approach assumes that for all kinds of pronouns impoverishment applies to the nominative forms. Since there are different marker sets for dual and plural on the one hand and singular pronouns on the other hand, an overt marker is inserted in the case of singulars, and the zero marker with duals and plurals.

3.3 Direct and inverse marking

On the basis of evidence from the Sino-Tibetan language Nocte, Aissen (1999) argues that her approach is capable of deriving direct-inverse marking as well. In Nocte, the hierarchically less marked direct form is not encoded overtly, but the hierarchically more marked inverse form is. The goal of this subsection is to point out that there are instances of direct-inverse marking that exhibit an alternation between two overt markers and hence cannot be derived within Aissen's system.

In Nocte, the direct form of the verb is chosen in the configurations 1-2, 1-3, 2-3 and 3-3 (where X is subject and Y is object in "X-Y"). In all other contexts, the inverse form is used. The inverse is encoded by an additional exponent, but the direct form is zero-marked. This is derived in Aissen's system by local conjunctions of constraints on subjects and constraints on objects, followed by local conjunction with a constraint penalizing zero marking ("*$Ø_D$" stands for "express direction"), as in (17).

(17)   *$Ø_D$ & *Su/3 & *Oj/loc

$$\gg \left\{ \begin{array}{l} (*Ø_D \ \& \ *Su/3 \ \& \ *Oj/3, \\ *Ø_D \ \& \ *Su/loc \ \& \ *Oj/loc \end{array} \right\} \gg *Ø_D \ \& \ *Su/loc \ \& \ *Oj/3$$

The ranking for Nocte is given in (18).

(18)   *Ranking in Nocte*

$$\left\{ \begin{array}{l} *Ø_D \ \& \ *Su/3 \ \& \ *Oj/loc, \\ *Ø_D \ \& \ *Su/2 \ \& \ *Ob/1 \end{array} \right\} \gg *\text{STRUC}_D \gg *Ø_D \ \& \ \text{GR/Pers}$$

with: GR = {Subj,Obj,Obl}; Pers = {1,2,3}

Evidently, this line of analysis only works for languages that have a morphologically unmarked direct form (such as Nocte). Consider, on the other hand, Algonquian languages (see Blake 1994 and Macaulay 2005, among others): In Menominee, for example, direct is marked by -ā, and inverse by -Eko. In Western Naskapi, the direct marker is -â, and the inverse marker is -ikw. In Plains Cree, the direct form is marked by -ā, and the inverse by attaching -ekw. In all three cases, two markers coexist. While it is unproblematic in Aissen's system to account for the fact that both the direct and the inverse forms are morphologically marked, there is no way of deriving that the direct is marked *less*, i.e., by a marker with fewer segments than there are on the inverse form. In other words, although Aissen acknowledges that the inverse is hierarchically marked with respect to the direct, this fact cannot be correlated with the markedness of the exponents themselves. Therefore, in Aissen's approach one would be forced to treat the Algonquian and Nocte cases as fundamentally different.

Within the present analysis, on the other hand, these facts can be derived by impoverishment in direct contexts. Under this perspective Nocte is only a special case, with impoverishment leading to the selection of the zero marker.

To sum up, in the preceding two subsections we have provided empirical evidence that Aissen's approach is too narrow: As it is confined to zero/non-zero alternations, generalizations across patterns that involve overt/overt alternations cannot be captured. In the remainder of this article we will illustrate our extension to overcome this problem.[11]

3.4 Assumptions

This subsection introduces the core theoretical concepts that our analysis of differential argument encoding rests on. The basic assumption about grammar

---

[11] Another possible example is Russian. In Russian, there exists a (system-defining) identity of nominative and accusative marking with neuters, which is arguably best analyzed by impoverishment in a Distributed Morphology approach: There is a deletion of case features with neuters. Neuter nouns are the prototypical inanimate objects, and it seems hard to deny that the underlying motivations for differential object marking are active in this domain. However, neuter nouns in Russian do not involve zero exponence in accusative contexts. Rather, they exhibit a choice of a less specific, more general case marker that is underspecified with respect to the nominative/accusative distinction (viz., -o), instead of the more specific accusative/genitive marker that would otherwise be expected (viz., -a; see Wunderlich 2004), given that neuters and masculines essentially belong to one and the same inflection class.

It seems that in Aissen's approach, one would have to strictly separate the two classes. Such a step could not easily capture the identical pattern (which is extended to all inflection classes and genders in the plural): Nominative and accusative are identical if the object is inanimate (see Comrie 1978 and Wiese 2004 for further discussion).

is that it is organized as assumed in Distributed Morphology: Syntax precedes inflectional morphology; and syntactic structures can be manipulated before morphological realization (i.e., *vocabulary insertion*) takes place. The only crucial difference to standard versions of Distributed Morphology is that we assume that impoverishment is brought about not by specific rules, but by a system of conflicting constraints.

Vocabulary insertion applies as in Halle and Marantz (1993): Functional morphemes contain fully specified bundles of morpho-syntactic features in syntax; however, they do not yet contain phonological material. Inflection markers are vocabulary items that pair phonological and (often underspecified) morpho-syntactic features; they are inserted post-syntactically in accordance with the Subset Principle. The Subset Principle can be defined as in (19) (see Halle 1997: among others).

(19) *Subset Principle*
A vocabulary item V is inserted into a functional morpheme M
iff (i) and (ii) hold:
(i) The morpho-syntactic features of V are a subset of the morpho-syntactic features of M.
(ii) V is the most specific vocabulary item that satisfies (i).

The Subset Principle relies on the concept of Specificity. We assume that Specificity is defined as in (20), based on a hierarchy of features (see the discussion of determiner inflection in German above), with quality emerging as more important than quantity.

(20) *Specificity of vocabulary items* (Lumsden 1992, Noyer 1992, Wiese 1999)
A vocabulary item V_i is more specific than a vocabulary item V_j iff there is a class of features $\mathbb{F}$ such that (i) and (ii) hold.
(i) V_i bears more features belonging to $\mathbb{F}$ than V_j does.
(ii) There is no higher-ranked class of features $\mathbb{F}'$ such that V_i and V_j have a different number of features in $\mathbb{F}'$.

Finally (and most importantly), we adopt the following approach to impoverishment (see Grimshaw 2001, Kiparsky 2001, Trommer 2001, 2006, Wunderlich 2004, Lahne 2010, Opitz 2008):

(21) *Impoverishment*
   a. Syntactic structures (inputs) are mapped onto structures (outputs) that in turn serve as the input to vocabulary insertion.
   b. This mapping is subject to optimization (see Prince and Smolensky 1993/2004).
   c. Markedness constraints may force feature deletion, in minimal violation of faithfulness (MAX) constraints.
   d. Vocabulary insertion may face an impoverished structure.

So, post-syntactically, underspecified markers compete for insertion into abstract syntactic heads. These latter heads can be underspecified if impoverishment has applied. The one marker that actually gets inserted into the syntactic head is chosen on the basis of two conditions that form part of the Subset Principle. First, only those markers can be inserted at all whose features form a subset of the syntactic head. Hence, vocabulary insertion can never add new information to a given head. Given underspecification of inflectional markers, there is potentially more than one marker fulfilling the Subset Principle's compatibility requirement (i). Among those residual markers the choice is conditioned by the specificity requirement (ii): The most specific marker is chosen.

Impoverishment interacts with these principles in the following way. Suppose there are four markers A, B, C and D, and assume further that these exponents are specified as in (22).

(22) a. A ↔ [+α, −β]
     b. B ↔ [+α]
     c. C ↔ [ ]
     d. D ↔ [+β]

Suppose that these markers compete for insertion into a syntactic head Γ comprising the features {+α, −β}. Then, first, the Subset Principle excludes D from the competition since its features do not constitute a subset of the head. Hence, specificity chooses among the remaining markers A, B and C. Assuming for the sake of simplicity that only set cardinality is relevant here (i.e., α and β count as equally ranked in the sense of (20)), A is most specific and consequently gets inserted into the head.

Now consider a minimally different case where, prior to marker insertion, an impoverishment rule applies to the head Γ, yielding deletion of the feature [−β]. This results in a head $Γ_{\{+α\}}$. As before, the Subset Principle directly excludes the (incompatible) marker D, but crucially, A now does not fulfill the Subset Principle either. Thus, the Specificity condition that is part of the Subset Principle only chooses between B and C, resulting in insertion of B. This illustrates how impoverishment influences marker insertion into a given syntactic head.

On this basis, we now turn to a number of case studies, beginning with Hindi.

4 Case studies

4.1 Differential encoding of subjects and objects in Hindi

The phenomenon of split ergativity in Hindi has been studied extensively (see, e.g., Mahajan 1990, Mohanan 1994, Woolford 2001, Lee 2003, Stiebels 2002, Butt and King 2004, Anand and Nevins 2006). Most of the existing approaches have in common that they view the distribution of the relevant case markers as syntactically derived. In contrast, in Keine (2007) it is argued that case assignment within syntax is uniform, but morphological impoverishment affects marker insertion depending on contextual features. Although the approach assumed a conventional concept of impoverishment rules because they were triggered by explicitly stating the relevant features specification, it can easily be modified so as to fit into the present approach. To do this, we will first give a brief overview over the data, followed by an outline of the approach in Keine (2007), with a subsequent implementation into the analysis presented here. Since the intention of this section is to illustrate the mechanisms at work the empirical survey is far from complete; see Keine (2007) for a more comprehensive discussion.

4.1.1 The phenomenon

The three case exponents under consideration here are -*ne* (traditionally called the ergative marker), -*ko* (accusative/dative) and -Ø (nominative). Both -*ne* and -*ko* alternate with the zero marker. Objects of transitive verbs are standardly marked by -*ko*. However, if the object is highly typical in the sense of the Hale/Silverstein hierarchy, i.e., non-specific and non-human, there is zero marking of the object. This is shown in (23) (for specificity) and (24) (for humanness/animacy).

(23) a. *Naadyaa=ne   gaaṛii   calaa-yii   hai*
       Nadya.F.SG=ERG   car.F.SG.NOM drive-PERF.F.SG be.PRES.3SG
       'Nadya has driven a car'

   b. *Naadyaa=ne   gaaṛii=ko   calaa-yaa   hai*
       Nadya.F.SG=ERG   car.F.SG=ACC   drive-PERF.M.SG be.PRES.3SG
       'Nadya has driven the car.'

(24) a. Ilaa-ne ek   bacce-ko /   *baccaa   utʰaa-yaa
       Ila-ERG one child-ACC   child.NOM   lift/carry-PERF.M.SG
       'Ila lifted a child.'

   b. Ilaa-ne ek   haar /   *haar-ko   utʰaa-yaa
       Ila-ERG one necklace.NOM necklace-ACC lift-PERF.M.SG
       'Ila lifted a necklace.'

This distribution can be derived by assuming that syntactically all transitive objects receive one and the same case feature (ACCUSATIVE) that, by default, yields attachment of -ko morphologically. Accusative case is not a primitive but a feature bundle (see Jakobson 1936, Bierwisch 1967, page 7 above, and below, for the decomposition of case categories into combinations of more primitive features). For present purposes, it suffices to assume that this feature bundle consists of a primitive case feature [+gov] plus other primitive case features. The marker -ko and the zero marker compete for insertion; -ko bears the feature [+gov], whereas, -Ø is radically underspecified, in accordance with the Iconicity Meta-Principle. Both markers thus realize a subset of the target specification, but -ko is more specific than the zero marker. However, if the object is highly typical, bearing the features [−specific,−human], impoverishment applies, deleting the feature [+gov] on the noun. In this case, the marker -ko no longer satisfies the compatibility requirement of the Subset Principle; it is therefore removed from the competition. Only the radically underspecified zero marker is left, which fulfills the Subset Principle by definition; this yields zero exponence. The cornerstones of this analysis are summarized in (25):

(25) a. *Case decomposition*
       ACCUSATIVE: [+gov,...]
   b. *Vocabulary items*
       /-ko/ ↔ [+gov]
       /-Ø/   ↔ [ ]
   c. *Impoverishment rule for objects*
       [+gov] → Ø / [−specific,−human]

The distribution of the marker -ne is treated along the same lines: -ne only shows up on the subjects of perfective clauses. Subjects of non-perfective clauses, on the other hand, are zero marked. Woolford (2007) argues that this constitutes a case of differential subject marking, since the appearance of the ending -ne is a clear indication that the sentence is in the perfective aspect. On this view, overt ergative marking in Hindi ultimately is functionally motivated. Woolford calls this phenomenon *parasitic marking*. It is illustrated in (26):

(26) a. *Raam-ne   Ravii-ko   piiṭaa*
       Ram-ERG   Ravi-ACC   beat.PERF
       'Ram beat Ravi.'
   b. *Raam   Ravii-ko   piiṭtaa   hai*
       Ram.NOM   Ravi-ACC   beat.IMPERF   be.PR
       'Ram beats Ravi.'

As before, it can be assumed that all subjects receive ergative case syntactically, regardless of aspectual information. The ergative case is made up of a set of primitive case features that includes the feature [+subject]. The two markers satisfying the compatibility requirement of the Subset Principle are *-ne* ([+subject]) and *-Ø*, which is again maximally underspecified in accordance with the Iconicity Meta-Principle. If the case feature is left unchanged by morphology, *-ne* is attached. However, if impoverishment deletes the feature [+subject] only the zero marker is available; and this is what happens in the context of non-perfective clauses. This is summarized in (27):

(27) a. *Case decomposition*
       ERGATIVE: [+subject]
   b. *Vocabulary items*
       /-ne/   ↔   [+subject]
       /-Ø/   ↔   [ ]
   c. *Impoverishment rule for ergatives*
       [+subject] → Ø / [−PERFECT]

4.1.2 Analysis

The analysis developed in Keine (2007), which was sketched in the preceding subsection, can easily be modified so as to be compatible with the assumptions adopted in the present paper. Recall that under present assumptions, impoverishment is not brought about by context-sensitive deletion rules, as in (25) and (27) above, but by interspersing a markedness constraint that forces deletion, into a subhierarchy of complex faithfulness constraints that is derived from harmonic alignment of scales.

As for the -*ko*/zero alternation, the relevant scales are those in (28):

(28) SCALES
    a. *Animacy Scale*

                      Non-Human

        Human > Animate > Inanimate

    b. *Definiteness Scale*
        ... > Specific > Non-Specific

    c. *GF Scale*
        Subject > Object

Harmonic alignment of the GF scale with the animacy scale yields the harmony scales in (29a); harmonic alignment with the definiteness scale derives the harmony scales in (29):

(29) *Harmony scales*
    a. (i)   Subj/Hum ≻ Subj/NHum
       (ii) Obj/NHum ≻ Obj/Hum
    b. (i)   Subj/Spec ≻ Subj/NSpec
       (ii) Obj/NSpec ≻ Obj/Spec

These scales are then converted to constraint alignments:

(30) *Constraint alignments*
    a. (i)   *Subj/NHum ≫ *Subj/Hum
       (ii) *Obj/Hum ≫ *Obj/NHum
    b. (i)   *Subj/NSpec ≫ *Subj/Spec
       (ii) *Obj/Spec ≫ *Obj/NSpec

Only the constraint alignments in (ii) will be relevant here. Local conjunction of the subhierarchies in (30aii) and (30bii) yields the rankings in (31), which can be notationally simplified (following Aissen 2003) as shown in (32):

(31) *Local conjunction*
    a. *Obj/Hum & *Obj/Spec ≫ *Obj/Hum & *Obj/NSpec
    b. *Obj/NHum & *Obj/Spec ≫ *Obj/NHum & *Obj/NSpec
    c. *Obj/Spec & *Obj/Hum ≫ *Obj/Spec & *Obj/NHum
    d. *Obj/NSpec & *Obj/Hum ≫ *Obj/NSpec & *Obj/NHum

(32) *Notational simplification of (31)*
   a. *Obj/Hum/Spec ≫ *Obj/Hum/NSpec
   b. *Obj/NHum/Spec ≫ *Obj/NHum/NSpec
   c. *Obj/Hum/Spec ≫ *Obj/NHum/Spec
   d. *Obj/Hum/NSpec ≫ *Obj/NHum/NSpec

Finally, to make these constraints relevant for case marking, they are locally conjoined with the faithfulness constraint MAX-C that penalizes deletion of case features from input to output; see (33).

(33) *Local conjunction with* MAX-C(ASE)
   a. *Obj/Hum/Spec & MAX-C ≫ *Obj/Hum/NSpec & MAX-C
   b. *Obj/NHum/Spec & MAX-C ≫ *Obj/NHum/NSpec & MAX-C
   c. *Obj/Hum/Spec & MAX-C ≫ *Obj/NHum/Spec & MAX-C
   d. *Obj/Hum/NSpec & MAX-C ≫ *Obj/NHum/NSpec & MAX-C

The constraint **Obj/Hum/Spec & Max-C* states that case features cannot be deleted on object DPs that are [+human] and [+specific]; **Obj/Hum/NSpec & Max-C* demands a preservation of case features with [+human], [−specific] objects DPs; and so forth.

The domination relations of the constraints in (33) can be illustrated as in (34) (see Aissen 2003 for this type of graphic representation of multi-dimensional differential argument encoding):

(34) *Inherent ranking of faithfulness constraints:*

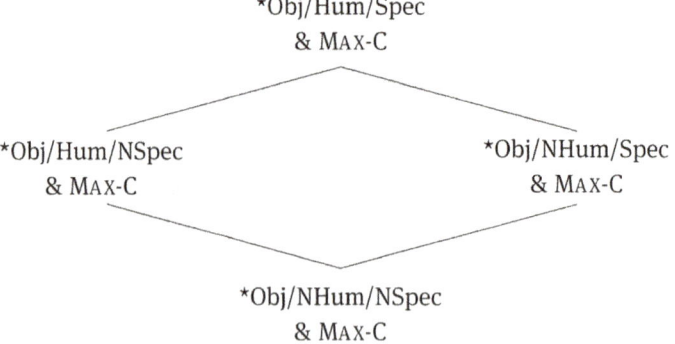

Thus, there is a fixed, invariable ranking that goes back to local conjunction for only some of the constraints in (33): While **Obj/Hum/Spec & Max-C* inherently outranks all other constraints, the relation between the constraints **Obj/Hum/*

NSpec & Max-C and **Obj/NHum/Spec & Max-C* is not intrinsically specified, and can be fixed in one way or the other. **Obj/NHum/NSpec & Max-C*, in contrast, is necessarily dominated by all the other constraints in (33).

All these constraints are faithfulness constraints that prohibit deletion of input information in outputs. In order to derive changes from input to output, the markedness constraint *[+gov] is inserted into the constraint ranking established so far. This constraint penalizes a case feature [+gov] in the output. It differs from Aissen's similar constraint *STRUC$_C$ in that it does not simply penalize any case feature but only the occurrence of the case feature [+gov]. If a syntactic case feature consists of the two features [+gov,+α], the constraint only triggers deletion of [+gov], leaving [+α] intact. Consequently, it is possible that *more than one* markedness constraint exists that penalizes case features.[12]

The relevant ranking for Hindi is the one in (35). The ranking of the first three contraints is ignored here since it is irrelevant for the present analysis (but **Obj/Hum/Spec & Max-C* must of course outrank the remaining two constraints; see (34)).

(35) Ranking for Hindi

$$\left\{ \begin{array}{l} \text{*Obj/Hum/Spec \& Max-C,} \\ \text{*Obj/Hum/NSpec \& Max-C,} \\ \text{*Obj/NHum/Spec \& Max-C} \end{array} \right\} \gg \text{*[+gov]} \gg \text{*Obj/NHum/NSpec \& Max-C}$$

This ranking triggers the deletion of [+gov] in exactly the same contexts that the stipulative impoverishment rule (25c) did: *[+gov] forces deletion of the case feature [+gov] in all those contexts where the corresponding faithfulness constraint is ranked lower. Given the ranking in (35), *[+gov] only outranks **Obj/NHum/NSpec & Max-C*. Therefore, impoverishment applies only to highly canonical objects, viz., those that are [–human] and [–specific]. In all other cases, the higher ranked faithfulness constraints prevent case feature deletion.

Let us go through one case in detail. Consider again the sentences in (23), which are repeated here in (36) (with zero marking in (36a) now glossed as accusative rather than nominative, in line with the analysis adopted here).

---

[12] As far as the case currently under consideration is concerned, a second constraint *[+α] could be inserted into the ranking independently of *[+gov]. This would yield *gradual impoverishment*: A highly atypical object DP might maintain all of its case features; for less marked ones, parts of their syntactic case features are deleted, whereas all case features of canonical objects are deleted. Such considerations are irrelevant for Hindi, but their usefulness will be demonstrated for Trumai in §4.3 and Finnish in §4.5 below.

(36) a. Naadyaa=ne   gaaṛii-Ø   calaa-yii   hai
        Nadya.F.SG=ERG car.F.SG-ACC   drive-PERF.F.SG be.PRES.3SG
        'Nadya has driven a car.'
    b. Naadyaa=ne   gaaṛii=ko   calaa-yaa   hai
        Nadya.F.SG=ERG car.F.SG=ACC   drive-PERF.M.SG be.PRES.3SG
        'Nadya has driven the car.'

By assumption, the structure generated by syntactic operations is used as the input for the mapping from syntax to morphology. Possible outputs (which in turn function as inputs to morphological realization) may either leave the feature specifications of the input unchanged, or they may carry out various kinds of deletion operations; deletion violates faithfulness constraints but may lead to a better constraint profile with respect to markedness constraints.[13] As shown in (37), deletion of [+gov] is optimal if the conflicting active faithfulness constraint is lower-ranked, but suboptimal (hence, blocked) if it is higher-ranked.

(37) a. *Tableau for (36a)*

INPUT: [obj, –hum, –spec][+gov]	*o/+h/+s & MAX-C	*o/+h/–s & MAX-C	*o/–h/+s & MAX-C	*[+gov]	*o/–h/–s & MAX-C
☞ [obj, –hum, –spec]					*
[obj, –hum, –spec][+gov]				*!	

b. *Tableau for (36b)*

INPUT: [obj, –hum, +spec][+gov]	*o/+h/+s & MAX-C	*o/+h/–s & MAX-C	*o/–h/+s & MAX-C	*[+gov]	*o/–h/–s & MAX-C
[obj, –hum, +spec]			*!		
☞ [obj, –hum, +spec][+gov]				*	

The outputs of the syntax-morphology mapping are then used as the inputs for morphological realization. Here, marker insertion takes place exactly as assumed in standard Distributed Morphology approaches, governed by the Subset Principle.[14] The relevant vocabulary items (accusative allomorphs) are repeated in (38).

---

13 The type of optimality-theoretic model adopted here also has to envisage the possibility of unfaithful feature *insertion* operations in outputs. This issue is irrelevant for the present discussion, but it certainly is an option in general. See Müller (2007a) for discussion, and for arguments that there is reason to adopt an operation that is complementary to impoverishment even in standard (rule-based) approaches to impoverishment.
14 Of course, the actual realization (or insertion) of exponents could also be handled by an optimization procedure that incorporates the compatibility and specificity requirements of the Subset Principle as separate constraints; see, e.g., Wunderlich (2004). However, we believe that

(38) *Vocabulary items for accusative contexts*
  /-ko/ ↔ [+gov]
  /-Ø/ ↔ [ ]

In the output of (37a) the case feature is deleted. Hence, only -Ø fulfills the Subset Principle, which results in zero marking. The optimal output of (37b), on the other hand, retains its case feature so that both -*ko* and the zero marker satisfy the compatibility requirement of the Subset Principle. This gives rise to the insertion of the more specific marker -*ko*. More generally, the zero marker can only be attached if impoverishment has applied, which in turn is only active for canonical objects ([–hum, –spec]). Consequently, the overt exponent only shows up on atypical objects, and this produces the effect of differential object marking.[15]

This analysis differs from the one in Keine (2007) in one respect: It does not explicitly state the context of the impoverishment rule but derives its application from the interaction of markedness and faithfulness constraints, the ordering among which is not arbitrary but conditioned by Hale/Silverstein hierarchies. As a consequence, the present approach is more restrictive. If the contextual features are simply listed as part of an impoverishment rule, there are no constraints on what kind of objects can trigger impoverishment. It would, in principle, be possible to impoverish in the case of highly typical and highly untypical objects and only in those cases. Take (34) as an example: If the impoverishment rule were to apply in exactly the topmost and lowermost kinds of objects, those two would be zero marked while the ones in between woul be marked with -*ko*.

---

there are two reasons for not adopting such an approach. First, the compatibility and specificity requirements embodied in the Subset Principle do not seem to be violable; accordingly, they always have to be assumed to be undominated in constraint rankings. In our view, this can be taken to suggest that these requirements are very different from constraints of the type in (37), and should therefore best be kept apart. Second, the two types of constraints concern different kinds of operations (optimization of abstract feature structures on the one hand, and insertion of concrete morphological exponents on the other), which again would seem to suggest a different formal treatment.

15 Upon closer scrutiny, this turns out to be an oversimplification. There are some verbs whose object is zero marked regardless of its definiteness/humanness properties. This class contains verbs such as *banaa* 'make', *padh* 'read', *gaa* 'sing', and *pii* 'drink'. One example is given in (i).

(i) Ilaa-ne   yah k^h at   / *is k^h at-ko lik^h aa
    Ila-ERG   this.NOM   letter.NOM   this.NONNOM   letter-ACC   write.PERF
    'Ila wrote this letter.'   (Mohanan 1994: 81)

In (i), the object *yah k^h at* 'this letter' may not bear -*ko* despite being definite. The simplest way to account for this class of verbs is to assume that they assign a distinct syntactic case, say, objective. Due to its case subfeatures the objective only and always receives default case exponence, i.e. -Ø. There is thus no impoverishment active here.

This would run counter to the well-established functional motivation of differential argument encoding. On the other hand, if impoverishment results from constraint ranking, such a problem does not emerge. No matter where *[+gov] is inserted into the ranking of faithfulness constraints in (34), there never can be a scenario with case feature deletion for only the topmost and the lowermost configuration. If *[+gov] dominates the topmost constraint it must dominate the constraints in the middle as well, resulting in zero marking for all kinds of objects. If, on the other hand, it does not dominate the constraints in the middle, it does not dominate the topmost constraint either, yielding overt marking for all those cases.[16]

So far, we have introduced our morphology-based approach to differential argument encoding on the basis of data from Hindi. However, since both instances of differential marking in Hindi involve zero/non-zero alternations, this does not yet constitute an empirical argument in favour of the present approach, and against the view taken by Aissen. The present approach differs from Aissen's in that it allows for alternations between two overt markers as well. This state of affairs would arise for Hindi if, in addition to the zero marker and -*ko*, there were a third marker that would also fulfill the Subset Principle for the impoverished feature specification but would be more specific than the zero marker; but there isn't. In the following subsections, we argue that the situation may be slightly different in other languages.

4.2 Differential encoding of objects in Mannheim German

4.2.1 The phenomenon

In all varieties of German, feminine, neuter and plural DPs are morphologically indistinguishable in nominative and accusative environments. In the variety of German spoken in and around Mannheim (and elsewhere in Palatine and Rhine areas), the same holds for non-pronominal masculine DPs (the so-called "Rheinischer Akkusativ"; see Behaghel 1911, Karch 1975, Müller 2003, and literature cited there). Crucially, this pattern is not extended to pronouns – masculine personal pronouns are marked differently in nominative and accusative contexts. Thus, Hale/Silverstein scales seem to be at work: Pronouns outrank nouns

---

16 One point that we would like to note only in passing here is that differential object marking in Hindi (amongst other languages) interacts with verbal agreement. Scale driven impoverishment of case features must hence likewise affect agreement. An account along the lines sketched here and incorporating questions of agreement may be found in Keine (2010).

on the definiteness scale (see (1f)). This suggests a unified approach; but a unified approach is not available if the theory of differential argument encoding can only account for a difference between zero and non-zero encoding. The reason is that the nominative forms of German determiner inflection are not strictly zero-marked.

For concreteness, consider the examples in (39), which exhibit case marking of non-pronominal masculine objects in Mannheim German.[17]

(39) a. *Ich wünsch Ihnen* [$_{DP}$ *ein-Ø schön-er Tag*] *noch*
I wish you.DAT a-NOM nice-NOM day PRT

b. *Wir haben* [$_{DP}$ *pädagogisch-er Planungstag*]
we have pedagogical-NOM planning day

c. *Ich hab auch* [$_{DP}$ *ein-Ø schön-er Ball*], *meinst du, bloß du*
I have also a-NOM nice-NOM ball think you, just you
hast [$_{DP}$ *ein-er*]?
have a-NOM

d. *Man müsste mal wieder so richtig* [$_{DP}$ *einer*] *drauf machen*
one should PRT again PRT really one-NOM on it make
'We should really have a night on the town again.'

e. *Hol mir mal* [$_{DP}$ *der Eimer*]
fetch me PRT the-NOM bucket

In all these cases, the accusative form of the masculine object DP is indistinguishable from the corresponding nominative form. Still, this does not mean that there is no nominative/accusative distinction left in Mannheim German: Masculine personal pronouns in (structurally governed) object positions are marked by the accusative exponent *-n*, and cannot be marked by the nominative exponent *-r*. Compare the case marking on the pronoun in (40) with the case marking on the minimally different non-pronominal DP in (39e).

(40) *Hol en/*er mir mal her*
fetch he-ACC/*he-NOM me-DAT PRT PRT

---

17 Case marking in German DPs is located mainly on determiners, to some extent on prenominal adjectives, and much less so on the nouns themselves. Note also that the glossing as 'NOM' is just for expository convenience; the assumption that the exponents are NOM markers will actually be abandoned below.

It would be highly implausible to assume that in two completely identical contexts, structural accusative case is assigned to pronominal objects whereas structural nominative case is assigned to non-prononominal objects. Therefore, we may conclude that the DP-internal case/number/gender markers in (39) are exponents that realize a syntactic accusative specification, just like their counterpart in (40) does. We develop such an analysis in the following subsection.

4.2.2 Analysis

Recall Wiese's (1999) underspecification analysis of determiner inflection in Standard German summarized in subsection 2.3 above.[18] Case and gender/number are subanalysed in the following way:

(41) *Case*   *Gender/Number*
    NOM: [−obl, −gov] MASC: [+masc, −fem]
    ACC: [−obl, +gov] FEM: [−masc, +fem]
    DAT: [+obl, +gov] NEUT: [+masc, +fem]
    GEN: [+obl, −gov] PL: [−masc, −fem]

The vocabulary items postulated by Wiese are repeated in (42), with the ones that are most relevant in the context of the present discussion rendered in boldface. At least for present purposes, we can assume that this inventory is identical in Standard and Mannheim German (there are minor phonological differences that we can ignore here).

(42) *Vocabulary items for determiner inflection in German*
    a. (i)   /m/ ↔ [+masc, +obl, +gov] (DAT.MASC.SG./NEUT.SG.)
        (ii) /s/ ↔ [+masc, +obl]   (GEN.MASC.SG./NEUT.SG.)
        (iii) /s/ ↔ [+masc, +fem]   (NOM./ACC.NEUT.SG.)
    b. (i)   **/n/ ↔ [+masc, +gov]**   (ACC.MASC.SG.)
        (ii) **/r/ ↔ [+masc]**   (NOM.MASC.SG.)
        (iii) /r/ ↔ [+obl, +fem]   (DAT./GEN.FEM.SG.)
        (iv) /n/ ↔ [+obl, +gov]   (DAT.PL.)
        (v) /r/ ↔ [+obl]   (GEN.PL.)
    c. (i)   /e/ ↔ [ ]   (NOM./ACC.FEM.SG./PL.)

---

[18] See Bierwisch (1967), Blevins (1995), Wunderlich (1997a), and Trommer (2005) for alternative suggestions, most of which could just as well be adopted for present purposes.

It is clear that that /n/ qualifies as more specific than /r/, under any definition of specificity. The relevant scales for the case of differential argument encoding in Mannheim German are the ones in (43).

(43) a. *GF scale* (basic)
Subject > Object

b. *Definiteness scale*
Pro(noun) > Name (PN) > Def(inite) > Indefinite Specific (Spec) > NonSpecific (NSpec)

Harmonic alignment applied to these scales yields the constraint ranking in (44).

(44) *Constraint alignment*
*Obj/Pro ≫ *Obj/PN ≫ *Obj/Def ≫ *Obj/Spec ≫ *Obj/NSpec

Finally, order-preserving local conjunction of these constraints with the constraint MAX-CASE (corresponding to Aissen's *$\emptyset_C$) that penalizes deletion of case features results in the ranking of faithfulness constraints in (45).

(45) *Local conjunction with* MAX-CASE
*Obj/Pro & Max-C ≫ *Obj/PN & Max-C ≫ *Obj/Def & Max-C ≫ *Obj/Spec & Max-C ≫ *Obj/NSpec & Max-C

Obj/Pro & Max-C is violated if a case feature of a VP-internal pronoun is deleted post-syntactically (i.e., before morphological realization); *Obj/PN & Max-C* is violated if a case feature of a VP-internal proper name DP is deleted post-syntactically; and so on.

The conflicting markedness constraint that prohibits a case feature from appearing in the output and hence triggers impoverishment of this case feature is (46). It constitutes a special case of Aissen's general *STRUC$_C$ constraint since it does not penalize *any* case feature in the output but only one special feature.

(46) *Markedness constraint triggering impoverishment*
*[+gov]

To derive the deletion of the case feature [+gov] everywhere except with pronouns in Mannheim German (i.e., to ensure a neutralization of nominative/accusative distinctions in all non-pronominal contexts), *[+gov] must be ranked in (45) just below the faithfulness constraint for object pronouns, but higher than the other faithfulness constraints:

(47) *Ranking in Mannheim German*

$$\text{*Obj/Pro \& Max-C} \gg \text{*[+gov]} \gg \begin{Bmatrix} \text{*Obj/PN \& Max-C} \\ \text{*Obj/Def \& Max-C} \\ \text{*Obj/Spec \& Max-C} \\ \text{*Obj/NSpec \& Max-C} \end{Bmatrix}$$

This ranking yields the result that [+gov] is maintained with object pronouns, and accordingly leads to a different realization of the pronoun in accusative and nominative contexts.[19] With all other (structurally case marked) objects, [+gov] is deleted due to the constraint *[+gov], which is ranked higher than the relevant faithfulness constraints that penalize deletion. Here, /n/ cannot be inserted anymore, and the more general marker /r/ must be chosen.[20] On this view, Standard German differs from Mannheim German (with respect to the syntax-morphology mapping in the nominal domain) only in that *[+gov] is ranked lower than all the faithfulness constraints in (47).

4.3 Differential object marking in Trumai

The line of argumentation for Trumai is identical to Mannheim German above, but the empirical evidence is more intricate in an interesting way: The alternation involves three overt exponents and one zero exponent. This confirms a prediction of the present analysis: In contrast to what is the case under the approach developed by Aissen (1999, 2003), the present approach does not envisage a single *STRUC-CASE constraint that penalizes *any* case feature in the

---

[19] This reasoning presupposes that personal pronouns follow essentially the same system of inflection as determiners. We would indeed like to contend that the inflectional exponents for personal pronouns are to a large extent those listed in (42). It is certainly not an accident that *e-r* (MASC.NOM.SG pronoun) parallels *dies-er* (MASC.NOM.SG inflected determiner); *ih-n* or its Mannheim German variant *e-n* (MASC.ACC.SG pronoun) parallels *dies-en* (MASC.ACC.SG inflected determiner); *ihn-en* (DAT.PL pronoun) parallels *dies-en* (DAT.PL inflected determiner); etc. Approaches that subanalyze personal pronoun forms into combinations of stem and inflectional exponent (including suppletion phenomena) along the lines of (42) are developed in Wiese (2001) and Fischer (2006).

[20] One might ask why the ranking in (47) does not lead to deletion of [+gov] in dative contexts. It obviously does not because masculine/neuter /m/ is not replaced with less specific /s/ with non-pronominal DPs, and plural /n/ is not replaced with /r/ either: **Ich danke dieses Mann*, **Ich danke dieser Männer*. One possible answer is that "Obj" means Comp(V) (see above), but dative arguments show up as Spec(V). The **Spec(V)/X & Max-C* constraints are all ranked higher than *[+gov].

output. Instead, there are more specific markedness constraints against certain case features (*[+gov] in Hindi and Mannheim German). Since these markedness constraints can be freely interspersed with the faithfulness constraints, it should be possible for objects that are slightly (i.e., not maximally) atypical to get one (decomposed, primitive) case feature deleted, which results in the choice of a less specific marker than would otherwise be expected (i.e., as it shows up with fully atypical objects). A second markedness constraint can now be ranked between the faithfulness constraints for slightly atypical and typical objects. This leads to deletion of a second decomposed case feature with typical objects. This results in a yet more impoverished head; consequently, an even less specific exponent is inserted in this context. In this case, a threefold division arises. Since there is no inherent boundary for this mechanism, more than three distinctions should also be possible. In this section, we will discuss differential object marking in Trumai, which involves three overt markers, differentiated along the lines just sketched.

Trumai, a language isolate spoken in central Brazil by 51 speakers, has three dative markers *-(V)tl*, *-ki*, and *-(V)s* (Guirardello 1999). The choice among them is conditioned by the factors *individuation* and *prominence*, as shown in (48). Some examples are provided in (49)–(51)

(48) Distribution of dative markers in Trumai (Guirardello 1999: 280)

-(V)tl	>	*-ki*	>	*-(V)s*
– individuated		– individuated but not identifiable		– not individuated, not identifiable
– identifiable		– individuated but not prominent		– not individuated not prominent
– prominent		– non individuated, identifiable		

(49) a. ha hu'tsa chï_in kasoro-tl
       I see   Foc/Tens dog-DAT
       'I saw the dog (I know it).'

   b. ha hu'tsa chï_in kasoro yi-ki
      I see   Foc/Tens dog   YI-DAT
      'I saw a dog/the dog (I do not know it well).'

   c. ha hu'tsa chï_in kasoro-s
      I see   Foc/Tens dog-DAT
      'I saw dogs.'   (Guirardello 1999: 276)

(50) a. hi fa-tke-a   hai-tl?
       I   kill/hit-DES-QUEST 1-DAT
       'Do you want to kill me?'

   b. ha fa   fa   chï_in   ine-tl²¹
      I   kill/hit kill/hit FOC/TENS   3-DAT
      'I beat him (someone that I know well).'

   c. ha fa   fa   chï_in   ine yi-ki
      I   kill/hit kill/hit FOC/TENS   3   YI-DAT
      'I beat him (somebody that I do not know; he is a stranger).'
      (Guirardello 1999: 271–2)

(51) a. ha sone-tke   misu-ki
       I   drink-DES water-DAT
       'I want to drink water (a little/a glass).'

   b. ha sone-tke   misu-s
      I   drink-DES water-DAT
      'I want to drink some water.'   (Guirardello 1999: 277)

The distribution of the three markers in terms of markedness scales corresponds to their phonological markedness: -(V)tl is most marked both for distribution and phonological complexity, followed by -ki; -(V)s is the least marked among the three. This correspondence can be straightforwardly derived within the present system as follows.

Assume the scales in (52). Harmonic alignment, conversion into a constraint ranking and local conjunction with the constraint MAX-CASE leads to the ranking in (53).

(52) a. *Individuation scale*
       Ind(ividuated) > Non-ind(ividuated)

   b. *Prominence scale*
      X > x
      (discourse-prominent argument > non-discourse prominent argument)

   c. *GF scale*
      Subject > Object

---

[21] The verb *fa* can mean both 'hit' and 'kill'. Duplication of the verb disambiguates it to the former meaning. Duplication, however, is not obligatory, even if the meaning 'hit' is intended (Guirardello 1999: 272 fn. 8).

(53) *Ranking of faithfulness constraints*
   a. *Obj/Ind/X & MAX-C ≫ *Obj/Ind/x & MAX-C
   b. *Obj/Non-ind/X & MAX-C ≫ *Obj/Non-ind/x & MAX-C

Analysing the dative as consisting of the subfeatures in (54), the three dative markers can be considered as being specified as in (55). Note that all three markers conform to iconicity.

(54) DATIVE: [+obl, −subj, +gov]

(55) *Vocabulary items*
   /-(V)tl/ ↔ [+obl, −subj, +gov]
   /-ki/   ↔ [−subj, +gov]
   /-(V)s/   ↔ [−subj]

Since markedness constraints are only sensitive to the presence of a certain case subfeature, two such constraints can be inserted into different positions within the ranking. This yields the three-way alternation of the dative. Here we assume the constraints *[+obl] and *[+gov]. Consider the ranking in (56).

(56) *Ranking for Trumai*
   *Obj/Ind/X & MAX-C ≫ *[+obl]
   ≫ { *Obj/Ind/x & MAX-C, *Obj/Non-ind/X & MAX-C } ≫ *[+gov] ≫ *Obj/Non-ind/x & MAX-C

This ranking has the effect that highly marked objects are not impoverished at all. For more canonical objects, [+obl] is deleted, but only highly canonical objects additionally have their [+gov] deleted. Due to iconicity, every impoverishment step is associated with insertion of a phonologically less marked exponent. This yields the pattern in (49) and (50): Prominent and individuated objects bear *-(V)tl*, less marked objects are marked with *-ki*, and non-prominent, non-individuated objects – the least marked object type – bear *-(V)s*.

In contrast, Aissen's approach is not appropriate for an analysis of the Trumai data as it does not involve a zero/non-zero alternation. That the principles at work here are the same as in the cases considered by her cannot be derived. The present approach, on the other hand, derives these alternations along the same lines and therefore captures their striking similarity.

4.4 Differential object marking in Cavineña

Another system that exhibits an overt/overt alternation is Cavineña, a Tacanan language spoken in Bolivia by less than 1,200 speakers (Guillaume 2008). There are two overt dative/genitive markers: -*kwe* and -*ja*. Their choice is conditioned by person and number of the stem: Highly non-canonical objects – local person and singular – bear -*kwe*. All other combinations select -*ja*. This distribution correlates with the phonological complexity of the two markers: -*kwe* is more marked phonologically than -*ja*. Hierarchical markedness thus corresponds to morphological markedness. This instantiates a more/less alternation in differential object marking. The distribution of the two markers is given in (57), along with some examples in (58).[22]

(57) Marker distribution

PERSON	SINGULAR	DUAL	PLURAL
1	e-Ø-kwe	ya-tse-ja	e-kwana-ja
2	mi-Ø-kwe	me-tse-ja	mi-kwana-ja
3	tu-Ø-ja	ta-tse-ja	tu-na-ja
3PROX	riya-Ø-ja	re-tse-ja	re-na-ja

(58) a. E-kwe   ani-kware   [maletero   ari-da$_{cc}$=ke$_{RC}$]$_S$
   1SG-DAT   sit-REM.PAST   bag   big-ASF=LIG
   'I had a big bag (lit. a big bag sat to me).'

   b. Sergio=ja   ani-ya   [ata   Ramón   bakani]$_s$
   Sergio=DAT   sit-IMPFV   relative   Ramsón   name
   'Sergio had a relative called Ramón (lit. a relative called Ramón was sitting to Sergio).'

   c. Tume   =tuna-ja   =tu-ke   =Ø$_A$ be-ti-wa   budari$_o$
   then   =3PL-DAT   =3SG-FM   (=1SG.ERG)   bring-GO.TEMP-PERF   banana
   'I will go and bring bananas for them.'   (Guillaume 2008: 575,567,603)

Since the distribution of these two markers depends on person and number, the person and number scale, along with the GF scale, are relevant for Cavineña.

---

[22] The following abbreviations are used in the glosses. ASF: adjective suffix; CC: copula complement; FM: formative; LIG: ligature; O: transitive object; RC: relative clause; S: intransitive subject; TEMP: temporarily.

(59) a. *Person scale*
       Loc(al) (1/2) > N(on)loc(al)
    b. *Number scale*
       Sg > Non-sg
    c. *GF scale*
       Subj > Obj

Harmonic alignment, conversion into a constraint ranking and subsequent conjunction with MAX-CASE leads to the ranking of faithfulness constraints in (60).

(60) a. *Obj/Loc/Sg & MAX-C ≫ *Obj/Loc/Non-sg & MAX-C
    b. *Obj/Nloc/Sg & MAX-C ≫ *Obj/Nloc/Non-sg & MAX-C

We assume that the dative comprises the subfeatures in (61). The markers *-kwe* and *-ja* are analysed as in (62), obeying iconicity.

(61) DATIVE: [+obl, +obj]

(62) *Marker specification*
     /-kwe/   ↔   [+obl, +obj]
     /-ja/   ↔   [+obj]

The markedness constraint *[+obl] is then inserted into the ranking of faithfulness constraints, cf. (63). This ranking leads to deletion of [+obl] for all except highly marked objects (local person, singular) because only the for this type of object does the faithfulness constraint outrank the markedness constraint. Given the markers as specified in (62), deletion of [+obl] bleeds insertion of *-kwe* and thus leads to a retreat to the more general marker *-ja*.

(63) *Ranking for Cavineña*

$$\text{*Obj/Loc/Sg \& MAX-C} \gg \text{*[+obl]} \gg \begin{Bmatrix} \text{*Obj/Loc/Non-sg \& MAX-C} \\ \text{*Obj/Nloc/Sg \& MAX-C} \\ \text{*Obj/Nloc/Non-sg \& MAX-C} \end{Bmatrix}$$

Notably, apart from being more restrictive, the constraint ranking in (63) has another advantage over an explicit impoverishment rule with the same effect: Impoverishment applies if the object is non-local *or* non-singular. As these contexts arguably do not form a natural class, the impoverishment rule at hand would have to involve a disjunction, as exemplified by (64).

(64) *System with explicit impoverishment rules*
 [+obl] → ∅ / __[3 ∨ –SG]

If, on the other hand, the context in which impoverishment takes place is derived by harmonic alignment of scales as in the present approach, the case feature is deleted in all environments that are dominated by the markedness constraint *[+obl]. (63) shows that this comprises exactly the domain of objects that are non-singular *or* non-local. What these contexts have in common, then, is that they form a homogenuous section of a constraint ranking: They are less marked than a certain cut-off point established by the insertion of the markedness constraint *[+obl]. The approach developed here is therefore superior on conceptual grounds.

The Cavineña data clearly conform to what is expected from the point of view of Hale/Silverstein hierarchies – more marking for unexpected objects. These data are nevertheless surprising if scales can only lead to a total reduction in morphological marking.

4.5 Differential encoding of objects in Finnish

The last system that we will discuss is object marking in Finnish. Recall that in the present proposal markedness constraints against case features do not simply penalize the presence of just any case feature. Instead, they are relativized to certain subfeatures. Consequently, several markedness constraints can be inserted into distinct positions, thereby outranking a different set of faithfulness constraints. Impoverishment then proceeds in several steps, giving rise to alternations between more than two markers. Object marking in Trumai instantiates such a system and thus provides further evidence for the present proposal. A second example of gradual impoverishment is provided by Finnish differential object marking, which comprises four markers.

4.5.1 The phenomenon

Finnish objects can be structurally case-marked by four different exponents, only one of which is zero: /t/, /n/, /a/ and /∅/. The principles that determine the choice of the correct exponents are exactly the ones that Aissen argues to underlie zero/non-zero alternations in differential argument encoding. This strongly suggests a unified approach; but a unified approach is not available if the theory of differential argument encoding is restricted to the difference between zero and non-zero encoding. We conclude from this that differential case marking of objects in Finnish is best treated as a morphological phenomenon.[23]

Variation in the case marking of objects in Finnish is illustrated by the examples in (65) (see Kiparsky 2001).

(65) a. *Tuo-n   he-t* b. *Tuo-n   karhu-n*
       bring-1.SG he-ACC   bring-1.SG bear-GEN
       'I'll bring him.'   'I'll bring the/a bear.'

   c. *Tuo-Ø   karhu-Ø* d. *Etsi-n   karhu-a*
      bring-IMP bear-NOM   seek-1.SG   bear-PART
      'Bring the/a bear!'   'I'm looking for the/a bear.'

Traditionally, it is assumed that the structural case markers for singular contexts in Finnish are those in (66).

(66) *Structural case markers (singular)* (traditional grammar)

	NOUNS: 'bear'	PRONOUNS: 'you'
NOM	/Ø/	/Ø/
ACC	/Ø/, /n/	/t/
GEN	/n/	/n/
PART	/a/	/a/

Based on the observation that the accusative form of nouns corresponds to either the nominative form or the genitive form in (66), Kiparsky (2001) argues for a re-interpretation of this system. On his view, there is no genuine accusative form for nouns; see (67).

(67) *Structural case markers (singular)* (Kiparsky's 2001 reconstruction)

	NOUNS: 'bears'	PRONOUNS: 'you'
NOM	/Ø/	/Ø/
ACC	–	/t/
GEN	/n/	/n/
PART	/a/	/a/

---

[23] To some extent, suggestions along these lines can already be found in Kiparsky (1998, 2001) and Wunderlich (2000), and what follows owes a lot to these works. However, the analysis below is much more radical in its treatment of objective case, and also fairly different in several other respects.

Assuming for the time being the correctness of (67), the following five generalizations hold.

(68) *Empirical generalizations* (Kiparsky 2001)
  (i) Objects of predicates that give rise to an *unbounded* (atelic) interpretation always take the partitive exponent.
  (ii) Objects of predicates that give rise to a *bounded* (telic) (resultative, or quasi-resultative) interpretation take the partitive marker if they have a "quantitatively indeterminate denotation.'
  (iii) Otherwise, objects of the latter predicates take the accusative marker if they are personal pronouns;
  (iv) and they take the genitive marker if they are non-pronominal, and c-commanded by an overt subject.
  (v) In all other cases, a structurally case-marked object DP takes the nominative marker.

Thus, we have a system where pronouns are marked differently from other DPs, and where non-specific DPs are marked differently from other DPs. In an Aissen-type approach, this strongly suggests harmonic alignment of the grammatical function scale with the definiteness scale as the underlying principle at work here.

4.5.2 Analysis

We claim that there is in fact only one kind of object case in all the examples in (65), viz., accusative.[24] Under this assumption, marker variation can be derived

---

[24] Needless to say, this makes a number of non-trivial predictions that will ultimately have to be explored further. To name just one consequence of the present, morphology-based approach to variation in object encoding in Finnish: If all object exponents in (65) are instantiations of one and the same syntactic case (accusative) – particularly, if what is called 'accusative' and what is called 'partitive' in (66) and (67) can emerge as a single case –, we do not expect syntactic operations to be sensitive of the morphological differences. Passiviziation is a case in point: Standardly, it is postulated that if two object cases behave differently with respect to absorption in the passive, they cannot be identical. There is some disagreement in the literature as to whether Finnish has a true passive construction in the first place (see Blevins 2003 vs. Manninen and Nelson 2004). Assuming that it does, it can be noted that 'partitive' markers (in the sense of (66), (67)) are maintained on objects in passive constructions (see (i e), with an epenthetic *t* accompanying the partitive exponent), whereas 'accusative' markers typically

as a morphological phenomenon resulting from impoverishment. Thus, suppose that structural cases in Finnish can be decomposed as in (69).[25]

(69) *Structural cases in Finnish*
   a. NOM: [−gov, −obl, +subj]
   b. GEN: [+gov, +obl, +subj]
   c. ACC: [+gov, −obl, −subj]

Relevant scales are the basic (binary) GF scale and the definiteness scale; see (70a,b) (= (43)). In addition, we will invoke a boundedness scale, as in (70c); recall from (68) that interpretational differences along this dimension (i.e., bounded vs. unbounded) give rise to different marker choices.

---

disappear (see (i-a)). However, there is an interesting exception: Pronouns that are [+human] retain the accusative marker in the passive (see (i-b)).

(i) a. *Jussi-Ø   murha-ttiin*
       Jussi-NOM   murder-PASS.PAST
       'Jussi was murdered.'

   b. *He-t   murha-ttiin*
       (s)he-ACC murder-PASS.PAST
       '(S)he was murdered.'

   c. *Etanoi-(t)a   tape-ttin*
       slugs-PART   kill-PASS.PAST
       'Some slugs were killed.'

Thus, if we were to conclude that the difference with respect to absorption implies that the object case assigned to the active counterpart of (i-c) is syntactically different from the object case assigned to the active counterpart of (i-a), the same reasoning would lead us to conclude that the object case assigned to the active counterpart of (i-b) is syntactically different from the object case assigned to the active counterpart of (i-a) – i.e., that human pronouns receive a different syntactic object case from non-pronominal DPs. This seems highly unlikely (and it would not be compatible with the labelling in (66), (67) either). We cannot offer a comprehensive analysis of case absorption in Finnish passive (or passive-like) constructions here. Suffice it to point out that the three groups of objects which are distinguished by this operation lend themselves to a description in terms of scales of the type investigated in this article, and that it might therefore eventually prove best to view case absorption in passive constructions as a morphological phenomenon (see Anderson 1992 for relevant discussion).

25 See Bierwisch (1967), Levin (1986), Alsina (1996), and Wiese (1999) for the primitive case features adopted here. The non-structural cases of Finnish can be assumed to be composed of primitive features encoding semantic concepts in addition to features of the type adopted here; but non-structural cases are of no importance in the present context. Note also that the classification of the Finnish genitive as [+subj] is motivated by its function as a DP-internal marker of possession, a subject-like property. Alternatively, the genitive could be taken to be defined by [−subj]. This would not radically change things; on the contrary, it would make it possible to invoke an arguably somewhat simpler concept of specificity. See below.

(70) a. *GF scale* (basic)
 Subject > object
 b. *Definiteness scale*
 Pro(noun) > Name (PN) > Def(inite) > Indefinite Specific (Spec) > NonSpecific (NSpec)
 c. *Boundedness scale*
 Bounded > unbounded (Bd > NBd)

By harmonic alignment, the constraint hierarchies in (71a) (for the definiteness scale) and (71b) (for the boundedness scale) are derived.

(71) *Constraint alignments*
 a. *Obj/Pro ≫ *Obj/PN ≫ *Obj/Def ≫ *Obj/Spec ≫ *Obj/NSpec
 b. *Obj/Bd ≫ *Obj/NBd

As seen before for Hindi, local conjuction then applies to the members of the two constraint hierarchies in (71), preserving order; see (72). This makes it possible to express the generalization that differential argument encoding in Finnish is two-dimensional (it involves degrees both of definiteness and of boundedness).

(72) *Local conjunction*
 a. *Obj/Pro & *Obj/Bd ≫ *Obj/PN & *Obj/Bd ≫ *Obj/Def & *Obj/Bd ≫ *Obj/Spec & *Obj/Bd ≫ *Obj/NSpec & *Obj/Bd
 b. *Obj/Pro & *Obj/NBd ≫ *Obj/PN & *Obj/NBd ≫ *Obj/Def & *Obj/NBd ≫ *Obj/Spec & *Obj/NBd ≫ *Obj/NSpec & *Obj/NBd

Again, a notational simplification can be carried out; compare (73) with (72).

(73) *Notational variant (simplification)*
 a. *Obj/Pro/Bd ≫ *Obj/PN/Bd ≫ *Obj/Def/Bd ≫ *Obj/Spec/Bd ≫ *Obj/NSpec/Bd
 b. *Obj/Pro/NBd ≫ *Obj/PN/NBd ≫ *Obj/Def/NBd ≫ *Obj/Spec/NBd ≫ *Obj/NSpec/NBd

Finally, the faithfulness constraint MAX-CASE (formerly $*\emptyset_C$) is locally conjoined with each of the constraints in (73a) and (73b), preserving the original order of constraints.

(74) *Order-preserving local conjunction with* MAX-CASE:
   a. *Obj/Pro/Bd & Max-C ≫ *Obj/PN/Bd & Max-C ≫
      *Obj/Def/Bd & Max-C ≫ *Obj/Spec/Bd & Max-C ≫
      *Obj/NSpec/Bd & Max-C
   b. *Obj/Pro/NBd & Max-C ≫ *Obj/PN/NBd & Max-C ≫
      *Obj/Def/NBd & Max-C ≫ *Obj/Spec/NBd & Max-C ≫
      *Obj/NSpec/NBd & Max-C

Thus, we arrive at invariant hierarchies of faithfulness constraints that penalize the deletion of case features depending on definiteness and boundedness features of the DP. For instance, *Obj/Pro/Bd & Max-C* is violated if a case feature of a VP-internal pronoun in a clause with a bounded interpretation of the predicate is deleted post-syntactically (before morphological realization). As a consequence of order-preserving local conjunction, this constraint must outrank all the other constraints in (74). Similarly, *Obj/NSpec/NBd & Max-C* is violated if a case feature of a VP-internal indefinite non-specific DP in a clause with an unbounded interpretation of the predicate is deleted post-syntactically (before morphological realization). This constraint is necessarily lowest-ranked (among the constraints in (74)). It will prove important to assume that constraints of this type are *gradient*; i.e., multiple violations add up, and a candidate α that differs from another candidate β only in that it incurs fewer violations of such a complex faithfulness constraint always has a better constraint profile.

In addition to the hierarchies of faithfulness constraints in (74a), there are conflicting markedness constraints that trigger deletion of decomposed, primitive case features (i.e., more fine-grained versions of Aissen's *STRUC$_C$*):; see (75).[26]

(75) *Markedness constraints that trigger case feature deletion*
   a. *[−obl]   b. *[+gov]   c. *[−subj]

The ranking that captures the variation in object encoding in Finnish is given in (76). Three groups of faithfulness constraints for case features of DP types can be identified (they are referred to as I, II, and III); members of each group exhibit a uniform behaviour with respect to the interspersed markedness constraints.

The overall system of multi-dimensional differential argument encoding in Finnish that arises under the present view looks as in (77) (as before, we use

---

[26] Note that it must be assumed that these markedness constraints cannot undergo local conjunction with the constraint hierarchies in (73). Otherwise, case features would preferentially be deleted in contexts with atypical objects, and retained in contexts with typical objects, thereby undermining the functional justification of differential object encoding. This is exactly as in Aissen (1999, 2003), where *STRUC$_C$ must be prevented from participating in local conjunction with constraint hierarchies; see footnote 4.

Aissen's (2003) method of graphically representing multi-dimensional differential object marking). On the basis of an initial (i.e., syntactic) accusative specification (viz., [+gov, –obl, –subj]), the markedness constraints in (75) trigger impoverishment operations for different kinds of objects (groups I, II, and III), with a different exponent emerging for each group.

(76) *Ranking in Finnish*
I: {*Obj/Pro/Bd & Max-C} ≫ *[–obl] ≫

II: $\left\{\begin{array}{l} \text{*Obj/PN/Bd \& Max-C} \gg \\ \text{*Obj/Def/Bd \& Max-C} \gg \\ \text{*Obj/Spec/Bd \& Max-C} \end{array}\right\}$ ≫ *[+gov] ≫

III: $\left\{\begin{array}{l} \text{*Obj/NSpec/Bd \& Max-C} \gg \\ \text{*Obj/Pro/NBd \& Max-C} \gg \\ \text{*Obj/PN/NBd \& Max-C} \gg \\ \text{*Obj/Def/NBd \& Max-C} \gg \\ \text{*Obj/Spec/NBd \& Max-C} \gg \\ \text{*Obj/NSpec/NBd \& Max-C} \end{array}\right\}$ ≫ *[–subj]

(77) *Differential object marking in Finnish*

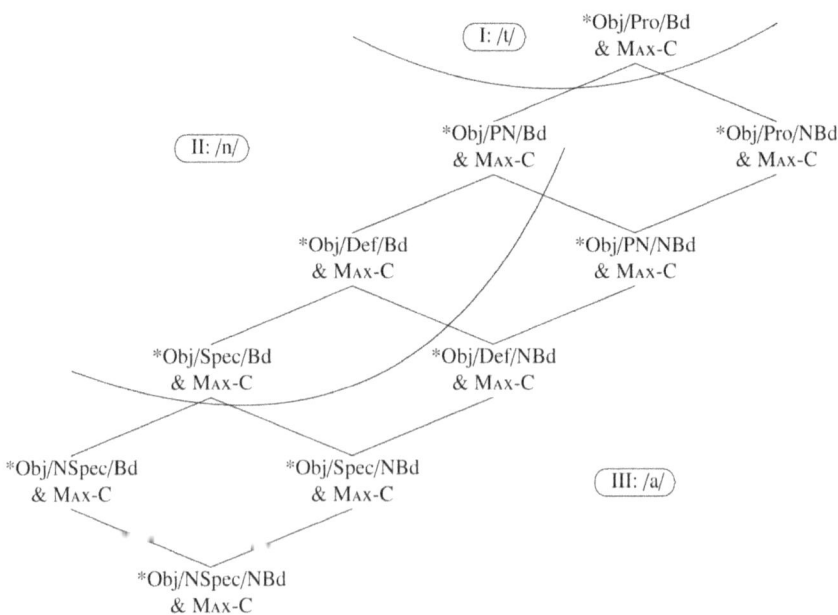

In order to derive the effect of the optimality-theoretic system in (76) by means of standard impoverishment rules, one would have to postulate the rules in (78).

(78) Impoverishment rules
   a. [−obl] → ∅/____[¬(Pro, Bd)]
   b. [+gov] → ∅/____[Nbd ∨ (NSpec, Bd)]

However, there are at least two reasons for why an approach based on the two rules in (78) is inferior to an approach based on (76). First, the optimality-theoretic analysis in (76) is based on fixed rankings of constraints that are derived from independently motivated scales; in contrast, the two rules in (78) are arbitary statements that stipulate, but are not inherently connected to, the functional motivation for differential object marking. And second, the form of the rules in (78) reveals that, in a canonical impoverishment approach that does not rely on optimization, it is extremely difficult to characterize the relevant environments in which impoverishment takes place as *natural classes*. Thus, negation and disjunction are needed: Rule (78a) applies to every object DP which is *not* a pronoun in a clause with a bounded interpretation of the predicate; the class of objects so defined is not a natural class. Similarly, rule (78b) applies to object DPs that *either* show up in a clause with an unbounded interpretation of the predicate, *or* qualify as nonspecific and show up in a clause with a bounded interpretation of the predicate; again, these contexts do not form a natural class. The same problem for a rule-based account emerged in Cavineña (see §4.4), where impoverishment applies if the object is non-singular *or* third person. In both Finnish and Cavineña, the only way out, it seems, would be to postulate a more fine-grained, highly abstract feature structure underlying the various categories. Such a step might be possible from a purely technical point of view, but seems poorly motivated linguistically. No such problem arises in (76): The classes of objects that show an identical behaviour vis-a-vis differential argument encoding are defined naturally, as being subject to constraints that show the same ranking with respect to the markedness constraints in (75).[27]

---

[27] A similar argument for defining natural classes by reference to discrete domains in linear orders (rather than by shared features) is provided by Wiese (2003) in his analysis of Latin noun inflection.

On this basis, the vocabulary items for encoding accusative case (i.e., [+gov, −obl, −subj]) in Finnish can be assumed to look as in (79).

(79) *Vocabulary items*
 /t/ ↔ [+gov, −obl, −subj]
 /n/ ↔ [+gov]
 /a/ ↔ [−subj]
 /∅/ ↔ [ ]

By assumption, /t/ is an exponent that is not underspecified: It completely matches the syntactic accusative specification. However, if deletion of [−obl] applies (triggered by *[−obl] if it outranks the relevant faithfulness constraint for a DP), /t/ cannot be inserted anymore, and the most specific exponent among the remaining (less specific) markers is inserted: /n/, which is marked as [+gov]. Note that, assuming that the genitive is defined as [+gov, +obl, **+subj**], /n/ cannot be characterized by [+gov, **−subj**] – if it were, the syncretism with the /n/ exponent in typical genitive contexts could not be captured by postulating a single entry. This assumption then necessitates a partial hierarchy of features [+gov] > [−subj] so as to ensure the correct choice of exponent in II contexts: /n/ must qualify as more specific than /a/.[28]

If deletion of [+gov] also takes place before morphological realization (forced by the markedness constraint *[+gov]), neither /t/ nor /n/ can be inserted, and the less specific marker /a/ is resorted to.

Let us go through a couple of derivations (one for each of the four accusative markers) that exemplify the basic working of the approach just outlined. Suppose first that the syntactic component delivers a pronominal object DP with structural accusative case ([+gov, −obl, −subj]) that occurs with a predicate which gives rise to a bounded interpretation (i.e., the object DP belongs to class I in (76)). The syntax-morphology mapping then takes this feature structure as the input and produces various outputs that selectively delete features of the input,

---

28 That said, it is not quite clear how strong the evidence is for assuming the genitive to be [+subj] rather than [−subj] in the first place (see footnote 25). If we were to assume that the Finnish genitive is defined as [+gov, +obl, −subj], the exponent /n/ could be associated with the features [+gov, −subj], and the fact that /n/ is more specific than /a/ would follow without resort to a feature hierarchy, just by comparing the size of the feature sets involved.

as in (80) (as noted in footnote 13 above, there may also be outputs that enrich the input's feature structure by adding material, but this option does not play a role in the present context).[29]

(80) *Sample optimizations 1:* /t/

INPUT: TYPE I [+gov, −obl, −subj], [Pro], [Bd]	I	*[−obl]	II	*[+gov]	III	*[−subj]
☞ O_1: [+gov, −obl, −subj]		*		*		*
O_2: [+gov, −obl]	*!	*		*		
O_3: [+gov, −subj]	*!			*		*
O_4: [−obl, −subj]	*!	*				*
O_5: [+gov]	*!*			*		
O_6: [−obl]	*!*	*				
O_7: [−subj]	*!*					*
O_8: [ ]	*!**					

Output O_1 emerges as optimal. It faithfully maintains all of the input's (i.e., the syntactic output's) feature structure by violating all markedness constraints that demand impoverishment because this is the only way to fulfill the highest-ranked constraint I (= *OBJ/PRO/BD & MAX-C). After optimization of syntactic structures before morphological realization, vocabulary insertion takes place in accordance with the Subset Principle. Since /t/ is the most specific vocabulary item that fits into the O_1 structure, it is inserted, thereby blocking the less specific markers /n/, /a/, and /Ø/.

Suppose next that the syntax has delivered an accusative-marked definite object DP in a clause in which the predicate receives a bounded interpretation; these pieces of information are encoded in the feature bundle {[+gov, −obl, −subj], [Def], [Bd]}. The object DP now falls under a faithfulness constraint of type II in (76); I is vacuously satisfied by all outputs. As shown in (81), the markedness constraint *[−obl] forcing deletion of [−obl] is ranked higher than the pertinent faithfulness constraint of class II (viz., *Obj/Def/Bd & Max-C). Therefore, output O_3 (with the features [+gov, −subj]) is optimal; there is impoverishment (postsyntactic deletion of [−obl]).

---

[29] I, II, III in (80) stand for the three ranked sets of constraints in (76). Features related to definiteness and boundedness are ignored in outputs since they are irrelevant for morphological realization.

(81) *Sample optimizations 2:* /n/

INPUT: TYPE II [+gov, −obl, −subj], [Def], [Bd]	I	*[−obl]	II	*[+gov]	III	*[−subj]
O_1: [+gov,−obl,−subj]		*!		*		*
O_2: [+gov,−obl]		*!		*		
☞ O_3: [+gov,−subj]				*		*
O_4: [−obl,−subj]		*!		*		*
O_5: [+gov]				**!		*
O_6: [−obl]		*!		**		
O_7: [−subj]				**!		*
O_8: [ ]				**!*		

Consequently, output O_3 is what morphological realization works on. Since the most specific exponent /t/ does not realize a subset of the (impoverished) syntactic structure anymore, the (compatibility requirement of the) Subset Principle ensures that it cannot be inserted in this context. There is a (minimal) retreat to the more general case: The next-specific marker /n/ is inserted; recall that /n/ is more specific than /a/, either because [+gov] belongs to a more specific feature class than [−subj], or because /n/ is in fact associated with more features to begin with (see footnote 28).

Next, consider a case where the syntactic component has produced an object DP belonging to class III, with, say, the feature set {[+gov, −obl, −subj], [Nspec], [Nbd]}. Higher-ranked faithfulness constraints active for class I and class II object DPs are now vacuously fulfilled, and the lower-ranked markedness constraint *[+gov] springs into action (in addition to higher-ranked *[−obl]), creating a more far-reaching impoverishment effect in violation of class III faithfulness. This is shown in (82): The optimal output is O_7, which has both [+gov] and [−obl] deleted in violation of the lower-ranked class III faithfulness constraint *Obj/NSpec/NBd & Max-C, maintaining only [−subj] – this latter primitive case feature cannot be deleted because deletion would incur a fatal violation of the class III constraint *Obj/NSpec/NBd & Max-C, given that the markedness constraint *[−subj] is ranked lower (cf. O_8).

(82) *Sample optimizations 3*: /a/

INPUT: TYPE III [+gov, −obl, −subj], [Nspec], [Nbd]	I	*[−obl]	II	*[+gov]	III	*[−subj]
O₁: [+gov, −obl, −subj]		*!		*		*
O₂: [+gov, −obl]		*!		*		*
O₃: [+gov, −subj]				*!		*
O₄: [−obl, −subj]		*!				*
O₅: [+gov]				*!		**
O₆: [−obl]		*!				**
☞ O₇: [−subj]						**
O₈: [ ]						***!

Consequently, morphological realization of a structure O₇ finds a feature specification that blocks insertion of both /t/ and /a/, due to the compatibility requirement of the Subset Principle. The most specific vocabulary item that can be inserted is /a/ (which blocks less specific /Ø/).

Finally, let us turn to the fourth, least specific, exponent for accusative contexts: /Ø/. Zero exponence results from massive impoverishment (a deletion of all case features). Simplifying a bit, it shows up when there is no overt subject argument present (e.g., in imperatives). Again, this would seem to suggest a clear functional motivation. There are two analytic possibilites:[30]

– Objects do not participate in harmonic alignment in the first place when they are not accompanied by an overt subject. Hence, sole objects do not obey any of the constraints in I-III, and the *[case] constraints demand full deletion of case features.
– Sole objects participate in harmonic alignment and thus fall under I-III. However, there is an undominated constraint that demands deletion of case features in object positions when no (relevant) subject is present.

Both options seem to us to be viable in principle. For the sake of concreteness, we adopt the first one here. The syntax-morphology mapping in cases where a structurally case-marked object DP is not accompanied by a subject then proceeds as shown in (83) (we may refer to this type of object as belonging to a further class IV).

---

[30] Both solutions presuppose that whether a subject argument is overtly present or not can be read off syntactic structures, before post-syntacatic morphology takes place.

(83) *Sample optimizations 4: /Ø/*

INPUT: TYPE IV [+gov, −obl, −subj], [no subject]	I	*[−obl]	II	*[+gov]	III	*[−subj]
O_1: [+gov, −obl, −subj]		*!		*		*
O_2: [+gov, −obl]		*!		*		
O_3: [+gov, −subj]				*!		*
O_4: [−obl, −subj]		*!				*
O_5: [+gov]				*!		
O_6: [−obl]		*!				
O_7: [−subj]						*!
☞ O_8: [ ]						

Since faithfulness constraints are irrelevant, the markedness constraints force deletion of all case features. Thus, output O_8 (with feature structure [ ]) is optimal; radical impoverishment takes place. Therefore, /Ø/ is the only remaining marker that fits; there is a full retreat to the general case.

Note finally that the system reveals iconicity, as argued by Wiese (1999) for German (see subsection 4.2 above): /t/ is less sonorous than /n/, which is less sonorous than /a/; /Ø/ is least marked.[31] This corresponds to the exponents' degree of specificity.

5 Concluding remarks

To sum up, we have seen that differential argument encoding regulated by Hale/Silverstein hierarchies is not necessarily confined to zero/non-zero alternations, as predicted under the approach developed in Aissen (1999, 2003). Rather, differential argument encoding may also involve two or more non-zero exponents, with Hale/Silverstein hierarchies determining marker choice in exactly the same

---

31 There is a proviso. In certain morpho-phonologically defined contexts, an initial *t* shows up with /a/. We assume this consonant to be truly epenthetic, and irrelevant to the more abstract system measuring sonority for the purposes of iconicity as such. In other words: The form accessed by the Iconicity Meta-Principle must be an underlying phonological representation, and need not directly correspond to the surface form.

way as in the data considered by Aissen, and the alternating markers exhibiting iconicity effects (less/more alternations in marker form corresponding to the degree of case information available). We have argued that an approach according to which case may or may not be expressed is therefore not fine-grained enough. The alternative that we have developed in this paper takes Aissen's optimality-theoretic approach to be essentially correct: There is harmonic alignment of markedness scales and (order-preserving) local conjunction with faithfulness constraints blocking case feature deletion; and the resulting constraint hierarchies can be interspersed with markedness constraints blocking case. However, the present approach relies on a more elaborate system of primitive case features that have independently been postulated in theories of inflectional morphology in order to derive instances of syncretism, and it relocates the deletion of case features from the syntax to the morphology – or, more precisely, the morphology-syntax interface. The main claim that we have tried to defend in this context is that the optimality-theoretic system of selective post-syntactic deletion of case features underlying instances of differential argument encoding should be viewed as a principled approach to impoverishment operations as they have been proposed in Distributed Morphology.[32]

The overall picture of grammar (and of the morphology-syntax interface in particular) that emerges is a fairly conservative one (though see Keine 2010 for a different view). It is essentially identical to the one standardly adopted in Distributed Morphology, with one minimal qualification: Impoverishment does not result from the application of specific, arbitrarily defined rules, but from the interaction of simple optimality-theoretic constraints, many of which show a fixed order (due to order-preserving nature of harmonic alignment and local conjunction). On this view, Optimality Theory emerges as a theory of the morphology-syntax interface.[33] Whether optimization procedures also affect the inner workings of the syntactic and/or morphological components proper is an issue that is for the most part orthogonal to the questions that we have pursued here (but recall footnote 14).

---

32 At this point, we have to leave open the question of whether *all* instances of impoverishment can ultimately be conceived of in this way, as functionally motivated; but assuming this to be the case does not seem unreasonable as a research hypothesis.
33 This corresponds to the assumption that Optimality Theory should in general be considered to be a theory of linguistic interfaces; see, e.g., Pesetsky (1998).

References

Aissen, Judith. 1999. Markedness and subject choice in Optimality Theory. *Natural Language and Linguistic Theory* 17:673–711.

Aissen, Judith. 2003. Differential object marking: Iconicity vs. economy. *Natural Language and Linguistic Theory* 21:435–483.

Alsina, Alex. 1996. Passive types and the theory of object asymmetries. *Natural Language and Linguistic Theory* 14:673–723.

Anand, Pranav, and Andrew Nevins. 2006. The locus of ergative case assignment: Evidence from scope. In *Ergativity: Emerging Issues*, eds. Alana Johns, Diane Massam, and Juvenal Ndayiragije, 3–25. Dordrecht: Springer.

Anderson, Stephen. 1992. *A-Morphous Morphology*. Cambridge: Cambridge University Press.

Baerman, Matthew, Dunstan Brown, and Greville Corbett. 2005. *The Syntax-Morphology Interface. A Study of Syncretism*. Cambridge: Cambridge University Press.

Bank, Sebastian. 2008. Kasus, Genus und Belebtheit im Wettbewerb: Synkretismus in der deutschen Nominalflexion. MA thesis, Universität Köln.

Behaghel, Otto. 1911. *Geschichte der deutschen Sprache*. Straßburg: Trübner.

Bickel, Balthasar. 2007. How good is the evidence for referential scales? Ms., Universität Leipzig.

Bickel, Balthasar, Alena Witzlack-Makarevich, and Taras Zakharko. 2015. Typological evidence against universal effects of referential scales on case alignment. This volume.

Bierwisch, Manfred. 1967. Syntactic features in morphology: General problems of so-called pronominal inflection in German. In *To Honor Roman Jakobson, Vol. 1*, 239–270. The Hague/Paris: Mouton.

Blake, Barry. 1994. *Case*. Cambridge: Cambridge University Press.

Blevins, James. 1995. Syncretism and paradigmatic opposition. *Linguistics and Philosophy* 18:113–152.

Blevins, Jim. 2003. Passives and impersonals. *Journal of Linguistics* 39:473–520.

Bobaljik, Jonathan. 2002. Syncretism without paradigms: Remarks on Williams 1981, 1994. In *Yearbook of Morphology 2001*, eds. Geert Booij and Jaap van Marle, 53–85. Dordrecht: Kluwer.

Bonet, Eulàlia. 1991. Morphology after syntax. Ph.D. dissertation, MIT, Cambridge, MA.

Brown, Jason, Karsten Koch, and Martina Wiltschko. 2004. The person hierarchy: Primitive or epiphenomenal? Evidence from Halkomelem Salish. In *Proceedings of the 34th Meeting of the North East Linguistic Society (NELS 34)*, eds. Keir Moulton and Matthew Wolf, 147–162. Amherst, MA: GLSA.

Butt, Miriam, and Tracy King. 2004. The status of case. In *Clause Structure in South Asian Languages*, eds. Veneeta Dayal and Anoop Mahajan, 153–198. Boston: Kluwer.

Carnie, Andrew. 2005. Some remarks on markedness hierarchies: A reply to Aissen 1999 and 2003. In *Coyote Working Papers in Linguistics 14*, eds. Daniel Siddiqi and Benjamin Tucker, 37–50. University of Arizona.

Chomsky, Noam. 1965. *Aspects of the Theory of Syntax*. Cambridge, MA: MIT Press.

Chomsky, Noam. 2001. Derivation by phase. In *Ken Hale: A Life in Language*, ed. Michael Kenstowicz, 1–52. Cambridge, MA: MIT Press.

Comrie, Bernard. 1978. Morphological classification of cases in the Slavonic languages. *The Slavonic and East European Review* 56:177–191.

Corbett, Greville, and Norman Fraser. 1993. Network morphology: A DATR account of Russian nominal inflection. *Journal of Linguistics* 29:113–142.
de Swart, Peter. 2007. Cross-linguistic variation in object marking. Ph.D. dissertation, University of Nijmegen.
Dixon, Robert M. W. 1972. *The Dyirbal Language of North Queensland*. Cambridge: Cambridge University Press.
Dixon, Robert M. W. 1994. *Ergativity*. Cambridge: Cambridge University Press.
Don, Jan, and Elma Blom. 2006. A constraint-based approach to morphological neutralization. In *Linguistics in the Netherlands 2006*, 78–88. Amsterdam: John Benjamins.
Fischer, Silke. 2006. Zur Morphologie der deutschen Personalpronomina – eine Spaltungsanalyse. In *Subanalysis of Argument Encoding in Distributed Morphology*, eds. Gereon Müller and Jochen Trommer, volume 84 of *Linguistische Arbeitsberichte*, 77–101. Universität Leipzig.
Frampton, John. 2002. Syncretism, impoverishment, and the structure of person features. In *CLS 38: The Main Session. Papers from the 38th Meeting of the Chicago Linguistic Society, Vol. 1*, eds. Mary Andronis, Erin Debenport, Anne Pycha, and Keiko Yoshimura, 207–222. Chicago: Chicago Linguistic Society.
Georgi, Doreen. 2008. A Distributed Morphology approach to argument encoding in Kambera. *Linguistische Berichte* 213:45–63.
Grimshaw, Jane. 2001. Optimal clitic positions and the lexicon in Romance clitic systems. In *Optimality-Theoretic Syntax*, eds. Géraldine Legendre, Jane Grimshaw, and Sten Vikner, 205–240. Cambridge, MA: MIT Press.
Guillaume, Antoine. 2008. *A Grammar of Cavineña*. Berlin: Mouton de Gruyter.
Guirardello, Raquel. 1999. A reference grammar of Trumai. Ph.D. dissertation, Rice University, Houston, Texas.
Hale, Ken. 1972. A new perspective on American Indian linguistics. In *New Perspectives on the Pueblos*, ed. Alfonso Ortiz, 87–103. Albuquerque: University of New Mexico Press.
Halle, Morris. 1997. Distributed Morphology: Impoverishment and fission. In *Papers at the Interface*, eds. Benjamin Bruening, Yoonjung Kang, and Martha McGinnis, volume 30 of *MIT Working Papers in Linguistics*, 425–449. Cambridge, MA: MITWPL. Republished 2000 in: *Research in Afroasiatic grammar: Papers from the third Conference on Afroasiatic Languages*, eds. Jacqueline Lecarme, Jean Lowenstein & Ur Shlonsky, Amsterdam: John Benjamins, 125–151.
Halle, Morris, and Alec Marantz. 1993. Distributed Morphology and the pieces of inflection. In *The View from Building 20: Essays in Linguistics in Honor of Sylvain Bromberger*, eds. Ken Hale and Samuel Jay Keyser, 111–176. Cambridge, MA: MIT Press.
Halle, Morris, and Alec Marantz. 1994. Some key features of Distributed Morphology. In *Papers on Phonology and Morphology*, eds. Andrew Carnie, Heidi Harley, and Tony Bures, volume 21 of *MIT Working Papers in Linguistics*, 275–288. Cambridge, MA: MITWPL.
Harbour, Daniel. 2008. The syntactic basis of phi-case interaction. Ms., Queen Mary College, University of London.
Harley, Heidi, and Rolf Noyer. 2003. Distributed Morphology. In *The Second GLOT International State-of-the-Article Book*, eds. Lisa Cheng and Rint Sybesma, 463–496. Berlin: Mouton de Gruyter.
Haspelmath, Martin. 2007. Prominence scales in differential object marking: A critique of Aissen (2003). Ms., MPI-EVA, Leipzig.

Jakobson, Roman. 1936. Beitrag zur allgemeinen Kasuslehre: Gesamtbedeutungen der russischen Kasus. *Travaux du Cercle Linguistique de Prague* 6:240–288. Reprinted 1966 in: *Readings in Linguistics II*, ed. by Eric Hamp, Fred Householder and Robert Austerlitz, Chicago: University of Chicago Press, pp. 51–89.

Karch, Dieter. 1975. *Zur Morphologie vorderpfälzischer Dialekte*. Niemeyer.

Keine, Stefan. 2007. Reanalysing Hindi split ergativity as a morphological phenomenon. In *1 2 Many*, eds. Jochen Trommer and Andreas Opitz, volume 85 of *Linguistische Arbeitsberichte*, 73–127. Universität Leipzig.

Keine, Stefan. 2010. *Case and Agreement from Fringe to Core: A Minimalist Approach*. Berlin: de Gruyter.

Kiparsky, Paul. 1998. Partitive case and aspect. In *The Projection of Arguments*, eds. Miriam Butt and Wilhelm Geuder, 265–307. Stanford University: CSLI Publications.

Kiparsky, Paul. 2001. Structural case in Finnish. *Lingua* 111:315–376.

Lahne, Antje. 2010. A multiple specifier approach to left-peripheral architecture. *Linguistic Analysis* 35:73–108.

Lee, Hanjung. 2003. Parallel optimization in case systems. Ms., University of Minnesota, Twin Cities.

Legate, Julie Anne. 2008. Morphological and Abstract Case. *Linguistic Inquiry* 39:55–101.

Legendre, Géraldine, Paul Smolensky, and Colin Wilson. 1998. When is less more? Faithfulness and minimal links in wh-chains. In *Is the Best Good Enough?*, eds. Pilar Barbosa, Danny Fox, Paul Hagstrom, Martha McGinnis, and David Pesetsky, 249–289. Cambridge, MA: MIT Press and MITWPL.

Levin, Lorraine. 1986. Operations on lexical forms: Unaccusative rules in Germanic languages. Ph.D. dissertation, MIT, Cambridge, MA.

Lumsden, John. 1992. Underspecification in grammatical and natural gender. *Linguistic Inquiry* 23:469–486.

Macaulay, Monica. 2005. On the 2 > 1 prominence hierarchy of Algonquian. *LSO Working Papers in Linguistics* 5:1–24.

Mahajan, Anoop. 1990. The A/A-bar distinction and movement theory. Ph.D. dissertation, MIT, Cambridge, MA.

Manninen, Satu, and Diane Nelson. 2004. What is a passive? The case of Finnish. *Studia Linguistica* 58:212–251.

Mohanan, Tara. 1994. *Argument Structure in Hindi*. Stanford: CSLI Publications.

Morphy, Frances. 1983. Djapu, a Yolngu dialect. In *Handbook of Australian Languages, Vol. 3*, eds. Robert M. W. Dixon and Barry Blake, 1–188. Amsterdam: Benjamins.

Müller, Gereon. 2003. Zwei Theorien der pronominalen Flexion im Deutschen (Versionen Standard und Mannheim). *Deutsche Sprache* 30:328–363.

Müller, Gereon. 2004. A Distributed Morphology approach to syncretism in Russian noun inflection. In *Proceedings of the 12th Formal Approaches to Slavic Linguistics (FASL 12)*, eds. Olga Arnaudova, Wayles Browne, Maria Luisa Rivero, and Danijela Stojanovic, 353–373. University of Ottawa.

Müller, Gereon. 2005. Syncretism and iconicity in Icelandic noun declensions: A distributed morphology approach. In *Yearbook of Morphology 2004*, eds. Geert Booij and Jaap van Marle, 229–271. Dordrecht: Springer.

Müller, Gereon. 2007a. Extended exponence by enrichment: Argument encoding in German, Archi, and Timucua. In *Proceedings of the 30th Annual Penn Linguistics Colloquium*, eds. Tatjana Scheffler, Joshua Tauberer, Aviad Eilam, and Laia Mayol, volume 13.1 of *Penn Working Papers in Linguistics*, 253–266. Philadelphia: University of Pennsylvania.

Müller, Gereon. 2007b. Notes on paradigm economy. *Morphology* 17:1–38.
Noyer, Rolf. 1992. Features, positions, and affixes in autonomous morphological structure. Ph. D. dissertation, MIT, Cambridge, MA.
Noyer, Rolf. 1998. Impoverishment theory and morphosyntactic markedness. In *Morphology and its Relation to Phonology and Syntax*, eds. Steven Lapointe, Diane Brentari, and Patrick Farrell, 264–285. Palo Alto: CSLI.
Opitz, Andreas. 2006. A reanalysis of definiteness-markers in Albanian noun inflection. In *Subanalysis of Argument Encoding in Distributed Morphology*, eds. Gereon Müller and Jochen Trommer, volume 84 of *Linguistische Arbeitsberichte*, 103–114. Universität Leipzig.
Opitz, Andreas. 2008. Case and markedness in Tlapanec. *Linguistische Berichte* 214:211–237.
Ortmann, Albert. 2002. Economy-based splits, constraints and lexical representations. In *More than Words: A Festschrift for Dieter Wunderlich*, eds. Ingrid Kaufmann and Barbara Stiebels, 147–177. Berlin: Akademie Verlag.
Pesetsky, David. 1998. Some optimality principles of sentence pronunciation. In *Is the Best Good Enough?*, eds. Pilar Barbosa, Danny Fox, Paul Hagstrom, Martha McGinnis, and David Pesetsky, 337–383. Cambridge, MA: MIT Press and MITWPL.
Plank, Frans. 1979. Ikonisierung und De-Ikonisierung als Prinzipien des Sprachwandels. *Sprachwissenschaft* 4:121–158.
Prince, Alan, and Paul Smolensky. 1993/2004. *Optimality Theory: Constraint Interaction in Generative Grammar*. Oxford: Blackwell. Revision of 1993 technical report, Rutgers University Center for Cognitive Science.
Richards, Marc. 2015. Defective Agree, case alternations, and the prominence of person. This volume.
Silverstein, Michael. 1976. Hierarchy of features and ergativity. In *Grammatical Categories in Australian Languages*, ed. Robert M. W. Dixon, 112–171. Canberra: Australian Institute of Aboriginal Studies.
Smolensky, Paul. 1993. Harmony, markedness, and phonological activity. Ms., University of Colorado. (Handout of talk at Rutgers Optimality Workshop 1). Available from ROA (no. 87).
Smolensky, Paul. 2006. Harmonic completeness, local constraint conjunction, and feature domain markedness. In *The Harmonic Mind*, eds. Paul Smolensky and Géraldine Legendre, chapter 14, 27–160. Cambridge, MA: MIT Press.
Stiebels, Barbara. 2000. Linker inventories, linking splits and lexical economy. In *Lexicon in Focus*, eds. Barbara Stiebels and Dieter Wunderlich, 211–245. Berlin: Akademie-Verlag.
Stiebels, Barbara. 2002. *Typologie des Argumentlinkings: Ökonomie und Expressivität*. Berlin: Akademie Verlag.
Stiebels, Barbara. 2008. Scales in the various types of argument linking. Talk, Workshop on Scales, Leipzig.
Stump, Gregory. 2001. *Inflectional Morphology: A Theory of Paradigm Structure*. Cambridge: Cambridge University Press.
Trommer, Jochen. 1999. Morphology consuming syntax' resources. In *Procceedings of the ESSLI Workshop on Resource Logics and Minimalist Grammars*, 37–55. University of Nijmegen.
Trommer, Jochen. 2001. Distributed optimality. Ph.D. dissertation, Universität Potsdam.
Trommer, Jochen. 2005. Markiertheit und Verarmung. Ms., Universität Leipzig. Presented at the Honorary Doctorate Colloquium for Manfred Bierwisch, Leipzig 2005.
Trommer, Jochen. 2006. Person and number agreement in Dumi. *Linguistics* 44:1011–1057.
Wiese, Bernd. 1999. Unterspezifizierte Paradigmen: Form und Funktion in der pronominalen Deklination. *Linguistik Online* 4. (www.linguistik-online.de/3_99).

Wiese, Bernd. 2001. Paradigmen aus formbezogener Sicht. Handout, IDS Mannheim.
Wiese, Bernd. 2003. Zur lateinischen Nominalflexion: Die Form-Funktions-Beziehung. Ms., IDS Mannheim.
Wiese, Bernd. 2004. Categories and paradigms: On underspecification in Russian declension. In *Explorations in Nominal Inflection*, eds. Gereon Müller, Lutz Gunkel, and Gisela Zifonun, 321–372. Berlin: Mouton de Gruyter.
Woolford, Ellen. 2001. Case patterns. In *Optimality-Theoretic Syntax*, eds. Géraldine Legendre, Jane Grimshaw, and Sten Vikner, 509–543. Cambridge, MA: MIT Press.
Woolford, Ellen. 2007. Aspect splits as contextual faithfulness. Ms., University of Massachusetts, Amherst.
Wunderlich, Dieter. 1996. Minimalist morphology: The role of paradigms. In *Yearbook of Morphology 1995*, eds. Geert Booij and Jaap van Marle, 93–114. Dordrecht: Kluwer.
Wunderlich, Dieter. 1997a. Der unterspezifizierte Artikel. In *Sprache im Fokus*, eds. Christa Dürscheid, Karl Heinz Ramers, and Monika Schwarz, 47–55. Tübingen: Niemeyer.
Wunderlich, Dieter. 1997b. A minimalist model of inflectional morphology. In *The Role of Economy Principles in Linguistic Theory*, eds. Chris Wilder, Hans-Martin Gärtner, and Manfred Bierwisch, 267–298. Berlin: Akademie Verlag.
Wunderlich, Dieter. 2000. Reconsidering structural case in Finnish. Ms., Universität Düsseldorf.
Wunderlich, Dieter. 2004. Is there any need for the concept of directional syncretism? In *Explorations in Nominal Inflection*, eds. Gereon Müller, Lutz Gunkel, and Gisela Zifonun, 373–395. Berlin: Mouton de Gruyter.
Wurzel, Wolfgang Ullrich. 1984. *Flexionsmorphologie und Natürlichkeit*. Berlin: Akademie Verlag.

Jochen Trommer
6 Ø-Agreement in Turkana

In this paper, I develop a formalism for morphological spellout which captures the conditioning of Ø-agreement by scales in a maximally simple way. As a test case, I show that this formalism allows a straightforward analysis of the complex verb agreement and direction marking patterns ("Quirky Inverse Marking") in Turkana.

1 Introduction

In her groundbreaking work on optimality-theoretic morphosyntax, Aissen (1999, 2003b) captures a wide array of morphological hierarchy effects by the combined force of Constraint Conjunction (Smolensky 1995) and Harmonic Alignment (Prince and Smolensky 1993). Although the resulting system is formally quite powerful, all morphological phenomena Aissen captures are cases of Ø-morphology. Thus for the Tibeto-Burman language Nocte, Aissen (1999) derives that direction (inverse) marking is Ø in configurations where the subject is higher in animacy than the object. In the same paper she accounts for split-ergative systems, hence for the distribution of Ø subject and Ø object case under specific alignment patterns of the verbal arguments. Similar examples of differential object marking are treated in Aissen (2003b). Again all patterns under consideration involve Ø-morphology for case under an appropriate constellation of different scales. In Aissen (2003a), a bidirectional extension of the system is employed to capture the distribution of Ø object-agreement in Takelma and Tzotzil.

To be sure, the restriction to Ø-morphology is not an idiosyncrasy of Aissen's work, but for the most part a general fact about typological and theoretical work on morphological hierarchy effects, and possibly about morphology in general. I make this generalization explicit as the hypothesis in (1):[1]

---

[1] I know of only two patterns which are possible counterevidence to (1). *First*, many typologists assume that Ø-marking is just a special case of the preference for short over long formatives in special contexts (cf. Haspelmath 2008). However, Keine & Müller (2015) argue that this tendency actually follows from Ø-exponence and general conditions on iconicity. *Second*, in some languages affix order seems to be sensitive to scales. For example in Wardaman (Merlan 1994), the linear order of agreement prefixes for subject and objects reflects the hierarchy 1 ≻ 2 ≻ 3. Unfortunately, there are no crosslinguistic studies which would show whether these ordering patterns are accidental properties of single languages, or the effect of general linguistic mechanisms. Other types of scales have been argued to play a role in the ordering of different morphological categories such as agreement and tense. See Trommer (2002) for critical discussion.

(1) **Scales-Ø-Generalization:**
Effects of prominence scales on morphological spellout are restricted to the Ø-realization of otherwise expected morphological formatives

I take the Scales-Ø-Generalization as an indication that the Harmonic-Alignment model of morphological hierarchy effects, which employs an all-purpose formalism, may be too general for the task at hand, and explore the possibility that these effects are due to a formal system which is far more restricted in its domain of application since it is capable of nothing else than to license Ø-realization of affixes.

The agreement- and direction-marking system of Turkana (Dimmendaal 1983, 1986, 1991), an Eastern Nilotic Language spoken by around 350,000 speakers in the east of Lake Turkana in Kenya, is a well-suited testing ground for the formalism because it shows three types of hierarchy effects in a small paradigm. *First*, the affixation of plural affixes is governed by an asymmetry of 1st and non-1st person. *Second*, the appearance of person markers for subject and object is governed by an intricate interaction of different prominence scales. *Third*, Turkana exhibits an inverse marker very similar to the one familiar from Nocte. The distribution of the inverse marker is especially interesting because its use also extends to intransitive 1st person plural forms, a context which should be impossible for an inverse marker under most current approaches. (2) contains the complete set of relevant affixes, where *-te* is the plural suffix, *k-* the inverse prefix, and all other prefixes (*a-*, *i-*, and *e-*) mark person:[2]

(2) **Turkana Verb Agreement**

			Object						Ø
			1		2		3		
			sg	pl	sg	pl	sg	pl	
Subject	1	sg			k-a-		a-		
		pl			k-i-		k-i-		
	2	sg	k-i-				i-		
		pl	k-i- -te				i- -te		
	3	sg	k-a-	k-i-	k-i-		e-		
		pl	k-a- -te	k-i- -te	k-i- -te		e- -te		

---

2 The segmentation in (2) is not uncontroversial. Cysouw identifies two affixes, *ka* and *ki-*, which are not related to *a-*, *i-*, and *k-*. See also section 5 for a discussion of whether plural *k-* is different from inverse *k-*.

The paper is structured as follows: In section 2, I introduce the formal framework. Sections 3, 4, and 5 apply the formalism to number agreement, person agreement, and inverse marking in Turkana respectively. Section 6 contains a short summary, and a final appendix (section 7) spells out the formal details of vocabulary insertion in the developed formalism.

2 The formal framework

The model of morphology I am developing here is realizational in the sense of Stump (2001): The morphology component of the grammar provides phonological spellout of abstract morphosyntactic features. Spellout happens in two stages, vocabulary insertion and Ø-licensing. (3) illustrates this architecture schematically for person marking in an intransitive Turkana 1st person verb form (*à-los-ı̀*, 'I go'), where subject agreement is marked by the prefix *a*-. In the analysis developed in the following sections, this is derived by inserting both the marker *a*- for the feature [+1] and the equally motivated *i*- for [−3]. However, *i*- is marked as phonologically invisible by Ø-licensing and therefore only *a*- is pronounced:

(3) **Grammatical Architecture**

Input:	[+1−3]		(Morphosyntactic heads)
Vocabulary Insertion:	a:[+1]	i:[−3]	(Vocabulary Items)
Ø-Licensing	a:[+1]	i:[−3]	(Licensing Conditions)
Phonological Interpretation	a		(Phonological Structure)

2.1 Vocabulary Insertion

As in other realizational frameworks such as Amorphous Morphology (Anderson 1992), Distributed Morphology (DM, Halle and Marantz 1993) and Distributed Optimality (DO, Trommer 2003b), the input to morphology is provided by syntax. Here it has the form of an ordered pair of a (phonologically specified) root, and a list of heads (multisets of morphosyntactic features).

Consider the following fragment of Georgian verb inflection (Carmack 1997; Trommer 2003b) for the verb *xedav*, to 'see', in (4) (omitting all forms involving 3rd person subjects and objects):

(4) **Georgian Verb Agreement**

		Object				
		1sg	1pl	2sg	2pl	Ø
Subject	1sg			g-xedav	g-xedav-t	v-xedav
	1pl			g-xedav-t	g-xedav-t	v-xedav-t
	2sg	m-xedav	gv-xedav			xedav
	2pl	m-xedav-t	gv-xedav-t			xedav-t

For 2pl → 1sg forms, the input to morphology looks like (5) ("+S" stands in the following for the case feature of subjects and "+O" for the case feature of objects:)

(5) xedav [+O+1–pl]$_1$ [+S+2+pl]$_2$

Vocabulary insertion is a function which maps every input structure to a sequence consisting of a root and additional vocabulary items (VIs), representations of affixes which pair phonological content and morphosyntactic features.[3] Thus given the lexicon of VIs in (6), vocabulary insertion maps the input in (5) to the output in (7), where indices are used as in optimality-theoretic Correspondence Theory (Wunderlich 2000; Trommer 2003b): the prefix is coindexed with the first head of (5), and the suffix with its second head.

(6) **VIs for Georgian**
 a. gv- : [+1+O+pl]
 b. m- : [+1+O]
 c. g- : [+2+O]
 d. v- : [+1+S]
 e. -t : [+pl]

(7) m:[+1+O]$_1$-xedav-t:[+pl]$_2$

Vocabulary insertion has four important properties: It allows underspecification, it allows many-to-many mappings (portmanteaus), it is maximal, and it is derivationally ordered:

---

[3] The description of the formalism here is rather informal. See the appendix for more details.

2.1.0.1 Vocabulary insertion allows underspecification:

A VI is inserted if all the feature structures it specifies are subsets of (i.e. proper subsets or identical to) feature structures in the input. This is illustrated by (7), where *m-* is inserted specifying a subset of the input head [+O+1–pl], and *-t* is inserted specifying a subset of the features in the [+S+2+pl] head.

2.1.0.2 Vocabulary insertion allows many-to-many mappings:

For example, Lakämper (2000) argues that in the Potosí Quechua verb form in (8), *-nqa* corresponds to tense and subject agreement, and *-sunki* to subject agreement and object agreement (Lakämper 2000: 119):

(8) rikhu-nqa-sunki '(s)he will see you (sg.)'
 see-3Fut-3 → 2

Thus assuming for (8) the input in (9), this might be captured by the portmanteau VIs in (10) resulting in the output in (11):

(9) rikhu [+Fut]$_1$ [+O+2–pl]$_2$ [+S+3–pl]$_3$

(10) **VIs for Potosí Quechua**
 a. -nqa : [+Fut][+3+S]
 b. -sunki : [+O+2][+3+S]

(11) rikhu-nqa:[+Fut]$_1$[+3+S]$_3$-sunki:[+O+2]$_2$[+3+S]$_3$

In (11), single VIs are linked to more than one input head (*-nqa* is linked to [+Fut]$_1$ and [+O+2–pl]$_2$, while *-sunki* is linked to [+O+2–pl]$_2$ and [+S+3–pl]$_3$). At the same time, the input head [+O+2–pl]$_2$ is linked to two VIs in the output: *-nqa* and *-sunki*. Note however that the possibility of many-to-many mapping does not extend to the level of the single feature structures in VIs. Thus a feature structure [+1+2] in an output VI may not correspond to two input feature structures where one specifies [+1] and the other one [+2] (or both are specified as [+1+2]). Technically this is ensured by the condition that feature structures in the output (and the input) must have exactly one index.

2.1.0.3 Vocabulary insertion is maximal:

For any possible linking of VIs to input feature structures, there is an insertion of a VI instance in the output. Hence the same VI can be inserted more than once if there are correspondingly many distinct mappings in the input. Moreover the same input feature may be realized more than once in the output unhampered by the Elsewhere Principle (Anderson 1992) or restrictions against redundancy (cf. Wunderlich and Fabri 1994). This is already illustrated by the Quechua example. A similar case arises if we consider a 2sg → 1pl form for Georgian. Given the VIs in (6) and the input in (12), we predict the output in (13), where m:[+1+O]- and -t:[+pl] are inserted even though the features they express are already spelled out by gv:[+1+O+pl]-:

(12)   xedav [+O+1+pl]$_1$ [+S+2–pl]$_2$

(13)   m:[+1+O]$_1$-gv:[+1+O+pl]$_1$-xedav-t:[+pl]$_2$

In fact, (13) does not correspond to the correct form which is *gv-xedav*. This problem will be addressed in subsection 2.2.

2.1.0.4 Vocabulary Insertion is derivationally ordered:

It is carried out through step-by-step affixation of VIs. Thus in (11), first *-nqa* is attached, and in a second step *-sunki*, accounting for the linear ordering of the affixes. The order of insertion follows the following principles ranked in the sense of Optimality Theory (Prince and Smolensky 1993):[4]

(14)   **Ordering of Vocabulary Insertion:**

VI$_1$ is inserted before VI$_2$ if:
1. the leftmost input head to which VI$_1$ corresponds is more leftwards in the input list than the leftmost input head to which VI$_2$ corresponds
2. VI$_1$ contains more feature structures than VI$_2$
3. VI$_1$ is ordered before VI$_2$ in the lexicon of VIs

---

[4] There are two crucial points where the use of constraint ranking in (14) departs from standard OT: First, optimization does not evaluate entire word forms, but single derivational steps (cf. McCarthy 2007 and Heck and Müller 2006 for similar approaches in phonology and syntax respectively). Second, the ranking in (14) is assumed to be crosslinguistically fixed.

(14-1) is illustrated by the Quechua form in (11): *-nqa* is inserted first because the highest input head to which it corresponds is the leftmost feature structure in the input, whereas the highest input head to which *-sunki* corresponds is only second in the list. (14-2) accounts for affix order in the following verb form from Potosí Quechua (Lakämper 2000: 121), which I represent as in (16).

(15) rikhu-nqa-sunki-chis   '(s)he/they will see you (pl.)'
     see-3Fut-3 → 2-PL2

(16) rikhu-nqa:[+Fut]₁[+3+S]₃-sunki:[+O+2]₂[+3+S]₃-chis:[+2+pl]₂

While *-sunki* and *-chis* are linked to the same highest input head (object agreement) making them indistinguishable for constraint 1 in (14), the VI of *-sunki* contains more feature structures and is therefore inserted first. Finally, constraint 3 in (14) simply allows for language-specific stipulation for affix order in cases where constraints 1 and 2 do not determine any ordering.

2.2 Ø-Licensing

All current approaches to morphological spellout have explicit means to enforce Ø-realization of affixal material whose pronunciation is otherwise expected. In DM, this is achieved by Ø-VIs, impoverishment rules or fusion of heads, in Anderson (1992) through arranging spellout rules in disjunctively ordered rule blocks or by applying spellout rules without phonological consequences (which therefore block phonologically visible rules of the same block; see also Stump 2001), and in optimality-theoretic approaches by specific constraints which block the realization of morphosyntactic features under specific circumstances (Grimshaw 1997; Wunderlich 2000).

Here, I propose a very conservative approach to Ø-realization. I take Ø-expression not to be the absence of a specific marker, but a form of presence which is not interpreted by the phonological interface. Licensing Ø-pronunciation of a morpheme which is morphosyntactically present is a concept familiar from decades of research on pro-drop, Ø-pronouns which are allowed in specific languages under specific circumstances. Thus, preceding many similar analyses, Rizzi (1986) argues that in Italian empty subject pronouns are licensed by the presence of a specific type of "strong" agreement. This is illustrated in (17) for the Italian sentence *lui trem-a*, 'he trembles', whose unmarked realization leaves the subject pronoun *lui* unpronounced:

(17) **Pro Licensing in Syntax (Rizzi 1986)**

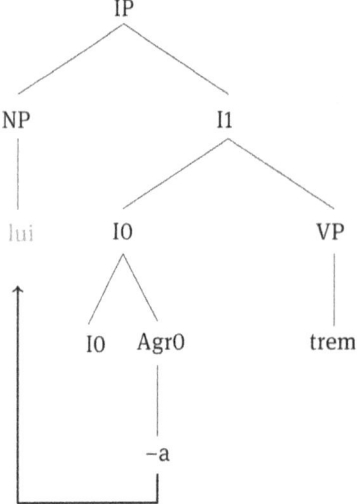

In fact, licensing of zero elements seems to be a more general principle of grammatical organization. Thus it plays a central role in Government Phonology (Kaye et al. 1990; Harris 1994), especially in its CVCV version (Lowenstamm 1996; Scheer 2004). CVCV-Theory has abandoned standard syllable theory in favor of a skeleton which consists of a strict concatenation of alternating CV-sequences (i.e. skeletal slots in the sense of Autosegmental Phonology). Thus the string *kata* might be syllabified as in (18):

(18) C V C V
      | | | |
      k a t a

Onset-less syllables correspond to an empty C-position, i.e. a C-slot which is not associated to a melodic element (a segment), and complex onsets (and codas) to empty vowel positions surrounded by filled consonant positions:

(19) C V C V C V C V
      | | | | | |
      i n a b   r a

Phonotactic generalizations crucially depend on general conditions licensing the possibility of Ø-V-positions. Thus a central axiom of the theory is that an empty V-position is only possible if it is "governed" by a following filled V-position. This is why vowels preceded by two consonants are in principle possible (e.g. in Czech), but vowels preceded by three consonants are generally impossible:[5]

(20) a.
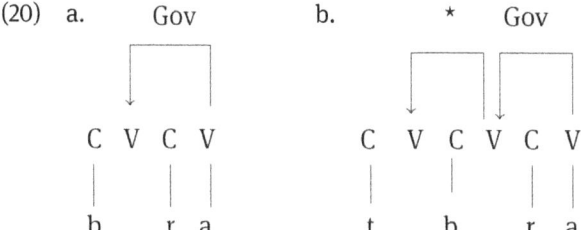

Here, I assume that Ø-exponence for affixes is an implementation of the same basic mechanism as the classical approach to pro-drop: Affixes can remain unexpressed if there is an appropriate licensing relation. In fact, I claim that affixes actually must be unexpressed if they are Ø-licensed (similarly to Ø-licensing in Government Phonology). This difference to pro-drop is probably related to the fact that to avoid pro-drop in pro-drop languages is only licit if the pronoun is linked to specific discourse functions (e.g. focus or more generally if it is a non-topic, cf. Grimshaw and Samek-Lodovici 1998). It is well known that inflectional affixes do not allow a similar integration into discourse relations, and this might motivate that Ø-licensing of affixes makes their Ø-expression obligatory.[6]

Ø-licensing is the effect of Ø-licensing conditions of the form in (21), where R (the "trigger" of the licensing condition) and T (the "target" of the licensing condition) are sets of feature structures:

(21) **General Format of Ø-Licensing Conditions:**
R licenses Ø-T under conditions $C_1, \ldots, C_n$

A licensing condition L Ø-licenses Ø-realization of a vocabulary item V in the output, iff (i) every feature structure in $T(L)$ subsumes at least one feature structure in V, (ii) every feature structure in V is subsumed by at least one feature structure in $T(L)$, and (iii) every feature structure in $R(L)$ subsumes at least one appropriate feature structure in the overall representation, under the conditions specified by $C_1, \ldots, C_n$. For simplicity, I will in the following often refer to

---

[5] Note here and in the following that sonorants may occur more freely than obstruents since they may be linked to vocalic positions. See Ségéral and Scheer (2008) for details.

[6] Constraints which require the Ø-realization of pronouns or, more generally, functional elements have been independently proposed in Chomsky (1981) ("Avoid Pronoun") and Pesetsky (1998) ("Telegraph").

"feature F" to designate the feature structure "$[F]$" (a feature structure containing the single feature F) to characterize triggers and targets.

Ø-licensing has similar formal properties to vocabulary insertion: Ø-licensing allows many-to-many-mappings: Portmanteau VIs corresponding to more than one input head can be Ø-licensed by the same licensing condition. Ø-licensing is maximal: A specific licensing condition is applied for all possible combinations of features which trigger it. Ø-licensing is derivationally ordered: Conditions licensing Ø-VIs corresponding to higher input feature structures are applied first, conditions licensing Ø-VIs corresponding to more input feature structures apply first, and licensing conditions ordered higher in the language-specific list of licensing conditions apply first, cf. (14). In addition, Ø-licensing has a fourth property not shared by vocabulary insertion:

2.2.0.5 Ø-licensing is mediated indirectly by prominence and entailment scales:

(22) is a typical example of a prominence scale (1st and 2nd person are ranked higher than 3rd person), and (23) is an entailment scale for person which will be crucial for the analysis of intransitive person marking in Turkana: The feature specification [+1] of a given head entails that the head is also [−3]:[7]

(22) **Prominence Scale for Person:** $\left\{\begin{matrix}+1\\+2\end{matrix}\right\} \succ +3$

(23) **Entailment Scale for Person:** $\left\{\begin{matrix}+1\\+2\end{matrix}\right\} \succ -3$

Any Ø-VI in a particular language is licensed by a specific licensing condition. Licensing conditions are derived from universal licensing schemata, which refer in a specific way to universal scales such as (22) and (23). Thus scales and schemata are universal, but whether a language adopts a specific licensing condition or not is a matter of arbitrary parametric choice. The single licensing scales and schemata I assume will be introduced and illustrated in the following sections.

---

[7] 1st person exclusive = [+1−2−3], 2nd person = [−1+2−3], and 3rd person = [−1−2+3] (cf. Trommer 2008).

2.3 An Illustrative Example: Georgian Verb Inflection

To illustrate the basic working of Ø-licensing, I will return to the Georgian data presented in (4). One interesting property of this paradigm is that the 1st person subject marker *v-* is suppressed in forms with 2nd person objects although this VI is predicted by the insertion formalism. Thus for the input in (24) ('I see you (sg.)') we get the incorrect output in (24-b) after vocabulary insertion:

(24) a. xedav [+2+O−pl]$_1$ [+1+S−pl]$_2$
 b. v:[+1+S]$_2$-g:[+2+O]$_1$-xedav

Previous research has characterized phenomena of this type as a kind of competition process ("hierarchy-based competition"): Affixes realizing different arguments compete for a single morphological slot, where prominence hierarchies determine the winner of competition (cf. Noyer 1992; Trommer 2006a). Here I show that this pattern can be fruitfully subsumed under the notion of Ø-licensing without losing the tight connection of these processes to prominence scales.[8] More evidence for the same approach will be found in the person marking system of Turkana. The central schema for linking prominence scales to Ø-marking in transitive agreement is given in (25), where F_1 and F_2 are features, H_1 and H_2 variables over input feature structures ("heads"), and C stands for a meta-feature such as [Per(son)] or [Num(ber)]:[9]

(25) **Schema for Superiority Licensing**

Condition:	$F_1 \geq F_2$ for scale S
Form:	Overt C of a F_1 head licenses Ø-C of a F_2 head

A licensing schema allows us to derive a specific licensing condition by instantiating (replacing) all variables in the schema by concrete values (features, meta-features, feature structures,...) which satisfy the condition(s) of the schema. Thus instantiating C by person and S by (22) we derive the following licensing condition, since according to S [+2] ≥ [+1] (the feature structure in brackets serves as an abbreviation for the condition):

---

[8] The following analysis owes a lot to Béjar (2003) although at a relatively abstract level.
[9] A meta-feature is an atomic expression which matches any feature of a specific type. Thus [Person] matches [+1], [−1], [+2], [−2], [+3] and [−3]. Note that different instances of a specific meta-feature in a licensing condition do not necessarily match the same instantiations of the meta-feature. Thus the first instance of [Per] in (26) matches [+2] in (27), while the second instance matches [+1].

(26) Overt [Per] of a [+2] head licenses Ø-[Per] of a [+1] head ([+2][+1])

(26) licenses Ø-realization of a person feature if this spells out a head H_1 which contains the feature-value pair [+1] and the same input list contains a head H_2 containing the feature-value pair [+2]. The full derivation of the 1sg → 2sg form is shown in (27):

(27) **Spellout: 1sg → 2sg**

Input:		xedav [+O+2−pl]$_1$ [+S+1−pl]$_2$
Insertion:		v:[+S+1]$_2$-g:[+O+2]$_1$-xedav
Ø-Licensing:	[+2][+1]	v:[+S+1]$_2$-g:[+O+2]$_1$-xedav
Phonology:		g xedav

Note also one general restriction on the application of Ø-licensing which is formulated in (28):

(28) **Vocabulary Suicide Condition:**
A feature structure in an overt vocabulary item *V* may not serve as trigger or target for Ø–licensing *V* itself.

Without (28), the schema for Superiority Licensing in (25) would allow for example the derivation of a licensing condition under which a VI expressing a first person would Ø-license itself, hence one could formulate unconditional Ø-exponence requirements for specific features (or feature combinations), which would deprive the Ø-licensing approach of much of its predictive power.

Let us now return to the problem raised in 2.1 that vocabulary insertion for 2sg → 1pl forms inserts *m-* and *-t* since they are compatible with the features of the underlying object agreement head [+O+1+pl] although these affixes don't show up phonologically.

In previous analyses of these data (Anderson 1992; Trommer 2003c), suppression of *m-* and *-t* follows from the Elsewhere Principle:[10] Insertion of a more specific marker blocks insertion of less specific markers. Here I reinterpret the basic insight underlying this approach: There is no blocking of less specific markers. All VIs which are compatible with a given input are inserted. However after insertion, VIs which realize for a specific input head a subset of the features which are already spelled out by a more specific marker are Ø-licensed and

---

10 The Elsewhere Principle is called the Subset Principle in Halle (1997).

hence not pronounced. Thus for a 2sg → 1pl form, vocabulary insertion produces in fact the structure in (29) (repeated from (13)):

(29) m:[+1+O]₁-gv:[+1+O+pl]₁-xedav-t:[+pl]₂

That *m-* and *-t* are not pronounced follows now from the licensing schema in (30):

(30) **Schema for Entailment Licensing**

Condition:	Feature structure F₁ entails feature structure F₂
Form:	Overt F₁ licenses Ø F₂ of the same head

Since the entailment scales in (31) trivially hold (every feature structure which is characterized as [+1+pl] is also characterized as [+pl] and as [+1]), (30) allows us to posit the licensing conditions in (32):

(31) **Entailment Scales**
   a. [+1+pl] > [+pl]
   b. [+1+pl] > [+1]

(32) **Licensing Conditions**
   a. Overt [+1+pl] licenses Ø [+pl] of the same head ([+1+pl+pl])
   b. Overt [+1+pl] licenses Ø [+1] of the same head ([+1+pl+1])

The full derivation of a 2sg → 1pl form is shown in (33):

(33) **Spellout: 2sg → 1pl**

Input:		xedav [+O+1+pl]₁, [+S+2−pl]₂
Insertion:		gv:[+O+1+pl]₁-m:[+O]₁-xedav-t:[+pl]₁
Ø-Licensing	[+1+pl+1]	gv:[+O+1+pl]₁-m:[+O]₁-xedav-t:[+pl]₁
	[+1+pl+pl]	gv:[+O+1+pl]₁-m:[+O]₁-xedav-t:[+pl]₁
Phonology:		gv- -xedav

Obviously the same analysis extends to most uncontroversial applications of the Elsewhere Principle to morphological spellout: Whenever one marker specifies a subset of the features of a second one, this induces an entailment scale resulting in a licensing condition which allows the less specific marker to be rendered phonologically invisible.[11] In section 4.1, we will see that entailment licensing also extends to cases which cannot be easily accommodated by conditions on subsets.

3 Number Agreement

We start the analysis of Turkana with the most simple morphological subsystem of Turkana verb agreement: subject marking for number, which consists basically of a plural suffix. Whereas there are a number of different allomorphs of this suffix, depending on verb classes and tense/aspect/mood, all behave roughly in the same way with respect to other agreement affixes, and in the following I will use the allomorph -te as representing all of its coallomorphs. As shown in (34), -te marks plural subjects independently from object agreement, but is blocked for 1st person subjects:

(34) **Turkana Plural Marking**

			Object						Ø
			1		2		3		
			sg	pl	sg	pl	sg	pl	
Subject	1	sg							
		pl					-Ø		
	2	sg							
		pl	-te				-te		
	3	sg							
		pl			-te				

The fact that the plural suffix is absent exactly in the first person is probably not an accident. As Nevins (2007) notes, based on a long tradition in the typological literature, there is a general tendency for inflectional systems to neutralize

---

[11] Note that the analysis here does not predict that the Elsewhere Principle holds without exceptions. Since languages may or may not adopt licensing conditions for specific entailment scales, languages may allow double exponence for specific features even if this violates the Elsewhere Principle. This might solve the problem of the often observed phenomenon of extended exponence (cf. Müller 2006 for recent discussion).

marked distinctions in the context of other marked distinctions (1st person is the most marked person, and plural the most marked number category in Turkana), and Noyer (1992) cites data similar to the Turkana case from Afro-Asiatic, where dual marking is systematically suppressed in the context of 1st person, but not in the context of 2nd and 3rd person.

I interpret markedness here as maximal prominence for a given scale, which predicts neutralization if a set of categories cooccurring in an input head are maximally prominent in distinct scales. This is implemented formally by the Ø-licensing schema in (35), where $F_1, F_2, \ldots, F_n$ are features (i.e., specific feature value pairs), and $S_1, S_2, \ldots, S_n$ prominence scales:

(35) **Schema for Cumulative Complexity Licensing**

Condition:	$F_1, F_2, \ldots, F_n$ are maximal in $S_1, S_2, \ldots, S_n$
Form:	$F_2, \ldots, F_n$ license Ø F_1 of the same input head

Instantiating (35) by the basic prominence scales for number and person in (36), we get the licensing condition in (37):

(36) **Prominence Scales for Number**

[+pl] is maximal in [+pl] > [−pl]

[+1] is maximal in $\left\{ \begin{matrix} [+1] \\ [+2] \end{matrix} \right\}$ > [+3]

(37) **Licensing Condition**
[+1] licenses Ø [+pl] of the same input head ([+1+pl])

If the plural suffix is specified as in (38), we get the derivation in (39). *-te* is inserted for all persons, but is rendered invisible for phonology by Ø-licensing in the 1st-person form.

(38) -te : [+pl+S]

(39) **Derivation of Number Spellout**

	1pl	2pl	3pl
Input:	[+1+pl]	[+2+pl]	[+3+pl]
Insertion:	-te	-te	-te
Ø-Licensing:	[+1+pl] -te	-te	-te
Phonology		-te	-te

4 Person Agreement

An intriguing characteristic of Turkana verb inflection is that the language has subject and object agreement for person, but at the same time only three distinct person markers, and maximally one person marker for any given verb form. Which person marker actually shows up in a particular verb form is crucially dependent on the relative prominence of person features in scales. In subsection 4.1, I discuss intransitive agreement, and in subsection 4.2 the more complex pattern in transitive forms.

4.1 Intransitive Person Agreement

As shown in (40), two of the person prefixes can be identified with traditional person categories: *a-* occurs only in 1st person forms, *e-* only in 3rd person forms. However *i-* appears not only in all 2nd person forms, but also in the 1pl:

(40) **Person Marking in Intransitive Forms**

			sg	a-
Subject	1	pl		
	2	sg	i-	
		pl		
	3	sg	e-	
		pl		

Therefore, I suggest the VIs in (41), where *i-* is characterized as [−3], which is compatible with both [+1] and [+2] (cf. footnote 8):

(41) **Vocabulary Items**
    a- : [+1]
    i- : [−3]
    e- : [+3]

Now the fact that *a-* is Ø in the 1pl while *i-* extends to this paradigm cell follows completely from the formal apparatus we have already developed. By reverting context and target for applying (35) to the scales in (36), we get the licensing condition in (42): Where (37) captures Ø-number in the context of overt person, (42) derives Ø-person in the context of overt number:

(42) **Licensing Condition**
[+pl] licenses Ø [+1] of the same input head ([+pl+1])

(43) shows how the licensing condition in (42) derives the correct marking for 2sg and 1pl forms. *i-* is inserted in both contexts; in the 1pl the additionally inserted *a-* is Ø-licensed and hence invisible:

(43) **Spellout: Intransitive Person**

		1pl	2sg
Input:		[+1−3+pl]	[+2−3−pl]
Insertion:		a-i-	i-
Ø-Licensing:	[+pl+1]	a-i-	−
Phonology:		i-	i-

This raises the question of why **i-** is Ø in 1sg forms where it should also appear given its lexical entry. Intuitively, *i-* is unnecessary in the 1sg because independently inserted *a-* makes it redundant to pronounce a separate [−3] marker. In other words, [+1] entails [−3] (in the assumed feature system, every [+1] head is also [−3], cf. footnote 8). Hence Ø-exponence can be derived by the entailment licensing scheme in (30) repeated as (44):

(44) **Schema for Entailment Licensing**

Condition:	Feature structure F_1 entails feature structure F_2
Form:	Overt F_1 licenses Ø F_2 of the same head

Applied to the entailment scale in (45), we get the licensing condition in (46):

(45) **Entailment Scale:** [+1] ≻ [−3]

(46) **Licensing Condition**
Overt [+1] licenses Ø [−3] of the same head ([+1−3])

(47) illustrates the spellout for all intransitive singular forms. Whereas the output of 2sg and 3sg corresponds to a single inserted VI, for 1sg two VIs are inserted, and *i-* becomes invisible by (46):

(47) **Spellout: Intransitive Person**

		1sg	2sg	3sg
Input:		[+1−3−pl]	[+2−3+pl]	[+3−pl]
Insertion:		a-i-	i-	e-
Ø-Licensing:	[+1−3]	a-i-	−	−
Phonology:		a-	i-	e-

Returning to the 1pl, (42) and (46) illustrate the important point that licensing conditions must be crucially ordered: In this context [+pl] would license Ø-realization of *a-* by (42), and (46) Ø-realization of *i-*, but only if *a-* is not rendered invisible. Hence [+pl+1] must be given priority over [+1−3]. Since both conditions target VIs corresponding to the same head, this order must be regulated by language-specific stipulation. The interaction of both licensing conditions is illustrated in (48) for all plural forms:

(48) **Interaction of Entailment and Complexity Licensing**

		1sg	1pl	2sg
Input:		[+1−3−pl]	[+1−3+pl]	[+2−3−pl]
Insertion:		a-i-	a-i-	i-
Ø-Licensing:	[+pl+1]	−	a-i-	−
	[+1−3]	a-i-	−	−
Phonology:		a-	i-	i-

4.2 Transitive Person Agreement

The distribution of person markers in transitive forms is quite complex. The same three affixes are used as in intransitive forms, but in some combinations they express phi-features of the object, not of the subject (e.g. in 3sg → 1sg forms):

(49) **Turkana Hierarchy-Based Competition**

			Object						
			1		2		3		Ø
			sg	pl	sg	pl	sg	pl	
Subject	1	sg			k-a-		a-		
		pl			k-i-		k-i-		
	2	sg	k-i-				i-		
		pl							
	3	sg	k-a-	k-i-	k-i-		e-		
		pl							

The appearance of person markers follows three crucial generalizations:
- In all forms, either subject or object trigger person agreement, but never both.
- 1st and 2nd person arguments always trigger agreement in the context of a 3rd-person argument.
- Otherwise the subject triggers agreement.

Obviously person-marking in Turkana exhibits a more general type of "hierarchy-based competition" for person than the one we have already seen for Georgian. The relevant licensing schema from (25) is repeated in (50):

(50) **Schema for Superiority Licensing**

Condition:	$F_1 \geq F_2$ for scale S
Form:	Overt C of a F_1 head licenses Ø-C of a F_2 head

Applied to the person scale in (51), and again inserting person for C, we get the licensing conditions in (52):

(51) **Person Scale:** $\left\{\begin{matrix}+1\\+2\end{matrix}\right\} \succ +3$

(52) **Licensing Conditions**
   a. Overt [Per] of a [+1] head licenses Ø-[Per] of a [+3] head ([+1][+3])
   b. Overt [Per] of a [+2] head licenses Ø-[Per] of a [+3] head ([+2][+3])
   c. Overt [Per] of a [+1] head licenses Ø-[Per] of a [+2] head ([+1][+2])
   d. Overt [Per] of a [+2] head licenses Ø-[Per] of a [+1] head ([+2][+1])

Thus (52-a) licenses Ø-realization of a person feature if this spells out a head H_1 which contains the feature-value pair [+3] and the same input list contains a head H_2 containing the feature-value pair [+1]. Now recall from section 2.2 that Ø-licensing – just as vocabulary insertion – follows the order of a given input list, hence Ø-licensing is applied first to VIs which correspond to higher feature structures on the input list. Assuming that object agreement in Turkana is closer to the verbal root than subject agreement, this derives the basic subject preference in the data. (53) shows the derivation of transitive forms with 2sg and 3sg arguments: *e-* is licensed to be Ø in both forms because it expresses person for a [+3] head in the context of overt *i-* which realizes person for a [+2] head (the licensing conditions not relevant here are omitted):

(53) **Spellout: 2sg ↔ 3sg**

		2sg → 3sg		3sg → 2sg	
Input:		[+3]$_O$	[+2–3]$_S$	[+2–3]$_O$	[+3]$_S$
Insertion:		e-	i-	i-	e-
Ø-Licensing$_O$:	[+2][+3]	e-	i-		–
Ø-Licensing$_S$:	[+2][+3]		–	i-	e-
Phonology:			i-	i-	

In forms with a 1sg and a 3sg argument, [+1][+3] and [+1–3] cooperate to ensure that only *a-* becomes phonologically visible:

(54) **Spellout: 1sg ↔ 3sg**

		1sg → 3sg		3sg → 1sg	
Input:		[+3]$_O$	[+1–3]$_S$	[+1–3]$_O$	[+3]$_S$
Insertion:		e-	a-i-	a-i-	e-
Ø-Licensing$_O$:	[+1][+3]	e-	a-i-		–
	[+1–3]		–	a-i-	e-
Ø-Licensing$_S$:	[+1][+3]		–	a-i-	e-
	[+1–3]	e-	a-i-		–
Phonology:			a-	a-	

The most intricate cases are transitive forms with 1st and 2nd person arguments. Here there is potentially Ø-licensing for all person markers for both arguments. However, the cyclic application of Ø-licensing to object markers before subject markers ensures that object agreement becomes invisible before Ø-licensing for subjects can use it as a licensing context in the second cycle. As a consequence only subject marking remains visible. Note also that for the 2sg → 1sg form both subject agreement markers undergo Ø-licensing by the same licensing condition:

(55) **Spellout: 1sg ↔ 2sg**

		2sg → 1sg		1sg → 2sg	
Input:		[+1–3]$_O$	[+2–3]$_S$	[+2–3]$_O$	[+1–3]$_S$
Insertion:		a-i-	i-	i-	a-i-
Ø-Licensing$_O$:	[+1][+2]			i-	a-i-
	[+2][+1]	a-i-	i-		
	[+1–3]				
Ø-Licensing$_S$:	[+2][+1]	–	–	–	–
	[+2][+1]				
	[+1–3]	–	–	i-	a-i-
Phonology:			i-		a-

5 Inverse Marking

In inverse-marking languages, transitive verb forms have a special marker if the object is higher (or equal) than the subject for a specific prominence hierarchy. While some inverse-marking languages also have an overt direct marker for transitive forms where the subject is hierarchically higher than the object (e.g. most Algonquian languages), in Turkana as in Nocte (Aissen 1999; Trommer 2003b), direct forms have no special affix. (56) shows the distribution of the inverse marker *k-* in Turkana. Basically, it occurs in forms where the subject is 3rd person and the object 1st or 2nd person, and in forms where both arguments are non-3rd person. Hence under the person hierarchy in (22), *k-* is restricted to contexts where the object is hierarchically higher than the subject as we would expect from a prototypical inverse marker:

(56) **Turkana Quirky Inverse Marking**

Subject		Object 1sg	1pl	2sg	2pl	3sg	3pl	Ø
1	sg			k-a-	k-a-	a-	a-	
1	pl			k-a-	k-a-	k-i-	k-i-	
2	sg	k-i-	k-i-			i-	i-	
2	pl	k-i-	k-i-			i-	i-	
3	sg	k-a-	k-a-					e-
3	pl	k-a-	k-a-					e-

What is unusual about Turkana *k-* is that it extends to intransitive 1pl forms, which is unexpected for an inverse marker, which by assumption singles out specific transitive configurations. Therefore most previous analyses of Turkana verbal inflection have assumed that the inverse *k-* and the *k-* found in intransitive 1pl forms are two different formatives (Dimmendaal 1983; Trommer 2003b). However, Cysouw (1998) provides compelling evidence against the assumption that this is a case of accidental homophony. As Cysouw shows in detail, other closely related Nilotic languages show basically the same pattern of syncretism between 1pl and inverse configurations even though the morphophonological details are quite different. To take just one example, in Karimojong, the allomorphs *iki-* and *itɔ-* are used for intransitive 1pl, but also for transitive 2 → 1 and 3 → 1 forms. Other forms which are marked as inverse in Turkana (transitive 3 → 1 and 1 → 2 forms) have the related prefix allomorphs *aka-*, *ɔkɔ-*, and *ɛkɛ-*:

(57) **Quirky Inverse in Karimojong (Novelli 1985)**

Subject		Object 1sg	1pl	2sg	2pl	3sg	3pl	Ø
1	sg			aka- ɔkɔ- ɛkɛ-	aka- ɔkɔ- ɛkɛ-	a-	a-	
1	pl			iki- itɔ-	iki- itɔ-	iki- itɔ-	iki- itɔ-	
2	sg	iki- itɔ-	iki- itɔ-			i-	i-	
2	pl	iki- itɔ-	iki- itɔ-			i-	i-	
3	sg	aka- ɔkɔ- ɛkɛ-	aka- ɔkɔ- ɛkɛ-					ɛ-
3	pl	aka- ɔkɔ- ɛkɛ-	aka- ɔkɔ- ɛkɛ-					ɛ-

While *iki-* bears some obvious resemblance to Turkana *k-*, *ito-* does not, which makes it unlikely that the syncretism of 1pl and inverse configurations is accidental. Interestingly enough, there are two sets of allomorphs which correspond to Turkana *k-*, but these do not single out intransitive 1pl from transitive inverse forms but specific inverse forms from other inverse and the 1pl forms. My analysis will therefore be based on the assumption that *k-* is in all contexts – transitive or intransitive – formally the same vocabulary item. More specifically, I will claim that *k-* fulfills both the criteria for being a number marker and an inverse marker. Now a necessary condition for the appearance of *k-* is that either (58-a) or (58-b) holds:

(58) **Necessary Conditions for the Appearance of k-**
 a. there is agreement with a plural argument **or**
 b. there is agreement with two (singular or plural) arguments

These apparently unconnected cases actually form a natural class once we adopt the Iconic Representation of Number (IRN), a theory of the formal representation of number developed in Trommer (2006b), which claims that different numbers are hierarchical trees containing instances of a single formal item, the number element "•". In a two-number system such as Turkana, singular and plural are represented as follows:

(59) **The Iconic Representation of Number (Trommer 2006)**

 Singular   Plural

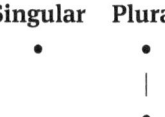

Here I will adopt a formally slightly simpler version of this theory where plural corresponds to a feature structure which contains two number elements [••], and singular to a feature structure with only one ([•]).[12] *k-* is now represented as in (60): It contains two feature structures where each contains a single number element:

(60) **Representation of k-**
 k- : [•+S] [•]

---

12 This means that feature structures are formally multisets. See the appendix for details.

Under this representation, *k-* is a number marker since it specifies number features, and adopting the claim that the class of direct/inverse-markers is in principle coextensive with the class of portmanteau agreement affixes (Trommer 2003a), it is also an inverse morpheme.

Crucially, the representation in (60) predicts that it can be inserted in exactly the configurations described in (58), as is schematically shown in (61). *k-* can be inserted in 3sg → 1sg forms (and more generally in all transitive forms) because each number element in the VI matches one number element in the input. The same is true for 1pl subject forms (and all other forms with a plural subject). In the 1sg (and all intransitive singular forms), *k-* cannot be inserted because the first number element of the VI matches the single number element of the input feature structure, but the input doesn't have a second • to match the second one:[13]

(61) **Possible Insertion Contexts for k-**

	1sg	1pl	3sg → 1sg
Input:	[•+S+1]	[••+S+1]	[•+S+3] [•+O+1]
VI:	[•+S] [•] *	[•+S] [•]	[•+S] [•]

(62) shows in which contexts *k-* is inserted:

(62) **Insertion of k-**

			Object						
			1		2		3		Ø
			sg	pl	sg	pl	sg	pl	
Subject	1	sg							
		pl							
	2	sg							
		pl							
	3	sg			k-				
		pl							

---

[13] Note that the first feature structure of *k-* cannot be linked to the object because the first feature structure of the VI is specified [+S]. This excludes a further conceivable linking of the number elements in forms with plural objects.

This predicts *k*- correctly for all paradigm cells where it actually occurs, but also for additional parts of the paradigm where *k*- does not appear, namely for the intransitive 2pl and 3pl forms, and for all forms with a 3rd person object apart from the 1pl subject forms. This discrepancy is shown in (63) where the forms for which *k*- is predicted but not pronounced are indicated by black shading:

(63) **Insertion vs. Pronunciation of k-**

			Object						
			1		2		3		Ø
			sg	pl	sg	pl	sg	pl	
Subject	1	sg			k-		■	■	
		pl							
	2	sg					■	■	
		pl	k-				■	■	
	3	sg					■	■	
		pl					■	■	

In the following, I will argue that all problematic forms where *k*- is inserted but not realized are cases which license Ø-exponence of *k*- for principled reasons. In particular, I will show that Ø-realization follows from the fact that *k*- is a number and an inverse marker at the same time.

5.1 *k*- as a Number Affix

Let us start with intransitive 2nd and 3rd person plural forms, where *k*- is inserted just as in 1pl forms. Recall from section 3 that these are exactly the forms where plural of the subject is already independently marked by the plural suffix which, adapting the entry from (38) to the Iconic Representation of Number, has the form in (64):

(64) -te : [••+S]

Now it is clear that the formal representation [••+S] entails the representation [•], which is a subset of [••+S]. Hence we have the entailment scale in (65), which, inserted in the schema for entailment licensing from (30) repeated in (66), gives us the licensing conditions in (67):

(65) **Entailment Scale for Number**
[••+S] > [•]

(66) **Schema for Entailment Licensing**

Condition:	Feature structure F_1 entails feature structure F_2
Form:	Overt F_1 licenses Ø F_2 of the same head

(67) **Licensing Condition:**
Overt [••+S] licenses Ø [•] of the same head ([•••])

According to the conditions on Ø-licensing introduced in section 2.2, overt -te: [••+S] Ø-licenses k-:[•+S] [•] under (67) since both [•+S] and [•] are subsumed by the single feature structure of the target ([•]), hence every feature structure of (67)'s target subsumes at least one feature structure in an output -te, and every feature structure in -te is subsumed by some feature structure of the target.[14]

(68) shows how this accounts for the correct realization of plural in all intransitive forms. In the 1pl, [+1••] Ø-licenses plural -te.[15] As a consequence there is no Ø-licensing for k- by [•••] since this depends on an overt plural marker in the word form. In contrast for 2pl and 3pl forms -te is phonologically visible and [•••] induces Ø-spellout for k-:

(68) **Spellout of k- and -t**

		1pl	2pl	3pl
Input:		[+1••]	[+2••]	[+3••]
Insertion:		k- -te	k- -te	k- -te
Ø-Licensing:	[+1••]	k- -te	–	–
	[•••]	–	k- -te	k- -te
Phonology:		k-	-te	-te

---

[14] Conversely, overt k- does not Ø-license -te under (66) because its trigger [••+S] does not subsume any single feature structure of k- ([•+S] and [•] are less specific than [••+S], hence subsume the latter, but not vice versa).

[15] Note that [+1••] does not Ø-license k-:[•+S] [•] since the target of the licensing condition – [••] – neither subsumes [•+S] nor [•].

5.2 *k-* as an Inverse Affix

The second set of data for which *k-* is predicted by its lexical entry, but does not actually appear phonologically, are transitive forms with 1st, 2nd, and 3rd-person subject and a 3rd person object. Crucially, these are direct forms (the subject is higher or equal than the object on the person hierarchy), and I will derive the non-pronunciation of *k-* in these cases from the fact that it has the formal characteristics of an inverse marker.

I will adopt the approach to inverse marking developed in Trommer (2003a), where inverse markers are characterized as VIs with two different feature structures specifying agreement features, and the distribution of inverse markers is only partially captured by their lexical entries, but derives in crucial respects from constraints on their realization in direct contexts.

More concretely I will use the licensing schema in (69), where a congruent scale contrast is a pair of feature pairs $(F_1/F_2, F_1'/F_2')$ such that $F_1 \succeq F_1'$, and $F_2 \succeq F_2'$. A direction marker is any VI of the form [ ]$_{Agr}$ [ ]$_{Agr}$, and a direction marker is linked *under* the congruent scale contrast $(F_1/F_2, F_1'/F_2')$ iff one of its feature structures realizes a head specified as F_1 and F_2, and the other one realizes a head specified as F_1' and F_2':

(69) **Schema for Direct Licensing**

Condition:	M is complex, C is a congruent scale contrast
Form:	Linking direction marker M under C licenses Ø M

For the scales in (70), and substituting [•+S][•] for M, we get the licensing conditions in (71):

(70) **Relevant Scales and Congruent Scale Contrasts**
  $[+1] \succeq [+3]$ and $[+S] \succ [+O] \Rightarrow ([+1]/[+S],[+3]/[+O])$
  $[+2] \succeq [+3]$ and $[+S] \succ [+O] \Rightarrow ([+2]/[+S],[+3]/[+O])$
  $[+3] \succeq [+3]$ and $[+S] \succ [+O] \Rightarrow ([+1]/[+S],[+3]/[+O])$

(71) **Licensing Conditions:**

a. Linking under $([+1]/[+S],[+3]/[+O])$ licenses Ø [•][•] $([\circ][\circ] \genfrac{}{}{0pt}{}{[+1][+3]}{[+S][+O]})$

b. Linking under $([+2]/[+S], [+3]/[+O])$ licenses Ø [•][•] $([\circ][\circ] \genfrac{}{}{0pt}{}{[+2][+3]}{[+S][+O]})$

c. Linking under $([+3]/[+S][+3][+O])$ licenses Ø [•][•] $([\circ][\circ] \genfrac{}{}{0pt}{}{[+3][+3]}{[+S][+O]})$

(72) shows the licensing conditions in action. *k-* is inserted in both 3sg → 1sg and 1sg → 3sg forms, but in the latter configuration, *k-* is marked as phonologically invisible:[16]

(72) **Spellout: 1sg ↔ 3sg**

		1sg → 3sg	3sg → 1sg
Input:		[+1•+S][+3•+O]	[+3•+S][+1•+O]
Insertion:		k- [•+S] [•]	k- [•+S] [•]
	[∘][∘] [+1][+3] / [+S][+O]	k- [•+S] [∘]	–
Ø-Licensing:	[∘][∘] [+2][+3] / [+S][+O]	–	–
	[∘][∘] [+3][+3] / [+S][+O]	–	–
Phonology:			k-

Exactly the same contrast is derived for forms with one 2nd and one 3rd person argument:

(73) **Spellout: 2sg ↔ 3sg**

		2sg → 3sg	3sg → 2sg
Input:		[+2•+S][+3•+O]	[+3•+S][+2•+O]
Insertion:		k- [•+S] [•]	k- [•+S] [•]
	[∘][∘] [+1][+3] / [+S][+O]	–	–
Ø-Licensing:	[∘][∘] [+2][+3] / [+S][+O]	k- [•+S] [∘]	–
	[∘][∘] [+3][+3] / [+S][+O]	–	–
Phonology:			k-

---

[16] That a direct configuration does not Ø-license plural *-t* or *k-* if it spells out plural of a single head follows from the definition of congruent scale contrast above: Being linked under a congruent scale contrast implies linking to two different feature structures in the input, whereas plural *-te/k-* are only linked to one feature structure in the input.

If both arguments are non-3rd person, *k*- is inserted, and retained because there is no licensing condition which would allow it to be suppressed phonologically:

(74) **Spellout: 1sg ↔ 2sg**

		1sg → 2sg	2sg → 1sg
Input:		[+1•+S][+2•+O]	[+2•+S][+1•+O]
Insertion:		k- [•+S] [•]	k- [•+S] [•]
Ø-Licensing:	[•][•] [+1][+3] [+S][+O]	–	–
	[•][•] [+2][+3] [+S][+O]	–	–
	[•][•] [+3][+3] [+S][+O]	–	–
Phonology:		k-	k-

5.3 Forms with *k*- as Inverse- *and* Number-Affix

A final complication arises with contexts where *k*- is inserted twice since it matches the number elements once by virtue of a plural subject, and once by matching number elements in the feature structures for subject and object agreement. In other words, *k*- is inserted once as a number affix and once as a direction affix. This happens for example in 1pl → 3sg forms:

(75) **Double Insertion for k-**

	1pl → 3sg	1pl → 3sg
Input:	[••+S+1] [•+O+3]	[••+S+1] [•+O+3]
VI:	[•+S] [•]	[•+S] [•]

Hence insertion leads actually to the distribution in (76), where some of the *k-k* cases here correspond to phonological *k*- and some to the complete phonological absence of *k*-:

(76) **Single and Double Insertion of k-**

			\multicolumn{6}{c}{Object}	
			\multicolumn{2}{c}{1}	\multicolumn{2}{c}{2}	\multicolumn{2}{c}{3}	Ø
			sg	pl	sg	pl	sg	pl	
Subject	1	sg					k-		
		pl					k-k-		k-
	2	sg	k-				k-		
		pl	k-k-				k-k-		k-
	3	sg			k-				
		pl			k-k-				k-

k-k-forms have three possible outcomes. *First*, in *k-k*-forms with a 2nd or 3rd person plural subject, both instances of *k-* are Ø-licensed, direction-marking *k-* by direct licensing, and number *k-* by entailment licensing triggered by plural *-te*. This is shown in (77) for a 2pl → 3sg form (here number elements bear indices to indicate by which match the VIs are licensed):

(77) **Spellout: 2pl → 3sg**

2pl → 3sg

Input:		$[+2\bullet_1\bullet_2+S][+3\bullet_3+O]$
Insertion:		k:$[\bullet_1+S][\bullet_2]$ k:$[\bullet_2+S][\bullet_3]$
	$[\bullet][\bullet]\begin{matrix}[+1][+3]\\ [+S][+O]\end{matrix}$	k:$[\bullet_1+S][\bullet_2]$ k:$[\bullet_2+S][\bullet_3]$
Ø-Licensing:	$[\bullet][\bullet]\begin{matrix}[+2][+3]\\ [+S][+O]\end{matrix}$	—
	$[\bullet][\bullet]\begin{matrix}[+3][+3]\\ [+S][+O]\end{matrix}$ $[\bullet\bullet\bullet]$	— k:$[\bullet_1+S][\bullet_2]$ k:$[\bullet_2+S][\bullet_3]$
Phonology:		

Second, in direct forms with a 1pl subject and a 3rd person object, direction *k-* (the one spelling out number elements of both heads) is Ø-licensed, whereas plural *k-* is maintained since it is not linked under a congruent scale contrast:

(78) **Spellout: 1pl → 3sg**

1pl → 3sg

Input:		$[+1\bullet_1\bullet_2+S][+3\bullet_3+O]$
Insertion:		k:[•₁+S][•₂] k:[•₂+S][•₃]
	[•][•] $\begin{array}{l}[+1][+3]\\ [+S][+O]\end{array}$	k:[•₁+S][•₂] k:[•₂+S][•₃]
Ø-Licensing:	[•][•] $\begin{array}{l}[+2][+3]\\ [+S][+O]\end{array}$	–
	[•][•] $\begin{array}{l}[+3][+3]\\ [+S][+O]\end{array}$ [••]	– –
Phonology:		k

Third, in forms with a 1pl subject and a 2nd person object, both instances of *k*- are retained in the morphology:

(79) **Spellout: 1pl → 2sg**

1pl → 2sg

Input:		$[+1\bullet_1\bullet_2+S][+2\bullet_3+O]$
Insertion:		k:[•₁+S][•₂] k:[•₂+S][•₃]
	[•][•] $\begin{array}{l}[+1][+3]\\ [+S][+O]\end{array}$	–
Ø-Licensing:	[•][•] $\begin{array}{l}[+2][+3]\\ [+S][+O]\end{array}$	–
	[•][•] $\begin{array}{l}[+3][+3]\\ [+S][+O]\end{array}$ [••]	– –
Phonology:		k k

Following Dimmendaal 1983, I assume that this is actually correct, and a rule of consonant degemination (Turkana has no geminate consonants) reduces *k-k* phonetically to *k*.

6 Summary and Discussion

In this paper, I have shown that hierarchy effects in pronominal agreement can be straightforwardly captured by licensing conditions which enforce Ø-realization of vocabulary items. This account differs in three substantial ways from the approach of Aissen (1999, 2003b) to Ø-spellout in morphology. *First*, the scope of both approaches overlaps while not being coextensive: Aissen's theory is an approach to hierarchy effects in morphosyntax in general, hence extends to syntax proper (for example, it also captures cases where obligatory passivization is driven by misaligned hierarchies), whereas the approach developed here is restricted to effects in low-level morphological spellout. Conversely, the Ø-licensing framework extends to an area of hierarchy-driven morphological spellout which is not captured by Aissen's account: the blocking of less specific items by more specific ones. Both morphosyntactic hierarchy effects as a whole and blocking effects at spellout form conceptually natural classes, but it is an open empirical question as to which degree these correspond to modules of grammatical knowledge. In fact, there is some evidence that hierarchical effects in syntax proper and in morphological spellout differ substantially in invoking different types of hierarchies (cf. McGinnis 2005, 2008). *Second*, the inherent prediction of the Ø-licensing approach is that the possible effects of hierarchies on morphological spellout are restricted to Ø-exponence of vocabulary items, whereas in Aissen's approach Ø-exponence is just a special case of markedness. Thus consider the constraint ranking in (80) which forms the core of Aissen's analysis of inverse marking in the Tibeto-Burman language Nocte (Aissen 1999: 707), where direction marking is restricted to appearance of the inverse suffix -*h* in transitive clauses in which the object is higher than the subject on the person hierarchy 1 ≻ 2 ≻ 3:

(80) {*Ø$_D$ & *Su/3 & *Oj/Loc, *Ø$_D$ & *Su/2 & *Oj/1}
 ≫ *STRUC$_D$ ≫ *Ø$_D$ & *GR/Pers

*STRUC$_D$ is an economy constraint which penalizes direction (direct/inverse) affixes. *Ø$_D$ is a markedness constraint against Ø-exponence for direction marking, which is linked via constraint conjunction to specific person configurations for subject and object. Thus the complex constraint *Ø$_D$ & *Su/3 & *Oj/Loc requires an overt direction marker for any clause with a 3rd person subject and a non-third (local) person. The fixed ranking of this constraint above the corresponding constraint for 1/2 → 3 clauses via Harmonic Alignment and the ranking of *STRUC$_D$ between them derives the fact that Nocte has direction marking in

3 → 1/2, but not in 1/2 → 3 clauses. Now crucially, in Aissen's theory, *STRUC$_D$ and *Ø$_D$ could be replaced by markedness constraints unrelated to Ø-exponence, e.g. constraints on linear order. Thus replacing *STRUC$_D$ in (80) by a constraint such as Aff ⇒ Right, which captures the universal preference for suffixation (Greenberg 1963; Cutler et al. 1985; Bybee et al. 1990), and *Ø$_D$ by Left ⇔ Person, which implements the counteracting typological tendency that person markers tend to be prefixal (Cysouw 2009; Trommer 2003d), we get a system where person affixes are consistently prefixed in inverse configurations, but suffixed in direct clauses, probably an unattested pattern. Thus Aissen's system implies that the **Scales-Ø-Generalization** formulated in (1) is too strong. However, as noted before, there is no systematic evidence for hierarchy effects on morphological spellout which are not related to Ø-exponence (cf. footnote 1). *Third*, the Ø-licensing approach predicts specific typological options categorically excluded by Aissen's account. In Aissen's system, due to universally fixed ranking by Harmonic Alignment, hierarchy effects such as direction marking can only surface in cases of equally prominent arguments (e.g. two non-third person arguments of a verb) if they are also attested in inverse contexts proper (e.g. 3 → 1/2 clauses). On the other hand, in the Ø-licensing account, Ø-licensing for symmetric and inverse configurations is independent, hence hierarchy effects should be possible in symmetric contexts even if they are absent in inverse contexts proper. There is some evidence that this prediction is in fact correct. Thus Dryer (1994) argues that the Amerindian language Kutenai has direction marking, but only in clauses with two 3rd person arguments. On the other hand, an inverse marker limited to local person would necessarily be restricted either to 1 → 2 or to 2 → 1 contexts (since languages typically do not allow more sub-differentiation of person categories in 1 → 2 and 2 → 1 forms). But under these premises, there is no empirical difference between strictly local inverse marking and portmanteau affixes marking specific combinations of subject and object. Thus every local portmanteau is also potential evidence for inverse marking restricted to local contexts. Now in fact the typological literature reports that portmanteau affixes are highly frequent in local contexts (Heath 1991, 1998) (cf. e.g. Guaraní which has person portmanteaus in all and only in 1 → 2 forms; Gregores and Súarez 1967: 131–132). Also many patterns of hierarchy-based competition in transitive person-number agreement are restricted to local (1/2 → 1/2) contexts. This holds for example for person agreement in Georgian, where the 2nd person object affix *g-* triggers Ø-exponence for the 1sg affix *v-*, but not for 3rd person affixes such as the 3sg suffix *-s* (cf. *v-xedav*, 'I see, '*g-xedav/*g-v-xedav*, 'I see you (sg.)', and *g-xedav-s*, '(s)he sees you (sg.)'). The same restriction to local contexts is found in the blocking of multiple plural affixes found throughout Algonquian languages (Béjar 2003; Henze and Zimmermann 2010). Thus the

system developed here is typologically less restrictive than Aissen's for specific configurations, but this "lack of restrictiveness" corresponds to cross-linguistically well-attested patterns.

Still, it remains a fruitful question whether the range of possible scale effects can be further narrowed down. A potentially relevant generalization emerges if we compare the licensing schemata introduced in this paper with respect to the relative prominence of Ø-licensors and Ø-licensees:

(81) **Types of Licensing**

	Licensor	Ø-Licensee	Conditions
Cumulative Complexity	High	High	same head different scales
Superiority	High	Low	different heads same scale
Direct	Congruent Linking	Complex Marker	different heads same scale
Entailment	High	Low	same head same scale

With the exception of direction licensing (which is difficult to classify in these terms because it targets portmanteaus, not simple markers), only input feature structures which correspond to high elements in scales can be licensors. Whether this generalization extends to other hierarchy effects and licensing schemata (e.g. for differential case-marking) is a question for future research.

7 Appendix: Details of Vocabulary Insertion

7.0.0.6 Features:

A feature is either an ordered attribute-value pair (e.g. (1, +), usually abbreviated as +1), or a single privative feature (e.g. •).

7.0.0.7 Feature Structures:

A feature structure is a multiset of features. Multisets are a mathematical construct which are largely equivalent to sets with the only exception that multisets can differ by having the same elements in different cardinality (cf. Knuth 1969 for details, and Gazdar et al. 1985 for another linguistic application). Thus the sets {a, b, c} and {a, a, b, c} are identical ({a, b, c} and {a, a, b, c} are different notations for the same set), but the multiset {a, b, c}$_m$ differs from the multiset {a, a, b, c}$_m$ since the first contains "a" once, and the latter twice. In the following and in the rest of the paper, I use the standard notation for morphological feature structures as a shorthand for multisets. Hence [+1–2••] is abbreviating the multiset {(1, +), (2, –), •, •}$_m$. An indexed feature structure is an ordered pair of a feature structure and a natural number (e.g. ([+3+Agr••], 1) abbreviated as [+3+Agr••]$_1$). To distinguish the *n* different instances of the same element in a multiset, I will assign distinct (superscripted) indices from 1 to *n* to them (e.g. [+3+Agr•^{1}•^{2}]$_1$).

7.0.0.8 Indexed Lists:

An indexed list is a set of indexed feature structures such that the indices of the feature structures impose a complete transitive order on the set. An example is given in (82), which abbreviates {[+3+Agr••]$_1$, [+3+Agr•]$_2$}.

(82) [+3+Agr••]$_1$ [+3+Agr•]$_2$

7.0.0.9 Inputs:

An input is an ordered pair of a lexical root (a string of phonemes) and an indexed list, e.g. (83), which abbreviates (xedav, {[+3+Agr••]$_1$, [+3+Agr•]$_2$}).

(83) xedav [+3+Agr••]$_1$ [+3+Agr•]$_2$

7.0.0.10 Vocabulary Items:

A vocabulary item is a triple (P, O, L), where P is a string of phonemes (the phonological content of the affix), O is either "prefix" or "suffix" (the affixal orientation of the affix), and L is an indexed list.

7.0.0.11 Possible Mappings:

To get a simple definition of the insertion algorithm, we need definitions of a number of auxiliary notions resulting in a precise definition of the mapping of a VI to an input:

(84) **Definition Partition:** A partition of an indexed feature structure F with index i is a multiset of indexed feature structures S = {F$_1$, ..., F$_n$}$_m$ such that all elements of S are non-empty, have the index i, and F$_1$ ∪ ... ∪ F$_n$ = F.

(85) and (86) enumerate all partitions of the indexed feature structures in (83):

(85) **Partitions of** $[+3+Agr\bullet]_2$:
    a. **P21:** $\{[+3]_2, [+Agr]_2, [\bullet]_2\}_m$
    b. **P22:** $\{[+3+Agr]_2, [\bullet]_2\}_m$
    c. **P23:** $\{[+3\bullet]_2, [+Agr]_2\}_m$
    d. **P24:** $\{[+3]_2, [+Agr\bullet]_2\}_m$

(86) **Partitions of** $[+3+Agr\bullet\bullet]_1$:
    a. **P11:** $\{[+3]_1, [+Agr]_1, [\bullet]_1, [\bullet]_1\}_m$
    b. **P12:** $\{[+3+Agr]_1, [\bullet]_1, [\bullet]_1\}_m$
    c. **P13:** $\{[+3]_1, [+Agr\bullet]_1, [\bullet]_1\}_m$
    d. **P14:** $\{[+3\bullet]_1, [+Agr]_1, [\bullet]_1\}_m$
    e. **P15:** $\{[+3]_1, [+Agr]_1, [\bullet\bullet]_1\}_m$
    f. **P16:** $\{[+3+Agr]_1, [\bullet\bullet]_1\}_m$
    g. **P17:** $\{[+3\bullet]_1, [+Agr\bullet]_1\}_m$
    h. **P18:** $\{[+3+Agr\bullet]_1, [\bullet]_1\}_m$
    i. **P19:** $\{[+3+\bullet\bullet]_1, [+Agr]_1\}_m$
    j. **P110:** $\{[+Agr+\bullet\bullet]_1, [+3]_1\}_m$

(87) **Definition Possible Split:** A possible split of an indexed list $I = \{F_1, \ldots, F_n\}$ is a multiset $S = S_1 \cup \ldots \cup S_n$ such that S_i is a partition of F_i $(1 \leq i \leq n)$.

For the input list in (83), every union of one partition of the first feature structure and one partition of the second feature structure is a possible split. (88) lists some examples:

(88) **Some Possible Splits of (83):**
    a. **P21 ∪ P11** = $\{[+3]_1, [+Agr]_1, [\bullet]_1, [\bullet]_1, [+3]_2, [+Agr]_2, [\bullet]_2\}_m$
    b. **P21 ∪ P13** = $\{[+3]_2, [+Agr]_2, [\bullet]_2, [+3]_1, [+Agr\bullet]_1, [\bullet]_1\}_m$
    c. **P24 ∪ P13** = $\{[+3]_2, [+Agr\bullet]_2, [+3]_1, [+Agr\bullet]_1, [\bullet]_1\}_m$

(89) **Definition Possible Mapping:** A *possible mapping* of a VI V to an input I is an injective function F from the indexed list of V to the indexed list of I such that
    a. the feature structure of F(FS) = the feature structure of FS
    b. for every ordered pair (a, a') and (b, b') in F:
        If Index(a) < Index(b) then Index(a') ≤ Index(b')

For example, two possible mappings of the VI in (90) and the input in (83) (based on (88-a)) are shown in (91) (recall that superscripts indicate the different occurrences of $[\bullet]_1$ in (88-a)):

(90) la- $[\bullet]_1$ $[\bullet]_2$

(91) a. $[\bullet]_1 \rightarrow [\bullet^1]_1$, $[\bullet]_2 \rightarrow [\bullet^1]_2$
      b. $[\bullet]_1 \rightarrow [\bullet^1]_1$, $[\bullet]_2 \rightarrow [\bullet^2]_1$

Finally, to avoid the proliferation of mappings which are basically identical, I define the notion of a minimal possible mapping:

(92) **Definition Minimal Possible Mapping:** M is a minimal possible mapping if it is a possible mapping, and there is no possible Mapping M' such that M can be transformed into M' by assigning lower token indices to multiset members in the range of M.

Thus (93-a) is a possible mapping, but not minimal because it can be transformed into the possible mapping (91-a) by changing $[\bullet^2]_1$ to $[\bullet^1]_1$. (91-b) could be transformed by the same replacement into (93-b), but (93-b) is not a possible mapping (it is not injective), hence (91-b) is also minimal.

(93) a. $[\bullet]_1 \rightarrow [\bullet^2]_1$, $[\bullet]_2 \rightarrow [\bullet^1]_2$
      b. $[\bullet]_1 \rightarrow [\bullet^1]_1$, $[\bullet]_2 \rightarrow [\bullet^1]_1$

7.0.0.12 Insertion Algorithm

The insertion algorithm basically produces an ordered list of all possible mappings for an input and a lexicon of VIs, and inserts the corresponding VIs. The ordering of the list corresponds to the ranked constraints in (14). The smallest input index of a possible mapping M (abbreviated as SIM(M)) is the smallest index of the indexed feature structures in the range of M, and the smallest output index of a possible mapping M (abbreviated as SOM(M)) is the smallest index of the indexed feature structures in the domain of M. The output is a list of base and affixes where affixes are ordered pairs of a phonological string and an indexed list. "←" assigns the value on its right to a variable on its left, and "+" is the concatenation operator for lists:

(94) **Insertion Algorithm:**

Input: An input I = (B, IL) and a list of VIs [$V_1 \ldots V_n$]
Create an ordered list O such that:
i)   O contains all minimal possible mappings from V_i to I, $1 \leq i \leq n$
ii) for every two members M_1 and M_2 of O the following holds:

   If M_1 precedes M_2 in O then:
   1. $SIM(M_1) \leq SIM(M_2)$
   2. If $SIM(M_1) = SIM(M_2)$ then $range(M_1) \geq range(M_2)$
   3. If $SIM(M_1) = SIM(M_2)$ and $range(M_1) = range(M_2)$ then $SOM(M_1) \leq SOM(M_2)$

For every element M of O corresponding to VI V = (P, O, L):
  Base ← [B]
  List ← L
  Replace the indices of L by the indices of the corresponding elements in M
  Affix ← [(P,L)]
  If O = prefix then: Base ← Affix+Base
  If O = suffix then: Base ← Base+Affix
Return Base

Bibliography

Aissen, J. (1999). Markedness and subject choice in Optimality Theory. *Natural Language and Linguistic Theory*, 17(4):673–711.

Aissen, J. (2003a). Differential coding, partial blocking, and bidirectional OT. In Nowak, P. and Yoquelet, C., editors, *Proceedings of BLS 29*, pages 1–16.

Aissen, J. (2003b). Differential object marking: Iconicity vs. economy. *Natural Language and Linguistic Theory*, 23(3):435–483.

Anderson, S. R. (1992). *A-Morphous Morphology*. Cambridge: Cambridge University Press.

Béjar, S. (2003). *Phi-Syntax: A Theory of Agreement*. PhD thesis, University of Toronto.

Bybee, J. L., Pagliuca, W., and Perkins, R. D. (1990). On the asymmetries in the affixation of grammatical material. In Croft, W., Denning, K., and Kemmer, S., editors, *Studies in Typology and Diachrony*, pages 1–42. Amsterdam: John Benjamins.

Carmack, S. (1997). Blocking in Georgian verb morphology. *Language* 73:314–338.

Chomsky, N. (1981). *Lectures on Government and Binding*. Cambridge MA: MIT Press.

Cutler, A., Hawkins, J. A., and Gilligan, G. (1985). The suffixing preference: A processing explanation. *Linguistics* 23(3). 723–758.

Cysouw, M. (1998). Pronoun descriptions: Nilotic. Ms., Max Planck Institute for Evolutionary Anthropology, Leipzig.

Cysouw, M. (2009). The asymmetry of affixation. *Snippets, Special Issue in Honor of Manfred Krifka*, 20(3):10–14.
Dimmendaal, G. J. (1983). *The Turkana Language*. Dordrecht: Foris.
Dimmendaal, G. J. (1986). Prominence hierarchies and Turkana syntax. In Dimmendaal, G. J., editor, *Current Approaches to African Linguistics*, pages 127–148. Dordrecht: Foris.
Dimmendaal, G. J. (1991). The geometry of verb paradigms in Teso-Turkana. In Plank, F., editor, *Paradigms: The Economy of Inflection*, pages 275–306. Mouton de Gruyter.
Dryer, M. S. (1994). The discourse function of the Kutenai inverse. In Givón, T., editor, *Voice and Inversion*, pages 65–100. Amsterdam: John Benjamins.
Gazdar, G., Klein, E., Pullium, G., and Sag, I. (1985). *Generalized Phrase Structure Grammar*. Oxford: Blackwell.
Greenberg, J. H. (1963). Some universals of grammar with special reference to the order of meaningful elements. In Greenberg, J. H., editor, *Universals of Language*, pages 58–90. Cambridge MA: MIT Press.
Gregores, E. and Súarez, J. A. (1967). *A Description of Colloquial Guaraní*. Mouton & Co.
Grimshaw, J. (1997). The best clitic: Constraint conflict in morphosyntax. In Haegeman, L., editor, *Elements of Grammar: A Handbook in Contemporary Syntactic Theory*, pages 169–196. Dordrecht: Kluwer.
Grimshaw, J. and Samek-Lodovici, V. (1998). Optimal subjects and subject universals. In Barbosa, P., Fox, D., Hagstrom, P., McGinnis, M., and Pesetsky, D., editors, *Is the Best Good Enough?*, pages 193–220. Cambridge MA: MIT Press.
Halle, M. (1997). Distributed Morphology: Impoverishment and fission. In Benjamin Bruening, Y. K. and McGinnis, M., editors, *Papers at the Interface*, volume 30 of *MIT Working Papers in Linguistics*, pages 425–449. Cambridge MA: MITWPL.
Halle, M. and Marantz, A. (1993). Distributed Morphology and the pieces of inflection. In Hale, K. and Keyser, S. J., editors, *The View from Building 20*, pages 111–176. Cambridge MA: MIT Press.
Harris, J. (1994). *English Sound Structure*. Blackwell, Oxford.
Haspelmath, M. (2008). Frequency vs. iconicity in explaining grammatical asymmetries. *Cognitive Linguistics*, 19(1):1–33.
Heath, J. (1991). Pragmatic disguise in pronominal-affix paradigms. In Plank, F., editor, *Economy of Inflection*, pages 75–89. Berlin: Mouton de Gruyter.
Heath, J. (1998). Pragmatic skewing in 1-2 pronominal combination in native american languages. *IJAL*, 64(2):83–104.
Heck, F. and Müller, G. (2006). Extremely local optimization. In Bainbridge, E. and Agbayani, B., editors, *Proceedings of WECOL 34*, pages 170–182. Department of Linguistics, University of Fresno, CA.
Henze, D. and Zimmermann, E. (2010). Hierarchy-governed insertion and RFD-markers in Potawatomi. In Bank, S., Georgi, D., and Trommer, J., editors, *2 in Agreement*, volume 88 of *Linguistische Arbeits Berichte*, pages 23–63. Universität Leipzig: Institut für Linguistik.
Kaye, J., Lowenstamm, J., and Vergnaud, J.-R. (1990). Constituent structure and government in phonology. *Phonology*, 7:193–232.
Keine, S. and G. Müller. 2015. Differential argument encoding by impoverishment. This volume.
Knuth, D. E. (1969). *The Art of Computer Programming*, volume 2. Reading, Massachusetts: Addison-Wesley.
Lakämper, R. (2000). *Plural- und Objektmarkierung in Quechua*. PhD thesis, University of Düsseldorf.

Lowenstamm, J. (1996). CV as the only syllable type. In Durand, J. and Laks, B., editors, *Current trends in Phonology. Models and Methods*, pages 419–441. Salford, Manchester: ESRI.

McCarthy, J. (2007). *Hidden Generalizations: Phonological Opacity in Optimality Theory*. London: Equinox.

McGinnis, M. (2005). On markedness asymmetries in person and number. *Language*, 81(3):699–718.

McGinnis, M. (2008). Phi-feature competition in morphology and syntax. In Harbour, D., Adger, D., and Béjar, S., editors, *In Phi-Theory: Phi-Features across Modules and Interfaces*, Oxford Studies in Theoretical Linguistics, pages 155–184. Oxford: Oxford University Press.

Merlan, F. C. (1994). *A Grammar of Wardaman*. Berlin and New York: Mouton de Gruyter.

Müller, G. (2006). Extended exponence by enrichment: Argument encoding in German, Archi and Timucua. Ms., University of Leipzig, available under http://www.uni-leipzig.de/~muellerg/mu227.pdf.

Nevins, A. I. (2007). Dual is still more marked than plural. Ms., Harvard University. Available as lingBuzz/000235.

Novelli, B. (1985). *A Grammar of the Karimojong Language*. Berlin: Dietrich Reimer.

Noyer, R. R. (1992). *Features, Positions and Affixes in Autonomous Morphological Structure*. PhD thesis, MIT.

Pesetsky, D. (1998). Some optimality principles of sentence pronunciation. In Barbosa, P., Fox, D., Hagstrom, P., McGinnis, M., and Pesetsky, D., editors, *Is the Best Good Enough?*, pages 337–384. Cambridge MA: MIT Press.

Prince, A. and Smolensky, P. (1993). Optimality theory: Constraint interaction in generative grammar. Technical reports of the Rutgers University Center of Cognitive Science.

Rizzi, L. (1986). Null objects in Italian and the theory of pro. *Linguistic Inquiry*, 17:501–57.

Scheer, T. (2004). *A lateral theory of phonology. Vol 1: What is CVCV, and why should it be?* Berlin: Mouton de Gruyter.

Ségéral, P. and Scheer, T. (2008). The coda mirror, stress and positional parameters. In ao de Carvalho, J. B., Scheer, T., and Ségéral, P., editors, *Lenition and Fortition*, pages 483–518. Berlin: Mouton de Gruyter.

Smolensky, P. (1995). On the internal structure of the constraint component Con of UG. Talk handout, UCLA, 7 April.

Stump, G. T. (2001). *Inflectional Morphology*. Cambridge: Cambridge University Press.

Trommer, J. (2002). The interaction of morphology and syntax in affix order. In DeCesaris, J., editor, *Proceedings of the 3rd Mediterranean Morphology Meeting, Barcelona, September 2001*, pages 343–355.

Trommer, J. (2003a). Direction marking as agreement. In Junghanns, U. and Szucsich, L., editors, *Syntactic Structures and Morphological Information*, pages 317–341. Berlin and New York: Mouton de Gruyter.

Trommer, J. (2003b). *Distributed Optimality*. PhD thesis, University of Potsdam.

Trommer, J. (2003c). Feature (non-)insertion in a minimalist approach to spellout. In *Proceedings of CLS 39*, pages 469–480.

Trommer, J. (2003d). The interaction of morphology and syntax in affix order. In *Yearbook of Morphology 2002*, pages 283–324. Dordrecht: Kluwer.

Trommer, J. (2006a). Hierarchy-based competition and emergence of two-argument agreement in Dumi. *Linguistics*, 44(5):1011–1057.

Trommer, J. (2006b). Plural insertion is constructed plural. In Müller, G. and Trommer, J., editors, *Subanalysis of Argument Encoding in Distributed Morphology*, volume 84 of *Linguistische Arbeits Berichte*, pages 197–228. Institut für Linguistik: Universität Leipzig.

Trommer, J. (2008). Third-person marking in Menominee. In Harbour, D., Béjar, S., and Adger, D., editors, *Phi-theory: Phi-features Across Modules and Interfaces*, pages 221–250. Oxford: Oxford University Press.

Wunderlich, D. (2000). A correspondence-theoretic analysis of Dalabon transitive paradigms. In Booij, G. and van Marle, J., editors, *Yearbook of Morphology 1999*, pages 233–252. Dordrecht: Kluwer.

Wunderlich, D. and Fabri, R. (1994). Minimalist morphology: An approach to inflection. *Zeitschrift für Sprachwissenschaft*, 20:236–294.

Marc D. Richards
7 Defective Agree, Case Alternations, and the Prominence of Person

1 Introduction: The Person-Animacy-Definiteness connection

The properties of animacy and definiteness/specificity are implicated in the triggering of a number of (otherwise seemingly unrelated) morphosyntactic phenomena (see Aissen 2003 for a comprehensive overview). Firstly, numerous case alternations have been identified that arise through the differential case-marking of arguments according to animacy and/or definiteness (thus animates and/or definites are overtly marked in languages such as Hindi, Persian, Turkish, Hebrew, Spanish and Romanian, contrasting with unmarked forms for inanimates and/or indefinites in these languages). Secondly, animate and/or definite arguments are prone to undergo displacement out of their base positions across the world's languages (e.g. Germanic, Mayan, Niger-Congo, and object clitics in Romance), whereas inanimates and indefinites are more readily accommodated in situ. Finally, direct objects in ditransitive constructions are widely subject to a class of agreement restrictions often called the Person-Case Constraint (PCC), such that they may not be first- or second-person (e.g. French – the '*me-lui* constraint'), animate (Mohawk, Southern Tiwa), or definite/specific (Akan).

One way to approach these phenomena is in terms of a referential hierarchy or prominence scale of the kind illustrated in (1).

(1) Silverstein person/animacy scale (simplified) (Silverstein 1976, Dixon 1994):
1/2-person (pron.) > 3-person (pron.) > animate (3-person) > inanimate (3-person)
← *more likely agents/subjects* ... *more likely patients/objects* →
← *more likely definite* ... *more likely indefinite* →

The relevant factors, animacy and definiteness/specificity, are all 'high-ranked' (salient) properties occurring towards the left of the scale. As such, they correlate with a further property, local person (i.e. first-/second-person). In connecting these three properties, prominence scales allow us to attribute the aforesaid morphosyntactic phenomena (or their likelihood of occurrence) to hierarchical position, in formal or functional terms. Thus differential case-marking, for example, may be viewed functionally as the overt marking of noncanonical argument types, such as inanimate agents and definite objects (see Comrie 1989); formally, nominals towards the left of the scale might be attributed greater internal structure than items towards the right, which in turn can feed morphological differences (see, e.g., Déchaine & Wiltschko 2002, Harbour 2007).

However, as discussed in Brown, Koch & Wiltschko (2004), the explanatory status of such scales is questionable from the formal perspective. Should they be taken as primitives of the theory (attributable to UG), or as epiphenomena proceeding from deeper or independent principles (perhaps language-independent)? Related to this question is that of formal implementation: do we assume hierarchies (as in OT approaches based on harmonic alignment – see, e.g., Aissen 2003, Keine & Müller 2015), feature geometries (cf. Harley & Ritter 2002), or phrase structure (e.g. the sequence of functional heads) to be responsible? Are the scales universal, or are they open to language-specific variation? And how many such scales must we recognize (e.g. perhaps (1) should be separated out into three separate scales for person, animacy, and definiteness)?

From the minimalist perspective of a blind, autonomous, local syntax and a maximally empty UG (in line with the Strong Minimalist Thesis as outlined in Chomsky 2004, 2007, 2008), the syntactic status of prominence hierarchies is dubious, as are the pseudo-semantic animacy and specificity features that might be postulated to derive their effects. The present paper thus seeks to answer two main questions: What is the syntactic source of the correlated phenomena outlined above – why do animates and definites pattern together in inducing PCC effects, case alternations and optional movements? And what is the formal relation between person, animacy and definiteness?

The strategy to be pursued in answering these questions is to take the correlations at face value, positing the simplest connection between them – that of identity. Our claim is that Person in the syntax *just is* animacy/definiteness at the (semantic) interface. That is, we assume that there is a single, discrete, binary property ([+/−Person]) whose presence vs. absence correlates with high- vs. low-prominence interpretations in the semantic component. Our goal is to show that these phenomena, or at least their core properties, may be amenable to an explanation in these simplest terms.

Implicational links between person and animacy, on the one hand, and person and definiteness/specificity, on the other, have already been drawn in the minimalist literature. Thus Adger & Harbour (2007) propose that the presence of a [Participant] feature on an argument implies animacy, and Richards 2004, 2008 argues that the presence of a Person specification on a nominal implies definiteness. Such claims would seem semantically well motivated. After all, local-person nominals, i.e. those at the leftmost end of the scale in (1), are always animate (Adger & Harbour 2007: 20) and always definite (Dixon 1994:

91). Furthermore, nominals at the rightmost end of the scale (non-specific indefinites, inanimates) are always third person (Richards 2004, 2008) – there are no semantically first- or second-person indefinites or inanimates. We thus identify two implications: (i) from 1/2-Person to [+animate] and [+definite]; and (ii) from [–animate] and [–definite] to 3-person. These are illustrated in the tables in (2) and (3).

(2) *Person-animacy*

	Animate	Inanimate
1	✓	✗
2	✓	✗
3	✓	✓

(3) *Person-definiteness*

	Definite	Indefinite
1	✓	✗
2	✓	✗
3	✓	✓

As can be seen, only [+animate/+definite] nominals have an indeterminacy for Person, i.e. may be first- *or* second- *or* third-person. Only animates and definites, then, require a person specification (the person of inanimates and indefinites can be filled in by default to {3}). On grounds of avoiding redundancy, we can therefore assume that Person is a (syntactic) property of definite and animate nominals only: a person specification on indefinites and inanimates is redundant and thus plausibly left unspecified. If correct, then indefinites and inanimates will bear only number (and gender) features – they are thus 'defective' in the agreement system (in the sense of Chomsky 2001).[1] This lends partial support to the common claim that "third person is absence of person" (cf. Kayne 2000, Sigurðsson 2001, Anagnostopoulou 2003, 2005; see Nevins 2007 for criticism): Third-person is indeed absence of Person (in the syntax), but only on indefinites and inanimates.

---

[1] This is not to deny that indefinites and inanimates may still appear with apparently agreeing verbs – thus, e.g., there is no difference between *A man **is** in the garden* and *The man **is** in the garden*. However, any apparent [3-person] agreement of this kind with inanimates and indefinites must be the result of a default realization in the morphology (of features that fail to receive a value through Agree(ment) in the syntax). The lack of syntactic Person, then, does not entail the lack of a Person exponent in the morphology; this exponent should just be the default, elsewhere form.

Further, given that bare nouns, too, are always inherently third-person (thus there is no first-person form of *cat*, no second-person form of *dog*, and so on), we can make the reasonable assumption that Person is a property of the category D, not N. Therefore, if indefinites and inanimates lack Person (as claimed above), then this equates syntactically to their lacking DP structure – that is, they are bare NPs. First- and second-person nominals, by contrast, will always be DPs, whereas third-person nominals may be either DPs or NPs, depending on whether they are animates/definites or not (i.e. depending on whether their Person feature is syntactically specified or not). The D head, then, can be thought of as contributing such interpretive properties as definiteness, animacy, and referentiality, yielding the following implications: a DP (i.e. [+Person] nominal) entails animacy/definiteness (cf. Adger & Harbour 2007, Heck & Richards 2010); inanimacy/indefiniteness entails an NP (i.e. [–Person]). Consequently, animate/definite NPs are still a logical possibility (see Heck & Richards 2010 for relevant evidence from Southern Tiwa incorporation, and footnote 2 below).

Returning to prominence scales, the above proposals can be (roughly) expressed as follows: Firstly, there are (just) *two* scales: person/animacy and person/definiteness. Person belongs to both scales, as the formal correlate of animacy and/or definiteness. Secondly, languages may differ as to whether they associate the presence of Person (i.e. a syntactic Person specification) on a nominal with animacy or definiteness (or both). If Person is a property of D and not N, as suggested, then this translates to whether a language interprets DPs (as opposed to NPs) as animate or definite (or both). Finally, the discrete, binary feature [+/–Person] (i.e. [+/–D]) is then associated with the two scales as shown in (4) and (5), perhaps with crosslinguistic variation as to the exact 'cut-off point' (see section 3 below).

(4) Person/animacy scale

        [+ *Person*] (= DP) | [–*Person*] (= NP)

1/2-pers. pron. > animate (3-pers., pron./noun) > inanimate (3-pers., pron./noun)

← *(likelihood/obligatoriness of) animacy*

(5) Person/definiteness scale

        [+ *Person*] (= DP) | [–*Person*] (= NP)

1/2-person (pron.) > 3-person (pron.) > definite > specific > nonspecific

← *(likelihood/obligatoriness of) definiteness*

In the remaining sections of this paper, I illustrate how the simple presence vs. absence of Person (i.e. of D), and thus of animacy and/or definiteness, might provide the syntactic basis of the various phenomena listed above. In section 2, agreement restrictions of the PCC kind, as well as associated interpretive restrictions, are shown to follow from the above proposal that a Person specification implies an animate and/or definite ('prominent') interpretation at the interface. Section 3 sketches an approach to case alternations (differential case-marking) in terms of defective Agree, in particular the idea that a defective (i.e. Person-less) probe may assign (value) a different case from its nondefective (+Person) counterpart in the Probe-Goal-Agree system of Chomsky 2000, 2001. Section 4 turns to Object Shift and optional movements, arguing that the EPP-feature of a probe may be associated with the entire probe (i.e. Person+Number) or else with just the Person feature of the probe, yielding differential argument movements. Section 5 provides a brief summary and a possible extension.

2 Defective (partial) Agree and interpretive restrictions

2.1 Person restriction (Person-Case Constraint, PCC)

Let us first consider the relation between Person and (syntactic) Agree. As is well known, Icelandic Quirky Subject (QS) constructions involving agreement with a nominative object (internal argument) across a dative subject are subject to two restrictions. These are given in (6) and illustrated in (7) for dative experiencers, in (8) for raising predicates, and in (9) for dative subjects of ditransitive passives (cf. Sigurðsson 1990, 1996, 2001, Taraldsen 1995, Boeckx 2000, Anagnostopoulou 2003, 2005, Rezac 2004 and many others).

(6) a. The nominative object can only be third person.

b. Agreement with the nominative object is *partial* (number only).

(7) a. *Henni   leiddust   strákarnir   / þeir*
       Her-DAT bored-3PL   the-boys-NOM / they-NOM

b. **Henni   leiddumst   við*
      Her-DAT bored-1PL   we-NOM

c. **Henni   leiddust   við*
      Her-DAT bored-3PL   we-NOM

d. **Henni   leiddist   við*
      Her-DAT bored-3SG   we-NOM

(8) a. Mér   höfðu   fundist   þær   vinna   vel
       Me-DAT   had-3PL   found   they-NOM   to-work   well

   b. *Mér   höfðum   fundist   við   vinna   vel
       Me-DAT   had-1PL   found   we-NOM   to-work   well

(9) a. Henni   voru   sýndir   þeir
       Her-DAT were-3PL shown   they-NOM

   b. *Henni   vorum   sýndir   við
       Her-DAT were-1PL shown   we-NOM

Boeckx (2000) equates (6a) with the Person-Case Constraint (PCC; Bonet 1991/4), sometimes also dubbed the *me-lui* constraint on the basis of familiar French examples such as (10a-b). Essentially, in double object constructions, local-person direct objects are barred. Such effects are pervasive across the world's languages; English, too, shows a similar restriction on weak (unstressed) object pronouns, (10c).

(10) a. Jean   le/*me   lui   a   recommandé   [French]
        Jean   it/me   him   has   recommended

   b. *I showed them it/*you/*me*   [English; 'you'/'me' = weak]

   c. *He showed you me

An influential class of analyses within the minimalist literature proposes that PCC effects arise where two arguments (goals) relate to the same functional head (probe), as in (11) – see Anagnostopoulou 2003, Rezac 2004.

(11) PCC: single probe, multiple goals
     [P ... G$_{DAT}$ ... G$_{NOM/ACC}$] → *NOM/ACC-$_{1/2}$

In terms of the hierarchies of section 1, the generalization to be derived is that the second argument cannot be more prominent (higher on the scale in (1)) than the first (cf. Haspelmath 2007). As analysed in Anagnostopoulou 2003, 2005, this effect follows from the multiple Agree (one probe – multiple goals) context in (11) if the first argument 'consumes' the Person feature of the probe, leaving only Number for the second argument. The second argument must therefore be 'personless' (equated with third person), i.e., it must bear only a number feature.

Richards (2004, 2008) offers an analysis of the Icelandic restrictions in (6) along similar lines, starting from the hypothesis that quirky case (Icelandic dative) is "inherent case with an additional structural Case feature" (Chomsky 2000: 127; 2001: 43, note 8). Assuming that Case features cannot be added in isolation (Case being simply an activating diacritic on goals (interpretable φ-sets)), the added Case feature must be attached to its own φ-set. Minimally, this dummy φ-substrate will be a defective and default φ-set, i.e. [3Person]. This means that QS should be characterized as in (12).

(12) QS = inherent case + **[3Person]**$_{Case}$

Since the added Case feature is now formally identical to an expletive (expletives, too, are arguably minimal goals, i.e. a Cased default Person feature), we can think of the reactivating 'shell' on QS as a *quirky expletive*.

The derivation of (7a) thus proceeds as in (13).

(13)

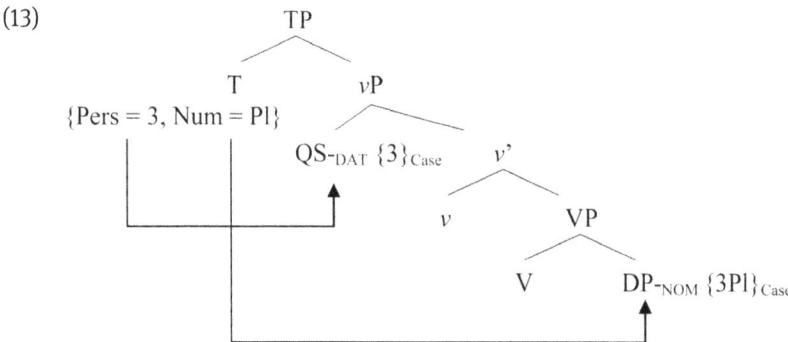

First the T probe meets (the quirky expletive on) QS, which values T's person as {3} via Agree. T's φ-set is then {Pers=3, Num=ø} at this point of the derivation. The PCC effect (6a) now follows simply from *nondistinctness* ("Match is nondistinctness rather than identity", Chomsky 2004: 13). An object with first- or second-person is distinct from the probe's third-person, hence fails to be matched by T. As a consequence, the object DP fails to enter Agree with T. The PCC effect in Icelandic thus reduces to a Case Filter effect: the object's Case goes unvalued, yielding a crash at the semantic interface.

The above analysis of the Icelandic PCC reduces it to the class of 'weak' PCC effects in terms of Anagnostouplou's (2005) *Multiple Agree* analysis: previously valued Person features 'count' for Matching of the second argument, which must therefore have a noncontradictory Person specification (i.e. {3} in Icelandic, due to the inherent third-person specification on the quirky expletive in (12);

{1}/{2} in Spanish, Italian, Catalan, etc.). We might therefore think of the weak PCC as the 'like with like' PCC.

However, more interesting for our present purposes is the existence of a stronger form of the PCC in which no direct object of any person is allowed (i.e. no matter whether it matches the person specification of the dative argument or not). Such cases of 'strong PCC' can be modelled in this system by assuming that previously valued Person features, here, do **not** count, so that Number probes alone for the second argument. In such cases, the second argument must indeed lack Person (i.e. be NP, and thus third-person) in order for Match and thus Agree to obtain. Given the 'Person=Animacy/Definiteness' proposal in section 1, this now makes the further prediction that the second argument in strong PCC environments will be subject to extra interpretive restrictions (in addition to the Person-agreement restriction). The type of restriction (animacy or definiteness) will depend on whether the language in question associates Person with animacy (cf. scale (4)) or with definiteness (scale (5)), or both. The following two subsections illustrate each of these two possibilities in turn.

2.2 Animacy restriction

Strong PCC effects in languages of the (4)-type are predicted to include an animacy restriction on the second (defective) goal. Certain dialects of Spanish, namely the *leísta* dialects, bear this out (Ormazabal & Romero 2007, Adger & Harbour 2007). In these dialects, the pronominal paradigm exhibits a dative-accusative syncretism for animate referents: *le* expresses third-person animates in dative and accusative alike, whereas inanimates have a distinct accusative form *lo/la* (3 ACC INANIM MASC/FEM). Given (4), the presence of Person is associated with [+animate]. Therefore, the agreement-restricted (third-person) direct object in a ditransitive PCC configuration is predicted to be subject to an animacy restriction: it must be inanimate, by virtue of having to lack Person.

PCC effects are thus predicted to occur not only with first- and second-person direct objects in such languages, but additionally with animate third-person direct objects too. This is indeed what we find:

(14) a. Te   lo   di
        2DAT.SG 3ACC.[−ANIM]   gave.1SG
        'I gave it to you.'

   b. *Te   le   di
        2DAT.SG 3ACC.[+ANIM]   gave.1SG
        'I gave him to you.'

The relevant derivation is given in (15). The Number-probe left over after valuation of T's Person (here, to {2}) can only match a personless goal. In these languages, this means not only that that goal must lack Person (i.e. be third-person), but also that it must be inanimate (since Person implies animacy).

(15)
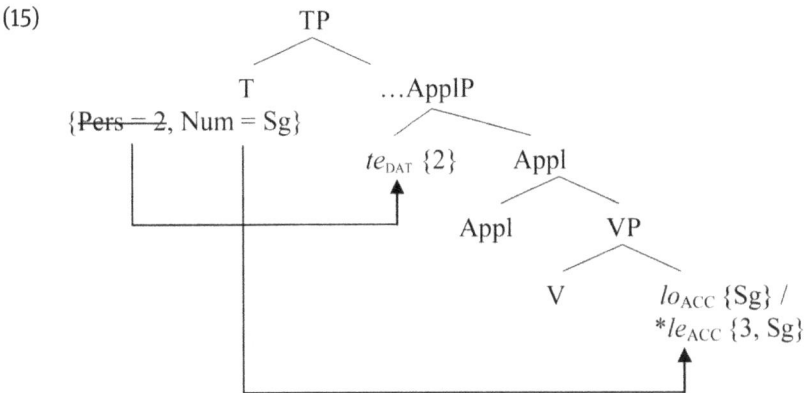

Another well-known example of a language that exhibits an animacy restriction accompanying direct objects in ditransitives is Mohawk (Ormazabal & Romero 2007, Baker 1996). As shown in (16), the theme may be the inanimate *car* but not the animate *girlfriend*.

(16) Ká'sere' / *Káskare' Λ-hi-tshΛry-a'-s-e'
      car   / girlfriend   FUT-1.SG.A/SG.MASC.O-find-BEN-PUNC
      'I will find him a car / girlfriend.'

A less direct example may be provided by the Tanoan language Southern Tiwa, which exhibits strong PCC effects in ditransitives: *DAT$_{1/2/3}$ – ABS$_{1/2}$. Rosen (1990), in her analysis of these restrictions, postulates a referential category *HiSpec* ('high specificity'), which she claims is associated with definite, specific and animate arguments – i.e. the very kinds of high-prominence arguments to which we have attributed a Person feature (see section 1 and Heck & Richards 2010). This now predicts that the agreement-restricted, third-person direct object in a ditransitive should lack the HiSpec property, by virtue of lacking Person. We concomitantly predict that it must be an NP, not a DP. These predictions are easily tested, since non-HiSpec absolutives (personless NPs) must obligatorily incorporate in Southern Tiwa. The agreement-restricted (third-person) absolutive in a ditransitive is thus predicted to obligatorily incorporate, as is borne out:[2]

(17) a. *Ka-'u'u-wia-ban*
 1SG:A:2SG-baby-give.PAST
 'I gave you the baby.'

 b. **'U'ude ka-wia-ban*
 baby 1SG:A:2SG-give.PAST (Rosen 1990: 687)

2.3 Definiteness restriction

Turning now to strong PCC effects in languages of the (5)-type; here we expect to find a definiteness/specificity restriction associated with the second (defective) goal. One candidate for such a language is Akan (Sááh & Ézè 1997, Haspelmath 2007). Given (5), the presence of Person is associated with [+definite]. Therefore, the agreement-restricted (third-person) direct object in a ditransitive is predicted to be subject to a definiteness restriction: it must be indefinite, by virtue of having to lack Person. As shown in (18), PCC effects on definite third-person direct objects are indeed attested in this language.

(18) a. *Ámá màà mè sìká* [Akan]
 Ama gave 1SG money
 'Ama gave me money.'

 b. **Ámá màà mè sìká nó*
 Ama gave 1SG money the
 'Ama gave me the money.'

More generally, we can extend this analysis to the classical definiteness effects found in existential expletive constructions such as English (19). These now emerge as simply the 'pure expletive' counterpart of the Icelandic 'quirky expletive' PCC effect in (13).

---

[2] Recall that the implication drawn out in section 1 is from [+Person] (DP) to animacy, not vice versa (cf. Adger & Harbour 2007). Animate NPs are thus a logical possibility, as the incorporated (NP) *baby* in (17a) now attests. Ormazabal & Romero make the related point (2007: 327, note 30) that there is a distinction to be drawn between 'real', 'biological' animacy and the formal, grammatical notion. The incorporated *baby* in (17a) is simply not formally, grammatically animate (cf. Baker (1996: 316) on the dehumanized, objectified interpretation of incorporated animates in Mohawk).

(19) a. *There arrived a / *the man.*
b. *There arose a / *the problem.*
c. *There appeared a / *the face at the window.*
d. *There was heard an / *the almighty explosion.*
e. *There seems to be a / *the man in the garden.*

The relevant derivation is given in (20). The second goal (here, the associate of the expletive) must be personless, and thus indefinite. The definiteness restriction in (19) can thus be given a formal syntactic explanation along the same lines as (13), i.e. it too reduces to a Case Filter violation, with Case going unvalued under partial Agree with a definite object (i.e. an object with a syntactic Person specification, which fails to be matched by the Number probe that remains after Agree between T and the expletive):

(20) a. *There arose a/*the problem*
b.

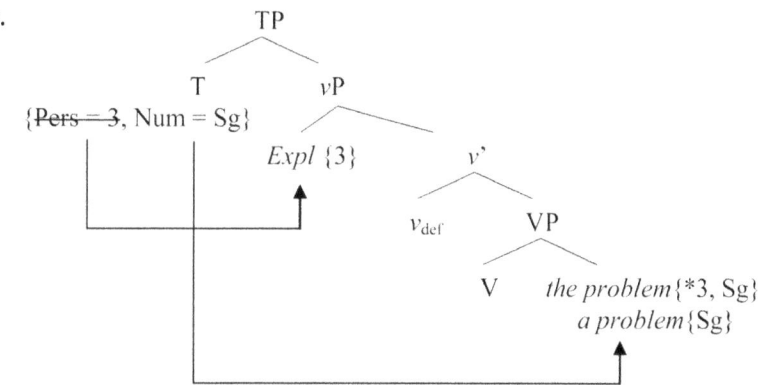

Conversely, weak PCC effects such as the Icelandic PCC in (7)–(9) can be characterized on this approach as a person-sensitive 'definiteness' effect.

A third potential example of a definiteness restriction that emerges under partial Agree with a defective probe is the Russian genitive of negation (GN), which exhibits all the hallmarks of a Person-related case alternation (see also next section).[3] Russian famously exhibits genitive case alternations on underlying internal arguments in the presence of sentential negation (see, e.g., Babby 1980, Pesetsky 1982, Franks 1995, Abels 2002, Harves 2001, 2002, 2004, 2005,

---

[3] For further details of the analysis of the Russian genitive of negation proposed here, see Richards 2008.

and many others), picking out the direct object of transitives (yielding a genitive-accusative alternation) and the 'subject' (i.e. S-argument) of passives and unaccusatives (yielding a genitive-nominative alternation): (21)–(23). It fails to obtain on true external arguments (i.e. the subjects of transitives and unergatives) or lexically/inherently case-marked objects: (24)–(26).

(21) Mal'čik ne čitaet knigi / knigu
 boy not reads book-GEN / book-ACC
 'The boy isn't reading a book / the book.'

(22) a. Otveta ne prišlo
  answer-GEN not came-3NS[4]
  'There was no answer.'

 b. Otvet ne prišel
  answer-NOM not came-3MS
  'The answer didn't come.'

(23) a. Ne bylo polučeno gazet
  not was-3NS received-3NS newspapers-GEN
  'No newspapers were received.' (Brown 1999: 47)

 b. Gazeta ne byla polučena
  newspaper-NOM not was-FS received-FS
  'The newspaper wasn't received.'

(24) *Mal'čika ne čital / čitalo knigu
 boy-GEN not read / read-3NS book-ACC

(25) *Ni odnogo mal'čika ne rabotalo
 not one-GEN boy-GEN not worked-3NS
 'Not a single boy was working.' (Neidle 1988: 75)

(26) Ja ne zvonil moej sestre / *moej sestry
 I not called [my sister]-DAT / [my sister]-GEN
 'I didn't call my sister.' (Brown 1999: 3)

Further, as indicated in the glosses for (21)–(23), GN correlates with an indefinite / nonreferential / existential reading of the GN-marked argument (i.e. the denial

---

[4] 3NS = third-person neuter singular. Similarly, MS = masculine singular, FS = feminine singular, etc.

of its existence), whereas the respective nominative/accusative alternant is associated with definite / referential / presuppositional semantics (the existential presupposition of the argument; cf. "individuation" in terms of Timberlake 1975; see also Pereltsvaig 1999, Harves 2001, Richards 2001 for discussion).

In sum, like Icelandic PCC-restricted nominative objects, GN is an unexpected case form on internal arguments, and like expletive-associate constructions, it is associated with an unexpected interpretive restriction (indefiniteness/ nonreferentiality) – the hallmark of partial-Agree-induced Case Filter effects, as we have seen.

The interpretive restriction is traditionally captured by the claim that GN-marked objects are interpreted within the *scope of negation* (cf. Babby 1980 and many others), as corroborated by quantified objects: GN-marking correlates with narrow scope ($\neg \ldots \forall$) in (27a), and accusative-marking with wide scope ($\forall \ldots \neg$) in (27b). (Examples from Neidle 1988: 39–40.)

(27) a. On   ne   rešil   vsex   zadač
       He   not   solved   [all   problems]-GEN.PL
       'He didn't solve all the problems.'
       [= At least one problem remained unsolved]

   b. On   ne   rešil   vse   zadači
      He   not   solved   [all   problems]-ACC.PL
      'He solved none of the problems.'
      [= No problem was solved]

Given the Probe-Goal system assumed here, Case is valued as part of φ-Agree. Thus a different case form implies a different probe. This means that the presence of negation must affect *v*'s case property by affecting its probe/φ-set. Following Rezac (2004: Chapter 5), we might expect a partially deactivated (i.e. defectivized) probe to value a different case from a full (φ-complete) one. Let us therefore propose the simple GN analysis in (28).

(28) Defective *v* values genitive in Russian

Assuming that negation (which we might take to be a separate head, Neg) can select either a defective or a nondefective (φ-complete) *v* as its complement (since both unaccusative and transitive *v*-types, of course, may appear in negative clauses, i.e. under sentential negation), then selection of the former will now yield a genitive object; selection of the latter will yield an accusative object.

Valuing of genitive case by defective v_{def} as in (28) and the concomitant interpretive restrictions (definiteness effects) now emerge as two sides of the same coin, instantiating the same syntactic scenario as English expletive-associate configurations (albeit with valuation by *v* instead of T):

(29)
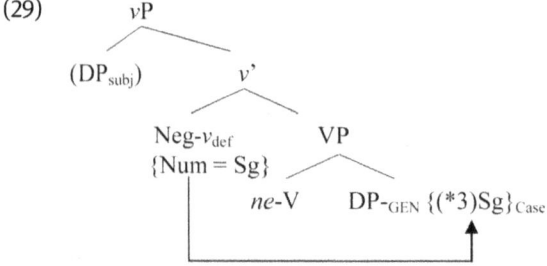

The 'negation-defectivized' *v* head can only Agree partially with the direct object (i.e. for Number only; it lacks Person as a defective head). Therefore, only personless objects (indefinite, bare NPs) can be fully matched and thus Case-valued (deactivated) by this defective GN probe. In effect, genitive emerges as the case of bare nouns, as independently proposed by Pesetsky (2007). Definite, specific (+Person) objects, on the other hand, require a φ-complete probe for convergence – either T or *v*, yielding nominative (cf. (22–23)) and accusative (cf. (21)), respectively. Further, the narrow scope (with respect to negation) of GN-nominals now follows from the Person-Specificity connection (cf. section 1). Weak, narrow-scoping quantifiers like nonspecific indefinites lack Person (i.e. they are NPs are not DPs) and thus may be valued genitive by defective *v*; strong, wide-scoping quantifiers like specific indefinites, however, are [+Person] and thus can only be valued accusative, by nondefective *v*.

In short, GN falls into place as another Case Filter effect in the context of defective Agree.

2.4 Section summary

In this section we have developed an approach to strong PCC effects that makes a strong connection between Person-related agreement restrictions and animacy/definiteness-related interpretive restrictions. Since defectiv(ize)d heads can only value (fully match) a defective argument (i.e. one that lacks a Person specification), defective heads will have the effect of forcing particular semantic/interpretive restrictions on their goals: non-specific indefiniteness/nonreferentiality in (5)-type languages; inanimacy in (4)-type languages. These restrictions reduce to Case Filter effects, in that the unvalued Case feature on a [+Person] nominal, i.e. on animate/definite DPs, cannot be valued by a defective, personless head.

The effects of the Case Filter are thus pervasive and fundamental under defective Agree: they now include Icelandic (and other) PCC effects, Mohawk animacy effects, expletive-associate definiteness effects, and Russian GN.

3 Case alternations (differential case-marking)

As we just saw with Russian GN, Person-agreement (Agree-DP) may result in a different case form from non-Person (e.g. Number-only) agreement (Agree-NP); the latter case forms ('defective cases') are associated with the interpretive restrictions that we argued in the previous section to result from defective (personless) agreement, namely PCC, animacy, and definiteness effects. We turn now to differential case-marking, the morphological consequence of differential Agree (i.e. defective vs. nondefective, complete vs. noncomplete).

Russian GN provides our first example of differential case-marking according to a nominal hierarchy (of the kind in (5) – nominals occurring towards the right of the hierarchy in (5) are 'more likely' to be marked genitive than accusative, as analysed in the previous section). This is a case of differential case-marking by *probe*: a defective probe values a different case form from its nondefective counterpart, as summed up in (30).

(30) *Russian GN*
    [v, +Person]   → accusative
    [v, –Person]   → genitive

The classical kinds of case alternations associated with Silverstein hierarchies of the kind in (1), namely split ergativity of the Pama-Nyungan kind, find an equally principled syntactic source in this model if we make our postsyntactic realization rules sensitive to the (non)defectivity of *goals*. That is, we keep the probe constant and realize different case forms according to which features on that probe are valued by the goal in the syntax (e.g. Person + Number in the case of a DP goal, but only Number in the case of an NP goal). Let us first illustrate with the textbook example of the Dyirbal person-split as presented by Dixon 1994.

As mentioned in section 1, a possibility that arises in the proposed system is that languages may differ as to which position along the scales in (4)/(5) is associated with the presence of a syntactic Person specification: nominals to the left of this point are [+Person] (i.e. DPs). The Dyirbal person split then arises from the association of Person with a higher point on the scale than in (4), e.g.:

(31) [+ Person] | [−Person]
   1/2-pers. pron. > animate (3-pers., pron./noun) > inanimate (3-pers., pron./noun)
   A/S = Ø   A = -ŋgu
   O = -na   S/O = Ø   (cf. Dixon 1994: 86)

We can now formulate simple realization rules, in which the marked combinations of T and a defective personless goal (i.e. a low-prominence A-argument) and *v* and a nondefective, [+Person] goal (i.e. a high-prominence O-argument) receive overt markings in the morphology.

(32) *Realization rules*: (cf. Aldridge 2007)
   a. [T, −Person]   → -ŋgu
   b. [*v*, +Person]   → -na
   c. elsewhere   → Ø

The uniform Ø-form found with intransitives (i.e. all S-arguments, regardless of Person) falls out easily on this approach (unlike many others, including Aissen 1999, 2003), due to the defective status of intransitive *v*, which lacks Person (cf. Chomsky 2000, 2001). Due to the defectivity of the probe in this case, the 'marked' rules (32a) and (32b) can never apply. Any defective, personless goal (i.e. low-prominence, third-person) will be a match for the defective *v* probe and thus be valued at the *v*-level, yielding the feature bundle [*v*, −Person], which only rule (32c) can realize. By contrast, any nondefective, [+Person] goal (i.e. high-prominence, first-/second-person) will only be matched and thus valuable by a nondefective, [+Person] probe, of which T is the only candidate. Valuation of [+Person] S-arguments thus takes place at the T-level, yielding the feature bundle [T, +Person], which again only rule (32c) can realize.

Perhaps more interesting is the split in related Djapu (Aldridge 2007), since this involves animacy as well as person: here, human nominals additionally follow the nom-acc pattern. This follows from the same system as (31) if in this language the [+Person]/[−Person] split occurs lower than in Dyirbal, i.e. between the animate and inanimate nouns, as in (33).

(33)   [+ Person] | [−Person]
   1/2-pers. pron. > animate (3-pers., pron./noun) > inanimate (3-pers., pron./noun)

Whilst more complex, three-way splits have yet to be investigated within this model, and its applicability to aspectual splits of the Hindi kind is unclear, the approach would seem straightforwardly extensible to other well-known alternations (such as Hindi *-ko* marking on animate and definite objects, Spanish 'animate datives', etc.; see also Adger & Harbour 2007 for an analysis of the Kiowa high tone as the realization of a [Participant] specification, in much the same spirit as the above). I leave these questions and extensions for further research.

4 EPP: Optional versus Obligatory

In the previous sections, we have examined the relation between Person and Agree and seen how the variable association of Person with nominals (DPs vs. NPs) can yield agreement restrictions and case alternations. However, as Carnie (2005) remarks in an insightful critique of markedness hierarchies, many languages differentiate between types of objects not through overt morphological marking, but through overt movement. Thus just as animates and definites receive differential morphological marking in languages with case splits, so animates and definites undergo differential syntactic placement (surface order) in other languages.

These optional movement operations, often termed *scrambling* in the literature, are pervasive across the world's languages, and are illustrated for all three argument roles (O, A, S) by the familiar examples in (34)–(36).

(34) Germanic Object Shift/Scrambling *(O-arguments)*

a. Er hat oft **ein Buch** gelesen [German]
he has often a book read
'He often read a (non-specific) book.'

b. Er hat **ein Buch** oft gelesen
he has a book often read
'There's a book that he often read.'

(35) Icelandic 'optional EPP' effects *(A-arguments)*

a. Í fyrra luku **þrír stúdentar** [$_{VP}$ víst öllum prófunum]
last year finished three students apparently all exams-the
'Three [=specific] students apparently finished all the exams last year.'

b. Í fyrra luku [$_{VP}$ víst **þrír stúdentar** öllum prófunum]
last year finished apparently three students all exams-the
'Last year, there were three students [=existential] who finished all the exams.'
(from Bobaljik & Thráinsson 1998)

(36) Mandarin objects *(S-arguments)*
   a. **Kèren** lái-le
      guest come-PFV
      '(The) guests came.'

   b. Lái-le **kèren**
      come-PFV guest
      'There came (some) guests.' (Li 1990: 136)

Crucially, movement to the relevant specifier positions (spec-*v*P for objects, spec-TP for subjects) is in each case associated with particular semantic effects (old, specific, and/or presuppositional readings), i.e. those that we have been associating with the presence of [Person] (cf. section 1).

Carnie (2005) then makes an important point, namely that a complete theory of the role of animacy and definiteness in differential case-marking should also be able to account for the role of these factors in differential ('optional') movement. Theories of hierarchy-based splits in the behaviour of nominals have to take into account more than just overt morphology (case alternations and differential case-marking), then; overt position is the equivalent syntactic phenomenon, with the same conditioning factor, and so a unified approach should be sought.

The question therefore arises as to whether the current analysis has anything to say about the relation between Person and Move (internal Merge), in addition to Person and Agree. Specifically, can it give us any insight into why [+Person] nominals, i.e. DPs, have a higher propensity to shift (undergo Object Shift etc.) than [−Person] ones, i.e. NPs?

In fact, the link between Person and movement is one that has already been noticed and established by a number of authors, including Boeckx (2006) and Sigurðsson (2002, 2007). Thus Boeckx 2006 suggests that EPP-effects (i.e. movement to spec-T) reduces to Person-valuation, on account of a number of special properties that single out Person and Person-agreement from other (φ-)features. These include the fact that Person-agreement is restricted to finite verb-agreement, being absent from participial and adjectival concord (see also Baker 2007); it is absent with in-situ (long-distance) subject-agreement, such as that found in expletive constructions of the kind exemplified in (19); and, as we have also seen, it is implicated in PCC effects. Boeckx proposes that what makes Person special is its anaphoric, context-dependent property, as a result of which it must be licensed by binding, not by Agree per se. This yields the Person-Move (EPP) connection: c-command by the goal is required for Person-binding, with valuer (goal) thus raising to bind the valuee (T).

However, Boeckx's central concern here, as noted, is the traditional, obligatory EPP characteristic of English (i.e. T's filled-specifier requirement). This raises two questions: why must this movement to spec-T be overt if it is only binding at stake (covert binding at LF would seem equally appropriate)? And more pressingly, what about optional EPP languages, those in which T's specifier may or may not be filled, with attendant extra semantic consequences (cf. (35))? Doesn't Person on T need obligatory binding in these languages too?

As the examples in (34)–(36) indicate, the role of Person (its presence versus absence) correlates precisely with the presence versus absence of movement, yielding optionality. This suggests that Person's role as movement trigger is in fact to be found precisely in cases of *optional*, 'discourse-driven' movement of the illustrated kind. By contrast, obligatory EPP of the English, spec-TP kind is precisely where *all* arguments are attracted to T, regardless of featural specification – i.e. both [+Person] DPs and [–Person] NPs alike. Since the latter (NPs) are Number-only on present assumptions (section 1), Number must be involved in obligatory EPP no less than Person.

We can therefore model the difference between optional and obligatory EPP in a maximally simple manner, making use of the generalized EPP-features (movement triggers) that are associated with probes in the Probe-Goal-Agree system of Chomsky 2000, 2001. The difference results from exactly which probe features the EPP-feature is associated with. Optional EPP effects (e.g. Object Shift) result from the association of a probe's EPP-feature with just the Person feature of the probe. Obligatory EPP, on the other hand, is the association of a probe's EPP-feature with the entire probe (Person+Number).

(37) a. Obligatory EPP = [uPerson, uNumber]$_{EPP}$
 b. Optional EPP   = [uPerson]$_{EPP}$

The EPP is thus centrally linked, but only partially reducible to, Person-valuation (since obligatory EPP involves Number-valuation too).

It follows immediately from (37) that English T (= (37a)) attracts all nominals with which T agrees into T's specifier (including expletives; cf. (20)), whereas, for example, Icelandic T (= (37b)) attracts to spec-TP only those nominals with which T's Person feature agrees, i.e. those with a Person specification – animate, definite, [+Person] DPs. Where a probe/head is of the (37b) type, then, definites and animates ([+Person] DPs) shift, whereas indefinites and inanimates ([–Person] NPs) remain in situ.

The simple, binary approach to hierarchy-based case/agreement phenomena proposed in the earlier sections thus extends simply and naturally to hierarchy-based displacement and information-structural phenomena too, a notable advantage if Carnie's (2005) critical observations are correct.

5 Conclusions and extensions

This paper has proposed a simple, binary approach to phenomena that distinguish among arguments according to a Silverstein prominence hierarchy (differential case-marking, differential displacement, agreement restrictions on certain argument types). The syntactic basis of these phenomena has been argued to be a single syntactic feature: Person. This feature is specified only on animate and/or definite arguments (since inanimates and indefinites are always inherently third-person), as part of the D head. Inanimates and indefinites are thus NPs, not DPs. The essential properties of the various hierarchy-based phenomena can be reduced to this single, binary syntactic source: the presence vs. absence of a Person specification (i.e. DP vs. NP). Where Person is absent on a probe, only defective Agree is possible, and this, in turn, yields 'unexpected' (alternative) Case forms correlating with 'unexpected' interpretive restrictions: PCC, animacy and definiteness restrictions. These restrictions all reduce to violations of the Case Filter: [+Person] goals cannot be valued by personless, defective probes.

The key characteristic of the proposed analysis is a nonuniform approach to third-person nominals (cf. Richards 2004, Adger & Harbour 2007): some lack a syntactic Person specification whilst others do not.

(38) *Two kinds of third-person nominals:*
   a. [**Person/Participant**, Number, (Gender)]   = "[+Person]"
   b. [Number, (Gender)]   = "[−Person]"

The claim is that it is third-person nominals of the (38a) kind that are barred in PCC-type environments in direct-object position, i.e. as the second goal of a single probe under a probe-sharing analysis of the PCC (cf. (11)). Then, by associating the syntactic presence of Person with such semantic properties as specificity/definiteness and animacy, we expand the empirical domain of the PCC to cover definiteness and animacy restrictions on direct objects. That is, whenever the presence of Person on a nominal is syntactically prohibited, as is the case for the direct object in PCC environments, the analysis has the empirical consequence in (39).

(39) *Prediction:* Person-related agreement restrictions (PCC) correlate with interpretive restrictions (animacy/definiteness).

The upshot, then, is that the direct object in probe-sharing (PCC) environments must lack Person and thus, if third-person, must be of the (38b) type, entailing interpretations of the inanimate and indefinite kind, i.e. interpretive restrictions as predicted in (39); these are summarized in (40), where DO = direct object and IO = indirect object.

(40) a. *1/2-person DO with IO → strong PCC
 b. *animate DO with IO → animacy-restricted PCC (cf. Mohawk)
 c. *definite DO with IO → definiteness-restricted PCC (cf. Akan)

In languages in which probe-sharing environments arise more generally, requiring even the subject and the object in simple transitive clauses to be licensed by a single probe/head, hierarchy-sensitive PCC-like effects will be even more commonplace, such that multiple [+Person] arguments will be barred in any single clause. The above approach thus readily expands to encompass such phenomena as direction marking (direct/inverse systems) (see Alexiadou & Anagnostopoulou 2006 for such an approach, with proximate arguments analysed as [+Person]) and Tagalog voice marking (Richards 2011).

In terms of the predicted interpretive restrictions on direct objects in probe-sharing (PCC) environments, the typology in (40) may be immediately extended to cover the ban on bound variables in clitic clusters, as discussed by Roca (1992), Ormazabal & Romero (2007), Bhatt & Šimík (2009) and others. As independently proposed in Richards 2012, bound variables must be analysed as [+Person] on unrelated grounds; that is, in our current terms, bound variables are to be included in the class of third-person nominals of the (38a) kind. This in turn predicts that bound variables should also count among the class of PCC-inducing direct objects; that is, they should be barred in PCC contexts. This is indeed borne out, as the above authors have observed, in languages such as Spanish, Catalan, French, Serbo-Croatian, and Czech. Example (41) provides a Spanish illustration.

(41) a. *Mateo$_i$ piensa que lo$_i$ entregaste a la policía.* [Spanish]
 Mateo thinks that him.ACC handed.2SG to the police
 'Mateo$_i$ thinks that you handed him$_i$ over to the police.'

 b. *Mateo$_i$ piensa que se lo$_{*i/j}$ entregaste a la policía.*
 Mateo thinks that 3.DAT him.ACC handed.2SG to the police
 'Mateo$_i$ thinks that you handed him$_{*i/j}$ over to the police.'

This PCC-like "obligatory disjoint reference effect" (Ormazabal and Romero 2007: 328) is dubbed the *Clitic Binding Restriction* by Bhatt & Šimík (2009):

(42) *Clitic Binding Restriction* (CBR)
When an indirect object (IO) clitic and a direct object (DO) clitic co-occur in a cluster, the DO clitic cannot be bound.

Thus, to the interpretive restrictions in (40) we may now add the following:

(43) *bound variable DO with IO → coreference-restricted PCC (CBR)

I leave further extensions to future research.

References

Abels, K. 2002. Expletive (?) Negation. In *Proceedings of FASL 10*.
Adger, D. and D. Harbour. 2007. Syntax and Syncretisms of the Person Case Constraint. *Syntax* 10: 2–37.
Aissen, J. 1999. Markedness and subject choice in Optimality Theory. *Natural Language and Linguistic Theory* 17: 673–711.
Aissen, J. 2003. Differential object marking: Iconicity vs. economy. *Natural Language and Linguistic Theory* 21: 435–483.
Aldridge, E. 2007. Case in Ergative Languages and NP Split-Ergativity. In *Texas Linguistics Society 9: Morphosyntax of Underrepresented Languages*, F. Hoyt et al (eds.).
Alexiadou, A. and E. Anagnostopoulou. 2006. From hierarchies to features: Person splits and direct-inverse alternations. In *Agreement Systems*, C. Boeckx (ed.). Amsterdam: Benjamins.
Anagnostopoulou, E. 2003. *The Syntax of Ditransitives. Evidence from Clitics*. Berlin: de Gruyter.
Anagnostopoulou, E. 2005. Strong and Weak Person Restrictions: a Feature-Checking analysis. In *Clitics and Affixation*, L. Heggie & F. Ordonez (eds). Amsterdam: Benjamins.
Anand, P. and A. Nevins. 2006. The Locus of Ergative Case Assignment: Evidence from Scope. In *Ergativity. Emerging Issues*, A. Johns, D. Massam and J. Ndayiragije (eds.), 3–25. Dordrecht: Springer.
Babby, L. 1980. *Existential Sentences and Negation in Russian*. Ann Arnor: Karoma.
Baker, M. 1996. *The polysynthesis parameter*. Oxford: Oxford University Press.
Baker, M. 2007. *The Syntax of Agreement and Concord*. Cambridge: Cambridge University Press.
Bhatt, R. and R. Šimík. 2009. Variable Binding and the Person-Case Constraint. Handout, paper presented at IATL 25.
Bobaljik, J. and H. Thráinsson. 1998. Two heads aren't always better than one. *Syntax* 1: 37–71.
Boeckx, C. 2000. Quirky Agreement. *Studia Linguistica* 54: 354–80.
Boeckx, C. 2006. The Syntax of Argument Dependencies. Paper presented at Linguistics Colloquium, University of Leipzig, November 2006.
Bonet, E. 1991. Morphology after syntax: Pronominal clitics in Romance. Ph.D. dissertation, MIT.
Bonet, E. 1994. The Person-Case Constraint: a morphological approach. In *The morphosyntax connection* (MITWPL 22), H. Harley and C. Phillips (eds.), 33–52.

Brown, J., K. Koch and M. Wiltschko. 2004. The Person Hierarchy: Primitive or Epiphenomenal? Evidence from Halkomelem Salish. In *Proceedings of NELS 34* (ROA 645).
Brown, S. 1999. *The Syntax of Negation in Russian: A Minimalist Approach*. Stanford: CSLI.
Carnie, A. 2005. Some remarks on markedness hierarchies: A reply to Aissen 1999 and 2003. *Coyote Working Papers in Linguistics* 14.
Chomsky, N. 2000. Minimalist Inquiries: the Framework. In *Step by step*, R. Martin, D. Michaels, and J. Uriagereka (eds), 89–156. Cambridge, MA: MIT Press.
Chomsky, N. 2001. Derivation by Phase. In *Ken Hale: A Life in Language*, M. Kenstowicz (ed.), 1–52. Cambridge, MA: MIT Press.
Chomsky, N. 2004. Beyond Explanatory Adequacy. In *Structures and Beyond. The Cartography of Syntactic Structures* (Vol. 3), A. Belletti (ed.), 104–131. Oxford: Oxford University Press.
Chomsky, N. 2007. Approaching UG from below. In *Interfaces + Recursion = Language? Chomsky's Minimalism and the View from Syntax-Semantics*, U. Sauerland & H.-M. Gärtner (eds.), 1–30. Berlin: Mouton de Gruyter.
Chomsky, N. 2008. On Phases. In *Foundational Issues in Linguistic Theory*, R. Freidin, C. P. Otero and M.-L. Zubizarreta (eds.), 133–166. Cambridge, MA: MIT Press.
Comrie, B. 1989. *Language universals and language typology*. Chicago: University of Chicago Press.
Déchaine, R-M. and M. Wiltschko. 2002. Decomposing Pronouns. *Linguistic Inquiry* 33: 409–442.
Dixon, R. 1994. *Ergativity*. Cambridge: Cambridge University Press.
Franks, S. 1995. *Parameters of Slavic Morphosyntax*. New York: Oxford University Press.
Harves, S. 2001. Genitive of negation and the syntax of scope. In *Proceedings of ConSOLE IX*.
Harves, S. 2002. Where have all the *Phases* gone? (Non-)defective categories and Case alternations in Russian. In *Proceedings of FASL 10*.
Harves, S. 2004. Unaccusativity and non-agreement in Russian. Handout: Paper presented at University of Cambridge.
Harves, S. 2005. Non-agreement, Unaccusativity, and the External Argument Constraint. Paper presented at FASL 14, May 2005.
Haspelmath, M. 2007. Ditransitive construction alternations: data and ideas. Handout (paper presented at Workshop on Grammar and Processing of Verbal Arguments, Leipzig, April 2007).
Heck, F. and M. Richards. 2010. A probe-goal approach to agreement and incorporation restrictions in Southern Tiwa. *Natural Language and Linguistic Theory* 28: 681–721.
Kawashima, R., and H. Kitahara. 2004. Phonological Content and Syntactic Visibility. In *Triggers*, A. Breitbarth and H. van Riemsdijk (eds), 205–230. Berlin: de Gruyter.
Kayne, R. 2000. *Parameters and Universals*. Oxford: Oxford University Press.
Keine, S. and G. Müller. 2015. Differential argument encoding by impoverishment. This volume.
Neidle, C. 1988. *The Role of Case in Russian Syntax*. Dordrecht: Kluwer.
Nevins, A. 2004. Derivations without the Activity Condition. In *Proceedings of the EPP/Phase Workshop* (MITWPL), M. McGinnis & N. Richards. (eds.).
Nevins, A. 2007. The Representation of Third Person and its Consequences for Person-Case Effects. *Natural Language and Linguistic Theory* 25: 273–313.
Ormazabal, J. and J. Romero. 2007. The Object Agreement Constraint. *Natural Language and Linguistic Theory* 25: 315–347.
Pereltsvaig, A. 1999. The Genitive of Negation and Aspect in Russian. *McGill Working Papers in Linguistics* 14: 111–40.

Pesetsky, D. 1982. Paths and Categories. Ph.D. dissertation, MIT.
Pesetsky, D. 2007. Russian case morphology and the syntactic categories. Paper presented at the Workshop on Morphology and Argument Encoding, Harvard, September 2007.
Rezac, M. 2004. Elements of Cyclic Syntax: Agree and Merge. Ph.D. dissertation, University of Toronto.
Richards, M. 2001. Russian Genitives Laid Bare: An Alternative Approach to Case Alternations. M.A. dissertation, University College London.
Richards, M. 2004. Object Shift and Scrambling in North and West Germanic: A Case Study in Symmetrical Syntax. Ph.D. dissertation, University of Cambridge.
Richards, M. 2008. Quirky Expletives. In *Agreement Restrictions*, R. d'Alessandro, G. Hrafnbjargarson, and S. Fischer (eds.), 181–213. Berlin: Mouton de Gruyter.
Richards, M. 2011. On A-type Discourse-Configurationality in Tagalog: Person prominence, Case-Agree and Case-Inheritance. Ms., Universität Leipzig.
Richards, M. 2012. Reappraising Copy Raising. Ms., Goethe-Univerität Frankfurt.
Richardson, K. 2005. Why Quirky Case is not so Quirky in Russian. Paper presented at LingSoc, University of Cambridge.
Roca, F. 1992. On the licensing of pronominal clitics: The properties of object clitics in Spanish and Catalan. Master's thesis, Universitat Autònoma de Barcelona.
Rosen, C. 1990. Rethinking Southern Tiwa: The geometry of a triple-agreement language. *Language* 66: 669–713.
Sáàh, K. and É. Ézè. 1997. Double objects in Àkán and Ìgbo. In *Object Positions in Benue-Kwa*, R-M. Déchaine & V. Manfredi (eds.), 139–151. The Hague: Academic Graphics.
Sigurðsson, H. 1996. Icelandic Finite Verb Agreement. *Working Papers in Scandinavian Syntax* 57: 1–46.
Sigurðsson, H. 2001. Case: abstract vs. morphological. *Working Papers in Scandinavian Syntax* 64: 103–51.
Sigurðsson, H. 2007. On EPP effects. Ms., University of Lund.
Silverstein, M. 1976. Hierarchy of features and ergativity. In *Grammatical Categories in Australian Languages*, R. Dixon (ed.), 112–171. Canberra: Australian Institute of Aboriginal Studies.
Taraldsen, K. 1995. On agreement and nominative objects in Icelandic. In *Studies in Comparative Germanic Syntax*, H. Haider, S. Olsen, and S. Vikner (eds.), 307–27. Dordrecht: Kluwer.
Timberlake, A. 1975. Hierarchies in the Genitive of Negation. In *Case in Slavic*, 1986, R. Brecht and J. Levine (eds.), 338–360. Columbus: Slavica.

Petr Biskup, Gerhild Zybatow
8 Prefixes, Scales and Grammatical Theory[1]

1 Introduction

This paper is concerned with the status of prominence scales in grammatical theory. It investigates the interaction of prefixation and the theta role scale and the case scale in Russian and Czech. We make a difference between particular scales – such as the case scale or the theta role scale – and a complex scale, which is composed of the two particular scales. We argue that the theta role scale and the case scale can be taken to be a reflection of syntactic structure and that they are determined by syntactico-semantic properties of the clause structure. The complex scale is a more interesting object. This scale is independent of syntactic structure and represents alignments of members of the theta role scale with members of the case scale. Although both types of scales are not necessary for deriving particular sentences, it is interesting that the complex scale – which itself is independent of the syntax – can predict the grammatical/ markedness status of particular sentences. Thus, the complex scale, whose abstractions seem to express more general patterns, can also have a certain explanatory power in language. Concretely, we argue that the form of the complex scale of a particular sentence parallels grammatical principles and operations. There is a correlation between the type of the complex scale tree, syntactic operations and the morphological marking/grammatical status of the sentence. We show that only certain types of crossings in the complex scale tree, which correspond to certain types of syntactic processes, are allowed in the grammar.

2 Data

In this section, we introduce the core data. We investigate case and theta role properties of transitive and intransitive predicates and their interaction with prefixes.

---

[1] We would like to thank the audience at the *Workshop on Scales* (Leipzig, 2008) for valuable comments. Particular thanks go to Marc Richards for his insightful comments and helpful suggestions.

2.1 Intransitive verbs

2.1.1 Unprefixed intransitive verbs

We begin with unprefixed intransitive verbs. The argument of intransitive verbs typically bears nominative case, as shown in the Czech examples below. This holds for both unergative verbs, as in (1), and unaccusative verbs, as in (2). The (b) examples demonstrate that the single argument cannot bear the accusative marker. There are only a few unaccusative verbs assigning accusative case in Czech.

(1) a. *Pavel   pracuje.*
       Pavel.NOM works
       'Pavel is working.'
       'Pavel works.'

   b. **Pavl-a   pracuje.*
       Pavel-ACC works

(2) a. *Oper-a   hoří.*
       opera-NOM burns
       'The opera is burning.'
       'The opera burns.'

   b. **Oper-u   hoří.*
       opera-ACC burns

There are also special classes of verbs, such as unaccusative psych verbs, which take a nominative object (patient), as shown in the Czech example (3). Example (3b) demonstrates that the patient argument cannot be assigned accusative case. (3c) shows the same for the experiencer argument and (3d) shows that if both arguments are realized as prepositional phrases, the verb bears default agreement.[2]

(3) a. *Pavl-ovi   se   líbil-a   ta   nová   pohádk-a.*
       Pavel-DAT self liked-SG.F   the   new   story-SG.F.NOM
       'Pavel enjoyed the new story.'

---

[2] We assume that dative arguments are prepositional phrases, hence *Pavlovi* in (3) is a prepositional phrase with a covert preposition (cf. Emonds 2007b: chapter 5, 2007a).

b. *Pavl-ovi   se   líbil-a   tu   novou   pohádk-u.
    Pavel-DAT self liked-SG.F the new   story-SG.F.ACC

c. *Pavl-a   se   líbil-a   ta   nová   pohádk-a.
    Pavel-ACC self liked-SG.F the new   story-SG.F.NOM

d. Pavl-ovi   se   líbil-o   v   Praze.
    Pavel-DAT self liked-SG.N in   Prague
    'Pavel enjoyed Prague.'

Another verbal class with a less common case pattern is the class of experiencer verbs taking a nominative patient and an accusative experiencer, as illustrated in the Czech example (4a). Example (4b) shows that cases on the arguments cannot be switched: the experiencer cannot receive nominative and the patient accusative. (4c) then shows that in addition to the nonstructural accusative on *Pavel*, the predicate cannot take another accusative argument.

(4) a. Pavl-a   bavil-a   ta   nová   pohádk-a.
         Pavel-ACC interested-SG.F the new   story-SG.F.NOM
         'Pavel was interested in/enjoyed the new story.'

   b. *Pavel   bavil   tu   novou   pohádk-u.
         Pavel.NOM interested.SG.M the new   story-SG.F.ACC

   c. *Pavl-a   bavil-o   tu   novou   pohádk-u.
         Pavel-ACC interested-SG.N the new   story-SG.F.ACC

2.1.2 Prefixed intransitive verbs

In this section, we investigate the question of what happens if a prefix is attached to intransitive verbs. As illustrated in the Russian example (5a), the stative predicate *mërz* 'froze' cannot be combined with the resultative prepositional phrase *v ajsberg* 'in iceberg'. However, the prefix *v-* attached to the verb can license the directional prepositional phrase, as shown in (5b).

(5) a. On   mërz   (*v   ajsberg).
         he.NOM froze   in   iceberg.ACC

   b. On   v-mërz   v   ajsberg.
         he.NOM in-froze   in   iceberg.ACC
         'He froze in the/a iceberg.'

In cases where a directional prepositional phrase can be combined with an unprefixed verb, prefixation brings about the result implication. In the Russian example (6a), there is an imperfective paradox; although there is an endpoint present in the sentence, it does not mean that the referent of *he* reached Moscow. In contrast, in (6b) the prefix *v-* brings about the telic type of perfectivity and the sentence means that the referent of *he* reached Moscow.

(6) a. *On echal v Moskv-u.*
    he.NOM drove in Moscow-ACC
    'He was driving to Moscow.'

  b. *On v"echal v Moskv-u.*
    he.NOM in-drove in Moscow-ACC
    'He drove to Moscow.'

Finally, the following Russian example shows that prefixes can also license an accusative object. In (7b) the verb *spal* 'slept' with the completive prefix *do-* 'to' can be combined with the accusative object *noč* 'night', in contrast to the unprefixed verb in (7a).[3]

(7) a. *On spal (*noč).*
    he.NOM slept night.ACC

  b. *On do-spal noč.*
    he.NOM to-slept night.ACC
    'He slept till the end of the night.'

We will now turn to transitive verbs. Let us begin with unprefixed predicates.

2.2 Transitive verbs

2.2.1 Unprefixed transitive verbs

Transitive verbs take a nominative and an accusative argument. The nominative case occurs on the agent argument and the accusative case on the patient argument, as demonstrated in the Czech example (8a). Example (8b) shows that the reversed alignment is not possible. A nominative patient can only occur in passive constructions with the instrumental agent, as illustrated in (8c).

---

[3] If the universal modifier *vsju* 'all' is added to the noun, (7a) with *noč* becomes grammatical.

(8) a. *Pavel   bil   Jirk-u.*
      Pavel.NOM beat Jirka-ACC
      'Pavel beat Jirka.'

   b. *Pavel   bil   Jirk-u.*
      Pavel.NOM beat Jirka-ACC
      *'Jirka beat Pavel.'

   c. *Pavel   byl   bit   Jirk-ou.*
      Pavel.NOM was beaten Jirka-INSTR
      'Pavel was beaten by Jirka.'

2.2.2 Prefixed transitive verbs

Prefixes attached to transitive verbs either just induce perfectivity or they also add a prepositional phrase; compare the Russian examples (9a,b,c). Example (9c) demonstrates that the nominative marker typically occurs on the agent argument, the accusative marker on the patient and the oblique marker on the goal. As shown in example (9d), the reversed alignment of the patient argument and the goal argument is not possible.

(9) a. *On   pisal   svoe   imja.*
      he.NOM wrote self name.ACC
      'He was writing his name.'

   b. **On   v-pisal   svoe   imja.*
      he.NOM in-wrote self name.ACC

   c. *On   v-pisal   svoe   imja   v   knig-u   počëta.*
      he.NOM in-wrote self name.ACC in book-ACC of honor
      'He wrote his name in the book of honor.'

   d. **On   v-pisal   v   imja   knig-u   počëta.*
      he.NOM in-wrote in name.ACC book-ACC of honour

3 Scales

3.1 Scales generally

Scales can be treated as hierarchies (certain approaches even use the term *hierarchy* instead of *scale*) and hierarchies in turn can be treated as a certain type of graph. To make clear that particular scales are just an abstraction of the more complex syntactic structure containing the appropriate scale members (cf. 3.2.), we will represent them as trees in this paper, connected acyclic graphs, as schematized in (10). Looking at (10), it is obvious that scales have a structure. Consequently, relations between scale members can be based on structural relations like c-command.

(10)

Let us now turn to particular prominence scales. We follow the standard proposals (for the case scale see e.g. Bobaljik (2008b) and for the theta role scale see The Research Proposal of FG 742 (2005)), as shown in (11a) and (11b).[4] (11a) means that nominative case is more prominent than accusative case and that accusative in turn is more prominent than dative or oblique case. Similarly, (11b) states that the agent theta role is more prominent than the patient theta role, which in turn is more prominent than the goal theta role.

(11) Prominence scales
    a. Case scale: nominative > accusative > dative/oblique
    b. Theta role scale: agent > patient > goal

Combining the tree of c-command relations in (10) with the scales in (11) results in (12a) and (12b). The nominative case, since it is the most prominent scale member, c-commands the accusative case and the dative or oblique case and the accusative case in turn c-commands the dative or oblique case. In a parallel fashion, the agent theta role, which is the most prominent one, c-commands the patient theta role and the goal theta role, and the patient theta role c-commands the goal theta role.

---

[4] Consider also the more general Case Realization Hierarchy (i) from Bobaljik (2008a, 2008b) and similarly Bittner and Hale (1996) and Marantz (2000). For our purposes, the case scale in (11a) is sufficient.

(i) unmarked case > dependent case > lexical case

(12) a.

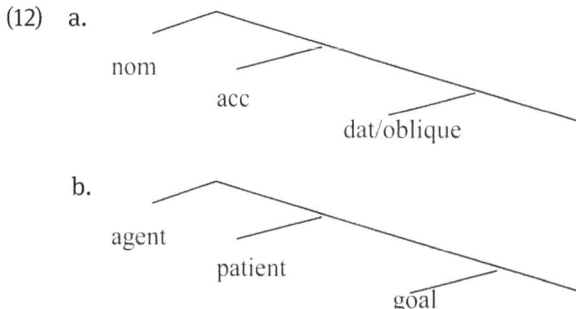

b.

To get more interesting theoretical statements, we put together the particular scales (12a) and (12b). If we keep the c-command relations between scale members and map members of one scale onto members of the other scale, we receive the complex scale tree (13), as shown below. This complex scale tree in fact represents the unmarked harmonic alignment of six particular scale members.[5]

(13)

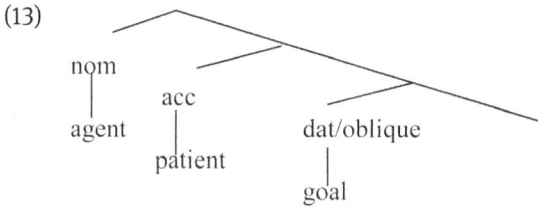

The generalization is that the unmarked alignment is a mapping between scale trees without crossing. To give a few examples of what we mean by a crossing, consider (14). In (14a) there is a one-way crossing, in (14b) a two-way crossing and in (14c) a two-way crossing, which in addition is reciprocal; we will see other types of complex scale trees in subsequent sections. A marked alignment then is mapping between scale trees with a crossing.[6]

(14) a. One-way crossing

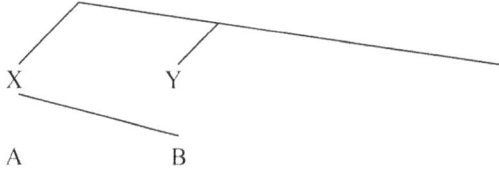

---

[5] According to Aissen (2003: 441), harmonic alignment applies to pairs of scales and aligns each element on one with each element on the other and then generates constraint subhierarchies expressing the relative markedness of each such association.

[6] Complex scale trees with crossings do not always satisfy the criteria for a tree but since nothing hinges on it here, we will call them trees as well.

b. Two-way crossing

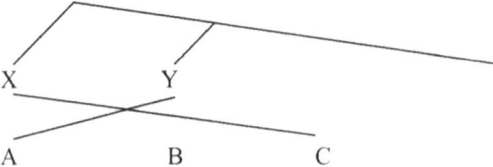

c. Two-way reciprocal crossing

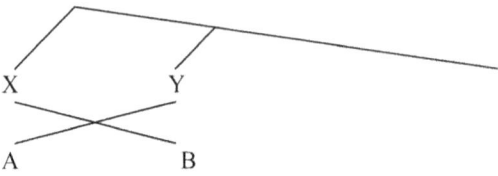

In the complex scale tree, the degree of markedness can also be determined by the c-command relations. The patient theta role c-commands the goal theta role in the complex scale tree; therefore a goal with the nominative marker is more marked than a patient with the nominative marker (and a patient with the nominative case would be more marked than an agent), as demonstrated in (15) also by the crossings of different lengths.

(15)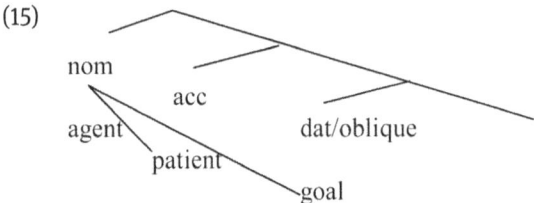

Markedness or crossings can go in both directions. Upwards, for instance, in the case of passivization in Czech, where the patient bears nominative, or downwards, like in the case of the antipassive voice in West Greenlandic, where the patient argument gets instrumental. It is important to note that this says nothing about the direction of operations in syntactic trees.

Languages generally do not have to reflect whole scales. Consider, for instance, case marking in ergative languages versus non-ergative languages. Languages also do not have to use whole scales in every sentence, as is obvious from cases like intransitive sentences.

3.2 Scales in a minimalist analysis

In this section, we deal with particular scales and show that both the theta role scale and the case scale are a reflection of the syntactic structure. Thus, they are determined by syntactico-semantic properties of the clause structure. The syntactic tree in (16) shows that both prominence scales in fact emerge from the syntactic structure and that c-command relations between members of particular scales are preserved. We see that the theta role scale is sandwiched inside the case scale. This is a consequence of the fact that structural cases are structurally higher than nonstructural cases (leaving aside adjunction). Specifically, structural cases are assigned or valued in the functional domain by the tense head and the aspectual head through the operation Agree and languages may differ with respect to whether or not the agreeing arguments move to the specifier position of the appropriate projection.[7] And nonstructural cases are assigned in the theta domain (vP) by the verb or prepositions through the operation External Merge.[8] One observes that only the goal argument and the dative or oblique case are mapped structurally, with unmarked harmonic alignment. The reason for this is that in the case of prepositional cases case goes hand in hand with the theta role.

(16)

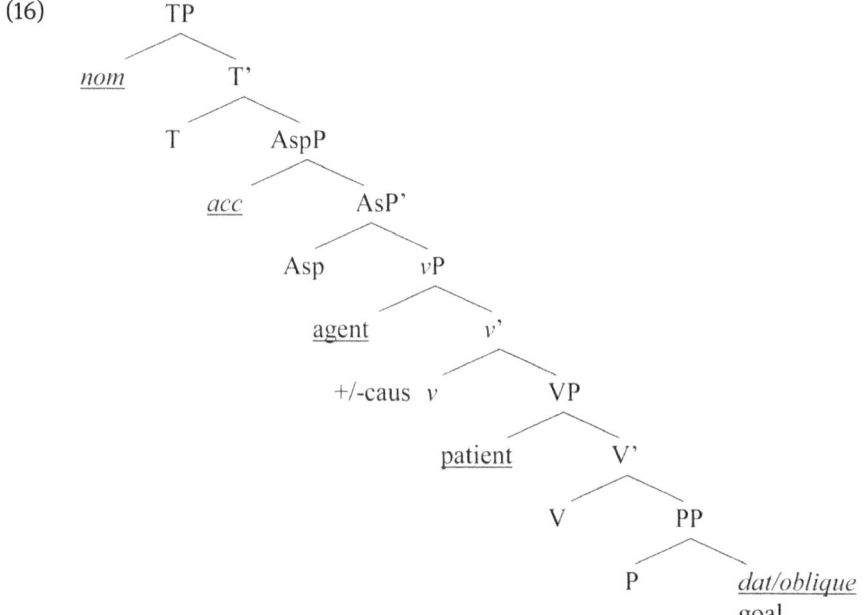

---

[7] For arguments supporting the claim that structural accusative is assigned in AspP in Russian and Czech, see Biskup (2009).

[8] Compare Babby's (1987) Syntactic Case Hierarchy (i) and Franks's (1995) Case Hierarchy (ii):

(i) Lexical Case takes precedence over a Configurational Case.
(ii) a. the +Oblique Cases are assigned at D-Structure,
  b. the −Oblique Cases are assigned at S-Structure.

The two prominence scales are (at least partially) determined by semantic properties of the syntactic structure. It is a well-known fact that there is a connection between structural cases and tense and aspect (e.g. Pesetsky and Torrego 2004). It has also been argued that tense and aspect relate two times (e.g. Klein 1995, Demirdache and Uribe-Etxebarria 1997). The head T can be treated as a dyadic operator that takes the reference time, which is related to AspP, and the speech time, and similarly the head Asp takes the event time, which is anchored in the verbal domain, and the reference time. Thus, T scopes over Asp and Asp over (the decomposed) *v*P. Therefore, nominative, which is connected to T, c-commands – is more prominent than – accusative, which is assigned in AspP. Accusative case then is more prominent than dative and oblique case, which are assigned in *v*P.

Parallel reasoning applies to the theta role scale. We assume that the event structure, that is *v*P, is decomposed. The (non-)causative *v* scopes over the process or stative V and V scopes over PP. Evidence for the event decomposition and ordering of subevents comes, for instance, from the contrast between the restitutive and the repetitive reading of the scope-taking adverb *again*. Von Stechow (1996) shows that in the restitutive reading, in contrast to the repetitive reading, *again* only scopes over VP (and PP) to the exclusion of *v*P. If theta roles are assigned configurationally as a result of DP-Merger (see Hale and Keyser 1993 and Ramchand 2008), then the agent theta role in Spec,*v*P c-commands – is more prominent than – the patient theta role in Spec,VP and the patient theta role in turn is more prominent than the goal theta role in PP.

4 Scales and derivations

In this section, we investigate several syntactic derivations and complex scale trees. Although the complex scale tree is not part of the syntactic derivation and is not necessary for deriving particular sentences, its form corresponds to certain syntactic processes and the grammatical/markedness status of the sentence.

4.1 Unprefixed intransitive verbs

We saw in section 2 that the single argument of intransitive verbs is typically realized as nominative. What is the reason for this? A possible answer is that nominative is the most prominent case. Let us look at how this proposal works.

Firstly, we need to introduce some basic properties of our theoretical framework. Pesetsky and Torrego (2004, 2006) argue that there is a relation between nominative and tense properties of the sentence and between accusative and aspectual properties and propose that structural case is an unvalued Tense feature on the nominal head N or D and that it is valued by head T and T_0 (the aspectual head). Biskup (2007, 2009) extends their proposal and suggests that all cases – not only structural cases – are an unvalued Tense feature on the nominal head D. This extension and the extension of φ-features to P heads allows us to use the Tense feature on P in the case assigning process and also to treat all cases uniformly with respect to the features participating in the case assigning relation. As shown in (17), the three heads P, T and Asp bear a valued Tense feature and unvalued φ-features at a certain stage of the derivation and agree with a DP, which gets case as a consequence of the Agree operation.[9]

(17) P: val T-f, unval φ-fs
     T: val T-f, unval φ-fs   Agree
     Asp: val T-f, unval φ-fs   ↔   DP: unval T-f, val φ-fs

Biskup (2009) proposes that the Tense feature on DPs, that is cases, can be revalued. This means that a DP can get multiple cases, but since morphological principles of Russian and Czech do not allow multiple overt case markers on one element, they are not visible, in contrast to languages like Japanese, Kayardild, Korean or Lardil, which allow more case markers.[10] Therefore, in Russian and Czech, the structurally highest Tense value always appears on the particular DP. Let us now look at unprefixed unergative verbs. The derivation of (1a), repeated here as (18a), looks like (18b).

(18) a. *Pavel   pracuje.*
         Pavel.NOM works
         'Pavel is working.'
         'Pavel works.'

---

9 The originally unvalued Tense feature on Asp is valued in the course of the derivation. Depending on whether or not a preposition (prepositions bear a valued Tense feature) incorporates into the verb, the verb emerges as perfective (prefixed) or as imperfective (unprefixed).
10 This means that we do not assume the Activity Condition. Data relying on the Activity Condition then need an alternative explanation.

b.

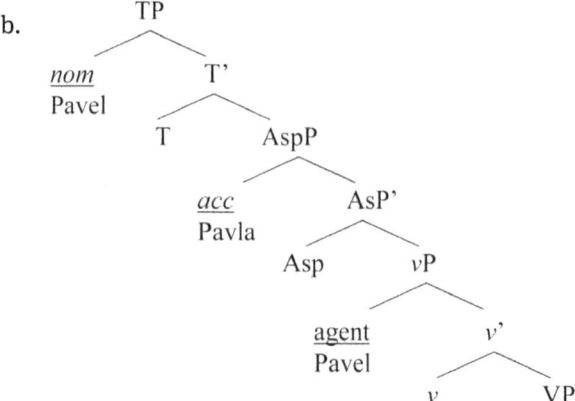

The agent *Pavel*, which is merged in Spec,vP, first agrees with the aspectual head and gets accusative. Given the principle of Full Interpretation in (19), which states that interfaces must contain only material that is interpretable (valued), unvalued φ-features on the head T must also be valued.

(19) Full Interpretation (Chomsky 1995: 27)
... there can be no superfluous symbols in representations (the principle of Full Interpretation, FI)...

Thus, *Pavel* also agrees with the head T and its Tense value (case) is revalued. Consequently, it is spelled out with the nominative marker.[11] Concerning the complex scale tree, we receive a one-way type of crossing, as illustrated in (20). For expository reasons, we put the particular exponents of the case scale and the theta role scale into the complex scale tree (in brackets). Note that complex scale trees do not have to say anything about whether or not the particular exponents are identical elements; they are just meant to represent alignments between cases and theta roles.

(20) Complex scale tree of (18a)

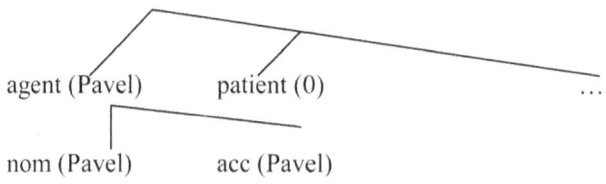

---

[11] It is not important here whether or not *Pavel* agrees with the heads Asp and T in situ. We put *Pavel* in Spec,AspP and Spec,TP just to show that it is marked with accusative and nominative case.

The tree demonstrates that the agent (*Pavel*) is marked with accusative case, which is usually unmarkedly aligned with the patient theta role; consider (13) again. It generally holds – not only for the language system – that a marked value or status is formally expressed (see e.g. Croft 1993 for a language typological point of view). However, there is no special verbal morphology (as e.g. in the case of passives) in (18a) and the argument is marked with the most unmarked case, namely, nominative. The reason for this is that there is no patient theta role in (18a). Thus, the morphologically unmarked alignment is a result of lacking the patient theta role, the principle of Full Interpretation and the case revaluation.

In the case of unprefixed unaccusative verbs, it works similarly. In (2a), which is repeated here as (21), patient *opera* bearing the unvalued Tense feature and valued φ-features first agrees with the head Asp, which results in the accusative Tense value on *opera*, and then it agrees with the head T and gets the nominative Tense value. Since this is the last (highest) Tense value, *opera* is spelled out with the nominative marker.

(21) *Oper-a   hoří.*
      opera-NOM burns
      'The opera is burning.'
      'The opera burns.'

In the complex scale tree (22), there is again a one-way crossing, now going from the patient theta role to nominative; compare (22) with the complex scale tree in (20). Similarly to the unergative example above, there is no special morphological marking on the elements in (21). The reason for this is that there is no agent theta role, as illustrated in (22).

(22) Complex scale tree of (21)

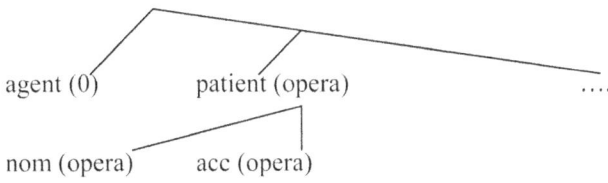

Let us now move to experiencer unaccusative verbs. Given the Binding Principle A asymmetries between the patient and the experiencer argument, we analyze example (23a)=(3a) as shown in (23b).[12]

(23) a. *Pavl-ovi   se   líbil-a   ta   nová   pohádk-a.*
Pavel-DAT   self   liked-SG.F   the   new   story-SG.F.NOM
'Pavel enjoyed the new story.'

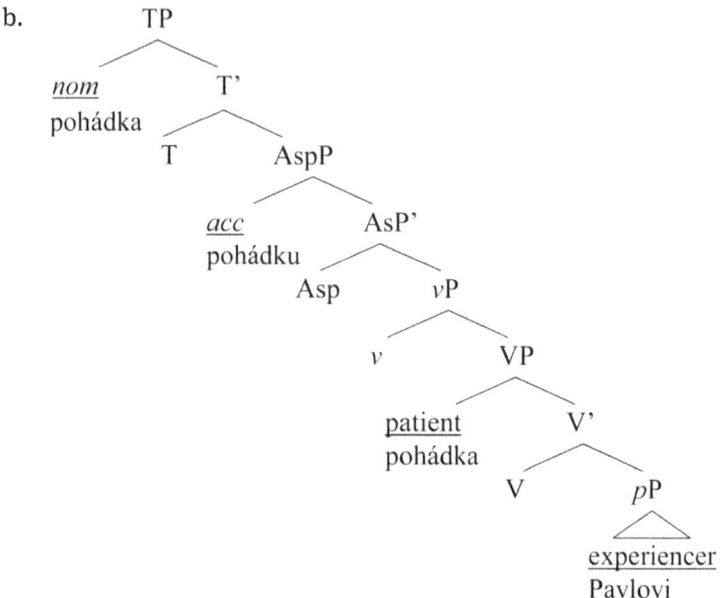

---

[12] The following example shows that the patient argument can bind into the dative experiencer (ia) and that in contrast the experiencer cannot bind into the patient (ib), which should be possible if the patient were generated below the experiencer. The control example (ic) shows that the ungrammaticality of (ib) is not due to the fact that the possessive reflexive is contained in the nominative argument.

(i) a. *Ten nový student   se   líbí   své   profesorce.*
the   new   student.M.NOM   self   likes   self.F.DAT   professor.F.DAT
'The professor likes his new student.'

b. **Svůj   student   se   líbí   profesorce.*
self.M.NOM   student.M.NOM   self   likes   professor.F.DAT

c. *Pavel   také   vystupuje   jako   svůj   žalobce.*
Pavel.M.NOM   also   acts   as   self.M.NOM   accuser.M.NOM
'Pavel also acts as the accuser of himself.'

Given the principle of Full Interpretation, unvalued φ-features on the heads Asp and T must be valued. This job is done by the patient argument *pohádka*. If all *v*Ps are phases (that is, unaccusative *v*Ps too) as argued by Legate (2003), then the patient argument must raise to the edge of *v*P. Then it agrees with the head Asp and T, which results in accusative and nominative case, as demonstrated in (23b). The final word order of (23a) is achieved by the topicalization movement of *Pavlovi*. Note that *Pavlovi* precedes the Wackernagel clitic *se*, which is standardly assumed to occur in a head position in the C domain.

It cannot be the dative argument *Pavlovi* that values unvalued φ-features on the heads Asp and T. We assume that nonstructural cases like the dative here are prepositional phrases, hence *Pavlovi* in (23a) is a prepositional phrase with a covert preposition, like in the case of free datives. Biskup (2009) proposes that the Tense value of the prepositional complement cannot be revalued because prepositional phrases are phases, that is, *p*Ps (see Abels 2003, who argues that prepositional phrases in Russian and other Slavic languages are phases). Since *Pavlovi* is trapped in the phase complement, then, given the Phase Impenetrability Condition (Chomsky 2000) in (24), it cannot enter into an Agree relation with φ-features on Asp and T and its dative case cannot be revalued as accusative or nominative.

(24) Phase Impenetrability Condition (Chomsky 2000: 108)
 In phase α with head H, the domain of H is not accessible to operations outside α; only H and its edge are accessible to such operations.

The phase status of the prepositional phrase, however, is not the only relevant factor since there are phases that allow extraction out of their complement, like *v*P phases. Another relevant factor is the ability of the appropriate argument to escape the phase. In this respect, we follow Biskup (2009) and Biskup and Putnam (2012), who propose that it is a certain type of the Tense feature that is responsible for the blocking of extraction. For instance, Biskup and Putnam (2012) propose that the prepositional complement cannot be extracted because of the A-over-A principle applied to categories with the bounded Tense feature. More concretely, since the head P bears a Tense feature with the value bounded and projects the category PP and this category includes the prepositional complement whose Tense feature has been valued as bounded, the complement cannot move across PP.

The fact that there is a default agreement on the predicate in (3d), repeated for convenience as (25), shows that prepositional complements (*Pavlovi* and *Praze*) indeed are not accessible for Asp and T and the operation Agree.[13]

(25) Pavl-ovi   se   líbil-o   v   Praze.
      Pavel-DAT   self   liked-SG.N   in   Prague
      'Pavel enjoyed Prague.'

The complex scale tree of (23a) is shown in (26). There is an unaccusative one-way crossing combined with the unmarked alignment of the experiencer with dative. Since the harmonic alignment of the experiencer theta role with the dative case is unmarked and there is no agent theta role – as in the case of the unaccusative complex scale tree – there is no reason for a special morphological marking (*se* in the predicate *líbit se* does not represent a special morphological marking because *líbit* cannot occur by itself).

(26) Complex scale tree of (23a)

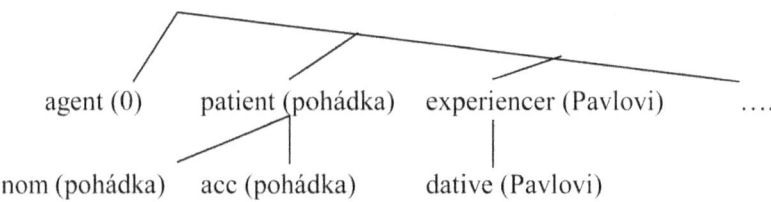

From the syntactic point of view, the morphologically unmarked alignment is a result of lacking the agent theta role, the principle of Full Interpretation and the impossibility of the revaluation of case on the prepositional complement.

In section 1 we saw that there is also a special class of experiencer verbs taking a nominative patient and an accusative experiencer. These verbs can be analyzed in the same way as the dative experiencer verbs. As to example (27a)=

---

[13] Dative experiencer constructions like (i), we analyze in the way that probes on the head Asp and T are valued by the postcopular adverbial, which in fact is a nominative DP, as argued by Caha and Medová (2009).

(i) Mně   je   zim-a   /   tepl-o.
     I.DAT is   coldness-SG.F.NOM   warmth-SG.N.NOM
     'I am cold/warm.'

(4a), we just put *Pavla* in the tree in (23b) instead of *Pavlovi* and change the predicate. As above, the experiencer argument is trapped in the phase complement of the covert preposition, hence its nonstructural accusative case cannot be revalued by nominative; therefore example (27b)=(4b) is ungrammatical.[14] The example in (27c)=(4c) shows that in addition to *Pavla* with the nonstructural accusative case, the predicate cannot take another accusative argument, which seems to be counterintuitive. However, unvalued φ-features on the head T must also be valued, which results in revaluing the structural accusative on *tu novou pohádku*.[15]

(27) a. *Pavl-a   bavil-a   ta   nová   pohádk-a.*
       Pavel-ACC   interested-SG.F   the   new   story-SG.F.NOM
       'Pavel was interested in/enjoyed the new story.'

   b. **Pavel   bavil   tu   novou pohádk-u.*
       Pavel.NOM interested.SG.M   the   new   story-SG.F.ACC

   c. **Pavl-a   bavil-o   tu   novou pohádk-u.*
       Pavel-ACC interested-SG.N   the   new   story-SG.F.ACC

Concerning the complex scale tree, we propose an analysis parallel to dative experiencer verbs; the only difference is that we put *nonstructural accusative* instead of *dative* in the tree in (26).

---

14 Compare accusative experiencer verbs in other languages, e.g., *interessieren*-type verbs in German (Sternefeld 2006), for some other languages see Pesetsky (1995). It is necessary to differentiate between the experiencer verb *bavit*, as in (27a), and the agentive *bavit*, as shown in (i). In contrast to (27a), the accusative case in (ia) is structural, therefore passivization is possible, as demonstrated in (ib).

(i) a. *Jan-a   bavila   Pavl-a.*
       Jana-NOM   amused   Pavel-ACC
       'Jana amused Pavel.'

   b. *Pavel   byl   baven   Jan-ou.*
       Pavel.NOM was   amused   Jana-INSTR
       'Pavel was amused by Jana.'

15 As pointed out to us by Marc Richards, our approach predicts that there are no single argument accusative intransitives, hence constructions like accusative unaccusatives may pose a problem for our analysis. With respect to these constructions, we follow Lavine and Freidin (2002), see also Harves (2006), who propose that T is a φ-incomplete head that does not have to enter into an Agree relation with an argument bearing φ-features.

4.2 Prefixed intransitive verbs

Example (5), repeated here as (28), shows that if the stative predicate *mërz* 'froze' is prefixed, it can be combined with the resultative prepositional phrase *v ajsberg* 'in iceberg'. Biskup (2007, 2009, 2012) argues that verbal prefixes are a spellout of a P element incorporated into the verb and that the valued Tense feature on the incorporated P element values the unvalued Tense feature on the aspectual head. This brings about perfectivity, concretely, in the case of (28b), the telic type of perfectivity, which licenses the resultative *p*P *v ajsberg*.

(28) a. *On   mërz   (*v   ajsberg).*
         he.NOM   froze   in   iceberg.ACC

   b. *On   v-mërz   v   ajsberg.*
      he.NOM   in-froze in   iceberg.ACC
      'He froze in the/a iceberg.'

Since prepositions are standardly analyzed as two-place predicates – as S/N/N or <e,<e,t>> or <l,<l,t>>, see Bierwisch (1988), Heim and Kratzer (1998), von Stechow (2006, 2007), respectively – that is, they localize the external argument with respect to the internal argument, we decompose prepositional phrases into PP and *p*P, following Talmy (1978), van Riemsdijk (1990) and Svenonius (2007). The internal argument is selected by the head P and is called *ground*, and the external argument, which is called *figure*, is introduced by the head *p*. The figure argument is the entity that is located, moved or somehow characterized with respect to the ground argument. Given this, (28b) is derived as shown in (29).[16]

---

[16] We put *on* in the specifier positions of Asp and T just for expository reasons, to show that it receives accusative and nominative (the same holds for the following syntactic trees). We are indifferent with respect to the final position of *on*. If every *v*P is a phase, then *on* must appear at least at the edge of *v*P.

(29)

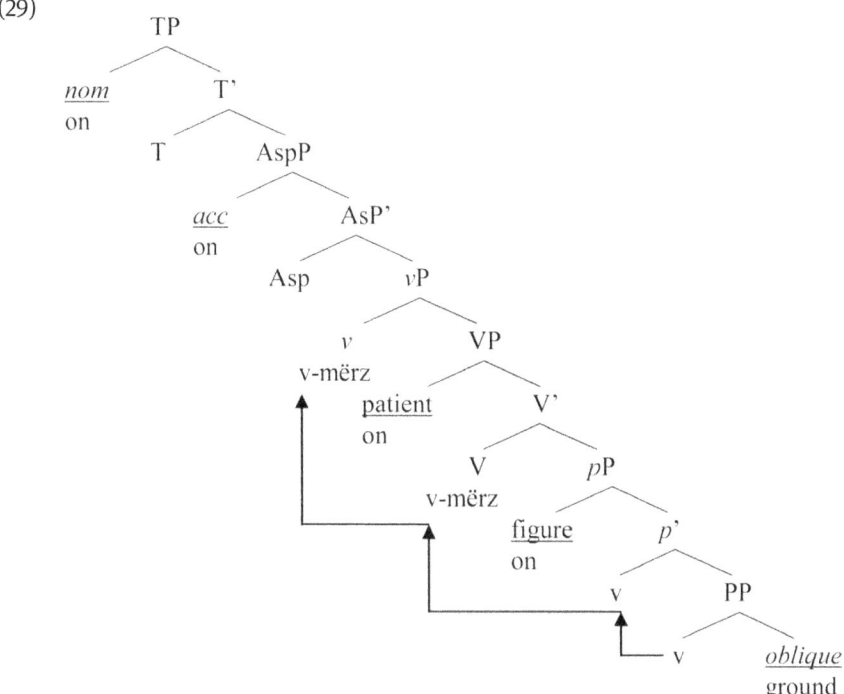

Figure arguments typically get accusative (which is revalued by nominative in intransitive constructions), hence this is the unmarked harmonic alignment and we put the accusative case on the case scale twice, as shown in (30). We assume that arguments can get multiple theta roles (see e.g. Hornstein 1999) and that every subevent must have an argument (Levin and Rappaport Hovav 2004).[17] From the scale point of view, movement (and the operation Agree) of *on* in the syntactic derivation (29) is represented as the unaccusative type of crossing with the unmarked alignment of figure with structural accusative combined with the unmarked alignment of the ground argument with oblique, as demonstrated in the complex scale tree (30).[18] Given this unaccusative one-way crossing and the

---

17 Given the fact that arguments can bear more theta roles and more cases, it may seem that our approach overgenerates with respect to possible argument structures. To avoid this complication, we assume in line with Ramchand (2008) that verbs are specified with respect to which subevents they can instantiate, which arguments they license, and whether or not the arguments can be identical.

18 As already mentioned, since complex scale trees are not meant to represent identity between particular exponents on the scales, there is no linking between the patient and the accusative below the figure or between the figure and the accusative below the patient. From now on, the term *goal* will be replaced with *ground*.

two unmarked alignments, we do not observe any special morphological marking in sentence (28b).

(30) Complex scale tree of (28b)

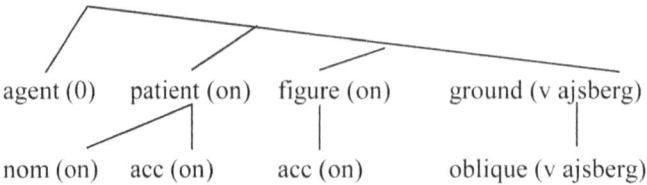

In contrast to the stative verb in (28), the motion verb *echal* 'drove' can be combined with a directional prepositional phrase, as shown in the following example. Since motion verbs have a path in their meaning, the directional prepositional phrase *v Moskvu* 'in Moscow' can be mapped onto the path of the event *echal* in (31a). In example (31b), the prefix *v-* incorporated into the verb values the Tense feature on the aspectual head, this again brings about the telic type of perfectivity, hence the sentence means that he reached Moscow, in contrast to the imperfective example (31a).

(31) a. On   echal   v   Moskv-u.
        he.NOM   drove   in   Moscow-ACC
        'He was driving to Moscow.'

   b. On   v"echal   v   Moskv-u.
        he.NOM   in-drove in   Moscow-ACC
        'He drove to Moscow.'

The event of *echal* has an agent and *on* bears the agent, patient and figure theta roles. At the same time, *on* bears nominative and structural accusative. Consequently, we arrive at the unmarked harmonic alignment of the agent theta role with nominative case, the patient with accusative case, the figure with accusative and the ground with oblique, as demonstrated in the complex scale tree (32). As to the markedness status, the complex scale tree (32) seems to be less marked than the one in (30). A comparison of the complex scale trees (30) and (32) and their appropriate sentences (28b) and (31) shows that the one-way type of crossing with the missing agent argument plays no role for morphological marking, as we already saw in the case of (20) and (??)

(32) Complex scale tree of (31)

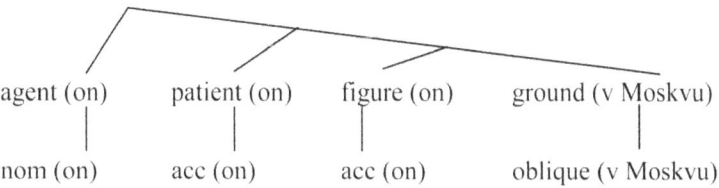

In section 1, we showed that prefixes can also add an argument with structural accusative; consider example (7)=(33) again. Since verbal prefixes are incorporated prepositions, they add a prepositional phrase to the verbal argument structure, which means that they also add new argument positions. This happens in the case of (33b), where *noč* 'night' is merged as the figure argument in Spec,*p*P.

(33) a. On   spal   (*noč).
        he.NOM slept   night.ACC

   b. On   do-spal   noč.
        he.NOM to-slept night.ACC
        'He slept till the end of the night.'

The ground argument is implicit in (33b). Taking into consideration the interpretation of this sentence and the prefix *do-*, the ground can be something like *do konca* 'till the end'.

4.3 Unprefixed transitive verbs

We will begin this section with the unmarked harmonic alignment of transitive verbs; consider example (34)=(8a). Given the Case Filter, every DP must have a case. However, the patient argument *Jirka* is not accessible for the head Asp and T because of the Phase Impenetrability Condition. Therefore, it must be moved by an Edge Feature to the edge of *v*P, more specifically, in accordance with the Extension Condition to the outer Spec,*v*P. In this position, *Jirka* can agree with the head Asp and its Tense feature is valued as accusative. Theoretically, the Tense feature on *Jirka* could be revalued by the head T as nominative – note that *Jirka* is closer to T than *Pavel* – but then *Pavel* would have no case and the derivation would crash, violating the Case Filter. Thus, *Pavel* must move. Note that *Pavel* precedes *Jirka* and can be interpreted as backgrounded (scrambled) in (34a). Since scrambled elements can take scope over negation (Biskup 2011) and negation is standardly positioned between T and Asp in Slavic, then in

(34), where no negation is present, *Pavel* scrambles (at least) to the specifier position of AspP. Since *Jirka* does not bear a Scrambling feature, in contrast to *Pavel*, it cannot block movement of *Pavel*. In the scrambled position then *Pavel* agrees with T and gets nominative case.

(34) a. *Pavel   bil   Jirk-u.*
       Pavel.NOM beat Jirka-ACC
       'Pavel beat Jirka.'

   b.
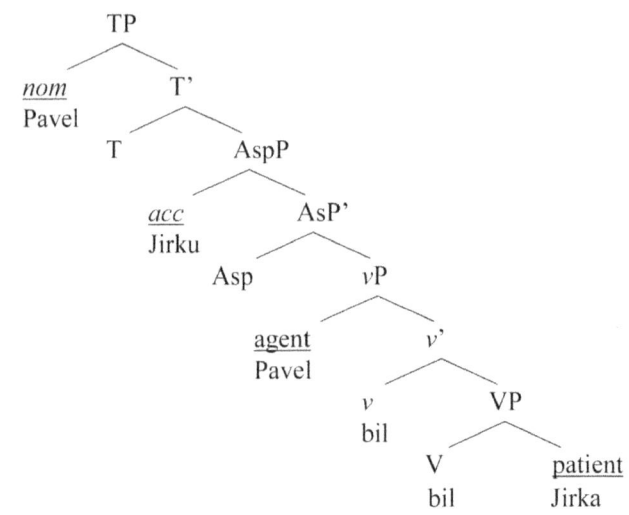

The form of the complex scale tree (35) corresponds to the syntactic tree (34b), which shows the alignment of *Pavel* and *Jirka*, not their overt syntactic positions. The unmarked alignment of the agent theta role with nominative and the patient theta role with accusative reflects the two Agree operations (and movements): between *Jirka* and Asp and between *Pavel* and T, which in turn are determined by syntactic conditions like the Phase Impenetrability Condition and the Case Filter. Since there are two unmarked harmonic alignments, hence no crossings in the complex scale tree, there is no special morphological marking in (34a).

(35) Complex scale tree of (34a)

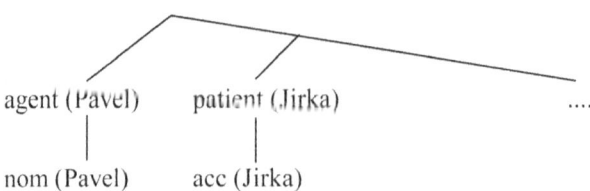

As demonstrated in example (8b), for convenience repeated as (36), the reversed alignment of the agent and patient argument is ungrammatical. The ungrammatical status is due to the violation of minimality principles. Following the argumentation above, in the derivation of sentence (36), the patient argument *Pavel* must move to the edge of vP across the agent argument *Jirka*. Then, however, the operation Agree between the aspectual head and *Jirka* (note that *Jirka* is marked with accusative) crosses *Pavel* in the outer Spec,vP.

(36) *Pavel   bil   Jirk-u.*
      Pavel.NOM   beat   Jirka-ACC
      *'Jirka beat Pavel.'

The complex scale tree of example (36) looks like (37). There is a two-way type of crossing that is reciprocal. Although (36) is ungrammatical because of the violation of minimality, the example seems to suggest that there is a relation between the reciprocal two-way type of crossing and the ungrammatical status. Generally speaking, if two entities interchange their forms, one cannot expect that the state of affairs remains normal.

(37) Complex scale tree of (36)

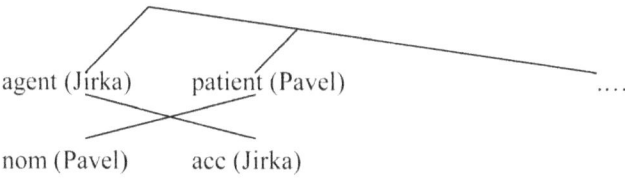

The way out of this problem is to mark the change. The state of affairs must be somehow repaired. Exactly this happens in the case of the passive sentence in (38); therefore the example is grammatical.

(38) *Pavel   byl   bit   Jirk-ou.*
      Pavel.NOM   was   beaten   Jirka-INSTR
      'Pavel was beaten by Jirka.'

If you take a look at the complex scale tree (39), you can see that the agent argument is marked with instrumental instead of the accusative case. Although there is a two-way type of crossing, as in (37) above, the crucial fact is that the crossing is not reciprocal. Note also that the verbal morphology in example (38) is more marked than the one in (36); it is more complex (see Greenberg 1966 and

Croft 1993, who argue that according to the structural markedness criterion, passives are usually more marked).

(39) Complex scale tree of (38)

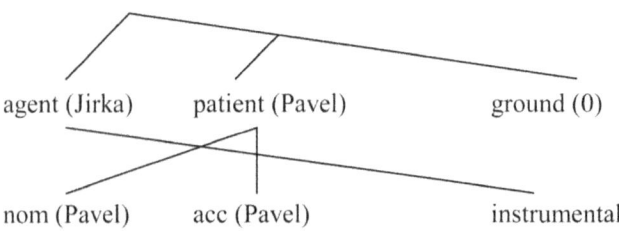

To show that this pattern is more general, consider a story from a fancy-dress party. The story nicely illustrates why the non-reciprocal two-way crossing is better than the reciprocal two-way crossing and worse than no crossing in the complex scale tree. Pavel dates Jana but he is going to split with her because he just began to be involved with Julie. He knows that at the fancy-dress party, Jana will wear a Snow White mask and Julie a cat mask. Imagine that in the evening, at the fancy-dress party, Pavel will come to the Snow White and tell her that their relationship is over and then he will tell the cat that he loves her. If the girls wear the right masks – if there is no crossing in the complex scale – then things go well for Pavel. However, if the girls exchange their masks – this is the reciprocal two-way crossing – Pavel will have two problems. Now consider the third scenario, that is, the morphologically marked case with the non-reciprocal two-way crossing. If Jana borrows Julie's mask and Julie borrows a mask from someone else, then Pavel will have only one problem.

As far as the syntactic derivation of (38) is concerned, the agent argument *Jirka* is trapped in the instrumental *p*P phase; therefore its Tense feature cannot be revalued by the head Asp or T and it is the Tense feature on *Pavel* that must agree with Asp and then with T.

Our analysis is supported by the following facts from Malayo-Polynesian languages spoken on the Philippines. A closer look at (40) with the Philippine-type voice system reveals that the passive voice is the unmarked alignment and that ergative case is used instead of accusative in the active voice.

(40) **active voice**   **passive voice**
     nom/direct (patient)   nom/direct (agent)
     ergative   (agent)   accusative (patient)

The situation in the active voice seems to be analogous to the passive example (38). The reciprocal crossing in the Philippine active voice must be somehow repaired, therefore ergative – which is often taken to be nonstructural (inherent) case; hence it can be put in the position of instrumental in (39) – replaces accusative, as demonstrated in the following complex scale tree.

(41) Complex scale tree of the Philippine active voice

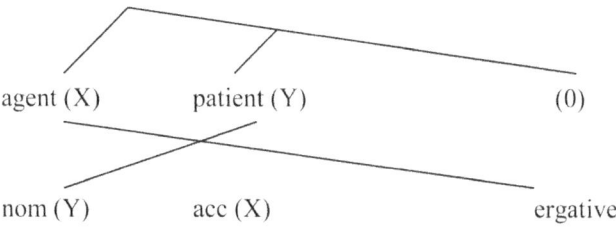

Another argument supporting our analysis comes from Rosen (1990). As pointed out to us by Fabian Heck (p.c.), Rosen analyzes the person/animacy hierarchy and the case hierarchy in Southern Tiwa in terms of a tiered model reminiscent of autosegmental phonology. What is important here is that according to Rosen, the hierarchy graph with crossing association lines is a prohibited configuration (for a purely syntactic approach, see Heck and Richards 2010). More concretely, Southern Tiwa does not have clauses like *The snake bit me* with a third person ergative and a first or second person absolutive. Such clauses represent the illicit configuration; consider the hierarchy graph with crossing lines in (42a), taken from Rosen (1990: 676), which resembles our reciprocal two-way crossing. Instead, Southern Tiwa uses the passive construction *I was bitten by the snake*, which represents the possible configuration; compare Rosen's graph (1990: 676) in (42b). This is in line with the Well-Formedness Condition on association lines in autosegmental phonology. Note that in our mapped complex scale tree, it is not the crossing itself but the two-way reciprocal crossing that is illicit.

(42) a.

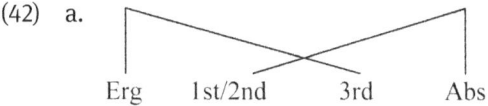

b.

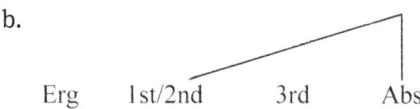

4.4 Prefixed transitive verbs

We have seen that verbal prefixes are incorporated prepositions, therefore they can add a prepositional phrase to the verbal argument structure; consider the contrast between (43a) and (43b). Sentence (43b) is represented by the complex scale tree in (44). There are four bidirectional unmarked harmonic alignments. The agent theta role is aligned with nominative, the patient theta role with accusative, the figure argument with accusative and the ground argument with the oblique case. Given these unmarked alignments, we do not observe any special morphological marking in sentence (43b).

(43) a. *On   v-pisal   svoe   imja.
         he.NOM in-wrote   self   name.ACC

  b.   On   v-pisal   svoe   imja   v   knig-u   počëta.
       he.NOM   in-wrote   self   name.ACC in   book-ACC of honor
       'He wrote his name in the book of honor.'

  c.   *On   v-pisal   v   imja   knig-u   počëta.
       he.NOM   in-wrote   in   name.ACC   book-ACC   of honour

(44) Complex scale tree of (43b)

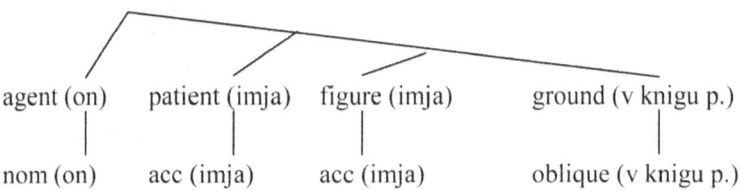

The example in (43c)=(9d) demonstrates that the reversed alignment of the figure (and patient) argument and the ground argument is not possible. *V imja* 'in name' cannot be interpreted as the figure argument and *knigu počëta* 'book of honour' bearing structural accusative cannot be interpreted as the ground.[19] The complex scale tree of (43c) then looks like (45). We again see the problematic reciprocal two-way crossing (plus the crossing going from the patient theta role to the oblique case and the unmarked alignment of the agent with nominative); hence, as expected, the sentence is ungrammatical.

---

[19] At first glance, in cases with more symmetrical arguments, the reversed alignment seems to be possible; see (i). In fact, it is not a reversed alignment; the prepositional argument is always interpreted as the ground argument.

(i) a. He stirred apple sauce into water.
    b. He stirred water into apple sauce.

(45) Complex scale tree of (43c)

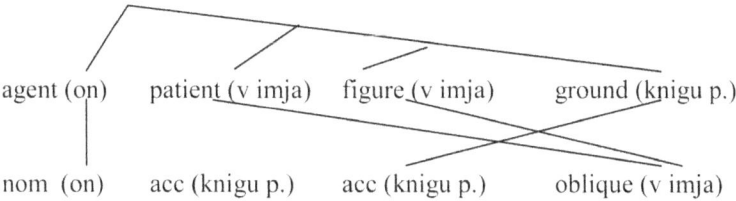

From the syntactic point of view, the problem lies in the fact that there are solid relationships in the prepositional phrase. Assuming that theta roles are assigned configurationally as a result of the DP-Merger, the argument merged in Spec,*p*P must be the figure and the argument merged as the complement of P must be the ground (see Svenonius 2007). Since the ground argument is trapped in the complement of the *p*P phase, it is not accessible for operations outside the *p*P phase and cannot get structural accusative. In addition, as discussed in section 4.1, the unvalued φ-features of the preposition are valued by its complement, that is, by the ground argument. Therefore, the preposition cannot serve as a probe any more and assign case to the figure argument.

There is no way to repair the reciprocal two-way crossing in (43c) with morphological marking, in contrast to the passive construction (38) and the Philippine active voice in (40). However, there are languages that have repairing tools for cases like this. Chukchi, which is an ergative language, has conversive antipassive constructions, in which the ground argument is promoted to the direct object and gets absolutive when the direct object, that is the figure, is demoted and gets oblique case, as demonstrated in (46), taken from Bobaljik (2007: 180–181, originally Kozinsky et al. 1988: 663–665).

(46) a. ətɬəγ-e   təkeč?-ən   utkuč-ək   peɬa-nen
         father-ERG bait-ABS   trap-LOC   leave-3SG>3SG
         'Father left the bait at/in the trap.'

      b. ətɬəγ-e   təkeč?-a   utkuč-ən   ena-peɬa-nen
         father-ERG bait-INSTR   trap-ABS   AP-leave-3SG>3SG
         'Father left the bait at/in the trap.'

The illicit two-way reciprocal crossing is repaired similarly to the examples in the preceding section; the predicate receives a special morphological marking, that is, the antipassive morpheme *ena*, and the figure argument gets instrumental, instead of the reciprocal locative case, as shown by example (46b).

5 Conclusion

We have argued that the theta role scale and the case scale are a reflection of syntactic structure; hence they are determined by c-command relations and semantic properties of the clause structure. As far as prefixes are concerned, we have shown that they can license case and add arguments to the verbal argument structure. In this way, they make the lower part of scales more complex. We wanted to draw attention to the fact that the complex scale expresses patterns more general than just language ones and that it can have a certain explanatory power in language. The form of the complex scale of particular sentences corresponds to grammatical principles, such as the principle of Full Interpretation and the Case Filter, and grammatical operations, such as the operation Agree and Move. We have drawn a parallel between the type of the complex scale tree, syntactic operations and the morphological marking/grammatical status of the sentence. Certain types of the complex scale tree correspond to the grammatical status, for instance, complex scale trees with the one-way crossing and a missing argument, certain types correspond to the morphologically marked status – complex scale trees with the non-reciprocal two-way crossing – and other types correspond to the ungrammatical status, the complex scale trees with the reciprocal two-way crossing. Although the complex scale tree of a particular sentence corresponds to grammatical principles and operations, the information about which types of the complex scale tree are problematic and which ones are not is of general nature and does not belong to the grammar itself.

References

Abels, Klaus. 2003. Successive cyclicity, anti-locality and adposition stranding. Ph.D. diss., University of Connecticut, Storrs.

Aissen, Judith. 2003. Differential object marking: iconicity vs. economy. *Natural Language and Linguistic Theory* 21: 435–483.

Babby, Leonard H. 1987. Case, prequantifiers, and discontinuous agreement in Russian. *Natural Language and Linguistic Theory* 5: 91–138.

Bierwisch, Manfred. 1988. On the grammar of local prepositions. In *Syntax, Semantik, Lexikon* (Studia grammatica 29), Manfred Bierwisch, Wolfgang Motsch, and Ilse Zimmermann (eds.), 1–65. Berlin: Akademie-Verlag.

Biskup, Petr. 2007. P(refixe)s and p(reposition)s. To appear in *Proceedings of the 2nd Congress of SLS, 2007*, Boštjan Dvořák (ed.).

Biskup, Petr. 2009. Prefixes as prepositions and multiple cases. In *Studies in Formal Slavic Phonology, Morphology, Syntax, Semantics and Information Structure. Proceedings of*

FDSL 7, Leipzig 2007, Gerhild Zybatow, Uwe Junghanns, Denisa Lenertová, and Petr Biskup (eds.), 3–17. Frankfurt am Main: Peter Lang.
Biskup, Petr. 2011. *Adverbials and the Phase Model*. Amsterdam: John Benjamins.
Biskup, Petr. 2012. Slavic prefixes and adjectival participles. In *Slavic Languages in Formal Grammar. Proceedings of FDSL 8.5, Brno 2010*, Markéta Ziková and Mojmír Dočekal (eds.), 271–289. Frankfurt am Main: Peter Lang.
Biskup, Petr, and Mike Putnam. 2012. One P with two spell-outs: the *ent-/aus*-alternation in German. Linguistic Analysis 38: 69–109.
Bittner, Maria, and Ken Hale. 1996. Ergativity: toward a theory of a heterogeneous class. *Linguistic Inquiry* 27: 531–604.
Bobaljik, Jonathan D. 2007. The limits of deponency: a Chukotko-centric perspective. In *Deponency and Morphological Mismatches. Proceedings of the British Academy*. Vol. 145, Matthew Baerman, Greville G. Corbett, Dunstan Brown, and Andrew Hippisleyet (eds.), 175–201. Oxford: Oxford University Press.
Bobaljik, Jonathan D. 2008a. From syntax to exponence: some Chukchi evidence. Paper presented at the *Exponence Network Meeting*. Universität Leipzig, 2008.
Bobaljik, Jonathan D. 2008b. Where's phi? Agreement as a post-syntactic operation. In *Phi-Theory: Phi Features across Interfaces and Modules*, Daniel Harbour, David Adger, and Susana Béjar (eds.), 295–328. Oxford: Oxford University Press.
Caha, Pavel, and Lucie Medová. 2009. Czech adverbs as case-marked adjectives. In *Studies in Formal Slavic Phonology, Morphology, Syntax, Semantics and Information Structure. Proceedings of FDSL 7, Leipzig 2007*, Gerhild Zybatow, Uwe Junghanns, Denisa Lenertová, and Petr Biskup (eds.), 31–42. Frankfurt am Main: Peter Lang.
Chomsky, Noam. 1995. *The Minimalist Program*. Cambridge, MA: MIT Press.
Chomsky, Noam. 2000. Minimalist inquiries: the framework. In *Step by Step: Essays on Minimalist Syntax in Honor of Howard Lasnik*, Roger Martin, David Michaels, and Juan Uriagereka (eds.), 89–156. Cambridge, MA: MIT Press.
Croft, William. 1993. *Typology and Universals*. Cambridge: Cambridge University Press.
Demirdache, Hamida, and Miriam Uribe-Etxebarria. 1997. The syntax of temporal relations. A uniform approach to tense and aspect. In *Proceedings of the 16th West Coast Conference on Formal Linguistics*, Emily Curtis, James Lyle, and Gabriel Webster (eds.), 145–159. Stanford, CA: CSLI Publications.
Emonds, Joseph. 2007a. Czech cases and the syntacticon: poznámky k, o, okolo, nad něčím a pro někoho. In *Czech in Generative Grammar*, Mojmír Dočekal, Petr Karlík, and Jana Zmrzlíková (eds.), 81–103. München: Lincom.
Emonds, Joseph. 2007b. *Discovering Syntax: Clause Structure of English, German and Romance*. Berlin: Mouton de Gruyter.
Franks, Steven. 1995. *Parameters of Slavic Morphosyntax*. Oxford: Oxford University Press.
Greenberg, Joseph Harold. 1966. *Language Universals, with Special Reference to Feature Hierarchies*. The Hague: Mouton.
Hale, Ken, and Samuel Jay Keyser. 1993. On argument structure and the lexical expression of syntactic relations. In *The View from Building 20*, Ken Hale, and Samuel Jay Keyser (eds.), 53–110. Cambridge, MA: MIT Press.
Harves, Stephanie. 2006. Non-agreement, unaccusativity, and the external argument constraint. In *Formal Approaches to Slavic Linguistics 14, The Princeton Meeting 2005*, James Lavine, Steven Franks, Mila Tasseva-Kurktchieva, and Hana Filip (eds.), 172–188. Ann Arbor, MI: Michigan Slavic Publications.

Heck, Fabian, and Marc Richards. 2010. A probe-goal approach to agreement and non-incorporation restrictions in Southern Tiwa. *Natural Language and Linguistic Theory* 28: 681–721.
Heim, Irene, and Angelika Kratzer. 1998. *Semantics in Generative Grammar*. Oxford: Blackwell.
Hornstein, Norbert. 1999. Movement and control. *Linguistic Inquiry* 30: 69–96.
Klein, Wolfgang. 1995. A time-relational analysis of Russian aspect. *Language* 71: 669–695.
Kozinsky, Isaac, Vladimir P. Nedjalkov, and Maria S. Polinskaja. 1988. Antipassive in Chuckchee: oblique object, object incorporation, zero object. In *Passive and Voice*, Masayoshi Shibatani (ed.), 651–706. Amsterdam: John Benjamins.
Lavine, James, and Robert Freidin. 2002. The subject of defective T(ense) in Slavic. *Journal of Slavic Linguistics* 10: 253–289.
Legate, Julie Anne. 2003. Some interface properties of the phase. *Linguistic Inquiry* 34: 506–516.
Levin, Beth, and Malka Rappaport Hovav. 2004. The semantic determinants of argument expression: a view from the English resultative construction. In *The Syntax of Time*, Jacqueline Guéron, and Jacqueline Lecarme (eds.), 477–494. Cambridge, MA: MIT Press.
Marantz, Alec. 2000. Case and licensing. In *Arguments and Case: Explaining Burzio's Generalization*, Eric Reuland (ed.), 11–30. Amsterdam: John Benjamins.
Pesetsky, David. 1995. *Zero Syntax: Experiencer and Cascades*. Cambridge, MA: MIT Press.
Pesetsky, David, and Esther Torrego. 2004. Tense, case, and the nature of syntactic categories. In *The syntax of Time*, Jacqueline Guéron, and Jacqueline Lecarme (eds.), 495–539. Cambridge, MA: MIT Press.
Pesetsky, David, and Esther Torrego. 2006. Probes, goals and syntactic categories. In *The Proceedings of the Seventh Tokyo Conference on Psycholinguistics*, Yukio Otsu (ed.), 25–61. Tokyo: Hituzi Syobo Publishing Company.
Ramchand, Gillian C. 2008. *Verb Meaning and the Lexicon: A First Phase Syntax*. Cambridge: Cambridge University Press.
van Riemsdijk, Henk. 1990. Functional prepositions. In *Unity in Diversity*, Harm Pinkster, and Inge Genée (eds.), 229–241. Dordrecht: Foris.
Rosen, Carol. 1990. Rethinking Southern Tiwa: the geometry of a triple agreement language. *Language* 66: 669–713.
von Stechow, Arnim. 1996. The different readings of *wieder* "again". A structural account. *Journal of Semantics* 13: 87–138.
von Stechow, Arnim. 2006. Spatial prepositions in interval semantics. Paper presented at the *Semantics Network Workshop*, Barcelona, September 2006.
von Stechow, Arnim. 2007. Schritte zur Satzsemantik II. www.sfs.uni-tuebingen.de/~astechow/Aufsaetze/SchrittelI.pdf
Sternefeld, Wolfgang. 2006. *Syntax. Eine morphologisch motivierte generative Beschreibung des Deutschen*. Tübingen: Stauffenburg Verlag.
Svenonius, Peter. 2007. Adpositions, particles, and the arguments they introduce. In *Argument Structure*, Eric Reuland, Tanmoy Bhattacharya, and Giorgos Spathas (eds.), 63–103. Amsterdam: John Benjamins.
Talmy, Leonard. 1978. Figure and ground in complex sentences. In *Universals of Human Language, Vol. 4, Syntax*, Joseph H. Greenberg, Charles A. Ferguson & Edith A. Moravcsik (eds.), 625–649. Stanford, CA: Stanford University Press.
The Research Proposal of Forschergruppe 742, 2005. *Grammatik und Verarbeitung verbaler Argumente*. Universität Leipzig, Max Planck Institute for Evolutionary Anthropology, Leipzig, and Max Planck Institute for Human Cognitive and Brain Sciences, Leipzig.

Jakob Hamann
9 Argument Encoding in Direction Systems and Specificity-Driven Agree

This paper presents a new, minimalist analysis of direct-inverse alternations which is fundamentally based on the assumption that specificity is a driving force in syntactic derivations (cf. Lahne 2008, 2009). It is argued that scale effects emerge because the dependency-forming relation Agree is specificity-driven in nature: Probes are sensitive to the specificity of matching goals such that it will always be the goal which is more specific for a probe that enters into an Agree relation. Specificity is understood in a quantitative sense, i.e. the number of matching features (the feature cardinality) determines the specificity of an element. As in morphological theory, the more features an element has, the more specific it is. Such an approach makes it unnecessary to refer to scales as primitive concepts of grammar in accounting for the facts, a desired result under minimalist tenets. As for direction marking, it is suggested that the realization of the direction marker as either "direct" or "inverse" is contingent on which argument enters into primary Agree with the agreement head T. An unvalued Case feature located on T indexes the value of the Case feature of the relevant argument. This is possible because all arguments receive their structural Case values early in the derivation, namely on the vP-level (cf. Sigurðsson 2000). Direction marking is thus reduced to Case.

1 Introduction and overview

Standardly, it is assumed that reference to so-called Silverstein or prominence scales (cf. Silverstein 1976, also see Hale 1972, Dixon 1994) seems unavoidable in order to account for certain effects that are especially pervasive in the realm of A-syntax, and that have considerable impact on agreement, word order, Case assignment and related syntactic processes.[1] What seems uncontroversial is that the notion of prominence must somehow be integrated into whatever theoretical framework one eventually assumes. However, the theoretical status of scales themselves remains notoriously unclear and is still a matter of debate. While

---

[1] Textbook examples typically include phenomena such as split ergativity, differential argument encoding and PCC effects.

some approaches crucially rest on the assumption that scales are primitive theoretical entities that syntactic and morphological operations can refer to (cf. e.g. Aissen 1999 and Keine and Müller 2015 for an optimality-theoretic approach that crucially relies on the operation of harmonic alignment of scales), precisely the opposite is called for by those approaches that seek to dispense with scales as genuine entities of grammar altogether (cf. e.g. Brown, Koch, and Wiltschko 2004, Wiltschko 2008 and Richards 2015 for proposals along these lines). In the latter group of approaches, the shared goal is to find a way of implementing the descriptive power of scales without actual reference to the concept itself, thereby deriving their effects from independently motivated principles of syntactic computation and the assumption that parametric variation between languages is lexical in nature: Languages vary with respect to the (featural) content of lexical items. This line of research will be assumed throughout the present paper, whose main goal is to outline a new approach to a particular phenomenon that is scale-driven in nature and that has been reported for many different languages: direct-inverse marking (cf. among others Comrie 1980, DeLancey 1981, Dahlstrom 1991, Klaiman 1991, 1992, Givón 1994, Palmer 1994, Fadden 2000, Zúñiga 2006).

Direction systems[2] are usually said to display a very prototypical hierarchy effect. Essentially, in such systems only the most prominent argument (of a transitive verb) can be cross-referenced via agreement on the verb, and the so-called "theme sign" (the direction marker) indicates whether this argument has subject or object status (i.e., it indicates the grammatical function of the agreed-with argument). The interaction between Φ-agreement and theme sign choice in direction systems leads to the impression of a non-local dependency holding between the verb and its core arguments: in order for the verb to decide which argument to agree with, it must have access to information about the properties (i.e., Φ-features) of both core arguments, simultaneously. But this seems a priori problematic, given a derivational organization of grammar, because at first sight one would seem to be forced to employ look-ahead or countercyclic operations (cf. also Georgi 2009a,b who reaches the same conclusion, in the empirical context of non-local Case assignment).

Obviously, direction marking is a phenomenon located at the interface between syntax and morphology, which makes it rather difficult to analyze. Hence,

---

2 A note on terminology. Other terms that are frequently used in the literature to refer to these systems are *direct-inverse system, inverse system* or *inverse voice system*. For the sake of consistency and clarity, I will henceforth use the term *direction system*.

there are many different approaches that are primarily or exclusively morphologically oriented and some which have a strong syntactic focus.[3] However, it seems that in several languages certain syntactic effects (e.g., binding relations) are contingent on whether the clause is in direct or inverse form, a fact that purely morphological approaches cannout account for, which supports a syntactic analysis to begin with.

The main goal of this paper is to argue that direct-inverse alternations can be derived via the operation Agree of Chomsky (2000, 2001). A small modification in the application of Agree will qualify as central to the analysis. It is proposed that Agree is not exclusively constrained by locality considerations as standardly assumed; it is specificity-driven in the sense that it can involve a goal G, although there is a potentially closer goal H, but only if G is more specific than H (cf. Lahne 2008, 2009). This is not to mean that locality is fully dispensed with; locality comes into play if two or more potentially accessible goals are equally specific. This necessitates an analysis according to which arguments are allowed to vary in their featural *specificity*. To this end, I adopt Béjar's (2003) and Béjar & Řezáč's (2009) decompositional approach to features according to which features are complex objects which consist of more primitive, elementary units (viz., segments). Under the assumption that scales essentially encode specificity (i.e., the elements on a scale differ not with respect to their "prominence", but with respect to their formal specificity, i.e. segment cardinality), the prediction is that syntactic objects which are more specific in this sense are preferred by Agree over syntactic objects which are less specific. Consequently, the conceptually problematic notion of "scale" can be fully dispensed with in this system, and the effects are derived with reference to principles and operations that already have independent empirical and conceptual motivation, namely the operation Agree in conjunction with a specificity principle, versions of which are employed in nearly every contemporary theory of inflection (cf. e.g. Halle and Marantz 1993, Stump 2001).

---

[3] Cf. e.g. the analyses developed in Ura (1996, 2000), Bruening (2001, 2005), Baker (2003), Alexiadou and Anagnostopoulou (2006) and Béjar and Řezáč (2009), which are primarily syntactic in nature and which focus on T as the locus of agreement (Béjar and Řezáč 2009 being an exception) and on v as housing direct-inverse morphology, which is analyzed differently (e.g., as a reflex of movement in Bruening 2001, 2005). Purely morphological approaches like Anderson (1992), Halle and Marantz (1993), Fabri (1996), and Trommer (2003, 2006), in contrast, often analyze direction marking as agreement plus Case, which is in accordance with the view envisaged in this article. A completely different approach in terms of realization rules is proposed in Stump (2001: 64) where direct-inverse languages make use of a so-called major-reference feature MR which can either be specified as MR:su (direct) or MR:ob (inverse). This might be closest to traditional approaches which treat direction as "flow of action" along some scale. For reasons of space, I am not able to discuss these approaches any further here.

Central to my proposal is that overt direction marking can be reduced to the theory of Case. Since the majority of direct-inverse languages lacks overt Case marking of nominals, it is evident that direction marking on the predicate replaces this "deficit." Under the assumption that grammatical functions must somehow be marked, whether on the arguments themselves, on their selecting predicate, or via word order, direction marking emerges as functionally equivalent to Case marking. It is suggested that the arguments of a transitive verb receive their Case values independently of Φ-agreement, namely on the vP level (via the functional head v, cf. Sigurðsson 2000). Thus I deviate from the standardly held assumption that (nominal) Case assignment and Φ-agreement are two sides of the same coin (a reflex of one and the same operation). The agreement head T, being equipped with a core Φ-probe, can then in turn index the Case value of the agreed-with argument due to the presence of an unvalued Case feature which is simultaneously checked off with the Φ-probe, and post-syntactically realized as a direction marker.

As for the surface realization of direct-inverse alternations, three types of languages will be identified in the course of the discussion. These are (i) languages that express direct-inverse alternations via morphological marking, (ii) languages that express these alternations via word order (movement), and (iii) languages that express them both via morphological marking and movement. Where other approaches fail to account for this typology, it is shown that all these language types are expected under the analysis to be developed here. A distinction between movement and non-movement direct-inverse languages is additionally fully compatible with the observation that direct-inverse alternations may give rise to grammatical function changing and certain other syntactic effects in languages exhibiting overt movement in inverse contexts, whereas languages of the non-movement type fail to show these effects.

The paper is organized as follows. Sections 2 and 3 discuss the general syntactic and morphological aspects of the phenomenon in detail and introduce the three basic inverse language types, providing empirical evidence in favor of a distinction between movement and non-movement inverse languages on the basis of grammatical function changing. Section 4 presents the analysis. Via specificity-driven Agree, I derive the empirical generalization that primary Φ-agreement can only affect the most prominent (= most specific) argument in a clause, and provide an explanation for the morphological reflex that manifests itself in the form of a direct or inverse marker in terms of Case agreement. Section 5 discusses an empirical prediction of the analysis which is shown to be borne out for a certain class of languages, and shows that the analysis developed in section 4 is applicable to the related phenomenon of agreement displacement as well. Finally, section 6 contains a short summary and some concluding remarks.

2 Data and generalizations

2.1 General features

In this section, I discuss the phenomenon of direct-inverse alternations in more detail, taking into account as many typologically different languages as possible. As indicated in the introduction, to a first approximation we can characterize a direction system as a special argument encoding system in which Φ-agreement tracks the features of a single argument which is the most prominent one according to some language-specific prominence scale.[4] The "theme sign" (henceforth called *direction marker*) indicates whether this argument acts as the subject or the object of the clause. Consider first the examples from Nishnaabemwin (Algonquian, Canada) in (1) (Valentine 2001: 270).

(1) a. *n-waabm-**aa***
 1-see-DIR
 'I see him.' [1 → 3]
 b. *n-waabm-**ig***
 1-see-INV
 'He sees me.' [3 → 1]

These sentences are completely identical with respect to agreement. The core agreement slot tracks the person feature of the most prominent argument

---

4 Obviously, this is a simplification. In direction systems, the less prominent argument may also induce agreement on the verb, a pattern that is comparatively frequently found. But the overall pattern that seems to hold rather consistently across direct-inverse languages is that there is a unique *core agreement slot* (cf. Béjar and Řezáč 2009) that tracks the features of one of the two arguments in a transitive context, and this is the most prominent one. Data like that from Passamaquoddy in (i) (from Bruening 2005: 1) might then at first sight look like potential counterexamples to this generalization, because the less prominent argument (3rd person here) does induce person and number agreement. In section 4, I suggest that these observations can be derived from the interaction between the activity condition on Agree and the relative ordering of operation-inducing features.

(i) a. *K-ucem-a-k.*
 2-kiss-DIR-3PL
 'You kissed them.' [2 → 3]
 b. *K-ucem-ku-k.*
 2-kiss-INV-3PL
 'They kissed you.' [3 → 2]

(namely 1st person, indicated by the prefix *n-*), prominence being determined by the scale in (2).⁵

(2) *Nishnaabemwin person scale:*
    2 > 1 > 3.PROX > 3.OBV > 3.INANIM

In both cases, (1) shows agreement with the 1st person argument, because 1st person outranks 3rd person on the person scale in (2). Since the subject (henceforth *external argument*; DP_{ext}) is 1st person and the object (henceforth *internal argument*; DP_{int}) 3rd person in (1-a) (i.e., DP_{ext} is more prominent than DP_{int}), the direct marker *-aa* is used. But if DP_{ext} is 3rd person and DP_{int} is 1st person (i.e., DP_{int} is more prominent than DP_{ext}), the inverse marker *-ig* is used.⁶

Although Algonquian languages like Nishnaabemwin are usually said to represent direction systems par excellence, the same pattern can be found in typologically very different languages. For example, Movima, an isolate language spoken in Bolivia, also exhibits the single argument agreement pattern, which is controlled by the Silverstein scale in (3) (Haude 2006: 276).

(3) *Movima person/animacy scale:*
    1SG > 1INCL/EXCL > 2SG > 2PL > 3HUM > 3NON-HUMAN

Since nominal Case is absent in Movima, the grammatical function (i.e., subject, direct object, indirect object, etc.) of the argument that controls agreement is

---

5 PROX and OBV stand for 'proximate' and 'obviative', respectively. These two terms describe the fact that 3rd person arguments are ranked according to their relative discourse salience (where 'proximate' denotes the more salient, 'obviative' the less salient 3rd person argument); see Aissen 1997.

6 Note that in this paper, I only look at transitive constructions with two core arguments. Ditransitive inverse constructions have been identified for several languages (Malchukov, Haspelmath, and Comrie 2010), e.g. Itonama (Isolate, Bolivia):

(i) *Direction Marking in Itonama ditransitive clauses (Malchukov, Haspelmath, and Comrie 2010: 44):*
  a. *Si-makï   uwaka   ya-dïlï   a-chipa ïwabï*
     1SG-give SP.meat DEM:MED-CLF:AN.seat.PL DU-two women
     'I gave the meat to those two women' [1A → 3R]

  b. *Wase'wa   sih-k'i-maki   pïlata   sah-nay-k'i-chuduwa'-ko   makaya*
     yesterday 1PL.EXCL-INV-give   SP.silver 1PL.EXCL-SUB-APPL-pay-NEUT clothes
     'Yesterday they gave us money to buy clothes.' [3A → 1R]

Malchukov, Haspelmath, and Comrie (2010) note that ditransitive inverse constructions always involve a competition for agreement between subject and indirect object, not between subject and direct object. Whether the analysis to be developed here can be extended to ditransitive contexts remains to be seen.

reflected in the form of the direction marker which attaches to the verb. Compare (4-a), a direct context and its inverse counterpart in (4-b). In (4-a), a 3rd person DP_{ext} which is human acts on a 3rd person DP_{int} which is animate (hence non-human). According to the animacy scale in (3), the more prominent human argument should induce agreement on the verb. This is indeed the case, as the presence of the clitic =sne indicates (agreement in Movima proceeds by cliticization). The same holds for (4-b), where one can identify the same agreement pattern. However, in (4-a) the agreed-with argument is DP_{ext}, in (4-b) it is DP_{int}. Thus we obtain direct marking in (4-a) and inverse marking in (4-b).[7]

(4) Direction marking in Movima (Haude 2006: 277):
    a.   tikoy-**na**=sne   os   mimi:di
         kill-DIR=FEM.A   ART.NEUT.PST   snake
         'She killed the/a snake.' [3HUM → 3NON-HUM]
    b.   tikoy-**kay**-a=sne   os   mimi:di
         kill-INV-LV=FEM.A   ART.NEUT.PST   snake
         'The snake killed her.' [3NON-HUM → 3HUM]

As has already been indicated, agreement with the less prominent argument is not strictly prohibited, but on the contrary is widely found in many direct-inverse languages. For example, in Mapudungun (Isolate, Chile), the core agreement slot encodes agreement with the most prominent argument in a clause according to the person scale in (5) (Arnold 1996), irrespective of this argument's grammatical function.

(5) Mapudungun person scale:
    1 > 2 > 3PROX > 3OBV

However, the other, less prominent argument obligatorily induces person agreement as well. This is illustrated in (6) for direct contexts, and in (7) for inverse contexts (data from Arnold 1996). The direct is unmarked, the inverse is marked by the morpheme e-.

(6)   a.   Ngilla-fi-n
            buy-3.OBJ-1SG.SUBJ
            'I bought it/him/her/them.' [1 → 3]

---

[7] LV in (67-b) means linking vowel, i.e., a phonologically conditioned epenthetic vowel.

b. *Ngilla-fi-imu*
buy-3.OBJ-2DU.SUBJ
'You two bought it/him/her/them.' [2 → 3]

c. *Ngilla-fi-y*
buy-3.OBJ-3.SUBJ
'He/she/they [prox] bought it/him/her/them [obv].'

(7) a. *Pe-e-n-Ø*
see-INV-1SG.SUBJ-2OBJ
'You saw me.' [2 → 1]

b. *Pe-e-y-ew*
see-INV-3SUBJ-3OBJ
'He/she/it/they [obv] saw him/her/it/them [prox].'

These data are especially interesting because they show that the thematic argument in inverse contexts is in fact expressed by the exponent which normally expresses subject agreement (compare (6-a) with (7-a)), which can be viewed as evidence for an analysis in terms of grammatical function changing (see section 3.2).

Another instance of two-argument agreement in direction systems can be found in Plains Cree (Algonquian, USA). The following examples from Klaiman (1992: 230) show that at least in some person-number combinations in both direct ((8-a)) and inverse contexts ((8-b)), both arguments trigger agreement on the verb, and the agreement morphology is completely identical in both cases. The only device that facilitates revelation of the grammatical functions of the arguments is the shape of the direction marker.

(8) a. *Ni-pēh-ā-nān-ak*
1-wait-DIR-1PL-3PL
'We await them.' [1 → 3]

b. *Ni-pēh-**iko**-nān-ak*
1-wait-INV-1PL-3PL
'They await us.' [3 → 1]

Languages with direction systems differ yet with respect to another factor, namely the relevant *direction domain* (cf. Zúñiga 2006). The direction domain restricts the range of arguments which participate in the direct-inverse alternation. In languages like Navajo (Athabaskan, USA), Kinyarwanda (Bantu, Rwanda) or Kutenai (Isolate, Canada), for example, direction marking only shows up if both

DP$_{ext}$ and DP$_{int}$ are 3rd person (termed *non-local direction*). In contrast, many languages of the Algonquian, Kiowa-Tanoan and Tibeto-Burman language families show a direct-inverse alternation pattern that involves a local (= 1st or second person) and a 3rd person argument (termed *core direction*). Some languages (like Nez Perce (Sahaptian, USA)) are argued to mark direct-inverse alternations only in local scenarios, i.e., if both DP$_{ext}$ and DP$_{int}$ are local persons (termed *local direction*).

2.2 Morphology

Turning to the morphological side, we can distinguish several possibilities of how direct-inverse alternations can be marked on the predicate. The first, arguably most common type, comprises those languages which only mark an inverse constellation with a special inverse morpheme; the direct one is left unmarked. This is the case in Nocte (Tibeto-Burman, India), Japhug Rgyalrong (Sino-Tibetan, China) and Kutenai, as the following examples show.

(9) Nocte (DeLancey 1981: 641):
   a. *Nga-ma   nang   hetho-e.*
      I-ERG   you   teach-1PL
      'I will teach you.' [1 → 2]
   b. *Nang-ma   nga   hetho-**h**-ang.*
      you-ERG   I   teach-INV-1SG
      'You will teach me.' [2 → 1]

(10) Japhug Rgyalrong (Jacques 2010: 129):
   a. *pɯ-mtó-t-a*
      AOR-see-PST-1SG
      'I saw him/her/it.' [1 → 3]
   b. *pɯ́-**wɣ**-mto-a*
      AOR-INV-see-1SG
      'He/she/it saw me.' [3 → 1]

(11) Kutenai (Dryer 1992: 185)
   a. *wu·kat-i   paɬkiy-s   titqat'*
      see-IND   woman-OBV   man
      'The man saw the woman.' [3PROX → 3OBV]
   b. *wu·kat-**aps**-i   titqat'-s   paɬkiy*
      see-INV-IND   man-OBV   woman
      'The man saw the woman.' [3OBV → 3PROX]

On the other hand, a number of languages marks both direct and inverse constellations alike. This is the case in many languages of the Algonquian language family (such as Plains Cree, Ojibwe, Passamaquoddy, etc.) and Movima; see (4), repeated here as (12).

(12) Movima (Haude 2006: 277)
  a. tikoy-**na**=sne   os   mimi:di
     kill-DIR=FEM.A   ART.NEUT.PST   snake
     'She killed the/a snake.'

  b. tikoy-**kay**-a=sne   os   mimi:di
     kill-INV-LV=FEM.A ART.NEUT.PST   snake
     'The snake killed her.'

Some languages distinguish non-local and core direction from local direction by a different set of direction markers. For instance, Nishnaabemwin/Ojibwe uses *aa-* (direct) and *-igw/-igo(o)/-ig* (inverse) with non-local and core direction (i.e., in 1/2 → 3, 3 → 1/2 and 3 → 3 predications), and *-i* (direct) and *-in(i)* (inverse) with local direction (i.e., in 2 → 1 and 1 → 2 predications) (Valentine 2001: 270):

(13) a. *n-waabm-aa*
        1-see-DIR
        'I see him.' [1 → 3]

     b. *n-waabm-ig*
        1-see-INV
        'He sees me.' [3 → 1]

     c. *g-waabam-i*
        2-see-DIR(local)
        'You see me.' [2 → 1]

     d. *g-waabm-in*
        2-see-INV(local)
        'I see you.' [1 → 2]

In yet other languages, a specific direction marker is lacking. Instead, there are distinct direct and inverse paradigms for the person-encoding affixes. A language that makes use of this strategy is the Carib variant spoken in Suriname (Fadden 2000: 33):

(14) a. *mi-kuupi-ya*
 2DIR-bathe-TNS
 'You bathe him.' [2 → 3]
 b. *a-kuupi-ya-ŋ̃*
 2INV-bathe-TNS-EVID
 'He bathes you.' [3 → 2]

Finally, languages may not at all mark a direct-inverse distinction overtly. Kinyarwanda and other Bantu languages are prototypical examples of this type (these languages are said to express these distinctions via movement, which is discussed in section 3.2.1). From these facts, one could draw the conclusion that the morphological realization of direction seems rather arbitrary, resulting from language-specific morphological idiosyncrasies. But there is a systematic pattern that can be observed: In none of the language data discussed above do we detect contexts in which direct constellations are marked, but inverse ones are unmarked. This fact is not surprising as it resembles a systematicity which is characteristic of many Case systems. These often show zero/non-zero alternations in the sense that marked Cases like ergative and accusative are expressed by richer morphology, whereas unmarked Cases like nominative and absolutive are often null or at least expressed by segmentally less complex markers. Furthermore, direction markers appear to have essentially the same function as Case markers: they reveal the grammatical function of the arguments which are not otherwise marked. Taken together, these observations lead to the conclusion that direction markers *are* Case markers (as already envisaged in Halle and Marantz 1993, Trommer 2003, 2006), and this is a desirable move, given that the grammatical apparatus is simplified by reducing direction marking to Case (this is further exploited in section 4.5).

Let me summarize what has been said so far. The generalization we arrive at is that verbs of transitive clauses first agree with one of the two core arguments, regardless of whether this is DP_{ext} or DP_{int}. The only prerequisite is that this argument is the most prominent one (according to the relevant scale active in the language). Subsequently, depending on the language, the verb can in principle agree with the less prominent argument. Again, it does not matter which grammatical function this argument has. It seems, then, that traditional notions like "subject agreement" or "object agreement" are simply not applicable to direct-inverse languages. I therefore suggest using the descriptive terms "primary" and "secondary" agreement to refer to these patterns. In section 4, I present an analysis that captures this division between primary and secondary agreement by invoking the independently motivated assumption that operation-inducing features on heads are ordered. In Hamann (2011), I also show that the very same mechanism is capable of deriving ordinary subject and object agreement.

We have also seen that direct-inverse languages naturally vary with respect to the relevant direction domain (i.e., the range of arguments which participate in the direct-inverse alternation), and their morphological properties. It was noted that direction systems show some similarities with canonical Case systems in that they frequently exhibit zero/non-zero alternations (as well as less/more patterns). The next three subsections center around the notion of grammatical function changing: First, I present the main arguments for a dissociation of direction systems from canonical active-passive systems (section 3.1). Subsequently (section 3.2), I illustrate why it is nonetheless reasonable to assume that in certain direct-inverse languages it is appropriate to speak of grammatical function changing in inverse contexts.

3 A-movement and grammatical function changing

3.1 Active-passive vs. direct-inverse

In the literature it is widely held that the direct-inverse alternation is a diathesis (or gramatical voice), just like the active-passive distinction known from more familiar languages like English (cf. Klaiman 1991, 1992 and Palmer 1994 for an overview). Despite their differences, some authors argue that passive and inverse are two terms for the description of a single phenomenon or that inverse is at least a special variety of passive (cf. e.g. Dryer 1992 on Kutenai). On the other hand, however, it is difficult to draw a sharp distinction between the two phenomena since they obviously cannot be viewed as holistic categories.[8] Nevertheless, the most basic formal difference between active-passive and direct-inverse systems is that the latter does not involve *detransitivization*. It is a defining property of passive systems that that active transitive verbs become intransitive when passivized, showing corresponding formal properties (such as intransitive agreement). Moreover, in direction systems one does not find argument demotion. In passive systems, the agent argument (i.e., the subject of an active clause) is semantically

---

8 This means that the phenomena under discussion cannot be reduced to a single instantiation; there is not *the* passive and *the* inverse. Rather, passive and inverse are descriptive terms for a number of morphological, syntactic and/or lexical operations which occur in different combinations across and even within individual languages.

"degraded" in the derived passive clause, such that it is often omitted or realized as an oblique. In inverse systems, this is not possible. Both core arguments of a transitive clause (no matter if in direct or inverse form) are obligatorily present and cannot be omitted. The following data demonstrate the core differences between the English active-passive system and the Navajo direct-inverse system (Navajo data taken from Witherspoon 1980: 5).

(15) a. The horse kicked the mule.
 b. The mule was kicked (by the horse).

(16) a. łį́į́' dzaanééz yi-ztał
  horse mule DIR-kicked
  'The horse kicked the mule.'
 b. dzaanééz łį́į́' bi-ztał
  mule horse INV-kicked
  'The horse kicked the mule.'

In the passive clause (15-b), the demoted agent *the horse* is marked by the preposition *by* and can be omitted without further ado (indicated by parentheses). The direct object of the active clause *the mule* becomes the subject of the passive clause, which is among other things visible through agreement marking on the verb. In the Navajo data in (16), none of the two arguments can be omitted. Both clauses are active and transitive and differ only in their word order and the morphological marking on the verb (*yi-* vs. *bi-*).[9]

A further argument that passive and inverse should be formally distinguished is that languages may exhibit both constructions. Plains Cree, for example, has an elaborate direction system, but marks passive voice by distinct morphology. Consider the following examples (Wolfart 1973: 24–25 and Dahlstrom 1991: 65).

(17) a. ni-sēkih-ā-enān atim
  1-scare-DIR-1PL dog
  'We scare the dog.'

 b. ni-sēkih-ekw-enān atim
  1-scare-INV-1PL dog
  'The dog scares us.'

---

9 On the basis of data from Plains Cree, Dahlstrom (1991) presents a number of tests which confirm that direct and inverse verbs are syntactically active and transitive. See Dahlstrom (1991, chapter 3) for details. Also see Fadden (2000, chapter 1).

(18) a. awīna ē=sākih-iht?
        who   love-PASS.3.CONJ
        'Who is loved?'

   b. *awīna ē=sākih-iht   omāmā-wa?
       who   love-PASS.3.CONJ   his.mother-OBV
       ('Who is loved by his mother?')

In contrast to an inverse clause like (17-b), the agent of a passive clause cannot be expressed, as (18-b) shows. That is, the agent is not only semantically demoted but entirely suppressed; it is impossible to express it overtly.

A similar pattern can be found in Kinyarwanda (Kimenyi 1980). Like Navajo, Kinyarwanda is assumed to employ overt movement to express the direct-inverse alternation. (19-a) is a direct clause, (19-b) its inverse counterpart (Kimenyi 1980: 141).

(19) a. Umuhuûngu   a-ra-som-a   igitabo.
        boy   HE-PRES-read-ASP   book
        'The boy is reading the book.'

   b. Igitabo   cyi-ra-som-a   umuhuûngu.
       book   IT-PRES-read-ASP   boy
       'The book is being read by the boy.'

In (19-a), word order is SVO, and the subject *umuhuûngu* 'boy' triggers agreement on the verb, indicated by the marker *a-*. In (19-b), however, word order is OVS; the direct object *igitabo* 'book' seems to have moved to subject position, which is motivated by the fact that it triggers agreement on the verb (by means of the marker *cyi-*).[10] Now consider the active-passive distinction in the language (Kimenyi 1988: 363):

(20) a. Abagóre   ba-a-boon-ye   mweébwe.
        women   THEY-PAST-see-ASP   you
        'The women saw you.'

   b. Mweébwe   mw-aa-boon-y-w-e   *(n')-âbagóre.
       you   YOU-PAST-see-ASP-PASS-ASP   BY-women
       'You were seen by the women.'

---

10 I follow Ura (1996, 2000) in assuming that there is obligatory V-to-T movement in Bantu languages, yielding the V/2 effect in both direct and inverse clauses.

The data illustrate that direct and active sentences are structurally identical. That is, in (20-a) word order is also SVO and the verb indexes agreement with the subject *abagóre* 'women'. The passive construction in (20-b) also seems to be identical to the inverse construction (19-b) with respect to word order, both exhibiting OVS, and with respect to agreement. However, whereas in the inverse clause the verb bears no overt morphological exponent, we can observe that it does so in the passive clause, and that this passive marker is obligatory. Furthermore, the subject is demoted to oblique status, indicated by the obligatory presence of the bound preposition *n'-*.

3.2 Evidence for A-movement and GF-changing

In the previous section, it was noted that direction systems are at first glance very similar to active-passive systems, but differ from them in several important ways. However, what they seem to have indeed in common is that they involve *grammatical function changing* (GF-changing), a term used to describe the fact that an argument's grammatical function (subject, object, indirect object) can change in the course of the derivation, although its thematic (θ-)role remains unaffected. That is, there are certain well-defined positions in the clause where specific θ-roles are assigned (θ-positions). These positions generally correspond to specific grammatical functions (i.e., they are simultaneously A-positions). So, an argument base-merged in the complement position of V receives the θ-role 'theme' or 'patient' and is in the position where it functions as the formal direct object of the clause. An argument base-merged in the specifier of vP receives the θ-role 'agent', and in this position, the argument functions as the formal subject of the clause. Now, there is one position in the clause in which no θ-role is assigned, but which is an A-position (hence assigns a specific GF to the argument which occupies that position): the specifier of TP. Given that movement can only target such $\bar{\theta}$-positions (see Chomsky 1981), an argument with whatever θ-role can therefore move to SpecT, the surface subject position. This is an instance of GF-changing, because an argument which has received a particular θ-role (and, correspondingly, a specific GF) at an earlier stage of the derivation moves to a position which is connected to a different GF, such that its original GF changes, while its thematic properties remain constant.

Such a GF-changing process is commonly held to take place in passive constructions. In passive clauses, the argument which receives the theme θ-role does not appear to carry out the direct object function. Instead, this argument seems to be the formal subject of the clause, in that it triggers certain processes connected to the GF subject (e.g., its ability of inducing subject agreement, binding subject-oriented reflexives, etc.). The original subject of the active clause seems to have disappeared or at least to have lost argument status. We thus have a GF-changing process that converts the GF 'object' of the theme argument in an active clause to the GF 'subject' of the same argument in the corresponding passive clause, and the former subject of the active clause is replaced by a new subject which has 'patient' properties.

Upon closer scrutiny, it turns out that direction systems might exhibit a kind of GF-changing in inverse contexts. This is again particularly clearly visible in Mapudungun (see (6-a) and (7-a), repeated below), where the agreement morphology seems to be completely inverted. For example, the 1st person subject marker -*n* expresses agreement with the agent argument in (21-a), but with the theme argument in (21-b).

(21) a. *Ngilla-fi-n*
    buy-3.OBJ-1SG.SUBJ
    'I bought it/him/her/them.'

   b. *Pe-e-n-Ø*
    see-INV-1SG.SUBJ-2OBJ
    'You saw me.'

We can thus tentatively presuppose the following descriptive characterization of 'subject' in Mapudungun (cf. Arnold 1996):

(22) *Subject:*
   The most prominent argument in a clause is the subject.

This enforces that by definition a prominent theme argument must change its GF 'direct object' to 'subject'. Given the structural approach to grammatical functions as described above (see Chomsky 1965, Baker 1988), the prominent argument must occupy SpecT, the subject position. GF-changing (hence A-movement), then, obligatorily takes place in inverse contexts, which might also be considered one of the reasons why passivization is generally in complementary distribution with the inverse.[11] There is indeed evidence that this view might

---

[11] At least in the languages I surveyed and that have been described as exhibiting both direct-inverse and active-passive constructions (e.g., Kinyarwanda), no examples were provided that might be viewed as instances of passivized inverse constructions. This, on the other hand, might suggest that there is an underlying abstract identity between passive and inverse constructions. But since both give rise to a similar process of GF changing, one cannot occur in the context of the other. This does not automatically imply an abstract identity between the two phenomena, it only implies that a certain core feature is shared by both constructions (also see fn. 8 on the non-holistic nature of these categories).

be correct, and I will discuss some of this evidence in the following two subsections.

3.2.1 Subject-object reversal in Bantu

Bantu languages such as Kinyarwanda, Kirundi and others as well as Apachean languages like Navajo are usually described as having rather fixed word orders in canonical declarative clauses: SVO for Bantu, SOV for Apachean. Both language groups have been argued to exhibit direct-inverse alternations that are not (exclusively) expressed by specific direct/inverse morphology, but by syntactic movement. The most straightforward evidence for this comes from the fact that the fixed word orders are disrupt in inverse contexts, resulting in OVS in Bantu languages, and OSV in Apachean.

Ndayiragije (1996) and Ura (1996, 2000) have convincingly argued that inverse constructions in Bantu languages involve syntactic A-movement of DP_{int} to the derived subject position SpecT. They motivate this analysis on the basis of certain formal properties including the circumvention of weak crossover (as in Passamaquoddy; see Bruening 2001, 2005), the form of the agreement marker, the shape of negation, the possibility of pro-drop in the subject position, and the fact that inverse clauses differ from clauses where Ā-movement (e.g. topicalization) has taken place in certain respects. Consider the Dzamba data in (23) (from Ura 2000: 41–42, who ascribes the data to Givón 1979).

(23) a. *oPoso a-tom-aki mukanda.*
    Poso HE-send-PAST letter
    'Poso sent a letter.'

   b. *I-mukanda mu-tom-aki oPoso.*
    the-letter IT-send-PAST Poso
    'The letter was sent by Poso.'

In Dzamba, as in Kinyarwanda (see section 3.1), the direct-inverse alternation is restricted to 3rd person arguments (non-local direction), and is constrained by the relative discourse prominence of the respective arguments (there is a non-overt proximate-obviative distinction). If DP_{ext} is given more discourse salience (proximate status), it precedes DP_{int} which is interpreted obviative, and obligatorily induces subject agreement (as in (23-a), indicated by the marker *a-*). On the other hand, if DP_{int} is proximate and DP_{ext} is obviative, then DP_{int} precedes DP_{ext} and induces subject agreement instead. We thus have a clear instance of a direct-inverse alternation: there is a unique core agreement slot whose controller is DP_{ext} in the direct, and DP_{int} in the inverse. Additionally, this agreement pattern is accompanied by syntactic movement: in the direct, DP_{ext} occupies the subject position, but in the inverse, DP_{int} is fronted to that position, preceding DP_{ext}.

One might raise the objection that this looks much like topicalization, which is also assumed to be an optional process. However, topicalization constructions in Dzamba are different from inverse constructions like (23-b) in that DP_{ext} additionally precedes the verb and induces agreement. Witness the contrast between (24-a) and the inverse clause in (23-b).

(24) Topicalization in Dzamba (Ura 2000: 43–44):
    a.   I-mukanda$_i$ oPoso   a-mu-tom-aki   t$_i$.
        the-letter   Poso   HE-IT-send-PAST
        'The letter$_i$, Poso sent t$_i$.'

    b.   *I-mukanda$_i$ oPoso   mu-tom-aki   t$_i$.
        the-letter   Poso   IT-send-PAST
        'The letter$_i$, Poso sent t$_i$.'

In contrast to object fronting in inverse contexts, topicalization is a true instance of Ā-movement which does not affect grammatical functions, although both topicalization and object fronting in inverse contexts involve movement of DP_{int} to a left-peripheral position in the clause. Thus, the topicalized object cannot induce subject agreement on the verb as in (24-b). If object fronting in inverse contexts is analyzed as an instance of A-movement, then GF-changing and its effects on agreement are fully predicted.

3.2.2 Variable binding in Passamaquoddy

Bruening (2001, 2005) provides data from Passamaquoddy involving variable binding that seem to confirm the hypothesis that there is a GF-changing process active in some direction systems. As mentioned before, the specifier position of TP is the subject position, hence movement to that position upon Agree between T and an argument in the syntax makes this argument formally a subject. In English, this is canonically DP_{ext} base-Merged in Specv: T looks for a goal DP to Agree with, in order to value and delete its uninterpretable Φ-features and to assign Case. Under standard assumptions, locality forces T to undergo Agree with the closest available matching goal. This cannot be DP_{int}, since DP_{int} is asymmetrically c-commanded by DP_{ext}, hence is protected from Agree. Given that T has some "EPP property" forcing an argument to occupy its specifier position, DP_{ext} moves from its base position to the derived subject position in SpecT upon Φ-Agree, checking T's EPP feature.

In some direction systems, we seem to have the case that sometimes DP_{ext}, and sometimes DP_{int} can act as the formal subject of the clause. The reason why only one argument can induce core (subject-)agreement on the verb can only be attributed to the fact that the T head in direction systems somehow differs from that in languages like English, in which it invariably affects the closest available goal (DP_{ext}) in a simple transitive context. We can thus postulate the generalization that T's behaviour is controlled by the language-specific prominence scale: it Agrees with the high-ranked DP_{ext} in a direct context, and with the high-ranked DP_{int} in an inverse context. We thus predict that in a direct-inverse language, given that EPP-movement is contingent on Agree, DP_{int} must also be able to move to the derived subject position SpecT, hence being able to act as the formal subject of the clause, like DP_{ext} in a direct context. This is shown in (25).[12] Indeed, Bruening provides empirical evidence from variable binding that corroborates this view.

(25) *Successive-cyclic A-movement in inverse contexts:*
 [$_{TP}$ DP_{int} T [$_{vP}$ DP_{ext} [$_{v'}$ t' [$_{v'}$ v [$_{VP}$ V t]]]]]

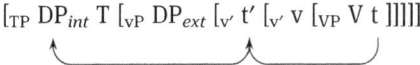

He argues that if DP_{int} moves to SpecT in an inverse context, it is predicted that variable binding into DP_{ext} (which has remained in an outer Spec of v) should be possible. Indeed, this prediction is borne out. First, in direct contexts as in (26), DP_{ext} (which is proximate) can bind a variable in DP_{int} (which is obviative), because DP_{ext}, not DP_{int}, has moved to SpecT, hence c-commands DP_{int} from an A-position.

(26) *Variable binding in direct contexts (Bruening 2005: 12):*
 a. *Kenoq olu yatte=hc wen 't-uwehkah-a-l 't-epeskom-akonu-m-ol.*
  however EMPH each=FUT who 3-use-DIR-OBV 3-play.ball-NOM-POSS-OBV
  'But each one₁ will use his₁ own ball.'

---

12 Bruening (2001) assumes that DP_{int} successive-cyclically raises to SpecT, hence the intermediate stop at the edge of vP. DP_{int} could also move in one fell swoop, or could even stop at every phrase edge on the way to its ultimate landing site, depending on the specific phase theory one assumes.

b. *Nit   msi=te   kehsi-htit   ehpic-ik*
   then all=EMPH   be.many-3PL.CONJ   woman-3PL

   '-pun-a-ni-ya   (')-nican-sis-uwa   sip-uk   apc   welaqiwik.
   3-put-DIR-N-3PL   3-child-DIM-3PL.OBV.PL   river-LOC again in.evening
   'That night, every one of the women₁ puts her₁ child into the river.'

In contrast, an object quantifier may not bind a variable in a proximate DP$_{ext}$ in a direct context (Bruening 2005: 13):

(27) [$_{NP}$ *Skitap musqitaham-ac-il*]   *'-koti-tqon-a-l*   *psi=te*   *wen-il.*
       man   hate-3CONJ-PART.OBV   3-FUT-arrest-DIR-OBV   all=EMPH   someone-OBV
   'A man that he*$_{i/j}$ hates will arrest everyone$_i$.'

The movement theory predicts that a proximate DP$_{int}$ should be able to A-bind a variable contained in an obviative DP$_{ext}$ in an inverse clause. The following data show that this is correct (Bruening 2005: 13):

(28) a. *Kat=op   wen   (')-nokol-oku-wihi-l   w-oli-witapi-hil.*
        NEG=would   who   3-leave-INV-NEG-OBV   3-good-friend-OBV
        'His₁ best friend would abandon no one₁.'

   b. *Yatte   wen   pilsqehsis   '-kis-cem-ku-l   w-ikuwoss-ol.*
       each   who   girl   3-PERF-kiss-INV-OBV   3-mother-OBV
       'Her₁ mother kissed each girl₁.'

   c. *Psi=te   wen   '-kosiciy-uku-l   w-ikuwoss-ol.*
       all=EMPH who   3-know-INV-OBV   3-mother-OBV
       'His₁ mother knows everyone₁.'

A further suggestive argument that direct-inverse alternations may indeed go hand in hand with syntactic movement in Passamaquoddy comes from reconstruction effects. In inverse contexts, an ambiguity arises that is totally expected under the movement theory: DP$_{int}$ may bind a variable in DP$_{ext}$, but the reverse is also possible, given that DP$_{int}$ can reconstruct to its base position, being in turn within the scope of DP$_{ext}$. This is illustrated for (29-a), whose structure is given in (29-b) (Bruening 2005: 14).

(29) a. *Mu=te   keq   utomeya-ku-w-on   [$_{NP}$ tepelto-k]*
        NEG=EMPH what   3.bother-INV-NEG-N   IC.own.TI-3.CONJ
        'Nothing₁ bothers the one who owns it₁.'

   b. [$_{TP}$ [$_{DP_{int}}$ the one who owns it] [$_{T'}$ T [$_{vP}$ nothing [$_{vP}$ bothers t$_{DP_{int}}$]]]]

4 Analysis

After having introduced the basic properties of direction systems and the empirical challenges imposed by them, the ensuing sections are devoted to a principled analysis of the facts within a general minimalist framework.

4.1 Basic assumptions

In what follows, I presuppose a strictly derivational, feature-driven approach to syntax (cf. Chomsky 1995, 2000, 2001) in which structure-building applies cyclically (respecting the *Strict Cycle Condition* in (30)) from bottom to top. There are two basic operations: Merge and Agree. Move is a special instance of Merge (namely internal Merge) and will not play a major role in what follows.

(30) STRICT CYCLE CONDITION (SCC, cf. Chomsky 1973):
No syntactic operation may exclusively apply within a domain Δ where Δ is a proper subtree dominated by the current root node of the phrase marker.

All elementary operations are triggered by designated features. Probe features ([∗F∗]) trigger Agree, structure-building features ([•F•]) trigger external and internal Merge.[13] Usually, it is assumed that operation-inducing features are unordered on heads. The approach to be developed here follows Müller (2010) in assuming that operations apply in a certain order, such that, given two features $[F]_1$ and $[F]_2$, either $[F]_1 \succ [F]_2$ or $[F]_2 \succ [F]_1$ holds. However, I do not fully dispense with the standard approach. Empirical evidence suggests that there is sometimes no inherent ordering between features. These features are discharged in parallel, and are pointed off by a comma (such that $[F]_1$, $[F]_2$) in what follows. The feature specification of a head is entirely lexically determined.

The necessity of deleting features is expressed in the *Last Resort Condition* in (31), which dictates that every syntactic rule application must discharge one of the two kinds of features introduced above and that all operation-inducing features must be discharged by the end of the derivation, in order to yield an interpretable expression at the level of Logical Form (LF).

---

[13] This notation is based on Adger (2003), Sternefeld (2006) and Heck and Müller (2007).

(31) LAST RESORT:
a. Every operation must discharge either [•F•] or [*F*]
b. Only the topmost feature on a stack is accessible.
c. Unordered features must be discharged simultaneously.

The clausal spine consists of CP, TP, vP and VP. DP_{int} is Merged as a sister of V, DP_{ext} is Merged as a sister of v′. Although the issue of what syntactic units (phrases, operations, etc.) count as phases (see Chomsky 2000, 2001, 2008, Epstein and Seely 2002, Müller 2004 and many others) is orthogonal to the main concerns of this paper and particularly the technical analysis proposed here, it should be noted that if the concept of phase is to be integrated into the current framework, it must be liberal enough so as to allow "long" Agree between T and the internal argument contained in VP, which is strongly supported by the data.[14]

Concerning the timing of inflection, I assume a Distributed Morphology architecture according to which morphology is located in the post-syntactic component (cf. Halle & Marantz 1993, 1994, Noyer 1992, Harley & Noyer 2003, Embick & Noyer 2007). Narrow syntax operates on phonologically empty, abstract heads which are bundles of morpho-syntactic features. Vocabulary items (pairings of phonological and morpho-syntactic information) are post-syntactically inserted into these abstract heads, according to the subset principle and the specificity principle (cf. Halle & Marantz 1993, Halle 1997).

4.2 Features and hierarchy effects

This section attempts to eliminate the descriptive concept "scale" as a primitive from the grammar. The principal motivation for doing so is that the concept is in general at variance with basic minimalist tenets (a number of works relating to this topic and with different solutions include Alexiadou and Anagnostopoulou 2006, Adger and Harbour 2007, Wiltschko 2008, Béjar and Řezáč 2009, Heck and

---

[14] This is not possible if vP and CP are taken to be (strong) phases, and is, a fortiori, not possible if every phrase counts as a phase. A technical solution is to employ a weaker version of the Phase Impenetrability Condition (PIC) as proposed by Chomsky (2001), according to which a strong phase is evaluated as soon as the next higher strong phase is reached. vP's domain is then spelled out after the CP phase has been completed, which makes it possible for T to probe into v's complement (namely VP containing DP_{int}). I do not see how this could be modelled if every phrase is a phase, even under the relaxed PIC. Another conceivable solution is to say that Agree is not subject to the PIC in the first place, as suggested by Bošković 2007. I will not discuss the issue further here.

Richards 2010 and Richards 2015, among many others). First, scales are conceptually problematic for theories that dispense with idiosyncratic, possibly language-specific constraints and rules, and instead elevate abstract, universal and externally motivated principles to the primary objects of investigation. Second, hierarchies have no theoretically relevant status in a minimalist framework which essentially makes use of a lexicon and a recursive computational device that generates structured expressions from lexical items, by employing a limited number of elementary operations. Third, the explanative power of hierarchies is relatively low, because they are too descriptively oriented, and it is not clear if they emerge from deeply rooted principles of universal grammar (cf. also Brown, Koch, and Wiltschko 2004).

It is undeniable that scales are to a large extent language-specific, idiosyncratic objects.[15] A standard minimalist account would therefore derive their cross-linguistic differences by appeal to variation in feature distribution and the featural build-up of lexical items. I adopt such an approach throughout the paper. Regarding the nature of features, I essentially follow Béjar (2003) and Béjar and Řezáč (2009), although their proposal is modified here to a certain extent (see below). To begin with, I adopt the following working hypothesis.

(32) *Working hypothesis:*
Scales encode *specificity*. Given a scale of the form $a > b > \ldots > n$, elements toward the left bear more features than elements toward the right, that is, a is the most specific, n the least specific element.

More precisely, this means that the number of elements on a scale displays the number of *features* that the leftmost element carries. There are proper superset relations among the elements from left to right: $A \supset B \supset \ldots \supset N$, with $A, B, N, \ldots$ representing the sets of features borne by the corresponding elements.

Adopting the terminology of Béjar and Řezáč (2009), a distinction is drawn between (complex) *features* and *segments* (or "atomic" features). A feature consists of a finite set of segments. The segments simultaneously encode the value of the feature. Features can be schematically represented as in (33).

(33) *Representation of a three-segmental feature:*
$$\begin{bmatrix} [s_1] \\ [s_2] \\ [s_3] \end{bmatrix}$$

---

[15] Certain universal restrictions on scales must nevertheless be recognized, including, for example, the fact that local persons are always higher ranked than non-local persons, or that animates always outrank inanimates.

As a concrete example, consider a language with a 1 > 2 > 3 person hierarchy. There are three elements on that scale. Consequently, '1st person' bears exactly three segments. These segments are a proper superset of the set of segments borne by '2nd person', which are in turn a proper superset of the set of segments borne by '3rd person'. The person features are then represented as in (34).

(34) *Representation of person features:*

$$\begin{bmatrix} [\pi] \\ [2] \\ [1] \end{bmatrix} > \begin{bmatrix} [\pi] \\ [2] \end{bmatrix} > [[\pi]]$$

Although their concrete nature is not of great importance here, the segments in (34) have a certain semantics. [1] represents 'speaker', [2] represents 'participant', and [π] is a general person feature which encodes 3rd person if it is the single segment in a feature matrix (see Béjar 2003 and Béjar and Řezáč 2009 for discussion). Of course, this procedure may be generalized to other features (such as animacy and definiteness) as well.

Consider a second example, a language with a hierarchy of the form 1/2 > 3, i.e., a language in which local persons are not distinguished from one another with respect to prominence status (i.e., specificity). This can be implemented by the following feature decomposition.

(35) $\begin{bmatrix} [\pi] \\ [2] \end{bmatrix} > [[\pi]]$

In this case, [2] representing 'participant' subsumes both 1st and 2nd person (since both are participants in a discourse).

Case features can also be implemented in this way. As person features contain a general π-feature, Case features are characterized by a general Case feature [κ], which, when it is the single segment in a feature matrix, encodes the less marked external Case (nominative and ergative). The internal Case (accusative and absolutive) is characterized by an additional feature [INT]; see (36).

(36) *Representation of Case features:*

$$\begin{bmatrix} [\kappa] \\ [\text{INT}] \end{bmatrix} > [[\kappa]]$$

Such a decomposition of Case features is completely parallel to the one given for Φ-features above, and is in line with the observation that the internal Case is inherently more marked (more specific) than the external Case. This will become especially relevant for the discussion of the agreement displacement data in section 5.2.

It should be evident that any hierarchy can be transformed into a corresponding specificity scale along these lines. Elements high on a scale are more specific, because they are encoded by a superset of the features that encode elements lower on the scale. In the next section, I will show how this conception of specificity can be formally integrated within the probe-goal theory of Agree.

4.3 Specificity-driven Agree

The operation Agree of Chomsky (2000, 2001) establishes a relation between a *probe* and a *goal* and is, inter alia, responsible for the surface effect that manifests itself in agreement morphology. By hypothesis, a probe feature enters the derivation unvalued and seeks the value that is provided by a matching goal feature. The probe must be checked and valued in order to be deleted. Deletion means LF-inaccessibility, a desired consequence, but not PF-inaccessibility (due to its phonetic effects).

A common property of syntactic dependencies is that they must be sufficiently local. In the case of agreement, feature-relativized minimality states that a probe π cannot enter into an Agree relation with an element α for a feature [F] iff there is a *closer* element β such that β also bears [F].[16] However, I would like to put forward the hypothesis that Agree is not exclusively locality-driven. More specifically, I argue that π can Agree with a more remote goal y if the segments borne by y match more probe segments of π than the segments of another matching goal y' (i.e., if the set of matching segments of y is a superset of the matching segments of y' with respect to π's probe segments), although y' is closer to π. Thus, Agree can involve the more distant goal in case it is more *specific* than the closer one. This general view of constraining syntactic operations via specificity is already envisaged in Lahne (2008, 2009).[17]

In section 4.2, I have introduced the feature-segment system based on Béjar (2003) and Béjar & Řezáč (2009). The proposed conception of "feature" as well

---

16 Closeness can be equalized with "closest c-command," in Chomsky's (2001) terms.
17 Lahne's (2009) argument for a Generalized Specificity Principle on Merge basically comes from certain empirical and conceptual issues relating to MLC effects. Anti-MLC effects like order-preserving movement (e.g. multiple *wh*-fronting in Slavic languages) are particularly problematic under an MLC-based account. A specificity principle does not only eliminate conceptually problematic constraints like the MLC or Equidistance, but derives their effects in a uniform way.

as "specificity" envisaged in this system must necessarily be integrated into the definition of Agree. I propose to reformulate the operation as follows:

(37) *Agree:*
A probe π Agrees with a goal y with respect to a feature [F], yielding valuation and deletion of [F] on π and y, iff (a)–(e) hold:
   a. Both π and y are active (see (42)).
   b. π and y match (i.e., there is at least one segment S such that S belongs to F on π and y).
   c. The set of *matching* segments G borne by y are a (proper or improper) subset of the set of probe segments P borne by π.
   d. π c-commands y.
   e. There is no alternative goal y' such that y' is more specific than y and is in the c-command domain of π.

(38) *Specificity:*
A goal y with a set of matching segments G is more specific for a feature [F] than a goal y' with a set of matching segments G' with respect to a c-commanding probe π iff either (a) or (b) hold:
   a. $|G| > |G'|$
   b. $|G| = |G'|$ and y asymmetrically c-commands y'.

According to (38), a goal counts as more specific if it bears more matching feature segments, or if it is closer to the probe. Trivially, the latter case becomes relevant only if the matching goals in the c-command domain of a probe are all equally specific. That is, if the goals cannot be distinguished by virtue of their feature cardinality, the probe selects by default the closest one. Thus, locality is not fully dispensed with in this system, as is desired on grounds of computational complexity.[18]

In accordance with the feature-segment approach developed in section 4.2, a probe feature is schematically represented as in (39).[19]

---

[18] One might object that the specificity approach envisaged here increases the computational burden, because the probing element has to compare several possible matching goals with one another in order to decide with which to Agree. In my opinion, this conceptually based argument loses much of its strength, given that the existence of phases already makes syntax computationally efficient (although, as pointed out earlier, I remain agnostic as to what actually counts as a phase). The PIC does constrain the search space of the probe, but within the search space, comparison of matching goals seems to be necessary on empirical grounds in the present context.

[19] For reasons of space, I will use the simplified horizontal notation [*s_1-s_2-s_3*] for features like (39) in all sample derivations throughout the rest of this paper.

(39) *Representation of a probe feature:*

$$\begin{bmatrix} [*s_1*] \\ [*s_2*] \\ [*s_3*] \end{bmatrix}$$

This entails that each probe segment is checked separately by a matching goal segment. Unmatched segments are deleted. That is, not all probe segments need to be checked and deleted; only one must. This is captured by the following condition on feature checking (which is a version of the *Match Requirement* in Béjar and Řezáč 2009: 45).

(40) CONDITION ON FEATURE CHECKING:
For convergence at LF, at least one probe segment must be checked via Agree. Segments that remain unchecked are ignored by the computational system. Features that remain unchecked are uninterpretable and lead to a crash of the derivation.

Note that in addition, something like Chomsky's (2001: 15) principle of *Maximize Matching Effects* must hold, because a probe feature must be checked at once and as fully as possible against a matching goal, "partial elimination of features under Match, followed by elimination of the residue under more remote Match, is not an option." This is the crucial difference between Béjar and Řezáč's (2009) approach and the one assumed here, because the gist of their analysis is that probe segments can be checked separately against different goals, under cyclic expansion of the search space (which may have various consequences). The present theory, however, demands that a probe feature can only Agree with one goal, and this goal must be the most specific one available in the c-command domain.

A question that arises in this context is how valuation is achieved in the system. That is, how can verbal agreement differentiate between specific values if the probe is already prespecified for particular segments? Valuation of a probe is achieved by deletion and copying. As indicated in (40), unmatched segments delete. If a goal feature has more segments than the probe, the missing segments are copied onto the probe. Thus it is possible for non-inverse languages like English or German to differentiate between person values, although these languages have prespecified *flat probes*. An abstract example for such a configuration is given in (41); added segments are underlined, '...' represents c-command.

(41) Valuation of a 'flat' probe:

$$[[*s_3*]] \ldots \begin{bmatrix}[s_1]\\[s_2]\\[s_3]\end{bmatrix} \Longrightarrow \begin{bmatrix}[*s_1*]\\[*s_2*]\\[*s_3*]\end{bmatrix} \ldots \begin{bmatrix}[s_1]\\[s_2]\\[s_3]\end{bmatrix}$$

I assume that in addition to probe features, certain goal features have to be checked as well (see the related *Person Licensing Condition* of Béjar and Řezáč 2009 and the *Feature Checking* constraint in Georgi 2009a and Georgi, Heck and Müller 2009). Relevant for the present purposes are Φ-features and Case features. As soon as the Φ-features or the Case feature of an argument have participated in an Agree relation, they are checked (as they are on the probing element). This has consequences for how long a syntactic object stays active during the derivation, because still unchecked features render a syntactic object (be it a probe or a goal category) active (see (42)).[20]

(42) *Activity Condition:*
A syntactic object α is *active* iff there is a feature F on α such that (a) or (b) hold:
a. F is an unchecked probe feature ([*F*]).
b. F is a goal feature which can be checked.

The specificity-based probe-goal system outlined so far is abstractly illustrated below.[21] In (43-a), a configuration is shown in which a probe targets a more distant goal ZP, although there is a potentially closer goal YP. The reason is that ZP outranks YP in the number of matching goal segments. The probe feature has three segments [*a-b-c*] which all search for a matching counterpart. The best matching candidate is ZP, because ZP's segment cardinality is 3, that of YP is 2. Both goals are in principle possible candidates for an Agree relation, but ZP is more specific than YP. Agree can thus never hold between H and YP in this configuration.

---

[20] Whereas unchecked (person) features lead to a violation of the Person Licensing Condition in Béjar and Řezáč 2009, I assume in contrast that goal features *can* be checked if the structural conditions for checking are met, but they do not necessarily need to. However, as noted in the main text, they are crucial in that they, if unchecked, render an argument visible for further syntactic computation.
[21] For reasons of space, I will hereafter use labeled bracketing notation instead of tree notation in all the example derivations that follow.

(43)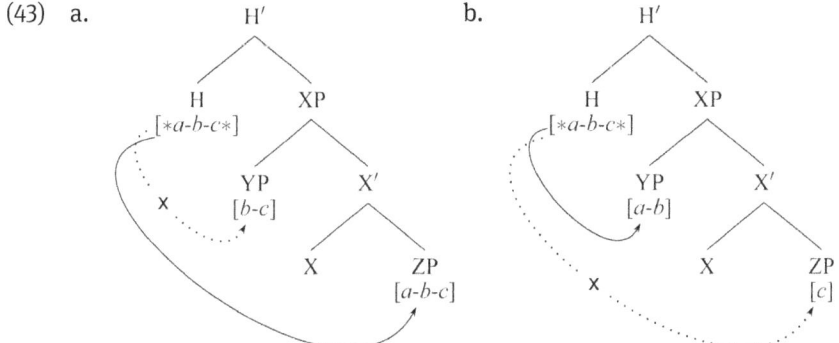

In (43-b) on the other hand, the closer goal YP is more specific than the more distant goal ZP, although ZP qualifies as a potential candidate for Agree. However, again, the segment cardinality of YP (2) outranks that of ZP (1). Therefore, Agree can, at least in the configuration shown in (43-b), never involve the more distant goal ZP.

4.4 Deriving the agreement patterns

With this much theoretical background, we can now derive the generalization that the controller of the core Φ-probe in direct-inverse languages is always the highest argument on the scale (i.e., the most specific one), a pattern which I referred to as core or primary agreement. The theoretical apparatus introduced in the last sections also allows us to derive the observation that there is secondary agreement in some direct-inverse languages. But before going into the details, let me first spell out some further assumptions. Recall that in order to circumvent the problem of look-ahead and countercyclicity, we must employ a uniquely high head that has both arguments in its scope. A possible candidate for such a head is T (as already envisaged by Alexiadou and Anagnostopoulou 2006 and subsequently adopted by others). v is not an option. The reason for this is two-fold. First, if v is the locus of agreement features, then look-ahead seems unavoidable, unless additional assumptions are made: at the v'-level, v cannot know whether DP_{int}, which is the only accessible goal for Φ-Agree at this stage of the derivation, is the most specific argument to Agree with. Therefore, v would have to look at the properties of DP_{ext}, which is not yet part of the structure. But if v does not perform Agree with DP_{int} at the v'-level, and waits until DP_{ext} is Merged, which eventually turns out not to be the most specific argument, then Agree has to apply countercyclically, thus violating the SCC in

(30) (because Agree applies within a subtree that is properly dominated by the current root node vP). Second, the c-command requirement on Agree is only satisfied for DP_{int}, but not for DP_{ext}.[22] Since Agree *must* take place under c-command, the empirically most appealing choice is T, which fits well with the GF-changing analysis proposed in section 3.2, given that potential EPP-driven movement to SpecT upon Φ-Agree results in a change of the relevant argument's GF to 'subject'.

T can then be specified in two ways: either it has a single core Φ-probe ([*Φ*]) which looks for the most specific goal argument to Agree with, or it has two probes which are ordered ([*Φ*]$_1$ ≻ [*Φ*]$_2$), such that the first probe Agrees with the most specific argument that is available in its c-command domain (so that [*Φ*]$_1$ Agrees with DP_{ext} in the direct, and with DP_{int} in the inverse), while the second probe Agrees with what is left over (so that [*Φ*]$_2$ Agrees with DP_{int} in the direct, and with DP_{ext} in the inverse). The former specification shows up, e.g., in Movima, where agreement can only be controlled by exactly one argument. The latter specification is present, for instance, in Mapudungun and Plains Cree, where both arguments generally induce agreement on the verb.

The process of Φ-agreement (or more precisely, in the present case, person agreement) in direct-inverse languages is abstractly illustrated in (44) (actual derivations follow in section 4.7), ignoring direction marking and Case for the moment. Suppose that the direct-inverse distinction in our hypothetical language is governed by a 1 > 2 > 3 hierarchy. Then there is a fully differentiated core person probe [*π-2-1*] on T. Suppose further that the language canonically shows agreement with both core arguments. Then there is a second person probe on T which is flat: [*π*].

Now imagine a transitive clause where DP_{ext} is 2nd person ([π-2]) and DP_{int} is 3rd person ([π]). The decisive steps of the derivation for such a direct clause are given in (44).

(44) *Direct context:*
    a. Step 1: Agree(T,DP_{ext}) → primary Agree
        [$_{T'}$ T$_{[*π-2-1*] ≻ [*π*]}$ [$_{vP}$ $DP_{ext[π-2]}$ [$_{v'}$ v [$_{VP}$ V $DP_{int[π]}$]]]]

    b. Step 2: Agree (T,DP_{int}) → secondary Agree
        [$_{T'}$ T$_{[*π-2*] ≻ [*π*]}$ [$_{vP}$ $DP_{ext[π-2]}$ [$_{v'}$ v [$_{VP}$ V $DP_{int[π]}$]]]]

---

[22] Expansion of search space or upward probing as it is assumed in Béjar and Řezáč (2009) is not possible in the system proposed here.

The operations apply in this order because DP_{ext} is more specific for the primary person probe on T than DP_{int}, although DP_{int} qualifies as a potential checker to begin with (that is, it meets the four conditions on Agree in (a)–(d) of (37)). But DP_{ext}'s segment cardinality (2) outranks that of DP_{int} (1), making it more specific than DP_{int} according to (38). Since DP_{ext}'s Φ-features are checked upon primary Agree, it does not intervene between T and DP_{int} anymore, such that secondary Agree can apply. Note that primary Agree deletes the unmatched [∗1∗] segment of the person probe.

Now suppose the situation is the other way round, with DP_{ext} being 3rd person ([π]) and DP_{int} being 2nd person ([π-2]). The derivation for such an inverse clause is given in (45).

(45) *Inverse context:*
    a. Step 1: Agree(T,DP_{int}) → primary Agree
       [$_{T'}$ T$_{[∗π-2-1∗] > [∗π∗]}$ [$_{vP}$ $DP_{ext[π]}$ [$_{v'}$ v [$_{VP}$ V $DP_{int[π-2]}$]]]]

    b. Step 2: Agree (T,DP_{ext}) → secondary Agree
       [$_{T'}$ T$_{[∗π-2∗] > [∗π∗]}$ [$_{vP}$ $DP_{ext[π]}$ [$_{v'}$ v [$_{VP}$ V $DP_{ext[π-2]}$]]]]

Now it is DP_{int} which is more specific for the core probe on T than DP_{ext}. Again, the unmatched [∗1∗] segment of the core probe is deleted, and secondary Agree can apply between T and DP_{ext} because DP_{int} is inactive at that point.

4.5 Direction marking as Case agreement

Thus far, we have seen how primary and secondary Φ-agreement can be derived via the mechanics laid out in section 4.1–4.3. Still, nothing has been said about what causes the appearance of a direction marker. It was already noted in passing that the direction marker is the only device that allows one to unambiguously determine the grammatical functions of the arguments, which are not otherwise marked (e.g., by Case-marking). From this striking fact, I concluded that the traditional view on direct-inverse marking is on the right track, viz. that direction markers are nothing else than Case markers, with the direct representing nominative or ergative (the 'external' Case) and the inverse representing accusative or absolutive (the 'internal' Case).

With this in mind, I argue in this section that direction marking can be derived from the simple assumption that there is an unvalued Case feature on T which occurs with the core Φ-probe.[23] This unvalued Case feature is valued and checked upon Φ-Agree with DP_{ext} or DP_{int} (recall that unordered probe features have to be discharged in one swoop). Importantly, this requires the additional assumption that both core arguments must have received their structural Case at an earlier stage of the derivation. I propose in line with Sigurðsson (2000) that arguments receive their Case values on the vP level. The functional head v assigns internal Case to DP_{int} and external Case to DP_{ext}.[24] This is achieved by two Case probes which are ordered on v as in (46).[25]

(46) [*κ-INT*] ≻ [*κ*]

Because only the topmost feature on a stack is accessible at each step of the derivation, the first Case feature is checked against DP_{int} because DP_{int} is the only accessible goal at that stage of the derivation (DP_{ext} is still in the workspace, waiting to be merged in Specv). At this point, it may be appropriate to introduce a further technical assumption. This centers around the problem that v does not c-command DP_{ext}. Recall that Agree requires c-command; therefore, specifier-head Agree, and hence checking of DP_{ext}'s Case feature, is by assumption precluded. To circumvent this problem, I suggest that the Case feature of a nominal is itself a probe (given that Case features are inherently uninterpretable, unlike Φ-features, which are interpretable on arguments but uninterpretable on functional categories). As a probe, it looks for the most specific goal to Agree with in the current phase. Note that nothing prevents a probe feature from Agreeing with another probe feature in the system proposed here, as long as both share matching segments. As for valuation, this has the consequence that the segments of the probe which is more specific are copied onto the less specific probe (this is exactly what the mechanism in section 4.3 predicts).

---

23 See Rackowski (2002) for a similar analysis of Case agreement in the Austronesian language Tagalog.
24 Here I deviate from standard analyses which employ two functional heads as Case assigners. For example, Chomsky (1993), Laka (1993), Bobaljik (1993), Řezáč (2003) and others assume that v assigns accusative or absolutive to DP_{int} and T assigns nominative or ergative to DP_{ext}. Murasugi (1992) and Müller (2009) propose a somewhat different analysis, according to which v assigns the more marked internal Case (subsuming ergative and accusative) to DP_{int} in nominative-accusative languages and to DP_{ext} in ergative-absolutive languages, and T the less marked external Case (subsuming nominative and absolutive) to DP_{ext} in nominative-accusative languages and to DP_{int} in ergative-absolutive languages. Note further that the analysis developed here is incompatible with the traditional insight that Case and agreement are "two sides of the same coin" (cf. George and Kornfilt 1981).
25 Thus, technically Case assignment is subsumed under Agree, triggered by appropriate probe features (this is very similar to the concept of κ-Agree proposed in Keine 2010).

Let me illustrate what that means for Case assignment. After DP_{int} has received internal Case ((47-a)), the [*κ*] feature of DP_{ext} looks for a matching goal to Agree with as soon as it is introduced into the derivation via Merge. The next specific goal to Agree with is the head v which still bears the unchecked [*κ*] feature. The decisive step of the derivation is given in (47-b).

(47)   *Structural Case assignment:*
   a. $[_{v'}\ V_{[*INT,\ κ*] \succ [*κ*]}\ [_{VP}\ V\ DP_{int[*κ*]}]] \rightarrow$

   $[_{v'}\ V_{[*κ\text{-}INT*] \succ [*κ*]}\ [_{VP}\ V\ DP_{int[*INT,\ κ*]}]]$

   b. $[_{vP}\ DP_{ext[*κ*]}\ [_{v'}\ V_{[*κ\text{-}INT*] \succ [*κ*]}\ [_{VP}\ V\ DP_{int[*κ\text{-}INT*]}]]] \rightarrow$

   $[_{vP}\ DP_{ext[*κ*]}\ [_{v'}\ V_{[*κ\text{-}INT*] \succ [*κ*]}\ [_{VP}\ V\ DP_{int[*κ\text{-}INT*]}]]]$

Once an Agree relation between the two probes on DP_{ext} and v is established, both are checked and deleted. v is now complete, as it has no further operation-inducing features. DP_{ext} and DP_{int} are still active by virtue of their Φ-features, which have not yet participated in an Agree relation. This is crucial for the analysis, because the Case features must be accessible at a later stage of the derivation, and the Φ-features are exactly the means that render the arguments visible for further syntactic computation (cf. clause (b) of (42)).

Given these assumptions, it is possible for the Case feature on T to Agree with the Case feature of the argument which has entered into a primary Agree relation with T (see the last section). If the relevant argument is DP_{ext}, then the Case feature on T is valued [*κ*]. If the relevant argument is DP_{int}, it is valued [*κ-INT*]. Post-syntactically, [*κ*] is realized by a "direct" marker /X/, while the feature bundle [*κ-INT*] is realized by an "inverse" marker /Y/. This is how direct-inverse alternations are modelled in the present theory. The next section once again takes up the issue of how to analyze the syntactic effects, especially GF-changing, that were briefly discussed in section 3.2.

4.6 Syntactic effects

As mentioned earlier (section 3.2), valuation of the core probe on T may give rise to certain syntactic effects, a fact that is often ignored by many approaches, especially those that attempt to derive direct-inverse alternations solely by referring to principles of morphological realization. Béjar and Řezáč (2009: 68) note that "the syntactic approach to PH [i.e. person hierarchy, J.H.] effects based on

Agree is fully compatible with possible syntactic displacement correlates of PH effects, though it correctly does not require them" (also see Řezáč 2011: 69). These effects were analyzed as being a direct result of syntactic A-movement of DP_{int} in inverse contexts, resulting in GF-changing. Languages may or may not show any of these effects, which is totally expected given that a movement-inducing EPP feature [•D•] on T is present or not. Such an analysis is completely parallel to the one standardly given for subject raising, which is mandatory in some languages but absent (or optional) in others. But how can we derive the fact that EPP-driven movement always affects the prominent (i.e., most specific) argument, given that it is blind to the Φ-specification of the arguments? I assume that the EPP property is associated with a Φ-probe (represented as [•Φ•]$_{EPP}$, or using the diacritic notation of Biberauer, Holmberg and Roberts (2010), as [•Φ•]^). In languages where there is just a single Φ-probe on T, EPP-driven movement follows immediately. However, in languages with primary and secondary agreement, the situation is not that clear. The EPP feature (or diacritic) could be associated with either probe, but the empirical evidence suggests that it must be associated with the one that is discharged first. As it stands, this is an ad hoc stipulation, and it remains to be seen whether it can be derived in a more general way.

4.7 Plains Cree

In this short section, I exemplify the mechanism laid out in the previous sections by going through some sample derivations in the Algonquian language Plains Cree (PC).[26] PC has a very complex agreement system (details are set aside here) and the direction domain covers all types of arguments (there is local, non-local and core direction). Basically, in the verbal system, three forms are distinguished: the Independent, Conjunctive and Imperative. I only look at independent indicative forms in this section. In the independent paradigms, PC displays agreement with both core arguments, which is expressed by prefixes and suffixes. The prefix always expresses person agreement with the most prominent argument, where prominence is determined by the hierarchy in (48). The suffixes generally express agreement with the less prominent argument, but they may additionally express features of the higher ranked argument.

---

[26] See Hamann (2011) for further exemplification of movement-based non-local direction in Kinyarwanda and subject agreement in German.

(48) PC person scale:
   2 > 1 > 3 PROX > 3 OBV

Like many Algonquian languages, PC ranks 2nd person over 1st person, and makes a distinction between proximate (more salient) 3rd persons and obviative (less salient) 3rd persons. The scale in (48) can be transformed into the specificity scale in (49).

(49) PC specificity scale:

$$\begin{bmatrix} [\pi] \\ [1] \\ [2] \end{bmatrix} > \begin{bmatrix} [\pi] \\ [1] \end{bmatrix} > [[\pi]] > [\,]$$

The proximate-obviative distinction is captured by assuming that obviative 3rd person arguments lack a person specification entirely (i.e., they lack a general $[\pi]$ feature). According to the specificity scale in (49), the core person probe on T in PC is fully differentiated (in the best case, the most specific goal to Agree with would be a 2nd person argument). The second person probe is flat, because the argument which is left over does not stand in competition with another argument anymore. In other words, the second person probe does not care which person specification the remaining argument has.

(50) Specification of T in PC:

$$\begin{bmatrix} [*\pi*] \\ [*1*] \\ [*2*] \end{bmatrix}, \quad [[*\kappa*]] \succ [[*\pi*]]$$

Consider a local context, i.e., a context where two local persons co-occur. The following data are from Fadden (2000: 3). In (51-a), a 2nd person subject acts on a 1st person object, hence according to the person scale in (48) a direct marker shows up. In (51-b), the opposite takes place: a 1st person subject acts on a 2nd person object. Therefore, an inverse marker appears.

(51) a. ki-pakamah-on
       2-hit-1DIR
       'You hit me.' [2 → 1]

   b. ki-pakamah-otin
       2-hit-1INV
       'I hit you.' [1 → 2]

Note that PC is special in that the Case feature of the primary argument and person features of the secondary argument are encoded in one marker (-*on* in the direct, -*otin* in the inverse). The decisive stage of the derivation underlying (51-a) is given in (52).

(52) *Step 1: Agree(T,DP$_{ext}$):*

$[_{T'} T_{[*\pi\text{-}1\text{-}2*],[*\kappa*]} \succ [*\pi*] [_{vP} DP_{ext[\pi\text{-}1\text{-}2],[*\kappa*]} \text{ v } [_{VP} V DP_{int[\pi\text{-}1],[*\kappa\text{-}INT*]}]]]$

$[_{T'} T_{[*\pi\text{-}1\text{-}2*],[*\kappa*]} \succ [*\pi*] [_{vP} DP_{ext[\pi\text{-}1\text{-}2],[*\kappa*]} \text{ v } [_{VP} V DP_{int[\pi\text{-}1],[*\kappa\text{-}INT*]}]]]$

Step 2: Agree(T,DP$_{int}$):

$[_{T'} T_{[*\pi\text{-}1\text{-}2*],[*\kappa*]} \succ [*\pi*] [_{vP} DP_{ext[\pi\text{-}1\text{-}2],[*\kappa*]} \text{ v } [_{VP} V DP_{int[\pi\text{-}1],[*\kappa\text{-}INT*]}]]]$

$[_{TP} T_{[*\pi\text{-}1\text{-}2*],[*\kappa*]} \succ [*\pi\text{-}1*] [_{vP} DP_{ext[\pi\text{-}1\text{-}2],[*\kappa*]} \text{ v } [_{VP} V DP_{int[\pi\text{-}1],[*\kappa\text{-}INT*]}]]]$

In the final representation, what is visible for morphological insertion is the unstructured feature set on T (there is no internal structure that morphology could refer to after the syntactic computation). The indices in (53) are just for expository purposes, denoting that the relevant features are different occurrences.

(53) $[[+T], [\pi]_1, [1]_1, [2], [\kappa], [\pi]_2, [1]_2]$

The relevant vocabulary items are given in (54) (whether they can be further subanalyzed is ignored here):

(54) a. /-otin/ $\leftrightarrow$ $\{[+T],[\kappa],[\text{INT}],[\pi],[1]\}$
     b. /-on/ $\leftrightarrow$ $\{[+T],[\kappa],[\pi],[1]\}$
     c. /ki-/ $\leftrightarrow$ $\{[+T],[\pi],[1],[2]\}$

Assuming successive feature discharge (cf. Noyer 1992), the first vocabulary item that is correctly inserted is (54-b), the direct marker, realizing the Case feature and the person features of the 1st person DP$_{int}$. The remaining features are discharged by the 2nd person marker /ki-/.

The corresponding inverse derivation where DP$_{ext}$ is 1st person and DP$_{int}$ is 2nd person is given in (55).

(55) *Step 1: Agree(T,DP$_{int}$):*

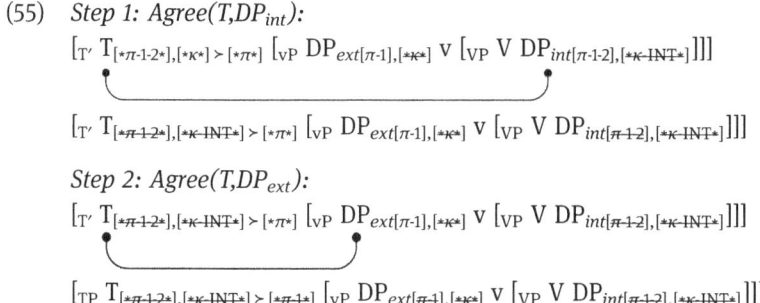

Step 2: Agree(T,DP$_{ext}$):

Now the inverse marker (54-a) is inserted into T, and the remaining features are again discharged by the 2nd person marker /ki-/. All the remaining contexts can be analyzed in the same way, which I will refrain from doing here for reasons of space. What should have become clear is that the distribution of the remaining Case markers (namely, the direct marker *āw-* and the inverse marker *-ik*, see Fadden 2000) showing up in contexts with a secondary 3rd person argument is fully accounted for if these markers additionally express person features, and this is possible because T undergoes Agree with both core arguments in the syntax.

5 Predictions and further applications

5.1 Direction marking in intransitive contexts

The analysis developed in section 4 makes an interesting prediction regarding Case agreement in intransitive contexts: Suppose one finds a direct-inverse language with an active argument encoding system, i.e. a system in which the external and internal argument of a transitive verb are marked differently (as in canonical accusative and ergative systems), but in addition are morphologically distinguished in intransitive contexts. Then one would expect to find "direct" marking on intransitive verbs that take an external argument, and "inverse" marking on intransitive verbs that take an internal argument, because both arguments receive different Case values from v, and T's Case feature in turn indexes these values, yielding accusative (or absolutive) Case agreement in inverse contexts, and nominative (or ergative) Case agreement in direct contexts.[27] In what follows, I show that this prediction is indeed borne out for certain Tupí-Guaraní (TG) languages.

---

[27] I would like to thank Doreen Georgi for bringing that point to my attention.

Payne (1994) argues that some TG languages have a direction system which is controlled by the person scale in (56).

(56) *TG person scale:*
1 > 2 > 3

TG languages have an active ergative argument encoding system. Since they are head-marking, argument encoding proceeds via prefixes on the verb, which Payne (1994) calls Set 1 prefixes (for external arguments) and Set 2 prefixes (for internal arguments).[28] Now, as is typical of inverse languages, a transitive verb can only agree with one of the two core arguments, and the decision is made with the help of the TG person scale in (56). The more prominent of the two arguments is chosen, resulting in a Set 1 prefix if it is the subject (DP_{ext}), and a Set 2 prefix if it is the object (DP_{int}). Thus, as Payne (1994: 318) notes, "sheer choice of Set 1 versus Set 2 prefixes formally constitutes a direct/inverse system." However, TG languages also appear to have a formal inverse marker *r-* (with a number of allomorphs) which shows up if a Set 2 prefix is used. The TG direction system is illustrated below.

(57) a. *Guajajara (Payne 1994: 327)*
 ere-sak
 2SG:I-see
 'You see him.'

 b. *Modern Wayampi (Payne 1994: 314)*
 Kwata jĩ-ga oro-esa.
 spider.monkey only-DIM 1PL.EXCL:I-meet
 'We saw some spider monkeys.'

(57) shows two direct contexts in which a local person subject acts on a non-local (i.e. 3rd person) object. The more prominent argument (1st or 2nd person) is cross-referenced on the verb, resulting in a Set 1 prefix in each case. Now consider (58), which shows two inverse contexts.[29]

---

28 Set 1 and Set 2 prefixes are marked in the glosses by 'I' and 'II', respectively.
29 Interestingly, the inverse marker also shows up in possessive constructions such as *e-r-uwy* 'my blood' in (58-b) (glossed as LK 'linker'). One might hypothesize that possessive constructions are in fact transitive nominal constructions (with the possessor being the 'subject' and the possessee being the 'object'), and it does not seem impossible to extend the analysis advanced in this paper from the verbal to the nominal domain. However, I will not delve into this issue here.

(58) a. *Guajajara (Payne 1994: 327)*
he-r-*esak*
1SG:II-INV-see
'He sees me.'

b. *Wayampi (Payne 1994: 315)*
E-r-*aty-pa*   *e-ke*   *pe*   *e-r-uwy.*
1SG:II-INV-cover-COMPL 1SG:II-sleep   in   1SG:II-LK-blood
'My blood completely covered me in my dream.'

In (58), a non-local person subject acts on a local person object (1st person in both cases). The person scale dictates that the local person induces agreement. Since it is the object in both cases, a Set 2 prefix is used. In addition, the inverse marker *r-* shows up in these configurations.

Now, as indicated above, one would expect that inverse marking shows up in contexts where an intransitive verb takes an internal argument, and that it does not in contexts where an intransitive verb takes an external argument. This prediction is borne out; consider the data from Guajajara in (59).

(59) *Guajajara (Payne 1994: 327)*
a. *he-r-urywete*
1SG.II-INV-happy
'I am happy.'

b. *a-zen*
1SG.I-run
'I run.'

The verb *urywete* 'be happy' in (59-a) is a stative verb that takes an internal argument. Consequently, under the analysis presented in the previous sections, it is totally expected that a Set 2 prefix and an inverse marker is chosen. In contrast to that, an active verb like *zen* 'to run' in (59-b) takes an external argument. Consequently, we expect a Set 1 prefix and nothing else. The decisive stages of the derivations underlying (59-a) and (59-b) are given in (60-a) and (60-b), respectively.

(60) a. $[_{T'} T_{[*\pi\text{-}2\text{-}1*],[*\kappa*]} [_{vP} V_{stat} [_{VP} \text{urywete DP}_{int[\pi\text{-}2\text{-}1],[\kappa\text{-}INT]}]]] \rightarrow$
$[_{T'} T_{[*\pi\text{-}2\text{-}1*],[*\kappa\text{-}INT*]} [_{vP} V_{stat} [_{VP} \text{urywete DP}_{int[\pi\text{-}2\text{-}1],[\kappa\text{-}INT]}]]]$

b. $[_{T'} T_{[*\pi\text{-}2\text{-}1*],[*\kappa*]} [_{vP} \text{DP}_{ext[\pi\text{-}2\text{-}1],[\kappa]} [_{v'} V_{act} [_{VP} \text{zen}]]]] \rightarrow$
$[_{T'} T_{[*\pi\text{-}2\text{-}1*],[*\kappa*]} [_{vP} \text{DP}_{ext[\pi\text{-}2\text{-}1],[\kappa]} [_{v'} V_{act} [_{VP} \text{zen}]]]]$

In (60-a), the Case probe is valued internal Case (absolutive) upon Φ-Agree with DP_{int}. In contrast, it is valued external Case (ergative) in the direct context in (60-b). In the post-syntactic component, the vocabulary items in (61) are inserted into the T head.

(61)   a.   /he-/ ↔ {[+T],[π],[2],[1]} / [_____ INT]
          b.   /a-/ ↔ {[+T],[π],[2],[1]}
          c.   /r-/ ↔ {[+T],[κ],[INT]}

An inverse marker is actually redundant, because the Set 2 prefix /he-/ could in principle encode all the relevant information (using distinct direct and inverse argument encoding prefixes, as in the Carib data given in (14)). However, this must be recognized as a simple morphological idiosyncrasy of the languages under discussion.

5.2 Agreement displacement

A further question arises as to whether the present approach can be extended so as to cover agreement displacement (AD) phenomena, of which ergative displacement in Basque is a prototypical example (Laka 1993). AD is very similar to direct-inverse marking in the sense that there is one core agreement slot for which multiple arguments compete, and the controller of that agreement slot cannot be determined on the basis of grammatical function (cf. Béjar and Řezáč 2009). However, in contrast to direction systems, in languages that have an AD system, agreement is preferably with DP_{int}, but may exceptionally be carried out with DP_{ext}. Béjar and Řezáč (2009: 37–38) point out:

> "We might characterize agreement displacement as a PH effect where the controller is given by some ranking of the EA and the IA on the basis of their π-specification, such that 1st > 2nd > 3rd person, where > means 'outranks'. This would indeed be an adequate characterization of a language like Algonquian or Mohawk, where the uniquely higher of the EA and the IA on such a scale is the agreement controller. However, it is inadequate for Basque-type languages."

The crucial contrast is thus that in direct-inverse languages, it is always the highest argument on a scale that induces primary agreement on the verb. AD languages also follow this pattern, but in case both arguments are equally specific (e.g. if two local person arguments co-occur in a language where 1st and 2nd person are inherently equally specific), agreement is with DP_{int}, not DP_{ext}. Basque is such a language (with a 1/2 > 3 person scale). The person scale effect of Basque is called *ergative displacement* and is illustrated in (62) (Béjar and Řezáč 2009: 37).

(62) a. ikusi **z**-in-t-u-da-n
 seen 2-X-PL-have-1-PAST
 'I saw you.'

 b. ikusi **n**-ind-u-en
 seen 1-X-have-PAST
 'He saw me.'

 c. ikusi **n**-ind-u-zu-n
 seen 1-X-have-2-PAST
 'You saw me.'

 d. ikusi **n**-u-en
 seen 1-have-PAST
 'I saw him.'

The crucial data are (62-a) and (62-c). At first sight, these would seem to run counter to what has been said in section 4.3 where it was pointed out that in case two potential goals are equally specific for a probe, the probe selects by default the closest one. Agree should thus affect the closer DP_{ext}, not DP_{int}.

In this section, I attempt to show that the AD data from Basque follow automatically from the system laid out in the previous sections. The only crucial difference between direction systems and AD systems is argued to be a lexical one: the approach developed so far in principle allows a Case probe feature on T to be structured as in (63).

(63) *Case probe on T specified for internal Case:*
$$\begin{bmatrix} [*\kappa*] \\ [*\text{INT}*] \end{bmatrix}$$

That is, a Case probe may be specified as being inherently "accusative" or "absolutive" (which is completely parallel to the differently structured Φ-probes). This is how preference for Agree with DP_{int} is modelled. Basque is a language in which local persons are not distinguished with respect to their relative specificity. That is, the language has the partially differentiated π-probe in (64).

(64) *Basque π-probe:*
$$\begin{bmatrix} [*\pi*] \\ [*2*] \end{bmatrix}$$

If two local person arguments co-occur in a transitive context, Agree with the internal argument will always win over Agree with the external argument, because the internal argument is inherently more specific for the Case probe in (63) which co-occurs with the core π-probe in (64). This is shown for a 1 → 2 context in (65), and a 2 → 1 context in (66).[30]

(65) [$_{T'}$ T$_{[*π-2*],[*κ-INT*]}$ [$_{vP}$ DP$_{ext[π-2-1],[*κ*]}$ v [$_{VP}$ V DP$_{int[π-2],[*κ-INT*]}$]]]

[$_{TP}$ T$_{[*π-2*],[*κ-INT*]}$ [$_{vP}$ DP$_{ext[π-2-1],[*κ*]}$ v [$_{VP}$ V DP$_{int[π-2],[*κ-INT*]}$]]]

(66) [$_{T'}$ T$_{[*π-2*],[*κ-INT*]}$ [$_{vP}$ DP$_{ext[π-2],[*κ*]}$ v [$_{VP}$ V DP$_{int[π-2-1],[*κ-INT*]}$]]]

[$_{TP}$ T$_{[*π-2-1*],[*κ-INT*]}$ [$_{vP}$ DP$_{ext[π-2],[*κ*]}$ v [$_{VP}$ V DP$_{int[π-2-1],[*κ-INT*]}$]]]

Post-syntactically, the exponent /z-/ will be inserted into the T head in (65), while the exponent /n-/ will be inserted into the T head in (66). Basque simply lacks an inverse marker, hence the Case feature on T is not realized. This is how AD can be derived under the present approach.

Béjar and Řezáč (2009) note that AD in Basque is not accompanied by syntactic effects, such as the emergence of new binding options, etc. What remains to be seen is whether other AD languages exhibit a similar grammatical function changing process like the one identified for direct-inverse languages, i.e. whether a similar distinction between morphology-based AD and movement-based AD can be drawn. I leave this issue open for future research.

6 Concluding remarks

Let me summarize the main results of this paper. The goal was to derive direct-inverse alternations from basic principles of syntactic computation, without adhering to "scale" as a primitive concept of grammar. This goal was achieved by decomposing features into more basic units (segments) in such a way that elements high on a scale are encoded by a superset of the segments that encode elements lower on the same scale. Such a decomposition made it possible for

---

30 In (65), I only illustrate primary agreement (i.e., the behavior of the core person probe). However, as the data in (62) show, there is also secondary agreement in these contexts. This can be derived by assuming that T bears a second π-feature which is discharged after [*π-2*], [* κ-INT*].

the core arguments to vary in their formal specificity. The operation Agree was in turn argued to be sensitive to this specificity in that it invariably targets the goal argument which has the greatest cardinality of matching segments. Potentially matching, even closer arguments are ignored by Agree in such configurations. If however both goal arguments are equally specific in terms of segment cardinality, the proposal was that Agree always targets the closer goal in such contexts. By applying this mechanism to direct-inverse languages, the apparently scale-driven agreement behavior could be accounted for, because the T head which was argued to be the locus of agreement features in these languages has both arguments in its scope, such that core Agree can in principle obtain with both of them. If DP_{ext} is more specific than DP_{int}, Agree(T,DP_{ext}) applies, and a direct context emerges. If DP_{int} is more specific than DP_{ext}, Agree(T,DP_{int}) applies, yielding an inverse context. A nice side effect of the analysis is that grammatical function changing in inverse contexts (where DP_{int} formally acts as the subject of the clause) can readily be accounted for if one assumes that a movement-inducing EPP feature on T is checked upon core Φ-Agree. Finally, the specific morphological reflex that manifests itself in a direct or inverse marker, respectively, was reanalyzed as agreement in Case, applying simultaneously with core Φ-Agree: There is an unvalued Case feature which is simultaneously checked off with the core Φ-probe whose value depends on the specific Case value borne by the respective argument. This is possible because all arguments were assumed to have received their structural Case values earlier in the derivation, namely on the vP level.

Generally, the analysis respects derivational principles of grammar and does not need to employ look-ahead or countercyclic operations. The approach makes reference to Silverstein scales completely unnecessary, which is a desired result under minimalist tenets. Another advantage is that the grammatical apparatus is simplified if the view on direction marking as a specific grammatical voice is abandoned, and instead is reduced to Case theory. Furthermore, the distinction between inverse and non-inverse languages reduces to a difference in feature structure, which is in accordance with the general view on parametric variation assumed in the Minimalist Program.

Needless to say, some (if not many) problems remain. Let me just single out two of those which appear to me to be rather pressing and which I already noted in passing. On the empirical side, it is unclear why Φ-probes which trigger primary Agree may induce movement to SpecT (i.e., may be associated with an EPP feature or movement diacritic), but Φ-probes which trigger secondary Agree may not. There might be a general principle which (probably pre-syntactically) assigns a movement diacritic to the topmost feature in a feature stack. As it stands, though, this has to be stipulated.

On the conceptual side, comparison of matching goals in the c-command domain of a probe strongly increases the computational complexity and does not contribute to computational efficiency. This criticism may be legitimate, but if such issues are taken seriously, one might on the other hand object that it is unclear how computational efficiency can be "measured" in the first place. The question whether such an approach is eventually reconcilable with conceptual conjectures of the Minimalist Program is surely an important one, but has to be left open for now.

On a more general level, the analysis can be viewed as an extension of the theory developed in Lahne (2008, 2009), with some minor qualifications. Further empirical investigation is necessary in order to assess the validity of the proposal that specificity is a fundamental force in driving the syntactic computation. For argument encoding in direction systems, this way of analysis seems to be highly suggestive, as I hope to have shown in this article.

Acknowledgments

I am grateful to Doreen Georgi and especially Gereon Müller for very helpful comments and suggestions. I would also like to thank the participants of the syntax colloquium at the University of Leipzig for their comments. An earlier, slightly different version of this paper was submitted as my BA thesis to the University of Leipzig in July 2011. The research documented here was carried out in project P5 *Argument Encoding in Morphology and Syntax* as part of DFG-Forschergruppe 742 *Grammar and Processing of Verbal Arguments*.

References

Adger, David. 2003. *Core Syntax: A Minimalist Approach*. (Oxford Core Linguistics 1) Oxford: Oxford University Press.
Aissen, Judith. 1997. On the syntax of obviation. *Language* 73 (4): 705–750.
Aissen, Judith. 1999. Markedness and subject choice in optimality theory. *Natural Language & Linguistic Theory* 17 (4): 673–711.
Alexiadou, Artemis and Elena Anagnostopoulou. 2006. From hierarchies to features: Person splits and direct-inverse alternations. In *Agreement Systems*, Cedric Boeckx (ed.), 41–62. Amsterdam: John Benjamins.
Anderson, Stephen R. 1992. *A-Morphous Morphology*. (Cambridge Studies in Linguistics 62) Cambridge: Cambridge University Press.
Arnold, Jennifer. 1996. The inverse system of Mapudungun and other languages. *Revista de Lingüística Teórica y Aplicada* 34: 9–48.

Baker, Mark C. 1988. *Incorporation: A Theory of Grammatical Function Changing*. Chicago: University of Chicago Press.
Baker, Mark C. 2003. On the loci of agreement: Inversion constructions in Mapudungun. In *Proceedings of the Thirty-Third Annual Meeting of the North East Linguistic Society (NELS 33)*, Makoto Kadowaki and Shigeto Kawahara (eds.), 25–49. Amherst, MA: GLSA.
Béjar, Susana. 2003. Phi-syntax: A theory of agreement. Ph. D. diss., University of Toronto.
Béjar, Susana and Milan Řezáč. 2009. Cyclic agree. *Linguistic Inquiry* 40 (1): 35–73.
Biberauer, Theresa, Anders Holmberg, and Ian Roberts. 2010. A syntactic universal and its consequences. Ms., Universities of Cambridge. and Newcastle.
Bobaljik, Jonathan. 1993. Ergativity and unvergative ergatives. In *Papers on Case and Agreement II* (Vol. 19 of MIT Working Papers in Linguistics), Colin Phillips (ed.), 48–88.
Bošković, Željko. 2007. Agree, phases, and intervention effects. *Linguistic Analysis* 33 (1–2): 54–96.
Brown, Jason, Karsten Koch, and Martina Wiltschko. 2004. The person hierarchy: Primitive or epiphenomenal? Evidence from Halkomelem Salish. In *Proceedings of the 34th Meeting of the North East Linguistic Society (NELS 34)*, Keir Moulton and Matthew Wolf (eds.), 147–162. Amherst, MA: GLSA.
Bruening, Benjamin. 2001. Syntax at the edge: Cross-clausal phenomena and the syntax of Passamaquoddy. Ph. D. diss., Massachusetts Institute of Technology.
Bruening, Benjamin. 2005. The Algonquian inverse is syntactic: Binding in Passamaquoddy. Ms., University of Delaware.
Chomsky, Noam. 1965. *Aspects of the Theory of Syntax*. Cambridge, MA: MIT Press.
Chomsky, Noam. 1973. Conditions on transformations. In *A Festschrift for Morris Halle*, Stephen R. Anderson and Paul Kiparsky (eds.), 232–286. New York: Holt, Rinehart and Winston.
Chomsky, Noam. 1981. *Lectures on Government and Binding*. Dordrecht: Foris.
Chomsky, Noam. 1993. A minimalist program for linguistic theory. In *The View from Building 20: Essays in Linguistics in Honor of Sylvain Bromberger*, Ken Hale and Samuel J. Keyser (eds.), 1–52. Cambridge, MA: MIT Press.
Chomsky, Noam. 1995. *The Minimalist Program*. (Current Studies in Linguistics 28) Cambridge, MA: MIT Press.
Chomsky, Noam. 2000. Minimalist inquiries: The framework. In *Step by Step: Essays on Minimalist Syntax in Honor of Howard Lasnik*, Roger Martin, David Michaels and Juan Uriagereka (eds.), 89–155. Cambridge, MA: MIT Press.
Chomsky, Noam. 2001. Derivation by phase. In *Ken Hale: A Life in Language*, Michael Kenstowicz (ed.), 1–52. (Current Studies in Linguistics 36) Cambridge, MA: MIT Press.
Chomsky, Noam. 2008. On phases. In *Foundational Issues in Linguistic Theory: Essays in Honor of Jean-Roger Vergnaud*, Robert Freidin, Carlos P. Otero and Maria Luisa Zubizarreta (eds.), 133–166. Cambridge, MA: MIT Press.
Comrie, Bernard. 1980. Inverse verb forms in Siberia: Evidence from Chukchee, Koryak, and Kamchadal. *Folia Linguistica Historica* 1 (1): 61–74.
Dahlstrom, Amy. 1991. *Plains Cree Morphosyntax*. New York: Garland.
DeLancey, Scott. 1981. An interpretation of split ergativity and related patterns. *Language* 57 (3): 626–657.
Dixon, R. M. W. 1994. *Ergativity*. (Cambridge Studies in Linguistics 69) Cambridge: Cambridge University Press.

Dryer, Matthew S. 1992. Subject and inverse in Kutenai. In *Papers from the American Indian Languages Conferences* (Vol. 16 of Southern Illinois University Occasional Papers on Linguistics), 183–202.
Embick, David and Rolf Noyer. 2007. Distributed morphology and the syntax-morphology interface. In *The Oxford Handbook of Linguistic Interfaces*, Gillian Ramchand and Charles Reiss (eds.), 289–324. Oxford: Oxford University Press.
Epstein, Samuel D. and T. Daniel Seely. 2002. Rule applications as cycles in a level-free syntax. In *Derivation and Explanation in the Minimalist Program*, Samuel D. Epstein and T. Daniel Seely (eds.), 65–89. Malden, MA: Blackwell.
Fabri, Ray. 1996. The inverse morphology of Plains Cree. In *Yearbook of Morphology 1995*, Geert Booij and Jaap van Marle (eds.), 17–41. Dordrecht: Kluwer.
Fadden, Lorna M. 2000. The inverse continuum. MA thesis, Simon Fraser University.
George, Leland and Jaklin Kornfilt. 1981. Finiteness and boundedness in Turkish. In *Binding and Filtering*, Frank Heny (ed.), 105–127. Cambridge, MA: MIT Press.
Georgi, Doreen. 2009a. Local modelling of global case splits. MA thesis, Universität Leipzig.
Georgi, Doreen. 2009b. A uniform analysis of global & local argument encoding patterns. Ms., Universität Leipzig. To appear in *Proceedings of Console XVII*.
Georgi, Doreen, Fabian Heck, and Gereon Müller. 2009. Maraudage. Ms., Universität Leipzig. (Talk at the Repairs Workshop of the DGfS conference 2009, Osnabrück, and at the Potsdam/Leipzig Workshop on Movement and Morphology, Leucorea, April 2009).
Givón, Talmy (ed.). 1994. *On Understanding Grammar*. New York: Academic Press.
Givón, Talmy (ed.). 1994. *Voice and Inversion*. (Typological Studies in Language 28) Amsterdam: John Benjamins.
Hamann, Jakob. 2011. A minimalist approach to argument encoding in direction systems. BA thesis, Universität Leipzig.
Hale, Ken. 1972. A new perspective on American Indian linguistics. In *New Perspectives on the Pueblos*, Alfonso Ortiz (ed.), 87–103. Albuquerque: University of New Mexico Press.
Halle, Morris. 1997. Distributed morphology: Impoverishment and fission. In *Papers at the Interface* (Vol. 30 of MIT Working Papers in Linguistics), Benjamin Bruening, Yoonjung Kang, and Martha McGinnis (eds.), 425–449.
Halle, Morris and Alec Marantz. 1993. Distributed morphology and the pieces of inflection. In *The View from Building 20: Essays in Linguistics in Honor of Sylvain Bromberger*, Ken Hale and Samuel J. Keyser (eds.), 111–176. Cambridge, MA: MIT Press.
Halle, Morris and Alec Marantz. 1994. Some key features of distributed morphology. In *Papers on Phonology and Morphology* (Vol. 21 of MIT Working Papers in Linguistics), Andrew Carnie, Heidi Harley, and Tony Bures (eds.), 275–288.
Harley, Heidi and Rolf Noyer. 2003. Distributed morphology. In *The Second GLOT International State-of-the-Article Book*, Lisa Cheng and Rint Sybesma (eds.), 463–496. Berlin: Mouton de Gruyter.
Haude, Katharina. 2006. A grammar of Movima. Ph. D. diss., Radboud Universiteit Nijmegen.
Heck, Fabian and Gereon Müller. 2007. Extremely local optimization. In *Proceedings of WECOL 26*, Erin Brainbridge. and Brian Agbayani (eds.), 170–183. California State University, Fresno.
Heck, Fabian and Marc Richards. 2010. A probe goal approach to agreement and non-incorporation restrictions in Southern Tiwa. *Natural Language & Linguistic Theory* 28 (3): 681–721.
Jacques, Guillaume. 2010. The inverse in Japhug Rgyalrong. *Language & Linguistics* 11 (1): 127–157.

Keine, Stefan. 2010. *Case and Agreement from Fringe to Core: A Minimalist Approach*. (Linguistische Arbeiten 536) Berlin: de Gruyter.
Keine, Stefan and Gereon Müller. 2015. Differential argument encoding by impoverishment. This volume.
Kimenyi, Alexandre. 1980. *A Relational Grammar of Kinyarwanda*. Berkeley: University of California Press.
Kimenyi, Alexandre. 1988. Passives in Kinyarwanda. In *Passive and Voice*, Masayoshi Shibatani (ed.), 355–386. Amsterdam: John Benjamins.
Klaiman, Miriam H. 1991. *Grammatical Voice*. (Cambridge Studies in Linguistics 59) Cambridge: Cambridge University Press.
Klaiman, Miriam H. 1992. Inverse languages. *Lingua* 88 (3): 227–261.
Lahne, Antje. 2008. Specificity-driven syntactic derivation: A new view on long-distance agreement. Ms., Universiät Leipzig.
Lahne, Antje. 2009. Specificity-driven syntactic derivation. Ms., Universität Konstanz.
Laka, Itziar. 1993. Unergatives that assign ergative, unaccusatives that assign accusative. In *Papers on Case and Agreement I* (Vol. 18 of MIT Working Papers in Linguistics), Jonathan Bobaljik and Colin Phillips (eds.), 149–172.
Malchukov, Andrej, Martin Haspelmath and Bernard Comrie. 2010. Ditransitive constructions: A typological overview. In *Studies in Ditransitive Constructions: A Comparative Handbook*, Andrej Malchukov, Martin Haspelmath and Bernard Comrie (eds.), 1–64. Berlin, New York: Mouton de Gruyter.
Müller, Gereon. 2004. Phrase impenetrability and *wh*-intervention. In *Minimality Effects in Syntax*, Arthur Stepanov, Gisbert Fanselow and Ralf Vogel (eds.), 289–325. Berlin, New York: Mouton de Gruyter.
Müller, Gereon. 2009. Ergativity, accusativity and the order of Merge and Agree. In *Explorations of Phase Theory: Features and Arguments*, Kleanthes K. Grohmann (ed.), 269–308. Berlin, New York: Mouton de Gruyter.
Müller, Gereon. 2010. On deriving CED effects from the PIC. *Linguistic Inquiry* 41 (1): 35–82.
Murasugi, Kumiko. 1992. Crossing and nested paths: NP movement in accusative and ergative languages. Ph. D. diss., Massachusetts Institute of Technology.
Ndayiragije, Juvénal. 1996. Case checking and OVS in Kirundi. In *Configurations: Essays on Structure and Interpretation*, Anna-Maria di Sciullo (ed.), 267–292. Sommerville, MA: Cascadilla Press.
Noyer, Rolf. 1992. Features, positions, and affixes in autonomous morphological structure. Ph. D. diss., Massachusetts Institute of Technology.
Palmer, Frank R. 1994. *Grammatical Roles and Relations*. Cambridge: Cambridge University Press.
Payne, Doris. 1994. The Tupí-Guaraní inverse. In *Voice: Form and Function*, Barbara Fox and Paul J. Hopper (eds.), 313–340. Amsterdam: John Benjamins.
Rackowski, Andrea. 2002. The structure of Tagalog: Specificity, voice and the distribution of arguments. Ph. D. diss., Massachusetts Institute of Technology.
Řezáč, Milan. 2003. The fine structure of cyclic Agree. *Syntax* 6 (2), 156–182.
Řezáč, Milan. 2011. *Phi-Features and the Modular Architecture of Language*. Dordrecht: Springer.
Richards, Marc. 2015. Defective agree, case alternations, and the prominence of person. This volume.

Sigurðsson, Halldór Ármann. 2000. The locus of case and agreement. *Working Papers in Scandinavian Syntax* 65: 65–108.
Silverstein, Michael. 1976. Hierarchy of Features and Ergativity. In *Grammatical Categories in Australian Languages*, R. M. W. Dixon (ed.), 112–171. Canberra: Australian Institute for Aboriginal Studies.
Sternefeld, Wolfgang. 2006. *Syntax: Eine morphologisch motivierte generative Beschreibung des Deutschen*. Tübingen: Stauffenburg. Two volumes.
Stump, Gregory. 2001. *Inflectional Morphology: A Theory of Paradigm Structure*. (Cambridge Studies in Linguistics 93) Cambridge: Cambridge University Press.
Trommer, Jochen. 2003. Direction marking as agreement. In *Syntactic Structures and Morphological Information*, Uwe Junghanns and Luka Szucsich (eds.), 317–340. Berlin, New York: Mouton de Gruyter.
Trommer, Jochen. 2006. Direction marking and case in Menominee. In *Case, Valency and Transitivity*, Leonid Kulikov, Andrej Malchukov and Peter de Swart (eds.), 91–111. Amsterdam: John Benjamins.
Ura, Hiroyuki. 1996. Multiple feature-checking: A theory of grammatical function splitting. Ph.D. diss., Massachusetts Institute of Technology.
Ura, Hiroyuki. 2000. *Checking Theory and Grammatical Functions in Universal Grammar*. Oxford: Oxford University Press.
Valentine, J. Randolph. 2001. *Nishnaabemwin Reference Grammar*. Toronto: University of Toronto Press.
Wiltschko, Martina. 2008. Person hierarchy effects without a person hierarchy. In *Agreement Restrictions*, Roberta D'Alessandro, Susann Fischer, and Gunnar Hrafn Hrafnbjargarson (eds.), 281–314. Berlin: Mouton de Gruyter.
Witherspoon, Gary. 1980. Language in culture and culture in language. *International Journal of American Linguistics* 46 (1): 1–14.
Wolfart, H. Christoph. 1973. *Plains Cree: A Grammatical Study*. Philadelphia: American Philosophical Society.
Zúñiga, Fernando. 2006. *Deixis and Alignment: Inverse Systems in Indigenous Languages of the Americas*. (Typological Studies in Language 70) Amsterdam: John Benjamins.

Andrej L. Malchukov
10 Towards a typology of split ergativity: A TAM-hierarchy for alignment splits[1]

1 The Animacy Hierarchy and noun-based alignment splits

1.1 Silverstein's Animacy Hierarchy: evidence and counterexamples

In recent years alignment splits have attracted much attention in the linguistic literature. The best known case of alignment splits is split ergativity conditioned by different types of nominals. The basic generalization going back to Silverstein (1976) is that nominals higher on the Animacy Hierarchy favor the accusative pattern (A=S≠P), while nominals lower on the Animacy Hierarchy prefer the ergative pattern (A≠S=P). This pattern has been attributed in work by Silverstein (1976), Comrie (1978) and Dixon (1979) to the discriminating function of cases (i.e., the need to discriminate between A and P arguments, more pressing if A is low on the animacy hierarchy and P is high). On this account, split ergativity is due to the fact that most natural agents (e.g. pronominal As) may remain unflagged (by ergative case), and most natural patients (e.g. inanimate Ps) need not be marked either (by accusative case). This approach has become known as the 'discriminating' approach to case marking, as opposed to the 'indexing' approach, which relates the function of case marking to the coding of role properties of the respective NPs (see Song 2001 for discussion).

More recently, the 'discriminating' approach has been taken over into Optimality Theory (OT) by Aissen (2003), who applied it to account for patterns of Differential Object Marking (DOM). Aissen recast the discriminating approach in terms of markedness hierarchies in interaction with economy constraints. Markedness hierarchies are derived through harmonic alignment of grammatical functions (Subject vs. Object) and values on the Animacy Hierarchy (which

---

[1] The present article was written in 2009, about the same time as Malchukov & de Hoop 2011, with which it shows some thematic overlap. I am grateful to Helen de Hoop for the useful feedback and discussions in the course of our collaborative work. I am also grateful to Marc Richards and Corinna Handschuh for comments on an earlier version of this paper. The usual disclaimers apply.

includes, apart from animacy proper, the dimensions of definiteness/specificity and person). Thus on Aissen's analysis, differential case marking in Hindi, where human objects take the accusative case, while inanimate objects need not be marked, is captured by the following hierarchy: *Obj/Human & *Ø$_C$ ≫ *Struc$_C$ ≫ ... *Obj/Inanimate & *Ø$_C$. (See Aissen 2003 for the full story, and Keine & Müller 2015 for further discussion.)

Aissen's approach has been highly influential and was followed up and refined in a number of respects in subsequent literature. De Hoop & Narasimhan (2005), De Hoop & Malchukov (2008), and de Swart (2007) proposed to subsume Aissen's markedness constraints under Distinguishability (as instantiation of the discriminating function of cases) in order to extend this analysis to cases where case assignment is 'global' (in terms of Silverstein 1976), that is, sensitive to properties of both arguments in a clause. Global distinguishability is arguably at work in languages like Fore, where A takes ergative case only when P is animate, and is left unmarked in clauses with inanimate patients where no disambiguation is necessary (de Hoop & Malchukov 2008; cf. an early discussion of the Fore pattern from an OT perspective in Donohue 1999). Kittilä (2006) and Malchukov (2008) showed the impact of distinguishability on ditransitives, pointing to cases where DOM is suspended in ditransitive constructions to avoid case doubling. Zeevat & Jäger (2002) proposed to reconstruct Aissen's analysis in OT semantics (Hendriks & de Hoop 2000), and Jäger (2007) framed a similar account relying on markedness and economy constraints in Evolutionary Game Theory. Keine & Müller (2015) show how Aissen's analysis can be extended to account for more subtle markedness patterns that involve a choice between two overt markers differing in "heaviness" /complexity. Finally, from a psycholinguistic perspective, de Hoop & Lamers (2006) explicitly argue for incremental optimization of case interpretation making use of distinguishability constraints. So it would appear that by now we have a complete story for differential case marking (DCM) based on the concept of markedness/distinguishability.

Yet at the same time, counterevidence to the 'discriminating' approach was mounting.[2] Recall that in typology a different 'indexing' approach has been developed, starting from Hopper & Thompson (1980), who explained patterns of differential case marking in terms of prominence rather than markedness. On Hopper & Thompson's (1980) approach, DOM arises from pressure to mark more prominent and/or canonical patients rather than untypical patients. A similar approach has been developed by Dowty (1991), who defines canonical As and

---

[2] I will disregard here other problems with the 'discriminating' approach, in particular, the question of how strong the empirical evidence is for (different subparts of) Silverstein's hierarchy; see Bickel et al (2015) for discussion.

Ps in terms of proto-Agent and proto-Patient properties. Although Dowty's approach has been designed to account for argument linking rather than case variation, subsequent work (in particular by Primus 1999 and Ackerman & Moore 2001) extended this approach to explain transitivity alternations as well, so this line of research started to converge with the literature on differential case marking (see Malchukov & de Swart 2009 for a brief review). In typology, this approach has been recently revived by Næss (2007), who attributes transitivity splits and alternations to the principle of Maximal Semantic Distinguishability between A and P arguments. Basically, this is a version of an indexing approach appealing to the notions of canonical Agents and Patients (or Proto-Agents and Proto-Patients, as in Dowty's approach).[3] Also, in OT, it has been observed that many alternations cannot be explained in terms of markedness, but should be due to other factors, such as variation in argument structure. Woolford (2001) was probably the first to highlight this point in the Optimality Theoretic context, but since then the evidence has been mounting (see many contributions to de Hoop & de Swart (eds) 2008). Of course, some sort of faithfulness constraints have always been taken for granted in analyses of oblique cases (see Wunderlich's Max constraints; Wunderlich & Lakämper 2001; Stiebels 2002), but more recently faithfulness has been found to be indispensable in analyses of variation in core cases as well (Lee 2003; cf. also Butt & King 2004 for discussion of the semantics of the core cases from an LFG perspective).

1.2 A two-factor approach to animacy-based ergativity splits

De Hoop & Malchukov (2007; 2008) and Malchukov (2008) propose to relate the scope of markedness and faithfulness constraints to different types of differential case marking (DCM). In particular, they argue that 'fluid' alternations (i.e. forms alternating, rather than being in complementary distribution) cannot be accounted for in terms of markedness. They also note that it is impossible to explain DCM in terms of markedness if a case alternation carries over to intransitive subjects (for which distinguishability considerations are irrelevant). This does not mean, however, that markedness constraints are epiphenomenal (as seems to be Woolford's position); rather both types of constraints are needed to explain cross-linguistic variation in case marking (De Hoop & Malchukov 2008; Malchukov 2008; see also Lee 2003 for a related proposal aiming at unifying both types of constraints). In our earlier work, we showed how this analysis can explain asymmetries between Differential Object Marking (DOM) and Differential Subject Marking (DSM), namely the fact that DOM is more consistent

---

3 This account is closest to the version of Dowty's approach advocated by Primus (1999), where proto-Agent and proto-Patient properties are seen as converses of each other.

cross-linguistically than DSM. Indeed, for the domain of DOM, the effects of both INDEX (Faithfulness) and DIFF (markedness-distinguishability) constraints converge on the same pattern, with more prominent/animate Ps preferentially marked (as predicted by Silverstein). In the case of DSM, however, the constraints are in conflict: DIFF penalizes case-marking of typical (animate, agentive) As, while INDEX penalizes marking of non-typical (non-agentive) As. Clearly, DIFF and INDEX constraints cannot be reduced to each other, as they lead to an opposite pattern in the domain of DSM, as illustrated here for Panmari (Amazonian) and Nez Perce (Sahaptian). Both languages are similar in that they have a DOM pattern manifested in preferential marking of prominent (in particular, pronominal) Ps. The two languages are also similar in that they display differential marking of As (ergative vs. zero marking) dependent on P-marking. Interestingly, however, the dependency between object and subject in these two languages yields an opposite pattern. In Panmari, when P is case marked, ergative case marking of A is dispensable (as in (1b)).

Panmari (Chapman & Derbyshire 1991: 164; 271)
(1) a. *Dono-a   bi-ko'dira-'a-ha   ada   isai   hoariha*
        Dono-ERG   3SG-pinch-ASP-M   DEM.M   child   other
        'Dono pinched the other boy'

   b. *Kada-amia   adani   a'oni-ra   va-ka-asar-ra*
       your-mother   DEM.PL   2PL-OBJ   3PL-TRZR-cry-IMMED
       'Your mothers are crying for you'

The alternation in (1) is clearly due to DIFF (distinguishability/markedness): in the presence of ACC marked P in (1b), A marking becomes dispensable, as no ambiguity arises. In Nez Perce, by contrast, the ergative case is mandatory only when P is case marked as well. Compare an example of a canonical transitive clause in (2a), with a construction with a low-prominent P (2b) where both arguments remain unmarked (Rude 1985):

Nez Perce (Rude 1985: 88; 86)
(2) a. *kawó   yasne   púutéye   piyéepim*
        then   poor.ACC   3TR.whip.PERF   brother.ERG
        'Then the elder brother whipped the poor one'

   b. *kícuy   hipap'lúutunu   sooyáapoo*
       gold   3NOM.PL.mine_go.PERF   whiteman
       'The white men went to mine gold'

Clearly, the DSM pattern in Nez Perce is due to INDEX (faithfulness) rather than DIFF (markedness): only strong/prominent As receive ERG case, and A qualifies as strong if the verb is transitive and has a prominent Patient. Thus dependency effects in the two cases are indeed opposite, being due either to Distinguishability (DIFF ≫ INDEX), as in Panmari, or to Faithfullness (INDEX ≫ DIFF), as in Nez Perce. Thus, it seems futile to try to reduce both factors (constraints) to one: the fact remains that in the domain of DSM we find two opposite patterns, a 'Silverstein-pattern' and an 'anti-Silverstein' pattern, even if the latter has been largely disregarded in the literature on alignment splits (see Malchukov 2008 and de Hoop & Malchukov 2008 for further discussion of asymmetries in differential case marking).[4]

2 Constraining TAM-based split ergativity

2.1 TAM (tense/aspect/mood) based splits: basic patterns

While noun-based alignment splits have been extensively studied in the literature, both typological and optimality theoretic, verb-based splits have attracted less attention. The only exception is provided by the tense/aspect based splits related to perfectivity: it has long been noted that perfective aspect and past tense favor ergative patterns, while imperfective/present favor an accusative pattern (see, e.g., Trask 1979; Comrie 1978; Dixon 1979; Plank 1985). The perfective/imperfective split is illustrated below with the familiar examples from Hindi, where ergative marking of subjects is restricted to (transitive) verbs in the perfective aspect:

Hindi (Mohanan 1990: 94)
(3) a. *Raam-ne   ek   bakraa   bec-aa*
       Raam-ERG one   goat.NOM   sell-PFV.SG.M
       'He sold a goat'

   b. *Raam   ek   bakraa   bec-taa   hae*
       Raam.NOM one   goat.NOM   sell-IMFV.SG.M   be.PRS.3SG
       'Raam sells a goat'

---

4 Cf., however, the following remark in Comrie (1978: 366): "... the close connection between ergativity and agentivity in some languages is counterbalanced by a close relation between ergativity and non-agentivity in some other languages."

In Georgian, the split is rather driven by tense: alignment is accusative in the present (and other 'Series 1'-tenses), but ergative in the past ('Series 2'-tenses).

Georgian (Hewitt 1995: 549)
(4) a. Šina.ber.a   jagl-s   jval-s   mi-ø-s-c-em-s
       spinster(NOM) dog-DAT bone-DAT Prev-(it)-it-give-TH-she
       'The spinster will give a bone to the dog' (Series 1)

   b. Šina.ber.a-m   jagl-s   jval-i   mi-ø-s-c-a
       spinster-ERG dog-DAT bone-NOM Prev-(it)-it-give-she.AOR
       'The spinster gave a bone to the dog' (Series 2)

Note that in Georgian, unlike in Hindi, agreement does not match case-marking. While the case pattern changes from accusative to ergative in the perfective, agreement remains accusative in both cases: A is cross-referenced by the subject agreement set ('Set-A' markers, in Hewitt's terms, as opposed to 'Set-B' agreement used for objects).

Similarly in many other languages (e.g., Indo-Arian, Caucasian and Mayan languages; Dixon 1994: 100) present/imperfective correlates with the accusative pattern, and past/perfective with the ergative pattern. The usual explanation for this split proposed in the literature (de Lancey 1981; Dixon 1994; Lazard 1994/8; Payne 1997) boils down to the statement that perfectives are P-centred, as they focus on the change of state of the P argument, while imperfectives are A-centred as the action is not completed (and P is not affected).[5] These accounts may be conceived as varieties of the markedness approach, even though they differ in certain respects. On the markedness approach, A is assumed to be the central argument in the imperfective, so P needs (case) marking to be identified. Conversely, P is assumed to be the central (unmarked) term in the perfective, while the role of A needs to be signalled.

There is, however, an alternative explanation to the attested split. Recall that on Hopper & Thompson's (1980) approach, the perfective aspect is one of the features contributing to high transitivity, so their approach seems to be equally suited to account for this kind of ergativity split. Yet this latter transitivity-based approach diverges from the markedness approach in one important respect. Indeed, the latter approach seems to predict that the perfective construction is more transitive than the corresponding imperfective construction,

---

[5] In terms of de Lancey (1981), P is a natural 'viewpoint focus' in a perfective construction, while A is a natural 'viewpoint focus' in an imperfective construction. Payne (1997) qualifies perfective constructions as P-oriented, and imperfective constructions as A-oriented.

instead of capturing the alignment reversal accompanying the shift from perfective to imperfective. For some languages this seems to be a conceivable analysis, at least in a diachronic perspective. Thus, for Georgian, it has been claimed that the non-ergative structure in the present tense series is historically a kind of antipassive construction (Harris 1985). Yet, synchronically, we are rather dealing with two different alignment patterns of a transitive clause in different tenses/aspects, which is, of course, also the usual interpretation of ergativity splits in the literature. So, it seems that the transitivity-based approach fails to explain the markedness reversal pattern conditioned by aspect splits (see Malchukov & de Hoop 2011 for a qualification, though). The markedness approach also has the advantage of being more general, in that it can be used to explain the alignment patterns beyond the imperfective/perfective splits to be considered in the next section. Indeed, as we move from perfectives into the domain of resultative perfects on the extended TAM hierarchy, the transitivity account seems to predict that the latter constructions score still higher in transitivity (as P is necessarily affected), yet in fact they often shift to an intransitive construction instead. This is at odds with the transitivity account, but is expected on the markedness account insofar as P remains unmarked in this construction (see §§3.1, 4.1 for further discussion and qualifications).

2.2 Extending the TAM-hierarchy

While perfective/imperfective (past/non-past) splits have been extensively discussed in the literature, it has not been sufficiently appreciated that this split is a part of a larger pattern. At least since Comrie (1976), it has been known that among tense categories the perfect shows a still stronger predilection for an ergative (or rather non-accusative) pattern. In particular, Comrie (1976) refers to Classical Armenian, which generally has accusative alignment, except for the (compound) perfect construction. The same conclusion has been reached by V.P. Nedjalkov (1979) for Chukchi, who showed that the 'degree of ergativity' increases as one moves down the following hierarchy:

imperfect > aorist > perfect

The situation in Chukchi is different insofar as the split manifests itself in agreement rather than case (case marking is ergative throughout),[6] yet the pattern is the same.

---

[6] On Nedjalkov's (1979) approach, "degree of ergativity" in Chukchi is established on the basis of the number of S/P vs. S/A agreement homophonies in verbal paradigms.

Note that this more complex hierarchy gives rise to further predictions, namely that if the aorist is non-accusative, the perfect (if available) will be non-accusative as well (the opposite need not be the case of course, as we have seen for Armenian). For the data at hand, this seems to be correct. Thus, in Georgian, where the perfective/past forms have non-accusative alignment, the perfect forms pattern non-accusatively as well: they show the so-called 'inverse pattern' (in terms of Harris 1985) with the subject in the dative case.

Georgian (Hewitt 1989)
(5) Šina.ber.a-s   jagl-is=tvis   jval-i   mi-ø-u-c-i-a
    spinster-DAT   dog-GEN=for   bone-NOM   Prev-(she)-OV-give-PF-it
    'The spinster apparently has given a bone to the dog'

The Georgian data conforms to the hierarchy with respect to agreement as well. While cross-referencing is accusative for both imperfective and perfective domains (where the same set of agreement cross-references A/S), in the perfect domain the same agreement cross-references P/S instead. A similar case to Georgian is found in Manipuri (Bhatt & Ningombo 1997), where perfective tenses (optionally) take an ergative subject, while the subject obligatorily switches to genitive in the perfect.

As shown by Lazard (1994/8), the TAM hierarchy above can be further expanded. Thus, Lazard added Future and Present to this pattern, yielding the following hierarchy:

Future > Present > Imperfect > Aorist > Perfect

Lazard (1998) cites, in particular, Kurdish and Burushaski as evidence for this extended hierarchy. Burushaski has accusative alignment in the future, and ergative alignment in the present and other tenses down the hierarchy. On the other hand, in Kurdish, future and present pattern accusatively, while other categories including imperfect (imperfective past) pattern ergatively.

2.3 Further extensions: imperatives and resultatives

It seems to be possible to further elaborate – in both directions – on the TAM hierarchy. First, as is well known from the literature on ergativity (e.g. Dixon 1979; 1994; Plank 1985; Comrie 1989), imperatives show a general preference for accusative (or maybe, rather, non-ergative) alignment. This preference is most evident in languages which show ergative (or non-accusative) alignment elsewhere. Dixon (1994: 101) refers, in particular, to Päri, Sumerian and Kuikúro, where all tense/aspect/mood forms have an ergative pattern except for the imperative. The following examples from Kuikúro, involving non-imperative and imperative forms, serve to illustrate this point.

    Kuikúro (Franchetto 1990: 414)
(6) a. *kagá   egé-la   kupehé-ni*
           fish   eat-PNCT 1INC.ERG-PL
           'We all eat fish'

      b. *e-g-egé-ke   kagá*
           2ABS-DETR-eat-IMP fish
           'Eat fish!'

In the Kuikúro example, ergative marking on the transitive subject is lost in the imperative (see (6b)). In part, this is clearly due to the tendency to omit the subject (the addressee) in the imperative construction, which naturally pertains to transitive subjects as well. This can explain the loss of the ergative pattern in the dependent-marking Dyirbal (Dixon (1994). Yet this explanation is insufficient, as realignment in imperatives may affect not only case, but also agreement. Note, in particular, that agreement in Kuikúro is absolutive in (6b). This does not mean, of course, that all ergative languages show this realignment. In some languages the alignment remains ergative throughout the tense/aspect paradigms. Thus for Shina (an Indo-Arian language) ergative case is retained on transitive subjects in all tense/aspect categories, including the imperative. Yet many ergative languages do show a tendency for realignment in imperatives. Thus, in Shipibo-Conibo (Valenzuela 1997), the ergative addressee (A) cannot be expressed in the imperative at all, while expression of the absolutive addressee (S) is optional:

    Shipibo-Conibo (Valenzuela 1997)
(7) a. *(*mi-n)   piti   pi-wé*
           (2-ERG)   fish.ABS   eat-IMP
           'Eat fish!'

      b. *(Mi-a)   ka.tan-we*
           (2-ABS)   go.do-IMP
           '(You) go!'

The tendency for realignment can also manifest itself in the use of antipassives in the imperative construction, either optionally (as in Dyirbal), or obligatorily (with the "categorical imperative" forms in Tzotzil; Aissen 2008).

One can also elaborate on the lower (ergative) part of the TAM-hierarchy, taking resultative forms into consideration. Here it is important to distinguish between two types of perfects: actional perfects (*He has gone*) vs. stative perfects (*He is gone*). The former will be opposed to the latter as 'perfects' vs. 'resultatives' following the convention introduced by Nedjalkov (ed. 1988). Importantly, transitive resultatives usually pattern ergatively even in accusative languages (Nedjalkov 1988; Comrie 1989: 119). This can be illustrated by the familiar data from European languages, where resultative forms take S/P as their subjects (cf. *He is gone*; *The door is open*). In that respect, resultatives differ from (actional) perfects, which normally preserve their alignment (cf. *He has gone*; *John has opened the door*).[7]

Admittedly, there are languages which also allow for resultative forms to pattern accusatively. Yet such patterns are usually marginal in these languages, which allow A-resultatives have P-resultatives as well. This is illustrated below for Even (a Tungusic language).

Even (Malchukov 1995 and f.n.)
(8) a. *Bej   il-ra-n*
       man   stand_up-AOR-3SG
       'The man stood up'

   b. *Bej   ila-t-ta-n*
      man   stand_up-RES-AOR-3SG
      'The man stands' (S-resulative)

(9) a. *Bej   urke-v   anga-n*
       man   door-ACC   open-AOR.3SG
       'The man opened the door'

   b. *Urke   anga-t-ta-n*
      door   open-RES-AOR-3SG
      'The door is open' (O-resultative)

   c. *Bej   urke-v   anga-t-ta-n*
      man   door-ACC   open-RES-AOR-3SG
      'The man holds the door open' (A-resultative)

---

7 The same alignment preferences are attested in attributive use of resultative forms. It has been proposed that these forms reveal split intransitive rather than ergative patterns (Donohue 2008), given that there is further variation among intransitives (cf. *the fallen leaf* vs. * *the sang choir*). What matters here is that the alignment is not accusative.

The effects of resultatives/perfects on subject marking is also evident in split-S languages of the active/stative type (Klimov 1977; Mithun 1991; Donohue & Wichmann (eds.) 2008). In many languages of this type, S patterns with A in a non-stative construction and with P in a (stative) perfect construction. For example, in Tuscarora (Mithun 1999: 235), verbs take object-style agreement to agree with the intransitive subject when used in the stative-perfective form. Thus, split intransitive languages too comply with the TAM hierarchy, even though they differ with respect to the cut-off points on the hierarchy. For example, in Mohawk (Mithun 1991, 233), the verbs follow an accusative pattern when used in the imperfective/habitual and perfective/aorist, and an ergative pattern when used in the perfect. And in Mayan languages, subject agreement switches to object agreement in the past, resulting in the ergative pattern (Primus 1999: 82). It can be objected that split-intransitive languages should not be confused with ergative languages; still, these examples are relevant insofar as past tenses show a dispreference for an accusative pattern.

3 A TAM-hierarchy for alignment splits

3.1 A one-dimensional TAM-hierarchy for alignment splits

At this point we are in a position to propose the following comprehensive TAM-hierarchy for alignment splits. The categories higher on the hierarchy favor accusative (and disfavor ergative) alignment, while the categories lower on the hierarchy favor ergative (and disfavor accusative) alignment.

(10) One-dimensional TAM-hierarchy for alignment splits
Imperative > Future > Present > Imperfect > Aorist > Perfect > Resultative
Acc/*Erg→   ←Erg/*Acc

The ranking of the hierarchy is motivated functionally, by markedness considerations, as discussed in §2.1 above. Thus, the categories lower on the hierarchy such as resultatives are P-centered insofar as the change of state of the P participant is at issue, while the categories higher on the hierarchy such as imperatives and futures refer to intended events and therefore are naturally A-centered. In this way, the markedness approach (correctly) predicts that in a P-centered resultative construction, P is the primary argument and remains unmarked. Similarly, in an A-centered imperative construction, the primary A argument remains unmarked.

The proposed hierarchy generates the usual predictions: for example, if the accusative pattern is found in the future in the predominantly ergative Burushaski, then it will be found in imperatives as well, as imperatives outrank futures on the hierarchy. This prediction is borne out (see Klaiman 1987 on Burushaski). Similarly, if the aorist (perfective past) patterns ergatively, the perfect will do so as well, insofar as the language under consideration distinguishes between perfective and perfect forms. This might be illustrated, for example, by Kashmiri (Wali & Koul 1997), where perfect has a separate form from aorist: predictably, both forms take an ergative pattern.

Some other cases may be more problematic, though. Thus, a language may not distinguish all the categories on the hierarchy: for example, it may fail to distinguish between perfective past vs. perfect (as in Hindi, which differs from Kashmiri in that respect), or between actional vs. stative perfect. This will not count as a counterexample, though, but rather as lack of supporting evidence for a particular ranking. More problematic is the case of Chukchi, where according to Nedjalkov (1979), imperatives show a higher degree of ergativity (again determined in terms of homophonies between S-agreement vis-à-vis A-agreement and P agreement), as compared to indicative forms. Yet it should be noted that the Chukchi imperative is unusual in a number of respects. First, it is not restricted to the 2nd person but is found throughout the person paradigm, which is more characteristic of optatives/subjunctives than of dedicated imperatives. Second, this form may also be used in interrogative contexts, which again is untypical of imperatives proper. Also morphologically, the Chukchi imperative patterns with the conditional mood, which again supports its qualification as a subjunctive mood rather than imperative proper. Note that the pressure for realignment observed for (dedicated) imperatives need not carry over to subjunctives: indeed, ergative languages like Basque, where a subjunctive form is used in the imperative function, retain the ergative alignment in this paradigm as well. Clearly, what is at issue here is a general question of cross-linguistic identifiability/comparability of linguistic categories. While this is a general question still open to discussion (see Haspelmath 2007, 2015, for discussion and proposals), it seems fair to state that here as elsewhere the predictions concerning individual categories on the hierarchy will hold insofar as language-specific categories comply with the prototype. In particular, the predictions will be stronger for dedicated forms than for forms combining several functions. We will take up the issue of polysemy in §4.2 below.

3.2 A two-dimensional TAM-hierarchy for alignment splits

Above we have presented our TAM hierarchy as a one-dimensional hierarchy comprising tense, aspect and mood categories. Yet, like the Animacy Hierarchy (which includes apart from animacy proper further dimensions of person and definiteness/specificity; see, e.g., Croft 2003; Aissen 2003), the TAM-hierarchy might also be viewed as a complex hierarchy subsuming several sub-hierarchies:

(i) Aspect Hierarchy: Imperfective > Perfective > Perfect > Resultative
(ii) Tense Hierarchy: Future > Present > Past
(iii) Mood Hierarchy: Imperative > Indicative (non-imperative)

The motivation behind the Aspect Hierarchy is most clearly related to the P-orientation of perfectives/perfects referring to a completed action in contrast to the A-orientation of uncompleted actions (recall the discussion in §2.1 above). The motivation behind the Mood Hierarchy is somewhat different: imperatives are inherently agent-oriented not only because an action does not extend to the P participant yet, but also because the imperative addressee should be a volitional subject (Dixon 1979; 1994). The Tense Hierarchy is arguably related to the other two hierarchies: the present vs. past distinction is functionally (and also diachronically) related to the imperfective vs. perfective distinction, while the future vs. non-future distinction is closer to the modal distinction between intended and realized action. Importantly, it also invokes a notion of a volitional (intentional) subject, inasmuch as future forms are related to the expression of intention.

Usually, the three hierarchies above do not conflict with each other and can be unified in a single dimension, as suggested in (10); sometimes, however, they do conflict. Consider the case of Newari discussed by Givón (1984),[8] where ergative marking is obligatory (for certain verb classes) in the past, optional in the future, and prohibited in the present:

Newari (Givón 1984: 155)
(11) a. Wō   manu-na   mē   ha-la
         the   man-ERG   song sing-PERF
         'The man sang (a song)'

   b. Wō   manu   mē   ha-yi   cō-gu   du
         the   man   song sing-IMPERF   be-NOM   be
         'The man is singing (a song)'

---

[8] In another variety of Newari (Dolakha Newari; Genetti 2006), there are no alignment splits: ergative is used throughout the hierarchy, and is also possible with imperatives.

c. Wō manu(nã) mē ha-yi
   the man(ERG) song sing-IMPERF
   'The man will sing (a song)'

On the basis of these data, Givón (1984: 153) proposed the following hierarchy governing alignment splits in Newari: **present > future > past**. Clearly, the ranking **present > future** contradicts the ranking of the two categories on the TAM-hierarchy in (10). Note, however, that this ranking can be derived from the Aspect Hierarchy: it is arguably due to the inherent imperfective value of the present which is absent in both past and future (cf. Malchukov 2009 for discussion of the "present perfective puzzle"). Yet, unless we want to allow for language-particular hierarchies, which would make the hierarchies void of any universal predictive power, such data seem to challenge the universal one-dimensional TAM hierarchy in (10). However, the Newari pattern can be easily accommodated once we decompose the hierarchy into several dimensions, as proposed above. On the latter 'multidimensional' view, the TAM-hierarchy can be conceived of as a combination of feature values from different sub-hierarchies. Here, for the sake of simplicity, we can represent it as a two-dimensional hierarchy which includes the Aspect Hierarchy (Imperfective > Perfective > Perfect > Resultative) as one dimension and the combined Mood-Tense Hierarchy (Imperative > Future > Present > Past) as another dimension. This would yield the two-dimensional hierarchy (lattice) in (12); cf. the two-dimensional animacy-definiteness hierarchy in Aissen (2003).

(12) **Two-dimensional TAM-hierarchy for alignment splits**

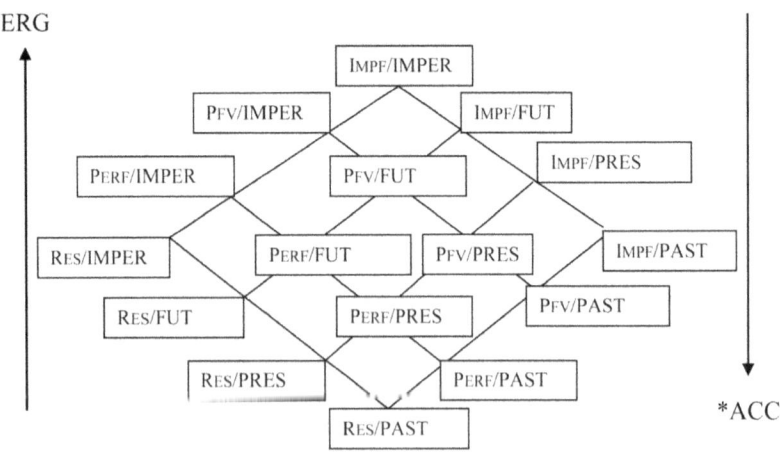

Note that this two-dimensional hierarchy allows us to account for the Newari pattern, as the combination of values <present; imperfective> is not universally ranked with respect to <future; perfective> (although both are lower than <future; imperfective> on the hierarchy). On the other hand, the proposed hierarchy seems to also be superior to a three-dimensional hierarchy projecting Tense, Mood and Aspect hierarchies as separate dimensions. Note that imperatives can be straightforwardly built into the Tense Hierarchy as they project into the future. Further, the two-dimensional hierarchy is more economical given that certain combinations of values (e.g., <imperative/past>) are disallowed, and certain other combinations (e.g., <imperative/future>) are redundant. Thus, only in some cases of plausible feature combinations (e.g., <future; imperfective> vs. <present; perfective>) do we observe cross-linguistic variation resulting from language-particular rankings. We conclude that a two-dimensional hierarchy is both necessary and sufficient to constrain possible alignment splits as well as to allow for (attested) language-particular variation. However, for ease of exposition, we will base our OT account of alignment splits on the simpler one-dimensional hierarchy.

4 Modeling alignment splits

4.1 Modeling the TAM-hierarchy

Now that we have established a TAM hierarchy, we can consider how to model it in Optimality Theory (Prince & Smolensky 1993). The choice of the theory is due to the fact that OT has already proved to be successful in modeling alignment splits conditioned by the Animacy Hierarchy (recall the discussion in §1.1). Further, we can build on some earlier proposals in the OT literature that aim at providing a unified account for TAM-based alignment splits, even though these accounts were so far restricted to the better attested perfective-imperfective splits. In particular, Sharma (2001) proposed to formalize De Lancey's (1981) account of alignment splits through harmonic alignment between the perfectivity scale and the grammatical function scale in a way reminiscent of Aissen's (2003) account of differential case marking (see also Lee 2003 and Stiebels 2002 for related proposals):

(13) a. *Subj/Perf & *øc ≫ *Subj/Nonperf & *øc
 b. *Obj/Nonperf & *øc ≫ *Obj/ Perf & *øc

Sharma's approach has been found problematic in a number of respects.[9] Most importantly, for this account to work, subject and object should be replaced by A and P, respectively, as argued by Stiebels (2002; cf. also Arkadjev 2008). With this amendment, the TAM hierarchy proposed above can be straightforwardly recast as a markedness hierarchy.

(14) a. *A& øc& Res ≫ *A& øc& Perf ≫ *A& øc& Aor ... ≫ *A& øc& Imper
b. *P& øc & Imper ≫ *P& øc & Fut ≫ *P& øc & Pres ≫ ... *A& øc& Res

Now alignment splits can be modeled through interpolation of economy constraints (*Case) into the constraint hierarchy. For example, the following constraint ranking models a situation in which ERG is disallowed only in Imperatives (as in Kuikúro; see (6))):

(15) ... *A& øc& Pres ≫ *A& øc& Fut ≫ *Erg ≫ *A& øc& Imper

The constraint ranking in (16) models a situation in which Acc is allowed in the present and disallowed in the past:

(16) ... *O& øc & Pres ≫ *Acc ≫ *O& øc& Past...

This pattern is found in Georgian (see (4ab) above), but also in Kashmiri, where DOM is found only in the present and suspended in the past (de Hoop & Malchukov 2008, citing Wali and Koul 1997).

Earlier we qualified the hierarchies above as markedness hierarchies, as they refer to relative (un)markedness of individual TAM features with respect to particular alignment patterns. Alternatively, they can be viewed as Faithfulness hierarchies, as proposed by Woolford (2001). Woolford (2001) speaks about contextually restricted faithfulness constraints (FaithLex), which force the ergative marking of subjects more forcefully in the perfective domain. This approach is more in line with the transitivity-based accounts of alignment splits inspired by Hopper & Thompson's (1980) work. However, as noted in §2.1 above, the transitivity-based approach does not readily extend to other categories on the

---

9 Lee (2003: 40) notes a potential problem with Sharma's approach as it presupposes a general ban on imperfective forms taking objects, and perfective forms taking subjects. This criticism seems to be justified for Sharma's initial proposal, but does not necessarily carry over to our approach making use of an extended hierarchy. For example, resultative forms indeed usually disallow expression of an A argument, A-oriented resultatives (as illustrated for Even) being exceptional.

TAM-hierarchy, such as perfects and resultatives. On the markedness account, by contrast, the ergative alignment of resultatives is expected: these constructions are P-centered (refer to a change of state of the P participant), hence the tendency to leave P unmarked.

This does not mean, however, that the transitivity-based faithfulness account should be totally discarded as an explanation for TAM-based ergativity splits. Note, first, that the markedness account is designed to account for 'asymmetric' patterns of differential case marking, with ergative and accusative marking alternating with zero in certain TAM forms, and is less applicable for 'symmetric' patterns of differential case marking involving two overt case markers (cf. de Hoop & Malchukov 2008). For the latter cases the faithfulness approach is to be preferred. Consider, for instance, the case of Finnish, where the choice between 'accusative' (genitive) and partitive object is determined by definiteness of P, on the one hand, and perfectivity, on the other hand (both factors are subsumed under 'event-boundedness' on Kiparsky's (1998) account). Here, as predicted by the faithfulness approach, the use of accusative correlates with higher transitivity. The markedness approach, by contrast, has nothing to say about this pattern, at least without some further assumption about (relative) markedness of the two case forms in variation. One could further argue that for cases of asymmetric alternations, faithfulness constraints are also at work but are 'masked' by (higher ranking) markedness constraints. This account might explain why perfective/imperfective splits are most common among TAM-based splits crosslinguistically: the ergative-perfective connection is equally supported by both factors/constraints (markedness and faithfulness). Finally, taking faithfulness into account can explain why a P-case involved in an imperfective construction rarely is a dedicated accusative marker. Rather the same case is also used as a dative (allative, oblique) marker elsewhere (cf., e.g., the functions of the dative-accusative marker *ko-* in Hindi). Now, while marking P with a (dedicated) Accusative in an imperfective pattern is at odds with the predictions of the faithfulness account, marking P with an oblique (dative/allative) marker is fully consistent with the faithfulness approach, predicting reduction of transitivity in an imperfective construction. Thus one can explain the recurrent polysemy of a P-case in an imperfective pattern, which remains puzzling under the markedness approach. Thus, ultimately, we might need both markedness and faithfulness constraints to explain the full range of facts involved in TAM splits (recall the two-factor analysis of differential case marking advocated by De Hoop & Malchukov 2008). In this paper, however, I will base my account on markedness alone, as it makes the right predictions about the patterns of asymmetric alignment splits under discussion.

4.2 Towards an integrated account of alignment splits

In the previous sections we discussed cases where alignment splits are due to the Animacy Hierarchy (in §1) and the TAM hierarchy (in §§2–3). In other cases, however, the splits are due to both factors ("mixed splits", in terms of Dixon 1994). For example, in Burushaski (Klaiman 1987), transitive subjects take ERG in the past, except for 1,2-person pronouns. Such combined splits can be straightforwardly captured through conjoining elements from both hierarchies. Thus the following constraint ranking accounts for the pattern of Burushaski:

(17) *A/human & øc & Past ≫ *A/3rd & øc& Past ≫ *Erg ≫ *A/1st, 2nd & øc& Past

In Kuikúro (Dixon 1994: 105), as exemplified in (6) above, the 1st person pronouns are unmarked only in the imperative (and some other 'interactive' moods); elsewhere (in indicative mood) they take the ergative case. Thus:

(18) ... * A/1st & øc & Fut ≫ *Erg ≫ *A/1st & øc & Imper

As can be seen from these examples, we can capture the mixed splits in a straightforward way by integrating Aissen-style hierarchies with the TAM-hierarchies above through the mechanism of constraint conjunction. Such integration is unproblematic, insofar as it does not interfere with the ranking on the TAM-hierarchy. In other cases, however, the TAM hierarchy can be violated due to interference of other factors.

Consider again the situation in Georgian (Hewitt 1989), where present and future (belonging to the "Series 1"-tenses) pattern accusatively, while aorist (and other related "Series-2" forms) take an ergative pattern. Now, the imperative shows an ergative pattern,[10] which is clearly at odds with the predictions of the TAM hierarchy. Importantly, in Georgian, imperatives (with a few exceptions) lack dedicated forms but are built on the corresponding aorist forms. Not surprisingly, imperatives inherit the ergative pattern from the aorist along with other derivationally related ("Series-2") forms. This shows that apart from functional constraints embodied in the TAM hierarchy, there are formal constraints due to polysemy and pattern inheritance, which may interfere with the markedness hierarchies. From an OT perspective, such constraints capturing effects of

---

[10] This is somewhat difficult to ascertain since pronominal subjects are usually missing in imperatives, and more importantly 1,2-pronouns lack a distinction between ergative and absolutive forms. However, insofar as the addressee of a (transitive) imperative is 3rd person and is overt, it takes the ergative case (T. Wier, p.c.).

analogical extensions can be conceived as constraints on Output-Output Correspondences (OOC; Prince & Smolensky 1993), which might be an appropriate account here as well (see Malchukov 2006 on interaction of function vs. form based constraints in the domain of nominalizations).

Thus, alignment splits are governed by several markedness hierarchies, including the Animacy Hierarchy and the TAM-hierarchy, which additionally interact with other constraints, some of them being functional (recall the discussion of the impact of faithfulness constraints in 4.2. above), some others structural. These latter constraints might interfere with (predictions of) markedness hierarchies, yet such violations are not fatal for the universal hierarchies insofar as these other factors (constraints) can be independently justified. Providing an integrated account of alignment splits driven by all these (potentially conflicting) factors is beyond the scope of this article, focusing on the TAM-hierarchy, yet it should be clear that Optimality Theory provides ready tools for modeling such interaction.

5 Conclusions

Above we addressed the feature hierarchies governing alignment splits. We started with the better-studied Animacy Hierarchy, which has been claimed to govern the distribution of ergative and accusative patterns (Silverstein's generalization). Based on earlier work, it has been argued that the markedness hierarchy implicated in such splits masks two different factors/constraints, Distinguishability and Indexing, which converge on one pattern of differential object marking, but give rise to different patterns in the domain of differential subject marking. Turning to the TAM-hierarchy, which is the focus of the present paper, I proposed (following Lazard) that this hierarchy can be extended far beyond the basic patterns of the perfective/imperfective splits. In view of some conflicting evidence, I further proposed to recast a one-dimensional TAM-hierarchy hierarchy as two-dimensional. The TAM-hierarchy (whether one or two-dimensional) is conceived of as a markedness hierarchy, which can be recast as a constraint hierarchy in Optimality Theory. Thus OT provides a natural way of integrating hierarchies from different domains (Animacy Hierarchy and TAM-hierarchy), as well as accounting for apparent counterexamples through taking other interfering factors (both functional and structural) into account.

References

Ackerman, F. and J. Moore. 2001. *Proto-properties and Grammatical Encoding: A Correspondence Theory of Argument Selection*. Stanford: CSLI Publications.

Aissen, J. 2003. Differential Object Marking: Iconicity vs. Economy. *Natural Language and Linguistic Theory* 21, 435–483.

Arkadjev, P. 2008. Differential argument marking in two-term case systems and its implications for a general theory of case marking. In De Hoop, H. & P. de Swart (eds.), 151–173.

Bickel, B., A. Witzlack-Makarevich, and T. Zakharko. 2015. Typological evidence against universal effects of referential scales on case alignment. This volume.

Bossong, G. 1985. *Differentielle Objektmarkierung in den neuiranischen Sprachen*. Tübingen: Narr.

Butt, M. and T. H. King. 2003. Case systems: beyond structural distinctions. In *New perspectives on case theory*. E. Brandner and H. Zinsmeister (eds). Stanford: CSLI.

Comrie, B. 1978. Ergativity. In *Syntactic Typology. Studies in the Phenomenology of Language*, Winfried P. Lehmann (ed.), 329–394. Austin, London: The University of Texas Press.

Comrie, B. 1989. *Language universals and linguistic typology*. Chicago: University of Chicago Press.

DeLancey, S. 1981. An interpretation of split ergativity and related patterns. *Language* 57: 626–657.

Dixon, R. M. W. 1979. Ergativity. *Language* 55, 59–138.

Dixon, R. M. W. 1994. *Ergativity*. Cambridge: Cambridge University Press.

Donohue, Cathryn. 1999. Optimizing Fore Case and Word Order. Stanford, CA: Stanford University.

Donohue, M. & S. Wichmann (eds). 2008. *Typology of languages with semantic alignment*. Oxford: Oxford University Press.

Dowty, D. 1991. Thematic proto-roles and argument selection. *Language* 67, 547–619.

Givón, T. 1984. *Syntax: a functional-typological introduction*. Vol. 1. Amsterdam: Benjamins.

Harris, Alice. 1985. *Diachronic syntax: the Kartvelian case*. Orlando: Academic Press.

Haspelmath, Martin. 2007. Pre-established categories don't exist: consequences for language description and typology. *Linguistic Typology* 11.1: 119–132.

Haspelmath, Martin. 2015. Descriptive scales versus comparative scales. This volume.

Hendriks, P., and H. de Hoop. 2001. Optimality theoretic semantics. *Linguistics and Philosophy*, 24.

Hewitt, G. 1996. *Georgian: A Learner's Grammar*. London: Routledge.

de Hoop, H., and M.J.A. Lamers. 2006. Incremental Distinguishability of Subject and Object. In *Case, Valency, and Transitivity*, L. Kulikov, A. Malchukov, and P. de Swart (eds.), 269–287. Amsterdam: John Benjamins.

de Hoop, H. & A.L. Malchukov. 2007. On fluid differential case marking: A bidirectional OT approach. *Lingua* 117: 1636–1656.

de Hoop, H. & A.L. Malchukov. 2008. Case-marking strategies. *Linguistic Inquiry* 39: 565–587.

de Hoop, H. & B. Narasimhan. 2005. Differential case-marking in Hindi. In *Competition and Variation in Natural Languages: the Case for Case*, M. Amberber & H. de Hoop, H. (eds.), 321–346. Elsevier.

de Hoop, H. & P. de Swart (eds.). 2008. *Differential Subject Marking*. Dordrecht: Springer.

Hopper, P., and S. Thompson. 1980. Transitivity in Grammar and Discourse. *Language* 56: 251–80.

Jäger, Gerhard. 2007. Evolutionary game theory and typology: a case study. *Language* 83: 74–109.
Keine, S. and G. Müller. 2015. Differential argument encoding by impoverishment. This volume.
Kiparsky, P. 1998. Partitive case and aspect. In *The projection of arguments: lexical and compositional factors*, Butt, M., Geuder, W. (eds.), 265–307. CSLI, Stanford.
Kittilä, S. 2006. The woman showed the baby to her sister. On resolving animacy-driven ambiguity in ditransitives. In *Studies in Case, valency and transitivity*, L. Kulikov, A. Malchukov, and P. De Swart (eds.), 291–309. Amsterdam: Benjamins.
Klimov, Georgij A. 1977. *Tipologija jazykov aktivnogo stroja*. Moskva: Nauka
Lazard, G. 1998. *Actancy*. Berlin: Mouton de Gruyter.
Lee, Hanjung. 2003. Parallel optimization in case systems. In *Nominals: inside and out* M.T.H. King (eds.), 15–59. Stanford: CSLI Publications.
Malchukov, A.L. 2006. Constraining nominalization: function-form competition. *Linguistics*, 44–45: 973–1008.
Malchukov, A.L. 2008. Animacy and asymmetries in differential case marking. *Lingua* 118: 203–221.
Malchukov, Andrej & Helen de Hoop. 2011. Tense, aspect and mood-based differential case marking. *Lingua* 121: 135–147.
Malchukov, Andrej & Peter de Swart. 2009. Differential case marking and actancy variation. In *Handbook of Case*, A. Malchukov & A. Spencer (eds.), 339–356. Oxford: Oxford University Press.
Mithun, Marianne. 1991. Active/agentive case marking and its motivations. *Language* 67: 510–546.
Mithun, Marianne. 1999. *The languages of Native North America*. Cambridge: Cambridge University Press.
Mohanan, T. 1990. *Arguments in Hindi*. Unpublished doctoral dissertation. Stanford University, Stanford.
Næss, Å. 2007. *Prototypical transitivity*. Amsterdam: Benjamins.
Nedjalkov, V.P. 1979. Degrees of ergativity in Chukchi. In *Ergativity*, Frans Plank (ed.), 241–262. London: Academic Press.
Nedjalkov, V.P. (ed.). 1988. *Typology of resulatative constructions*. Amsterdam: Benjamins.
Plank, Frans. 1985. The extended accusative/restricted nominative in perspective. In Frans Plank (ed.), *Relational Typology*, 269–311. Berlin: Mouton.
Primus, B. 1999. *Cases and thematic roles*. Tübingen: Niemeyer.
Prince, A., and P. Smolensky. 2004. *Optimality Theory: Constraint Interaction in Generative Grammar*. Oxford: Blackwell.
Sharma, Devyani. 2001. Kashmiri case clitics and person hierarchy effects. In *Formal and empirical issues in Optimality Theoretic syntax*, P. Sells (ed.), 225–257. Stanford: CSLI Publications.
Song, J.J. 2001. *Linguistic typology: morphology and syntax*. London: Longman.
Silverstein, M. 1976. Hierarchy of features and ergativity. In Dixon, R. M. W. (Ed.), *Grammatical categories in Australian languages*, 112–171. Canberra: Australian Institute of Aboriginal Studies.
Stiebels, Barbara. 2002. *Typologie des Argumentlinkings: Ökonomie und Expressivität*. Berlin: Akademie Verlag.
de Swart, P. 2007. *Cross-linguistic variation in object marking*. PhD thesis, Radboud University Nijmegen.

Trask, R. 1979. On the Origin of Ergativity. In F. Plank (Ed.). *Ergativity; Toward a Theory of Grammatical Relations*, 385–404. New York: Academic Press.
Valenzuela, P. 1997. *Basic verb types and argument structures in Shipibo-Conibo*. Ph.D. University of Oregon.
Woolford, E. 2001. Case patterns. In *Optimality-theoretic syntax*, Legendre, G., Grimshaw, J., Vikner, S. (eds.), 509–545. Cambridge, Mass: MIT Press.
Wunderlich, D. & R. Lakämper. 2001. On the interaction of structural and semantic case. *Lingua* 111: 377–418.
Zeevat, H., and G. Jäger. 2002. A reinterpretation of syntactic alignment. In *Proceedings of the Third and Fourth International Tbilisi Symposium on Language, Logic and Computation*, D. de Jongh, H. Zeevat, and M. Nilsenova (eds).

Corinna Handschuh
11 Split Marked-S Case Systems

1 Introduction

This paper discusses the kinds of split-alignment systems found in languages of the rare marked-S system. In the following section (2) I will introduce this kind of alignment, which exists in two 'flavors': Marked-nominative and marked-absolutive. Afterwards I will discuss different kinds of splits found in the languages of the marked-S type. The main focus lies on split-alignment systems in which the split can be interpreted as the effect of prominence scales of some kind. A prominence hierarchy of nominals is considered by many linguists as the driving force behind split-alignment systems. However, splits between alignment systems based on various other factors apart from a hierarchy of nominals are attested cross-linguistically. Even within the limited sample of languages of the rare marked-S type quite a number of such splits can be found. The following domains of splits are presented and discussed in this paper: nominal prominence hierarchy (section 3); clause types (section 4); and gender (section 5). Not for all of these does an explanation along the lines of an accessibility hierarchy seem as convincing as for the nominal splits.

2 Marked-S alignment

Syntactic typology traditionally distinguishes between nominative-accusative and ergative-absolutive systems as the main types of alignment. They can be easily distinguished by how they treat the single argument of an intransitive verb (S). If S is treated like the most agent-like argument of a transitive verb (A) – e.g. by means of case marking – but different from the more patient-like argument of a transitive verb (P), one speaks of nominative-accusative alignment. If on the other hand S is treated like P and distinct from A, the language is referred to as being of the ergative-absolutive type (cf. Comrie 1978, Dixon 1994). It has been observed that the marking of the transitive role which is encoded in the same form as S is usually the case form with the smallest amount of overt marking. This has been formulated as universal 38 in Greenberg (1963: 75) – if any case form is not overtly marked it will be "the one which includes among its meanings that of subject of the intransitive verb".

Nominative-accusative: Marked nominative:

```
     S                      S
  A     P                A     P
        |                      |
   overtly coded          used in citation
                          might be zero-coded
used in citation
might be zero-coded       overtly coded
```

Figure 1: Nominative-accusative vs. marked-nominative coding

However, there are some languages which behave in the opposite way. They have long been known within the nominative-accusative system as so-called 'marked-nominative' languages. While being of nominative-accusative alignment type these languages use a radically different coding pattern than the standard nominative-accusative languages. These languages use an overtly coded form in the Nominative case (S and A function) while the case covering the P function is zero-coded. The standard nominative-accusative coding is contrasted with the marked nominative system in Figure 1. For the languages of the marked-nominative type it has been observed that the P case covers more functions than just marking transitive objects (König 2006), the most wide-spread function of zero-coded P case being to provide the citation form of a noun.

The other possibility for a language to violate the Greenberg Universal is marked-absolutive alignment. This is a parallel structure to the ergative-absolutive system. There a zero-coded case-form marking the A function (Ergative) contrasts with an overtly-coded form of the noun covering S and P function. Marked-absolutive coding – although claimed to be non-existent (Dixon 1979: 78) – is attested for the Austronesian language Nias (Brown 2001). Both marked-nominative and marked-absolutive languages use an overtly coded form to mark the S function while one of the transitive roles is left zero-coded. Therefore I employ the term marked-S languages to refer to both types of coding system.

The marked-nominative system is seen by many as a hybrid between nominative-accusative and ergative-absolutive alignment. Dixon (1979: 77) proposed 'extended-ergative' as an alternate name for this alignment type, since this would "ensure that 'ergative' and 'accusative' are always used to name the marked case choices, and 'absolutive' and 'nominative' unmarked choices."

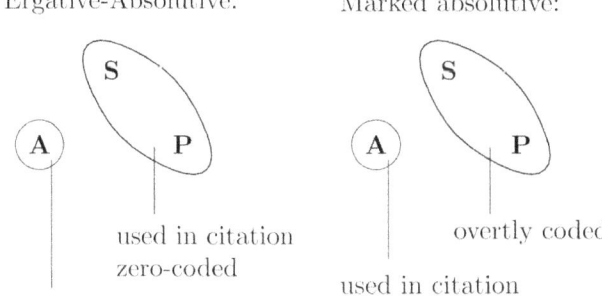

Figure 2: Ergative-absolutive vs. marked-absolutive coding

This view reflects the idea that in terms of markedness (in the sense of actual overt morphological marking) the marked-nominative system is closer to the ergative-absolutive than the nominative-accusative alignment. Conversely, the overt marking relations of the marked-absolutive system are more similar to the standard nominative-accusative system than to the ergative-absolutive. As we will see in the remainder of this paper, the mixed status of the marked-S system – alignment behaving like one type but the marking relations behaving according to another type – might prove to be a crucial factor when investigating alignment splits.

3 Splits on the prominence hierarchies of nominals

Split systems of case-marking are most prominently known from languages of the ergative type (Dixon 1994). However, they also occur in languages of the marked-S type, which has shared properties with nominative-accusative as well as ergative-absolutive languages. The association of certain alignment systems with specific parts of a nominal prominence scale can be broken down into two different factors both pointing in the same direction for languages of the standard nominative-accusative and ergative-absolutive types. I will refer to these two factors as the 'overt marking hypothesis' and the 'alignment hypothesis'. Since for the languages in which split systems have traditionally been studied the two factors make the same predictions, they are not usually discussed separately as two different motivations for split alignment systems. For languages of the marked-S type, however, the two factors point in different directions.

Therefore marked-S languages are the ideal test case to compare two hypotheses intended to account for the types of splits in alignment one finds along the prominence scale of Silverstein (1976). In this section I will give a brief review of the split patterns studied by Silverstein and others following him. Afterwards, I will discuss two different factors that could be taken into account as possible explanations for the so-called Silverstein Pattern, which I will refer to as the overt-marking and alignment hypotheses, and discuss the predictions these explanations make for the split behavior of marked-S languages. I will also consider these explanations in relation to the two common functions of case marking which are discussed in the literature, the 'discriminating' and 'identifying' functions. The subsequent subsections introduce the different types of splits along the nominal prominence scale found in languages of the marked-S type.

That languages often do not exhibit a uniform alignment system throughout all domains of their grammar has been stated many times and been dealt with in the linguistic literature of all orientations (an incomplete list contains Silverstein 1976, Dixon 1994, Aissen 2003). Based on these alignment splits, scales are constructed in which the parts of the grammar that share the same alignment system constitute continuous parts of the scale.

Silverstein's hierarchy of "'inherent lexical content' of noun phrases" (1976: 113) is one of the first and probably the most prominent example of a referential scale. Based on data from languages with a split-alignment system that depends on the type of nominal which is used, Silverstein has derived the ordering shown in figure 3. Languages with classical Silverstein splits in their case marking, e.g., have 1st and 2nd person pronouns which behave differently from 3rd person pronouns, which behave differently from full noun phrases, etc. Comparing languages with this or similar types of split alignment, many linguists noted that the different splits appeared to follow a parallel pattern. It was observed that the same kind of alignment tends to be associated with the same kinds of nouns. This has led to claims about the ordering of those parts of grammar in terms of cognitive prominence (ultimately reflected in the hierarchy itself). Furthermore, proposals have been made to universally assign particular alignment systems to particular parts of the scale.

On the scale set up by Silverstein (and many similar ones proposed by other scholars) – so is the prediction – ergative-absolutive alignment will be found on the lower end and nominative-accusative on the upper end. This is often said to be due to the low potential of inanimate and non-human referents to be the agent of a clause, therefore making overt agent-marking necessary, whereas pronouns (especially 1st and 2nd person) are said to be "natural agents", thus making special agent marking unnecessary. I will refer to this hypothesis as the

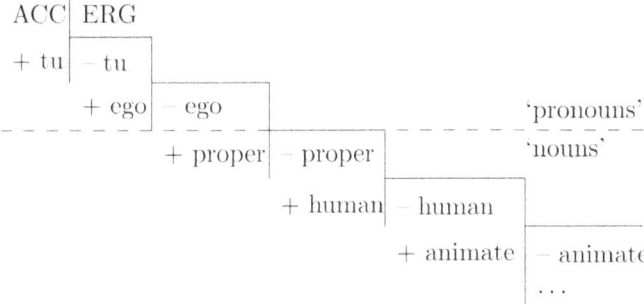

Figure 3: The Silverstein hierarchy (Silverstein 1976: 122)

OVERT MARKING HYPOTHESIS from now on. Given the reasoning of the overt marking hypothesis the split between alignment systems is a coincidental one since it is purely based on the overt marking relations of the two arguments of transitive verbs (A and P) and does not take into account the encoding of the single argument of intransitive verbs (S). In the previous section I discussed the ergative-absolutive-like properties of the marked-nominative alignment system in terms of overt case-marking. According to the overt coding hypothesis marked-nominative alignment should be found on the lower end of the animacy-hierarchy, just like ergative-absolutive systems.

Another line of argumentation that makes a prediction about the association of different parts of the prominence scale with certain alignment patterns is the ALIGNMENT HYPOTHESIS. Following this train of thought, it is not the necessity to overtly mark a certain case form (for a subset of nominals) that leads to splits in the alignment system of a language. Rather, the mechanisms leading to splits on the hierarchy are really based on the alignment system itself, which either favors a grammatical relation linking S and A arguments (nominative-accusative) or S and P arguments (ergative-absolutive). Support for this hypothesis is gained from a different domain of what is often considered a subfield of split ergativity, namely so-called split- or fluid-S languages, also referred to as semantic alignment (Donohue & Wichmann 2008). Languages of this type employ two different alignment patterns for intransitive S arguments based on the semantics of the verb. The S argument of intransitive verbs with a more agentive nature (unergative verbs) uses the same encoding as is employed for transitive A arguments, while less agentive verbs (unaccusative verbs) choose the same marking as used with transitive P arguments. The verbs that choose the transitive-A marking for their S arguments are expected to occur with nominals found on the upper part of the prominence hierarchy. Rather than being of the dependent-marking type, i.e. encoding grammatical relations through nominal case, these languages overwhelmingly choose verbal cross-referencing devices to encode grammatical relations. Further, these languages have two sets of verbal agreement markers, one used to cross-reference A (and some S) arguments and one to cross-reference P (and some S arguments). Therefore both A and P arguments are encoded through overt material. Since unergative verbs in languages with semantic alignment encode S arguments like A arguments for these verbs one can speak of a nominative-accusative alignment. Since, as noted above, unergative verbs are expected to appear with nominals high on the prominence scale, this part of the scale is associated with nominative-accusative alignment, i.e. identifying an S+A relation, irrespective of the question whether this S+A relation is overtly coded or zero-coded. The nouns on the lower part of the prominence scale, conversely, would almost exclusively be found with unaccusative verbs, which in languages with semantic alignment use the same coding for their S arguments as is used on transitive P arguments. As a result the ergative-absolutive pattern which associates S and P arguments with each other is more prominent for nominals on the lower part of the hierarchy, again irrespective of the type of encoding they receive.

While the overt-marking hypothesis is probably the most referred to explanation of alignment splits, the alignment hypothesis can explain the patterns equally well. The data from languages with semantic alignment shows that there is a motivation for languages to associate different nominals with different alignment patterns irrespective of the overt marking relations. Since this line of argumentation is likely to be less familiar I will briefly summarize the alignment hypothesis: First, unergative verbs are used with nominals high on the prominence hierarchy. Unergative verbs provide support for an S+A versus P alignment in languages with a semantic alignment system, since the same markers are used for S and A arguments. Therefore the S+A versus P alignment pattern (i.e. nominative-accusative) can be associated with nominals on the upper part of the hierarchy. Second, nominals on the lower part of the hierarchy typically occur with unaccusative verbs. In languages with a semantic alignment system unaccusative verbs support a relation of S+P versus A arguments. Thus the ergative-absolutive pattern should be expected to occur with nominals on the lower part of the hierarchy. According to this hypothesis marked-nominative systems behave just like standard nominative-accusative systems in terms of split marking, i.e. they should both be found with nominals on the upper part of Silverstein's scale.

These two hypotheses on the association of different alignment systems with specific parts of the prominence scale can be related to the two prominent explanations of case marking, which are often referred to as the discriminating and the identifying function of case (cf. Mallinson & Blake 1981: 91–93). The discriminating function of case in a nutshell states that case is used to distinguish between A and P arguments in transitive clauses. In order to do so, marking of one of the arguments is sufficient, thus the other arguments can be left zero-coded. Since no need for distinction of arguments arises with intransitive verbs, S arguments can be left zero-coded as well. For a more detailed illustration of the discriminating function of case see Comrie (1989: 125ff.), who, however, does not propose this function to be all-explaining and acknowledges the identifying function as well. The overt marking hypothesis on split alignments that I discussed above uses the same rationale, which can be abbreviated as: Use overt marking if there is the danger of misinterpreting the syntactic role of one of the transitive arguments. However, there is a fundamental difference between the two. According to the discriminating hypothesis overt marking of S arguments as it is found in all marked-S languages is superfluous and should not occur at all (as predicted by Greenberg's Universal cited above). Therefore marked-S languages cannot adequately be described by this principle (alone) and must make some use of the identifying function of case, which is to be discussed now. The identifying function of case proposes that different case forms overtly code intrinsic features of the arguments they mark.[1] This approach is often associated with Hopper & Thompson (1980), who list a number of semantic properties that are associated with the two arguments of transitive verbs. Similarly the alignment hypothesis associates the nominals on the upper part of the hierarchy to the nominative-accusative alignment pattern highlighting their high potential to be agents (an intrinsic property of highly animate and individuated entities).

In their optimality-theoretic approach de Hoop & Malchukov (2008), Malchukov (2008), Malchukov & de Hoop (2011) use constraints that are motivated by the two different functions of case marking to derive a number of alignment systems split between nominative-accusative, ergative-absolutive and/or neutral[2] systems. All languages discussed use the more typical pattern of using overtly encoded forms for accusative and/or ergative case. I will not attempt here to propose a complete optimality-theoretic style analysis of languages of the marked-S type. One property of any such analysis would have to be that ECONOMY constraints as proposed in de Hoop & Malchukov (2008), Malchukov

---

[1] This function is also sometimes referred to as the 'indexing function', as for example by Malchukov (2008, 2015).
[2] Neutral alignment is a system in which S, A and P arguments do not show any difference in their encoding.

(2008) must be ranked low in these languages, otherwise the overt marking of the S argument of intransitive verbs should not be possible.

3.1 Marked-S only with 3rd person: Datooga

Nouns in Datooga – a Nilotic language spoken in Tanzania – have distinct forms for S+A function (Nominative) and P-function (referred to as the Absolute form of the noun). The two forms can be distinguished through their contrasting tonal patterns. Since the base form of a noun – i.e. the form used in citation and to derive non-basic forms – is the Absolute rather then the Nominative, Datooga must be considered a marked nominative language.[3] Absolute and Nominative forms of the nouns *gùdéedà* 'dog' and *ɲáawùudà* 'cat' are shown in (1).[4]

(1) **Datooga** (Nilotic; Tanzania; Kiessling 2007: 153)
   a. qòo-dâw   ɲáawuúdá   gùdéedà
       S3-give   cat.NOM   dog.ABS
      'The cat gave (it) to the dog.'

   b. qòo-dâw   gúdéedá   ɲáawùudà
       S3-give   dog.NOM   cat.ABS
      'The dog gave (it) to the cat.'

Yet this situation does not hold for all the nominals in Datooga. While full nouns and 3rd person pronouns distinguish between Nominative and Absolute case via tonal marking (2), 1st and 2nd person independent pronouns on the other hand do not have distinct forms for the two cases as the paradigm in Figure 4 demonstrates.

---

[3] Kiessling (2007) convincingly states that the Nominative form is clearly derived from the Absolute and not vice-versa. Knowing the tonal shape of the Absolute form one can tell which tonal shape the Nominative will have. Predicting the Absolute from the Nominative is, however, not unambiguously possible. A reviewer pointed out that there might be a fundamental difference in the markedness relation between this situation and languages in which one case form of a noun is zero-coded and the other form consists of the zero-coded form plus affixal morphology. However, if one does not limit oneself to a view of morphology as a concatenating process but allows for more abstract representations of morphemes such as through (suprasegmental) features, the difference is rather the frequency with which a given pattern is found in the world's languages and not a fundamental one.

[4] The following glosses are used: 1,2,3 = first, second, third person; ABS = absolute (zero-coded accusative); ACC = accusative; COP = copula; DR = different referent; EX = exclusive; IRR = irrealis; LOC = locative; M = masculine; MUT = mutated form of a noun in Nias; NEG = negation; NOM = nominative; OBL = oblique; PL = plural; POL = polite; POSS = possessor; PRV = perfective; Q = question; S = subject agreement; SG = singular; SR = same referent.

	absolute	nominative
1SG	ánììní, ání	
2SG	áɲììɲí, áɲíi	
3SG	nìɲ	níɲ
1PL	éesèesá, èesà	
2PL	óogòogá, òogà	
3PL	sàawà	sáawá

Figure 4: Case on personal pronouns in Datooga (Kiessling 2007: 160)

(2) **Datooga** (Kiessling 2007: 162)
   a. gwà-éeʃà   nòʊt
       S3-say   other.ABS
       'She/he told another one.'

   b. gwà-éeʃà   nóʊt
       S3-say   other.NOM
       'Another one said.'

The Datooga situation does mirror the expected findings for split-ergative marking (as would be predicted by the overt marking hypothesis), since the marked-Nominative case is only found with entities at the lower end of this hierarchy, i.e everything from 3rd person pronouns downwards. The following scale visualizes the split case-marking in Datooga.

(3) 1st, 2nd > 3rd, full NP
     neutral > marked nominative

3.2 Marked-S only on Pronouns: Oirata

While the last section showed an example where the marked-nominative system exhibits the same split in marking as a well-behaved split-ergative system, we will now discuss an example of a marked-nominative system behaving the other way around. In Oirata – a non-Austronesian language spoken on the island Timor – pronouns functioning as S or A arguments of the verb are marked by the suffix *-te* – i.e. Nominative case.

(4) **Oirata** (Timor-Alor-Pantar; Timor; Donohue & Brown 1999: 66, 67)
    a. in-te   ee   asi
       1PL.EX-NOM 2SG.POL see
       'We saw you.'

b. ee-te in asi-ho
2SG.POL-NOM 1PL.EX see-NEG
'You didn't see us.'

c. an-te ete na'a ippa
1SG-NOM tree OBL fall
'I fell out of the tree.'

d. Nahi ee-te mede-pe'e-é
tomorrow 2SG.POL-NOM eat-IRR-Q
'Are you going to eat tomorrow?'

There are no 3rd person pronouns. Demonstratives can take over the function of third person pronominal elements, yet they receive no case-marking. The same is true for all full noun phrases: they do not receive any marking in S, A or P function. In other words, Oirata exhibits neutral alignment for full NPs, as demonstrated in (5).

(5) **Oirata** (Donohue & Brown 1999: 66, 67)
a. maaro [mede-n] kopete-he
person [eat-REL] black-NEG
'The person who is eating isn't black.'

b. ira eme modo ina-to tutu
water take child give-DR drink
'Give the child some water to drink.'

c. ihar ani asi-le mara
dog 1SG.ACC see-SR go
'The dog$_i$ saw me$_j$ and Ø$_i$ left.'

Thus in Oirata we find the marked-nominative alignment system in that region of the Silverstein scale where we would expect to find marking of the nominative-accusative type. Rather than behaving like an ergative-absolutive system, which it should according to the overt marking hypothesis, Oirata's marked nominative maps like a nominative-accusative system on the Silverstein scale, thus supporting the alignment hypothesis. The Oirata system is visualized in (6).

(6) 1st, 2nd > full NP
marked nominative > neutral

3.3 Marked-S only on full noun phrases: Kab'eena

The two examples of the previous sections showed a split between marked-nominative alignment in one domain of the Silverstein hierarchy and neutral alignment for the rest of the hierarchy. In this section we will turn to a system where the split lies between marked-nominative and standard nominative-accusative alignment.

In some approaches the marked-nominative system is not defined in terms of the overt marking of one form (i.e. the Nominative) versus the zero-coding of another form (i.e. the Absolute). Rather the notion of 'functional markedness' is called upon. A case form is functionally marked if its use is limited to a small range of functions while another case form (the functionally unmarked one) is employed in a wide range of functions. Zero-coding is not a necessary prerequisite, though it often correlates with functional unmarkedness (cf. e.g. König 2006).

In Kab'eena – a Cushitic language of Ethiopia – the functional (un)markedness of nominals does not obviously correspond to the zero-coding/overt coding distinction. Crass (2005: 86) argues that the Absolute (or Accusative in his terminology), though not morphologically zero-coded, is still less marked than the Nominative since the Nominative is derived from the Absolute through vowel-change and/or suprasegmental marking (i.e. tonal change). Given this analysis Kab'eena is marked-nominative in terms of formal marking. Furthermore the Absolute form of a noun clearly seems to be the unmarked member of the Absolute-Nominative pair in terms of the functional definition of marked-nominative. It is for example the Absolute form of a noun that is used in citation.

While for full noun phrases the Nominative is a marked case in terms of its distribution, for pronouns the opposite seems to be true. For example if we compare the two nominal predications in (7), we see that the case form of the predicate nominal differs. While pronominal predicate nominals are in the Nominative case (7a), full noun phrases are in the Absolute when functioning as predicate nominals (7b).

(7) **Kab'eena** (Cushitic; Ethiopia; Crass 2005: 124, 263)
    a.   'aneet^i hi'riyoommii-h^u
        1SG.NOM.COP buy.PRV.1SG-M.NOM
        'It is me, who bought [it].'

    b.   'is^u haakimee-h^a
        3SG.M.NOM   doctor.ABS-COP.M
        'He is a doctor.'

If we take the range of uses of a case form as an indicator of its functional markedness, we should analyze the Kab'eena pronominal system as an instance of the standard nominative-accusative alignment (as opposed to the marked-nominative of full noun phrases). Thus Kab'eena nominals are split into marked-nominative for full noun phrases and nominative-accusative for pronouns. Finding the standard nominative-accusative on the upper part of the hierarchy is what we would expect from the overt marking hypothesis. The Kab'eena system is illustrated in (8).

(8)   1st, 2nd, 3rd   >   full NP
      nominative-accusative >   marked nominative

3.4 Summary: Nominal Hierarchy Splits

Given the overall rarity of languages with marked-S alignment it is difficult to draw conclusions from the data which would yield statistically significant results – a point also made in general for split-ergative systems by Bickel (2008). The three examples discussed in this paper should therefore be understood as an impressionistic overview on the split case-marking of nominals in marked-S languages.

We have seen that one finds examples of marked-S alignment on the upper part of the Silverstein hierarchy (Oirata) as well as on the lower end (Datooga, Kab'eena). As stated before, marked-nominative case marking in domains where one would expect ergative-absolutive alignment (i.e. the lower part) is to be seen as supporting the overt marking hypothesis of split alignment, while marked-nominative alignment on the upper part of the hierarchy – the part where standard nominative-accusative systems should be found according to Silverstein – would corroborate the alignment hypothesis. Based on this (very small scale) survey the overt marking hypothesis appears to have more explanatory power, being able to account for two out of three splits. However, it fails to explain all instances of marked-S split systems and thus cannot be the ultimate explanation for alignment systems split along the Silverstein hierarchy.

4 Splits between clause types

Clause types are another area of grammar often split between the use of one type of alignment in one domain and another type of alignment in a different domain. In his survey of splits within ergative systems Dixon (1994: 101 ff.) discusses them as *'main' versus 'subordinate' clause splits*, and indeed it seems to be the case that many languages with a split between clause types differentiate between main clauses and at least some subordinate clauses. In the following sections data from the languages that restrict the marked-S pattern based on clause type will be presented.

4.1 Main clause vs. relative clause

The most common pattern among the marked S-languages seems to be to have a split between main clauses (and possibly some minor clause types) on the one hand and relative clauses on the other hand. For marked-S languages this split can be found in two flavors. In the first variant main clauses have the marked-S pattern while relative clauses have neutral alignment – i.e. they do not distinguish between subject and object marking in terms of case – combined with a more rigid word order. This is the case in almost all languages of the Yuman family and the Wappo language, all spoken on the North-American Pacific coast. The second pattern is more astonishing. In the Austronesian language Nias the use of the case forms switches between main and relative clauses. The form used for A marking in main clauses is employed for S and P marking in relative clauses and vice versa – note that Nias is of the marked absolutive type. Both systems are presented in the following.

4.1.1 Neutralization: Yuman and Wappo

Neutralization of case marking for relative clauses is the most common interaction of split-S alignment and clause types found within my sample of Marked-S languages. Such a system can for example be found in the Yuman languages of Northwestern America, as illustrated by Mojave in (9) and (10).

(9) **Mojave** (Yuman; California; Munro 1976: 188)
    a. **Pava:-č**   nʸəməsa:-m
       house-NOM white-TNS
       'The house is white.'

    b. **hatčoq-č** poš   taver-m
       dog-NOM   cat   chase-TNS
       'The dog chased the cat.'

(10) a. ʔava: kʷ-nʸəməsavc-lʸ ʔ-iva-m
house REL-white-LOC 1-sit-TNS
'I am in the white house.'

b. **hatčoq** poš kʷ-taver ʔ-iyuː-pč
dog cat REL-chase 1-see-TNS
'I saw the dog that chased the cat.'

In main clauses S (9a) and A arguments (9b) are marked by the Nominative case suffix -č. However, arguments serving as S (10a) or A (10b) within a relative clause are left zero-coded. Since P arguments are zero-coded in main (9b) as well as in relative clauses (10b), Mojave relative clauses have neutral case alignment contrasting with marked-S alignment in other clause types. A parallel pattern is found in most of the Yuman languages, as for example in Maricopa (Gordon 1986: 37), Yavapai (Kendall 1976: 203ff.) and Jamul Tiipay (Miller 1990: 137).

Wappo, a non-related language of the same macro-area, has the same pattern of marked-S main versus neutral relative clauses.

(11) **Wappo** (Wappo-Yukian; California; Thompson et al. 2006: 4, 117)
a. ce ew ce k'ew-i t'um-taP
DEM fish DEM man-NOM buy-PST
'That fish, the man bought (it).'

b. [ce k'ew ew t'um-ta] cephi i naw-taʔ
DEM man fish buy-PST.DEP 3SG.NOM 1SG see-PST
'The man who bought the fish saw me.'

Li et al. (1977) analyze the split alignment of Wappo as evidence of the recent innovation of the marked-nominative pattern in Wappo. They note that subordinate clauses are known to be more conservative than main clauses. Thus, they propose that the neutral case alignment combined with a rigid word order found in Wappo relative clauses reflects an earlier stage of the language where main clauses followed the same pattern. However, in the Yuman language family a very recent innovation of the marked-S system seems to be ruled out by the fact that all languages of the family except Kiliwa, which supposedly was the first language of that family to split off, share the pattern of overtly coded Nominative versus zero-coded Accusative. It thus seems plausible that the innovation of that pattern can at least be traced back to the proto-language of the non-Kiliwa part of the family tree, the time depth of which is not completely clear.

4.1.2 Switch of marking: Nias

Nias (Brown 2001, 2005) is the only known language with a straightforward marked-absolutive alignment. While S and P arguments are in the so-called mutated form of the noun, the A argument is in the non-derived unmutated form. Relative clauses in Nias use the mutated and unmutated form of a noun in the opposite way to how main clauses employ the forms. Compare the S in (12a) with the relativized S in (12b).

(12) **Nias** (Austronesian, Western Malayo-Polynesian; Indonesia; Brown 2001: 559, 2005: 580)
    a. mate   zibaya-nia   meneßi
        die   uncle.MUT-3SG.POSS yesterday
        'His uncle died yesterday.'
    b. nihs   si=ma=mate   fo'omo   meneßi
        person REL=CPL=die   wife   yesterday
        'the man whose wife died yesterday.'

The same is true for the P argument, as can be seen by comparing the a and b sentences in examples (13–14).

(13) **Nias** (Brown 2001: 414, 415)
    a. i-usu   ndrao   asu
        3SG.RLS-bite 1SG.MUT   dog
        'The dog bit me.'
    b. Andrehe'e   nasu   si=usu   ya'o
        DIST   dog.MUT   REL=bite   1SG
        'That's the dog that bit me.'

(14) a. i-halö   mbua   mbala   moroi   ba
        3SG.RLS-take fruit.MUT papaya.MUT come.from LOC
        mbua   hö'ö
        fruit_tree.MUT DIST
        'He took the papaya from the tree.'
    b. Andrehe'e mbua   si=ma   i-halö   bua
        DIST   fruit_tree.MUT REL=PERF 3SG.RLS-take fruit
        mbala   andre
        papaya   DIST
        'That is the tree that he took those papaya from.'

The A argument of a relative clause on the other hand is realized as a noun in the mutated form.[5]

(15) **Nias** (Brown 2001: 422)
    a. Ma=i-bözi nasu ono matua ba
       PERF=3SG.RLS-hit dog.MUT child male CNJ
       ma=m-oloi ya
       PERF=DYN-run 3SG.MUT
       'The boy hit the dog and ran away.'

    b. Andrehe'e nohi si=löna ni-lau
       DIST coconut_tree.MUT REL=NEG PASS-climb
       nono matua
       child.MUT male
       'That is the coconut tree the boy did not climb.'

The status of relative clause A arguments, however, is somewhat unclear, since the verb of the relative clause usually bears the prefix *ni* glossed as passive. None of the existing descriptions of Nias gives an extensive discussion of the passive. While the passive subject is in the unmutated (A) form in (16a), in (16b) the mutated form is used.

(16) **Nias** (Brown 2001: 556, 573)
    a. ya'o ni-be-ra si=a da'i manu
       1SG PASS-make-3PL.POSS REL=eat faeces.MUT chicken.MUT
       'I was humiliated' (lit. 'I was made into a person who eats chicken scat')

    b. ma=oya=ae mbalatu ni-nößö-i-nia
       PERF=many=already knife.MUT PASS-make-TR-3SG.POSS
       'He had already made a lot of knifes' (lit. 'The knifes made by him were already a lot')

The 3rd person possessive suffix on the passivized verb could indicate that this is rather an impersonal construction than a true passive.

---

5 Another strategy to realize the A argument of a relative clause is to have the A as a possessor.
  (i) **Nias** (Brown 2001: 420, 422)
    a. i-rökhi zekhula
       3SG.RLS-grate coconut.MUT
       'She grated the coconut.'
    b. u-fake zekhula ni-rökhi-nia
       3SG.RLS-use coconut.MUT PASS-grate-3SG.POSS
       'I used the coconut which she grated.'

Some passivized verbs have a transitivizer (TR) affixed to their stem (17a), which makes the whole situation even less transparent. But compare (17b), where the TR-marker occurs also with the non-passivized form of the same verb.

(17) **Nias** (Brown 2001: 556, 555)
   a. ya'ia   ni-bali-'ö-ra   saßuyu
        3SG   PASS-turn-TR-3PL.POSS slave
       'He was made a slave.'

   b. la-bali-'ö   ya   saßuyu
       3PL.PLS-turn-TR 3SG.MUT slave
      'They made him a slave.'

Although the details are not absolutely clear yet because of the situation with the passivization in relative clauses, it is clear that some extraordinary effects can be found with the case marking in Nias relative clauses.

4.2 Main clause vs. imperative, purposive and cleft sentences: Päri

Päri has a split between ergative-absolutive alignment in main clauses and marked-nominative alignment in a number of what Andersen (1988: 316) calls 'non-basic' clauses, which include imperatives, purposive clauses and cleft-sentences.[6]

(18) **Päri** (Nilotic; Sudan; Andersen 1988: 293, 309)
   a. dháagɔ̀ mìɛl̀
      woman dance
      'The woman is dancing.'

   b. lùum   á-waáŋ   cɔ̀ɔww-ì
      grass   COMPL-burn men-ERG
      'The men burnt the grass.'

The examples in (18) demonstrate the ergative-absolutive alignment found with main clauses in Päri. S arguments are zero-coded (a) while A arguments bear the Ergative suffix -ì.

---

[6] As Andersen (1988) shows, this split is not limited to case marking of S, A and P arguments but also shows up in verbal agreement, basic word order and optional zero-realization of arguments. Given the focus of this paper, we will only consider case marking.

(19) **Päri** (Andersen 1988: 318, 319)
    a. pìr   ŋɔ̀   ì   pʌʌr   cícɔ̀-ɛ̂
       why1 why2 LOC jump man-NOM
       'Why did the man jump?'

    b. pìr   ŋɔ̀   dháagɔ̀ ì   cɔ̀ɔl yí ɲìpɔ̀nd´-ɛ̀
       why1 why2 woman LOC call 3SG child-NOM
       'Why did the child call the woman?'

In the non-basic clauses on the other hand S and A behave alike in terms of case marking (and also other morpho-syntactic properties as noted above). Both arguments are marked with the same suffix, -ɛ̀, which is a variant of the Ergative marker seen before. The P argument is zero-coded just like S and P in the main clause. We are dealing with a marked nominative pattern for the non-basic clauses, while the main clauses exhibit an ergative-absolutive pattern.

4.3 Summary: splits by clause type

If one wanted to propose a hierarchy of clause types parallel to the nominal hierarchy against which we have viewed the splits in section 3, we would be confronted with the same problem as before. The marked-S pattern cannot uniquely be identified with one section of that prominence scale. Given the tentative hierarchy in (20) the marked-S pattern associates with the upper part of the scale in the Yuman languages, Wappo and Nias, but with the lower part of the scale in Päri.

(20)   main clause > subordinate clause

    Conversely, neutral alignment is associated with the lower part of the scale in all the examples given – Yuman and Wappo – and yet languages behaving the other way around may well exist. Ergative-absolutive alignment on the other hand is associated with the lower part of the hierarchy in Nias but with the upper part in Päri.

    Dixon (1994: 101f.) suggests an interesting way out of this dilemma. He argues for a semantic difference between different types of subordinate clauses which motivate different kinds of alignment. For the Päri data his prediction points in the right direction. "For this type of subordinate construction [i.e. purposive clauses, C. H.], we would surely expect S and A to be treated in the same way within the complement clause" (ibid. 102). For relative clauses on the other hand he argues that no type of alignment is more plausible than any other, so different types should be possible with this type of clause.

Note that this reasoning does not make reference to any kind of universal hierarchy in order to account for the splits found between main clauses and other clause types. Indeed any attempt to derive some hierarchy from this very limited data on splits by clause type would appear quite forced. Moreover for relative clauses one needs to distinguish between different types and different historical origins of the construction (e.g. through nominalization) before one can make any general claims about their behavior in terms of case alignment, since these factors certainly influence the case-marking behavior. Due to lack of time and historical material on most of the languages involved this investigation has not been carried out yet.

5 Splits between genders

Another pattern often noted in case languages is the tendency to neutralize formal distinctions of case in the feminine and neuter gender and in the plural number. This is for example the case in German (among other European languages), where the formal distinction between Accusative and Nominative case is lost for all nominals (pronouns as well as full NPs) for the feminine and neuter nouns. This pattern is not traditionally analyzed as a split in the alignment system but rather as an instance of syncretism. However, a similarity with the splits discussed before cannot be denied. In this section I will discuss alignment splits based on the categories of gender and/or number in the languages of the marked-S type.

5.1 Alignment split by gender: Mangarayi

In the Australian language Mangarayi nouns belong to one of the three genders, Feminine, Masculine or Neuter. Each of these genders has a distinct system of marking the S, A and P relations. Feminine nouns have an overt marker for the S+A relation (21a, 21b) and another distinct marker for P (21c), and thus exhibit a standard nominative-accusative pattern.

(21) **Mangarayi** (Non-Pama-Nyungan; Australia, Northern-Territory; Merlan 1989: 59, 61, 64)
    a. **ŋaḷa-gaḍugu**   Ø-ya-ɟ
        NOM.F-woman   3SG-go-PP
        'The woman went.'

    b. buy?   ɲan-wu-na   **ŋaḷa-bugbug**   ŋaḷa-X?
        show   3SG>2SG-AUX-PP   NOM.F-old_woman   NOM.F-X
        'Did old woman X (name deleted) show you?'

    c. **ɲan-guḍugu**   buy?   wuḷa-wu-na   **ŋani**
        ACC.F-woman   show   3PL>3SG-AUX-PP   language(N)
        'They taught the woman language.'

Masculine nouns use identical forms for the S+A relation as well (22a, 22b), but have a zero-coded P form (22c), thus exhibiting the marked nominative pattern.

(22) **Mangarayi** (Merlan 1989: 59, 61, 63)
    a. **ṉa-malam**   Ø-gala+wu-yi-ni   ṉa-landi-yan
        NOM.M-man   3SG-hang-MP-PC   LOC.N-tree-LOC
        'The man was hanging in the tree.'

    b. **ṉa-muyg**   ŋan-daḷag
        NOM.M-dog   3SG>1SG-bite.PP
        'The dog bit me.'

    c. **malam**   ŋa-ḍaṛa+wu-b
        man(M)   1SG>3SG-find-PP
        'I found the man.'

Neuter nouns on the other hand exhibit an ergative pattern with zero-coded S+P (23a, 23b) and overtly coded A (23b). Note that the Neuter Ergative marker is identical in form to the Masculine Nominative.

(23) **Mangarayi** (Merlan 1989: 59, 61)
    a. wumbawa **ḷandi** ɟir   Ø-ɟaygi-ni   wuburgba ṉa-budal-an
        one   tree(N) stand 3SG-AUX-PC halfway   LOC.N-billabong-LOC
        'One tree is standing in the middle of the billabong.'

    b. **ṉa-gunbur** ŋan-gawa-ɟ   **ɟib**-ŋanju
        ERG.N-dust 3SG>1SG-bury-PP eye(N)-mine
        'Dust buried (i.e. blew into) my eye.'

With Mangarayi nouns the three different alignments of nominative-accusative, ergative-absolutive and marked-nominative can all be found depending on which gender a noun has. For this system an argumentation along the lines of case syncretism does not work, since a distinction between A and P is found for all genders.

5.2 Neutralization by gender: Qafar

Whereas in Mangarayi all three genders encode transitive A distinctly from transitive P, in some of the Cushitic languages the distinction between A and P is only found with masculine nouns (or a subset of masculine nouns) while feminine nouns have no distinct forms for the two functions.

One of these languages is Qafar as shown in the following. Vowel-final masculine nouns have distinct Nominative and Accusative forms (24).

(24) **Qafar** (East Cushitic; Ethiopia; Hayward 1998: 629)
    a. awkí   yemeetéh   'A/the boy has come.'
    b. àwka   'boy (acc.)'

Feminine nouns on the other hand have no special Nominative form. Instead the Accusative[7] is also used for the Nominative functions (S and A marking) (25).

(25) **Qafar** (Hayward 1998: 629)
    a. awká   temeetéh   'A/the girl has come.'
    b. awka   'girl (ACC)'

This system is similar to the one mentioned for a number of European languages. The only difference is that Qafar has marked-nominative alignment for (some) masculine nouns and neutral alignment for all others, while for German and others the standard nominative-accusative contrasts with neutral alignment.

5.3 Summary: splits by gender

The (notably very limited) data from marked-S languages does give a consistent picture of the alignment of a particular case system with a particular nominal

---

[7] In Hayward's (1998) terminology the case covering P function and citation form is called the Absolutive. In order to avoid confusion between the case used for S and P function in ergative-absolutive languages the term Absolute is used in this paper, which is the label used for the respective case in a number of related languages.

gender. Marked-nominative systems are found with masculine nouns, whereas other alignment systems are found with other genders. However, if one considers data such as the data from German and other languages mentioned in the introduction to this section, this clear picture becomes blurred, for in German it is the standard nominative-accusative alignment found with masculine nouns (and not the feminine nouns like in Mangarayi). Of course those differences in behavior (here in terms of case alignment) are to be expected. After all, we are comparing two different and unrelated languages, which happen to use the same label, i.e. masculine, to describe a distinct subclass of nouns. These two language-specific groupings of nouns cannot be expected to have the same properties. So even if one wants to analyze these effects as the result of some prominence hierarchy of genders, the prominence difference between the genders would quite possibly be based on at least two factors: first, which nouns belong to the respective genders in a language, and second, are there any cultural reasons for assigning a higher level of prominence to the nouns of one gender than to the nouns of another gender? Summing this up, alignment splits by gender might well be a reflex of some prominence scale of the respective genders, but this prominence scale will most likely be rooted culturally rather than on pure linguistic grounds.

6 Conclusion

Apart from the well known splits between different types of nominals, marked-S languages exhibit a wide variety of split alignment systems. Only a selection could be presented here; there are a number of further areas of grammar where the alignment changes in those languages. All of these could be analysed in terms of splits. Notable is the neutralization of case marking for emphatic elements (e.g. focus or contrastive topic) in a number of African and Pacific languages, and also the opposite situation found in some Papuan languages where a marked-S system only exists for emphatic arguments. Another phenomenon are such lexical tendencies as the association of negative existentials with one alignment while positive existentials trigger another alignment, as found in Ajie (Fontinelle 1976, Lichtenberk 1978) and Nias (Brown 2001).

While for the nominal splits a hierarchy analysis has been proposed for many languages, for the marked-S languages the results do not point in one direction or the other in terms of association of a type of alignment to a certain part of the hierarchy. However, as mentioned before, non-marked-S languages might equally be lacking any clear correlations in this domain of grammar (Bickel 2008). Furthermore, for the marked-S languages the absence of any clear generalization about the direction of splits could also be attributed to the two different motivations I discussed for associating types of nominals with parts of the prominence scale that point in different directions for these languages.

Whether there is a – possibly universal – prominence hierarchy of nominals is and probably will remain an issue of hot debate. For alignment splits based on other factors such explanations have not been proposed as prominently. However, the effects are strikingly similar in some cases, and if one is in favor of a nominal hierarchy, one should seriously consider the possibility of different hierarchies governing different kinds of splits. Otherwise one would have to provide a good explanation for why there should be such a hierarchy to account for splits in one domain of grammar, but seemingly parallel splits in another domain have some other source. Or in other words, if factors distinct from any sort of hierarchy can account for splits within the gender system or between different clause types, why do we need an accessibility hierarchy in order to explain alignment splits between pronouns and full noun phrases?

References

Aissen, Judith. 2003. Differential object marking: Iconicity vs. economy. *Natural Language & Linguistic Theory* 21, 435–483.

Andersen, Torben. 1988. Ergativity in Pari, a Nilotic OVS language. *Lingua* 75, 289–324.

Bickel, Balthasar. 2008. On the scope of the referential hierarchy in the typology of grammatical relations. In Greville Corbett & Michael Noonan (eds.) *Case and grammatical relations. Studies in honor of Bernard Comrie*. Amsterdam: John Benjamins.

Brown, Lea. 2001. *A Grammar of Nias Selatan*. Ph.D. thesis, University of Sydney.

Brown, Lea. 2005. Nias. In Alexander Adelaar & Nikolaus P. Himmelmann (eds.) *The Austronesian Languages of Asia and Madagascar*, 7 of *Routledge Language Family Series*, 562–589. London, New York: Routledge.

Comrie, Bernard. 1978. Ergativity. In Winfred P. Lehmann (ed.) *Syntactic Typology*, 329–394. Hassocks (Sussex): The Harvester Press.

Comrie, Bernard. 1989. *Language Universals and Linguistic Typology*. Chicago, IL: University of Chicago Press, second edn.

Crass, Joachim. 2005. *Das K'abeena. Deskriptive Grammatik einer hochlandkuschitischen Sprache*, 23 of *Cushitic Language Studies*. Köln: Köppe.

Dixon, Robert M. W. 1979. Ergativity. *Language* 55(1), 59–138.

Dixon, Robert M. W. 1994. *Ergativity*. Cambridge Studies in Linguistics. London: Cambridge University Press.

Donohue, Mark & Lea Brown. 1999. Ergativity: Some additions from Indonesia. *Australian Journal of Linguistics* 19(1), 57–76.

Donohue, Mark & Søren Wichmann (eds.). 2008. *The Typology of Semantic Alignment*. Oxford: Oxford University Press.

Fontinelle, Jacqueline de la. 1976. *La langue de Houailou (Nouvelle-Calédonie). Description phonologique et description syntaxique*. Paris: SELAF.

Gordon, Lynn. 1986. *Maricopa Morphology and Syntax*. Berkeley, Los Angeles, London: University of California Press.
Greenberg, Joseph H. 1963. Some universals of grammar with particular reference to the order of meaningful elements. In Joseph H. Greenberg (ed.) *Universals of Human Language*, 58–90. Cambridge, MA: MIT Press.
Hayward, Richard J. 1998. Qafar (East Cushitic). In Andrew Spencer & Arnold M. Zwicky (eds.) *The Handbook of Morphology*, 624–647. Oxford, Malden: Blackwell.
de Hoop, Helen & Andrej L. Malchukov. 2008. Case-marking strategies. *Linguistic Inquiry* 39(4), 565–587.
Hopper, Paul J. & Sandra A. Thompson. 1980. Transitivity in grammar and discourse. *Language* 56(2), 251–299.
Kendall, Martha B. 1976. *Selected Problems in Yavapai Syntax. The Verde Valley Dialect*. New York, London: Garland Publishing Inc.
Kiessling, Roland. 2007. The "marked nominative" in Datooga. *Journal of African Languages and Linguistics* 28(2), 149–191.
König, Christa. 2006. Marked nominative in Africa. *Studies in Language* 30(4), 655–732.
Li, Charles N., Sandra A. Thompson & Jesse O. Sawyer. 1977. Subject and word order in Wappo. *International Journal of American Linguistics* 43, 85–100.
Lichtenberk, Frantisek. 1978. A sketch of Houailou grammar. In *Working Papers in Linguistics* 10, 76–116. Manoa, HI: Department of Linguistics, University of Hawaii.
Malchukov, Andrej L. 2008. Animacy and asymmetries in differential case marking. *Lingua* 118, 203–221.
Malchukov, Andrej L. 2015. Towards a typology of split ergativity: A TAM-hierarchy for alignment splits. This volume.
Malchukov, Andrej & Helen de Hoop. 2011. Tense, aspect, and mood based differential case marking. *Lingua* 121, 35–47.
Mallinson, Graham & Barry J. Blake. 1981. *Language Typology. Cross-linguistic Studies in Syntax*. Amsterdam, New York, Oxford: North-Holland Publishing Company.
Merlan, Francesca. 1989. *Mangarayi*. London, New York: Routledge.
Miller, Amy Whitmore. 1990. *A Grammar of Jamul Diegueño*. Ph.D. thesis, University of California, San Diego.
Munro, Pamela. 1976. *Mojave Syntax*. New York, London: Garland Publishing Inc.
Silverstein, Michael. 1976. Hierarchy of features and ergativity. In Robert M. W. Dixon (ed.) *Grammatical Categories in Australian Languages*, 112–171. Canberra: Australian Institute of Aboriginal Studies.
Thompson, Sandra A., Joseph Sung-Jul Park & Charles N. Li. 2006. *A Reference Grammar of Wappo, 138 of University of California Publications in Linguistics*. Berkeley, Los Angeles, London: University of California Press.

Ina Bornkessel-Schlesewsky and Matthias Schlesewsky
12 Scales in real-time language comprehension: A review[1]

In recent years, cross-linguistic comparisons have become increasingly important in the fields of psycholinguistics and neurolinguistics. In addition to shedding some initial light on which language comprehension strategies are universal and which are subject to cross-linguistic variation, this line of research has revealed that prominence scales appear to play an exceptionally important role in online language comprehension. For example, the animacy scale has been shown to yield comparable neurophysiological reactions during the processing of simple transitive sentences across a wide range of languages (Bornkessel-Schlesewsky & Schlesewsky, 2009b). Strikingly, at least certain aspects of this response appear to be independent of whether animacy is grammatically relevant in the particular language under examination or not. This chapter reviews the available evidence on the impact of scales in language comprehension, focusing both on the question of which brain regions support the use of this information and on the temporal dynamics of its application. It also discusses the question of whether scales should be viewed as extragrammatical heuristics which help the processing system to make decisions in the absence of full and unambiguous information, or as functionally equivalent to morphosyntactic information in the form-to-meaning mapping.

1 Introduction

The most fundamental goal of linguistic research is to identify the underlying characteristics of language, i.e. to determine why human languages are organised in the way that they are. The particular approach adopted in order to address this question differs between the various linguistic subdisciplines: grammatical theories seek to explain which utterances occur in the languages of the world and how these serve to mediate between form and meaning; language typology is concerned with cross-linguistic generalisations and distributions and the question of which patterns occur frequently and which do not; psycholinguistic

---

[1] The research reported here was supported by the German Research Foundation (grant BO 2471/3-2) and by the Max Planck Society (Research Group Neurotypology at the Max Planck Institute for Human Cognitive and Brain Sciences awarded to IBS).

theories attempt to account for the way in which linguistic utterances are produced and comprehended in real time. In spite of the fact that all of these fields approach language from fundamentally different perspectives, they (and the additional linguistic subdisciplines not mentioned here, e.g. historical linguistics) all engage in the common endeavour of uncovering the hidden "pressures" that serve to shape languages. Arguably, the strongest conclusions as to what these pressures might be can be drawn when there is converging evidence from several different domains. This chapter argues that prominence scales may constitute one such area of convergence.

The remainder of the chapter is organised as follows. We begin by providing a brief introduction to basic concepts of language comprehension (section 2), before turning to basic research questions in and theoretical approaches to the domain of scales and comprehension (section 3). Section 4 goes on to discuss neurophysiological correlates of processing prototypical and atypical roles (in terms of scales). A potential model for deriving the ubiquity of scales in the language comprehension process, the notion of an actor attractor network, is presented in section 5 and supported with additional evidence from neuroimaging in section 6. Finally, section 7 offers some conclusions.

2 Language comprehension: Crucial concepts

In order to meet the demands of efficient communication, language must be produced and understood in real time. This means, for example, that the human language processing system cannot "wait" until the end of a sentence is reached in order to begin comprehending it – if this were the case, natural dialogue would be virtually impossible. Rather, it is standardly assumed that interpretation is "incremental" in the sense that each incoming word is immediately integrated with the representations already established and interpreted as fully as possible (e.g. Marslen-Wilson, 1973; Crocker, 1994; Stabler, 1994). Consequently, interpretive choices must often be made in the absence of complete and unambiguous information. Consider, for example, the following German sentence fragments (from beim Graben et al., 2000):

(1) a. Welche Studentin   besuchte ...
        [which student]:NOM/ACC.SG visited.3SG ...
    b. Welche Studentin   besuchten ...
        [which student]:NOM/ACC.SG visited.3PL ...

Both (1a) and (1b) begin with the wh-phrase *welche Studentin* ('which student'), which is morphologically ambiguous between nominative and accusative case marking and, thereby, between a subject and an object reading. In terms of generalised semantic roles, it could either be an S, A or P argument.[2] When it encounters *welche Studentin*, the language comprehension system therefore cannot be sure which of these multiple potential readings will turn out to be correct. In spite of these various interpretive options, however, the processing system adopts an analysis in which the wh-phrase is taken to be the argument that agrees with the finite verb (i.e., the subject or "privileged syntactic argument"). This processing choice is evidenced by the increased processing costs that can be observed at the position of the adjacent plural verb *besuchten* in (3) in comparison to a singular verb in the same position, i.e., when the "subject-first preference" is disconfirmed. This tendency to analyse an initial ambiguous argument as the subject of the sentence is a robust processing strategy that has been observed in a number of languages (e.g. Italian: de Vincenzi, 1991; Dutch: Frazier and Flores d'Arcais, 1989; German: Schriefers et al., 1995; Turkish: Demiral et al., 2008; Chinese: Wang et al., 2009).

All available evidence suggests that incremental interpretation is a very basic property of the human language comprehension architecture (e.g. Crocker, 1994; Stabler, 1994) in the sense that it can be observed at all levels of comprehension and even under circumstances of massive ambiguity. Thus, it appears to hold even in consistently head-final languages such as Japanese, in which – in addition to ambiguities regarding case, grammatical function and generalised semantic role as described above – it may not even be clear to which of several potential clauses an argument belongs. Evidence that the processing system nonetheless does not delay interpretation until disambiguating information is encountered was provided by Kamide and Mitchell (1999) using sentences such as (2).

(2) Kyooju-ga   gakusee-ni   toshokansisho-ga
     professor-NOM student-DAT   librarian-NOM

     kasita mezurasii komonjo-o   miseta.
     lent   unusual   ancient.manuscript-ACC showed

     'The professor showed [the student] the unusual ancient manuscript which the librarian had lent [the student].'

---

[2] Note that, here and in the following, we use the labels S, A, and P for generalised argument roles in the spirit of Comrie (1978) and Dixon (1994): S, the sole argument in an intransitive event; A, the more "agent-like" argument in a transitive event; and P, the more "patient-like" argument in a transitive event.

In (2), the dative NP gakusee-ni could either be an argument of the main clause (in which case the professor showed the manuscript to the student) or of the relative clause (in which case the librarian lent the manuscript to the student). By comparing globally ambiguous sentences like (2) with sentences disambiguating towards one of the two possible readings (by way of including either main clause or relative clause verbs which did not take a dative argument), Kamide and Mitchell (1999) were able to show that the matrix argument reading is, in fact, preferred. This observation provides strong converging support for the assumption of incremental interpretation.

As is apparent from the discussion of examples (1) and (2), the endeavour to maximise interpretation at each point within a sentence can only be upheld if the processing system is able to select an interpretation from several available candidates.[3] While it is thus generally uncontroversial that the system engages in ambiguity resolution during online comprehension, the precise mechanisms leading to a preference for one reading over the other for a particular phenomenon are often subject to much debate. For example, the subject-preference has been attributed to a preference for minimal filler-gap distances (Frazier, 1987), for minimal dependencies (in the sense of an initial object triggering the expectation for a subject but not vice versa; Gibson 1998) or simply to a higher frequency of occurrence (Vosse and Kempen, 2000) to name just a few of the available explanations.

Finally, given the need for ambiguity resolution during online comprehension, it follows that the processing system may sometimes commit to an analysis that turns out to be incorrect at some later point in the sentence. For example, an ambiguous initial argument may turn out to be an object rather than the subject (as in example 1b). In this case, the system must initiate a reanalysis in order to attempt to come up with the correct reading as quickly and efficiently as possible. Depending on the type of information needing to be revised, reanalyses range from imperceptible to massively disruptive in real time communication (see, for example, Sturt and Crocker, 1996).

---

[3] Note that this does not necessarily imply that the processing system pursues only a single reading to the exclusion of all others ("serial processing"). Preferences of this type may also come about in an architecture in which several readings are maintained in parallel, but with different weightings ("ranked parallel processing"). For an introduction to these more fine-grained architectural issues, see Mitchell (1994).

3 Prominence scales in language comprehension: Basic research questions

The aim of this chapter is to provide a review of how prominence scales impact upon the process of incremental language comprehension that was described in the previous section. In this regard, we focus on the processing of simple sentences (rather than, for example, relative clause constructions) and primarily on transitive events. Following the typological literature, we assume that transitive events involve the transfer of activity between participants, with an information flow from the A to the P argument (Hopper and Thompson, 1980; Comrie, 1989; DeLancey, 1981). We will discuss how transitive events are comprehended in real time and which neurocognitive mechanisms underlie this comprehension process. Specifically, we focus on two basic questions (see also Bornkessel-Schlesewsky and Schlesewsky, 2009b):

(a) *Role identification:* How does the human language comprehension system identify who is who in the information transfer situation (i.e. how does it identify which is the A and which is the P participant)?
(b) *Role prototypicality:* To what degree is on-line comprehension affected by the role-prototypicality of the arguments, i.e. does a less prototypical A and/or P participant render a transitive construction more difficult to process?

We will argue that both role identification and role-prototypicality are crucially influenced by prominence scales (e.g. animacy, definiteness). We will further review evidence that, within the comprehension process, prominence features (which would traditionally be classified as semantic or pragmatic) are functionally equivalent to information types such as word order and morphological case marking (which are traditionally viewed as syntactic) within the language processing architecture. This evidence speaks against a view of prominence information according to which it used as a heuristic "shortcut" to interpretation, which either precedes a full algorithmic analysis (Townsend and Bever, 2001) or serves to produce semantic representations that are merely "good enough" interpretations rather than accurate representations of the message actually conveyed by the speaker (Ferreira et al., 2002). Rather, we argue that prominence scales play a fundamental role during language processing across typologically different languages and that this state of affairs may be grounded in more general cognitive characteristics of how we understand actions in the world around us.

3.1 Prominence in language processing: two competing traditional views

In the literature on sentence processing, the role of prominence information has traditionally been conceptualised in two different ways. We will refer to these as the algorithmic and heuristic perspectives, respectively.

According to the algorithmic perspective, role identification during incremental comprehension is based on the syntax. This view is based, at least in part, on the tenet of Chomskyan generative grammar, according to which different sentential meanings / role assignments correlate with different syntactic structures. Accordingly, how a sentence is interpreted during online processing can be viewed as amounting to a choice of syntactic structure. In the words of Miller (1962, p. 752): "the proper functioning of our syntactic skill is an essential ingredient in the process of understanding a sentence". By contrast, non-syntactic information types such as animacy are thought to be crucially involved in the evaluation of role prototypicality. Thus, they serve to determine how well the event participants fit into the roles assigned to them by the syntax. From this perspective, the distinction between role identification and role prototypicality can essentially be subsumed under the broader dissociation between syntax and semantics (or, more generally, between syntactic and non-syntactic information). Notably, however, different models within this broader group differ markedly with respect to how they conceptualise the interplay between the aspects of processing which we have termed role identification and role prototypicality. Modular (or "two-stage") approaches (e.g. Frazier, 1978; Frazier and Rayner, 1982; Frazier and Clifton, 1996) assume an initial stage of analysis that only draws upon syntactic category information and a small set of structural preference principles. Non-syntactic information types such as animacy, plausibility, and frequency of occurrence only influence processing choices in a post-initial stage. From this perspective, (syntactically-determined) role identification precedes the (extra-syntactically-determined) assessment of role prototypicality. Interactive models, by contrast, assume that all available information types are jointly taken into account from the very first stages of processing (e.g. MacDonald, Pearlmutter, & Seidenberg, 1994; Trueswell & Tanenhaus, 1994). In this type of architecture, the potential role prototypicality of an argument may serve to guide the choice of syntactic structure, hence influencing role identification. (For a more detailed illustration of how these two classes of models differ with regard to the predictions that they make for online comprehension and how this relates to prominence information, see Bornkessel-Schlesewsky and Schlesewsky, 2009b.)

The heuristic perspective, by contrast, challenges the assumed division of labour between the syntax as a locus for role identification and non-syntactic information sources as defining role prototypicality. Specifically, approaches of this type posit that sentence interpretation may not always be determined by the syntax (e.g. Bever, 1970; Townsend and Bever, 2001; Ferreira, 2003; Ferreira and Patson, 2007; Kolk et al., 2003; van Herten et al., 2005; van Herten et al., 2006; Kim and Osterhout, 2005). The idea is that the processing system does not always (or immediately) establish a complete and accurate representation of the linguistic input with which it is confronted, but that it may rather employ a number of heuristics that serve as quick and efficient shortcuts to interpretation. Several famous examples of comprehension heuristics date back to Bever's seminal (1970) paper "The Cognitive Basis for Linguistic Structures". Two of these are given in (3):

(3) Two examples of comprehension heuristics (from Bever, 1970)

Strategy C: Constituents are functionally related according to semantic constraints. (p. 296)

Strategy D: Any Noun-Verb-Noun (NVN) sequence within a potential internal unit in the surface structure corresponds to "actor-action-object". (p. 298)

According to Strategy D (also known as the "NVN strategy"), sentences deviating from the actor-action-object schema (e.g. passives, object relative clauses, or object clefts) are prone to being misunderstood (Ferreira, 2003). However, it is not always the case that passive sentences, for example, are more difficult to understand that actives: *The cookie was eaten by the dog* is as easy to process in a sentence-picture verification task as *The dog ate the cookie*, while *The horse was followed by the cow* is more difficult than *The cow followed the horse* (Slobin, 1966; examples from Bever, 1970). Bever explains this observation in terms of Strategy C, arguing that unambiguous semantic relations may allow for "syntactic factors to be bypassed entirely" (Bever, 1970, p. 276).

As is apparent from the example *The cookie was eaten by the dog*, semantic heuristics may involve prominence information such as animacy. Indeed, some heuristically-based accounts specifically emphasise the role of animacy as a factor in sentence interpretation, i.e. they assume that thematic roles may be assigned purely on the basis of an argument's animacy status and independently of the syntax (see, for example, Ferreira, 2003, for a discussion of an animacy-based interpretation heuristic).[4]

The idea of interpretation heuristics thus calls into question the classic algorithmic assumption that role identification is primarily determined by the syntax. Rather, it may also be driven by non-syntactic information types, including prominence features such as animacy. Nevertheless, these heuristic processing strategies are mostly not viewed as fully-fledged sentence comprehension mechanisms, but rather as surrogate strategies that are applied in lieu of a full syntactic analysis. For this reason, Ferreira and colleagues have subsumed them under the broader cover-term of "good enough" representations during language processing (see Ferreira and Patson, 2007, for a review). Hence, while the heuristically-based approach differs from the traditional assumptions discussed above in that it allows non-syntactic information types to determine role identification, it nevertheless maintains a subdivision between syntactic analysis and other types of interpretation processes. Only the former is viewed as providing a complete and accurate analysis of the linguistic input. Accordingly, some heuristic approaches even posit that "we understand everything twice" (Townsend and Bever, 2001), once via fast – but possibly inaccurate – heuristics, and subsequently via a complete (algorithmic) syntactic analysis.

3.2 An alternative view on scales during language comprehension: The interface hypothesis

In the last subsection, we discussed two distinct perspectives on the function of prominence information during language comprehension. The first of these (the

---

[4] Over approximately the past decade, this perspective has gained additional backing from studies with event-related brain potentials (ERPs), i.e. a technique that measures changes in the electrical activity of the brain which are timelocked to the processing of a stimulus (e.g. a critical word within a sentence). For an introduction to this technique directed at a linguistic audience, see Bornkessel-Schlesewsky and Schlesewsky (2009a) and Appendix A. For example, Kim and Osterhout (2005) observed that implausible sentences such as *The hearty meals were devouring the kids* do not engender the electrophysiological response traditionally associated with semantically anomalous sentences (the so-called "N400"). Rather, they give rise to an ERP signature that is also engendered by syntactic violations (a so-called "P600"). Findings such as these have been interpreted in the spirit of Bever's Strategy C, i.e. as providing evidence for a syntax-independent level of semantic composition that is based primarily on semantic associations (for a review, see van de Meerendonk et al., 2009). While the effects of animacy which appear in this context are most often subsumed under a more general plausibility heuristic (Kolk et al., 2003; van Herten et al., 2005; van Herten et al., 2006; Kim and Osterhout, 2005), a specific animacy-based assignment of thematic roles has also been proposed (Hoeks et al., 2004; Kuperberg et al., 2003; Kuperberg et al., 2007). (For alternative perspectives on findings such as these, see Bornkessel-Schlesewsky and Schlesewsky, 2008a; Brouwer et al., 2012.)

classic "algorithmic view") assumes that prominence features such as animacy determine role prototypicality, but not role identification. The second (the "heuristic view") posits that prominence information may influence role identification (via role prototypicality), but in a qualitatively different manner to syntactic information. In the following, we will argue in favour of a third perspective, namely for the view that prominence information is an integral part of the form-to-meaning mapping during language comprehension and that, in this respect, it is functionally equivalent to information types that are typically considered syntactic (e.g. case marking, word order). According to this "interface view" (Bornkessel-Schlesewsky and Schlesewsky, 2009b), prominence information influences both role prototypicality and role identification, though not as part of a heuristic. In the following, we begin by introducing the basic assumptions of the interface view, before discussing the cross-linguistic evidence which supports it.

The basic assumptions of the interface view are given in (4):[5]

(4) *The interface hypothesis of incremental argument interpretation*
(Bornkessel-Schlesewsky and Schlesewsky, 2009b, p. 28)
Incremental argument interpretation (i.e. role identification and assessment of role prototypicality) is accomplished by the syntax-semantics *interface*, i.e. with reference to a cross-linguistically defined set of prominence scales and their language-specific weighting. The relevant prominence scales are:
a. morphological case marking (nominative > accusative / ergative > nominative)
b. argument order (argument 1 > argument 2)
c. animacy (+animate > -animate)
d. definiteness/specificity (+definite/specific > -definite/specific)
e. person (1st/2nd person > 3rd person)

The notion of a direct interaction between semantic prominence features and morphosyntactic information sources during language comprehension that is posited by the interface hypothesis is also a central claim of a model of language comprehension that was first developed in the late 1970s / early 1980s: the Competition Model (e.g. Bates et al., 1982; MacWhinney and Bates, 1989).

---

[5] Note that, here and in the following, we use "prominence" as a cover term for (traditionally "semantic") features such as animacy/definiteness/person *as well as* (traditionally "syntactic") features such as case marking and linear order. This is in line with the assumption that all of these information types play a functionally equivalent role for the form-to-meaning mapping during language comprehension.

This model envisages sentence comprehension as a direct form-to-function mapping based on a variety of interacting information types ("cues"; e.g. word order, animacy, agreement, stress). The relative importance of a particular cue is language specific and determined via the notion of "cue validity": a cue that is highly valid in a particular language exerts the strongest influence on interpretation. Cue validity is determined by the combination of "cue applicability" (which is high when a cue is always available) and "cue reliability" (which is high when a cue is always unambiguous and never misleading). The interpretation of a sentence (e.g. with respect to the question of which argument is identified as the actor of the event being described) is thought to result from a competition between different cues. As all cues interact directly and only differ in their language-specific weighting, the Competition Model was the first proponent of an "interface"-type sentence processing architecture in the sense introduced above. However, since it has relied almost exclusively on behavioural findings (e.g. how often speakers of a particular language judge a particular noun phrase to be the actor of the sentence and how long it takes them to make this judgement), the competition model has not provided direct evidence for the assumption that the different types of cues are processed in a qualitatively similar manner.

The Competition Model is thus compatible with what might be termed a "weak version" of the interface hypothesis (see 5b), according to which the interaction between prominence information of different types essentially amounts to a differential weighting of the various prominence cues, while individual cues could be processed in qualitatively dissociable subsystems. According to a stronger version of the interface hypothesis (see 5a), by contrast, different prominence cues are processed in a qualitatively similar manner.

(5) a. *The interface hypothesis of incremental argument interpretation (strong version)*
Prominence information from different linguistic domains (e.g. semantic and morphosyntactic prominence information) are processed in a *qualitatively* similar manner by the neural language comprehension system.

b. *The interface hypothesis of incremental argument interpretation (weak version)*
Prominence information from different linguistic domains (e.g. semantic and morphosyntactic prominence information) interacts in determining overall sentence interpretation. Distinct information sources may, however, be processed by qualitatively different systems during online comprehension.

In the following, we review neurocognitive evidence for the strong version of the interface hypothesis. We first draw upon data from a number of cross-linguistic event-related potential (ERP) studies in order to demonstrate that features such as animacy have a *qualitatively* similar impact upon the assessment of role prototypicality in languages of different types (i.e. across languages with very different relative weightings of animacy information). In a second step, we discuss findings from functional magnetic resonance imaging (fMRI), which provide converging support for the proposed functional equivalence of ("semantic") features such an animacy and ("syntactic") information such as case marking. Note that, with respect to both issues, our arguments are based entirely upon studies using *grammatical* and *plausible* sentences.[6] Furthermore, as all critical sentences are unambiguous with respect to grammatical functions, none of the findings discussed are due to the reanalysis of a local ambiguity.

4 The neural correlates of role prototypicality

The aim of this section is to show that the neural response to role prototypicality mismatches is qualitatively similar across languages of different types and from different language families. Even more importantly, existing findings suggest that the reaction to prototypicality mismatches involving a particular prominence feature is independent of the weighting of that feature in the language under consideration. We will demonstrate this on the basis of event-related brain potential (ERP) findings on the processing of inanimate A arguments across languages.

In order to examine whether the electrophysiological response to role prototypicality mismatches is qualitatively similar or different across languages with a different weighting of the prominence feature under consideration, we must first have some idea of how to determine feature weightings in a given language. To this end, we can draw upon the results of experimental studies conducted within the framework of the competition model, which provide evidence for the relative influence of factors such as word order, agreement, animacy and definiteness in different languages. Animacy, in particular, was shown to be a

---

6 In our view, the use of non-anomalous sentences constitutes an important step forward from the violation paradigms that were traditionally used in a great deal of research on the neurocognition of language. However, it is of course only a step towards fully naturalistic stimuli, which present a whole host of challenges for data analysis in order to rule out confounding influences on the factors of interest.

cross-linguistically applicable cue for the (offline) interpretation of sentential arguments. Furthermore, the degree to which animacy determined argument interpretation varied from language to language: the effects of this feature were relatively weak in English, somewhat stronger in Italian, and relatively strong in German and Mandarin Chinese (MacWhinney et al., 1984; Li et al., 1993). Overall, these studies showed that animacy may determine which argument is interpreted as A and which as P, even in languages in which animacy is not grammaticalised as the primary determinant of role identification (e.g. German and Chinese). However, these experiments were neither suited to revealing the influence of animacy during online sentence interpretation nor, as already noted above, to determining whether it may have qualitatively different effects depending on its relative importance in a particular language.

Both of these issues (online processing and possible qualitative differences) can be addressed by examining the effects of animacy on role prototypicality processing using neuroscientific methods. Event-related potentials (ERPs) are particularly well suited to the question at hand because they provide a direct measure of the electrical activity of the brain and can therefore reveal neural correlates of language comprehension as a sentence unfolds. They are also multidimensional, thereby revealing possible *qualitative* differences between effects of interest. For a brief introduction to the ERP methodology and its application to language processing, see Appendix A.

The first electrophysiological investigation of role prototypicality effects was conducted by Weckerly and Kutas (1999) using sentence stimuli such as (6).

(6) Example stimuli from Weckerly and Kutas (1999)
   a. The novelist that the movie inspired praised the director for staying true to the complicated ending.
   b. The movie that the novelist praised inspired the director to stay true to the complicated ending.

Among several other effects, Weckerly and Kutas (1999) observed a central negativity between approximately 200 and 500 ms (N400) for an inanimate (vs. animate) head noun and for an inanimate (vs. animate) A-argument within the relative clause. This finding provided a first indication that the N400, an ERP component that is traditionally associated with lexical-semantic integration or lexical preactivation (see, for example Kutas and Federmeier, 2000; Hagoort, 2000, Lau et al., 2008), may also be sensitive to role prototypicality mismatches during online comprehension. From this perspective, the initial inanimate NP leads to a mismatch with the preference for the first argument to bear the highest-ranking role in English. The finding of a similar conflict for the second argument, which is unambiguously identified as an A-argument by its structural position, supports this perspective. However, an interpretation along these lines is subject to the caveat that the N400 might also be due to the lexical difference between animate and inanimate nouns.

Several further findings attest to the cross-linguistic stability of the N400 as a correlate of role prototypicality mismatches and to the fact that this effect is not grounded in lexical differences or the infrequency of inanimate subjects. Consider the following German examples (from Frisch and Schlesewsky, 2001; Roehm et al., 2004):

(7) Example stimuli from Frisch and Schlesewsky
 Paul fragt sich, ...
 Paul asks himself, ...
 a. ... welchen Angler   der Jäger   gelobt   hat.
    ... [which angler]:ACC [the hunter]:NOM praised has.
    '... which angler the hunter praised.'

 b. ... welchen Angler   der Zweig   gestreift hat.
    ... [which angler]:ACC [the twig]:NOM brushed has.
    '... which angler the twig brushed.'

In a reanalysis of Frisch and Schlesewsky's (2001) data (in which sentences such as 7 served as control stimuli for another manipulation) Roehm et al. (2004) found an N400 for inanimate vs. animate nominative arguments following an initial accusative (e.g. *der Zweig*, 'the twig', in 7b vs. *der Jäger*, 'the hunter', in 7a; see Figure 1A). By contrast, in an experiment using the identical sentence stimuli, no comparable effect was observed for *initial* inanimate nominatives (Ott, 2004; see Schlesewsky and Bornkessel, 2004). Similar findings have been reported for Tamil, a Dravidian language spoken in southern India, in a study that employed a within-experiment control of animacy at the position of the first and second arguments (Muralikrishnan et al., 2008). These observations indicate that the N400 in (7b) is neither due to a lexical difference between animate and inanimate nouns nor to a principled mismatch between inanimacy and nominative case marking or to the infrequency of inanimate nominative arguments. Rather, it suggests that the role prototypicality mismatch effect results when the language comprehension system is confronted with an A argument after it has already processed a P argument. This might be due to the fact that, at the position of an initial nominative in German, the processing system cannot

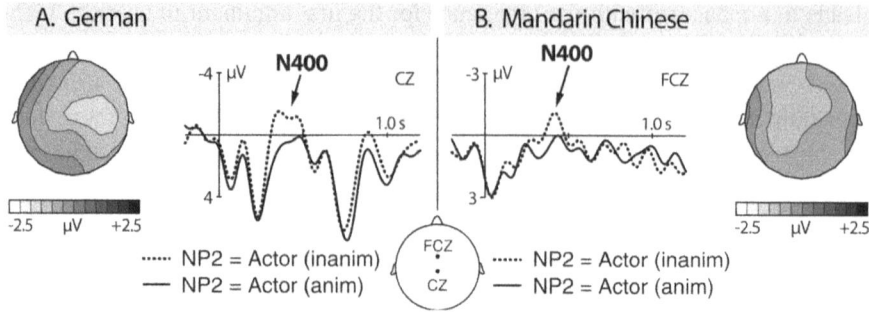

Figure 1: Grand average event-related brain potentials at the position of inanimate (dotted line) vs. animate (solid line) A arguments following a P argument in German (panel A) and Mandarin Chinese (panel B). The data are taken from Roehm et al. (2004) and Philipp et al. (2008), respectively (figure adapted from Bornkessel-Schlesewsky & Schlesewsky, 2009b). In each case, the onset of the critical argument is signalled by the vertical bar and negative voltage is plotted upwards. The topographical maps depict the scalp distribution of the N400 effect at its maximum (inanimate NP – animate NP). Note that the study on German employed visual stimulus presentation, while the stimuli in the experiment on Mandarin Chinese were presented auditorily.

unambiguously identify this argument as an A. Rather, it could also be an S argument, or even the P argument in a transitive construction.[7] Hence, a nominative NP is only clearly recognisable as an A argument after an accusative-marked NP has already been processed.

The notion that the role atypicality N400 is only apparent for arguments that are unambiguously an A receives further converging support from studies on Mandarin Chinese (Philipp et al., 2008). This language differs fundamentally from all of the languages discussed so far (English, German, Tamil) in that role

---

[7] Note that we define S, A and P in strictly semantic terms, i.e. the more agent-like and more patient-like arguments in a transitive construction are defined as A and P irrespective of their case marking (see Bickel, 2010). Accordingly, an example of a nominative-marked P-argument in German is given in (i):

(i) Gestern wurde dem Jungen das Fahrrad gestohlen.
 yesterday was [the boy]:DAT [the bicycle]:NOM stolen
 'The boy had his bicycle stolen yesterday.'

In example (i), the inanimate nominative *das Fahrrad* ('the bicycle') is the P-argument, thereby illustrating that the overt morphological case marking of a single argument does not unambiguously determine the argument role of that argument in German. Note, however, that nominative-marked P arguments only occur in sentences with dative-marked co-arguments (see, for example Fanselow, 2000; Wunderlich, 1997). Therefore, a nominative following an initial accusative can be unambiguously identified as an A argument.

identification is governed neither by word order (as in English) nor by morphological case marking (as in German and Tamil). Notably, Chinese allows considerably more word order variation than English, permitting OSV, SOV and VOS orders in spoken language (Li et al., 1993; for acceptability ratings of SOV and OSV orders with varying combinations of argument animacy, see also Wang et al., 2012). Nevertheless, just as in German, the processing of an unambiguous inanimate A argument following a P argument gave rise to an N400 effect in the bèi-construction in Mandarin Chinese (8b vs. 8a; Philipp et al., 2008; see also Figure 1B).[8] This finding corroborates the conclusion that prototypicality effects appear to be tied to A-arguments for several reasons. Firstly, using further experimental conditions, Phillip and colleagues contrasted the same groups of animate and inanimate nouns that engendered an N400 difference for sentences such as (8b) v.s (8a) in the sentence-initial position and found no difference in terms of ERPs. Thus, once again, the effect in question does not appear to result from simple animacy differences at the single argument level. Secondly, Philipp and colleagues also examined A-before-P orders in the so-called bǎ-construction (8c/d). In this case, no animacy-based N400 effects were observed, neither at the position of bǎ (at which point it becomes clear that the first argument is an A rather than an S) nor at the position of the second argument (at which point the relation between A and P becomes clear). These results thus suggest that the N400 for atypical A arguments only occurs when the A is encountered *after* a P.[9]

(8) Example stimuli from Philipp et al. (2008)
 a. 王子　　被　　挑战者　　　刺死　了。
    wáng zǐ bèi tiǎo zhàn zhě cì sǐ le
    prince   bèi contender   stab   PFV
    'The prince was stabbed by the contender.'

---

[8] While the bèi-construction is often described as a type of passive, it in fact differs from "European-style" passive constructions in that it is traditionally associated with an adversative reading, i.e. a reading in which the first NP (the P) is negatively affected by the event described (e.g. Bisang, 2006; Chappell, 1986).

[9] This interpretation was corroborated by an additional experiment (Philipp et al., 2008, Experiment 2), in which the order of the arguments was reversed by the use of relative clause constructions (e.g. 把挑战者刺死了的小刀褪色了。lit: bǎ contender stab-PERF de knife bleach-PERF, 'The knife that stabbed the contender was bleached.'). At the position of the head noun (e.g. knife), an N400 was observed for inanimate vs. animate head nouns (i.e. for inanimate A arguments encountered after a P argument) in exactly the same bǎ-constructions that did not engender such an effect when the A argument preceded the P argument.

b. 王子　　被　　绳子　　勒死　　了。
   wáng zǐ　bèi　shéng　zilēi sǐ　le
   prince　bèi　cord　strangle　PFV
   'The prince was strangled by the cord.'

c. 王子　　把　　挑战者　　　刺死　　了
   wáng zǐ　bǎ　tiǎo zhàn zhě　cì sǐ　le
   prince　bǎ　contender　stab　PFV
   'The prince stabbed the contender.'

d. 小刀　　把　　挑战者　　　刺死　　了。
   xiǎo dāo　bǎ　tiǎo zhàn zhě　cì sǐ　le
   knife　bǎ　contender　stab　PFV
   'The knife stabbed the contender.'

When taken together, the results discussed in the preceding paragraphs provide evidence for the following five claims:

(i) *Atypical role assignments are reflected in N400 effects*. In terms of event-related brain potentials, atypical role assignments are reflected in modulations of N400 components.
(ii) *Verb-independence*. As these effects are observable prior to the verb, they attest to the verb-independence of role prototypicality assessment, i.e. to abstract, verb-independent role categories.
(iii) *Role based asymmetry*. Role atypicality effects are not observable for all roles (S/A/P) in an equal manner. Specifically, they appear to be tied closely to A arguments, rather than to S or P arguments. In addition, the asymmetry of the effect (i.e. the "A-after-P" requirement) indicates that it cannot be reduced to the degree of lexical fit (or semantic association) between the arguments.
(iv) *Relationality*. Role atypicality effects for A arguments are only observable in the context of a second argument, e.g. in a P-before-A order. This suggests that the effect is tied to the relation between the arguments rather than arising from a simple matching to a single prototype for A arguments.
(v) *Cross-linguistic generalisation*. The N400 effects for role atypicality are qualitatively similar across a range of typologically different languages from different language families. Moreover, previous behavioural results show that the languages discussed here differ considerably with respect to the relative weighting of animacy as a cue to role identification (MacWhinney et al., 1984; Li et al., 1993). This observation suggests that the neural response to role prototypicality mismatches is, at least to some degree, independent of the weighting of a particular prominence feature within the language under consideration (for further details, see Bornkessel-Schlesewsky and Schlesewsky, 2009b).

In summary, the finding of role atypicality-based N400 effects in grammatical and plausible sentences across the range of languages studied here provides converging support for the interface view: it shows that the brain's reaction to a particular dimension of prominence is independent of that dimension's language-specific weighting / degree of grammaticalisation. This observation speaks against the assumption of functionally separable roles for syntactic and non-syntactic features during sentence processing. It also calls into question whether prominence features such as animacy exert a "heuristic" influence on role identification that is qualitatively distinguishable from a full, algorithmic syntactic analysis.

In addition, the data discussed above show an intriguing generalisation, namely that role atypicality effects appear to be specific to A-arguments encountered in the context of other arguments. In the following section, we describe a model that (a) provides a cognitive motivation for the cross-linguistic importance of prominence scales in language comprehension; and (b) accounts for the asymmetries with regard to the locus of role atypicality effects.

5 Why prominence scales? The actor role as a possible cognitive (neural) attractor

The preceding section discussed in detail how prototypical and non-prototypical roles are processed across languages of different types. The evidence reviewed there provides compelling support for the notion that prominence features such as animacy affect processing in a qualitatively similar manner in a range of typologically diverse languages. In this section, we will argue that these findings – and particularly the fact that they are not distributed equally across all roles and all sentence contexts – can be explained with reference to a general processing strategy, which we term the "actor identification strategy" (AIS). The AIS is described in (9)

(9) Actor Identification Strategy (AIS)
 The processing system attempts to identify the actor role – i.e. the participant primarily responsible for the state of affairs under discussion – as quickly and unambiguously as possible.
 Corollaries:
 a. The processing system prefers actor-initial orders.
 b. (Potential) arguments compete for the actor role.

Actor is a prototype concept, with a number of characteristic properties. These are given in (10).

(10) Properties characterising the actor prototype (Primus, 2006, p. 55)
    a. ctrl(x,s)   x controls the situation s denoted by the predicate
    b. exp(x,y)   x is sentient of y
    c. phys(x,y), x physically contacts or moves y;
        phys(x)   x moves or is active
    d. poss(x,y)   x possesses y

In the basic predicates in (10), x is the actor and y is the undergoer. Crucially, the way in which the y-participant is involved in the event is dependent on the type of involvement of the x-participant, i.e. a y-participant is controlled via the presence of a controller, moved via the presence of a mover, experienced via the presence of an experiencer etc. (for a detailed motivation via basic notions of causality, see Primus, 2006, section 3). An additional generalisation over all the basic predicates in (10) is that only the actor argument need exist independently of the event described, while the undergoer need not (for the property of independent existence, see also Dowty, 1991). There is thus a fundamental asymmetry between the actor and undergoer roles in that only the actor is associated with a set of prototypical properties, while the undergoer is not (i.e. its properties depend on those of the actor).[10] A consequence of this is that S arguments are never categorised as undergoers: "[A]rguments of different intransitive verbs can only be distinguished by the number of agentive properties they accumulate or by aspectual factors. An argument that does not bear any involvement property (e.g. John is tall) does not automatically qualify for a Patient or Theme" (Primus, 200659). Crucially, the actor properties in (10) are closely correlated with the prominence features discussed in the preceding sections of this chapter. These are repeated in a slightly revised fashion in (11).

---

[10] In accordance with this observation, there has been some debate in language typology as to whether, across the languages of the world, a prototypical transitive construction involves an inanimate or an animate undergoer (Hopper and Thompson, 1980; DeLancey, 1981; Comrie, 1989). By contrast, there is a general consensus regarding the status of prototypical actors (i.e. that they should be animate).

(11) Prominence features correlating with the actor role (Primus, 1999; Bornkessel-Schlesewsky and Schlesewsky, 2009b; Bornkessel-Schlesewsky and Schlesewsky, 2013b)

+animate (vs. – animate)
+human (vs. -human)
+definite (vs. -definite)
+1st person, "self" (vs. other)
+nominative (vs. -nominative) (in accusative languages)
+1st (argument) position (vs. other positions)

As we have argued extensively elsewhere (e.g. Schlesewsky and Bornkessel, 2004; Bornkessel and Schlesewsky, 2006; Bornkessel-Schlesewsky and Schlesewsky, 2009b), we assume that the language comprehension system makes use of the prominence features in (11) in order to deduce which argument is the actor in the sentence currently being processed. In other words, arguments compete for the actor role in accordance with their "potency to act" as indicated by their overall prominence value (i.e. their combined ranking on all of the prominence scales in 11, for a computationally more precise formulation, see Alday et al., 2014; for a model of actor-centred comprehension that aspires towards neurobiological plausibility, see Bornkessel-Schlesewsky & Schlesewsky, 2013a). Crucially, since it proceeds via prominence information, this competition can take place even in the absence of verb information. Indeed, it is this verb-independent competition for the actor role that we will focus on in the following in order to highlight the relevance of prominence scales.[11]

Evidence for the first corollary of the AIS (actor-initiality) stems from a range of electrophysiological studies in typologically varied languages, including Turkish (Demiral et al., 2008), Chinese (Wang et al., 2009) and Hindi (Choudhary et al., 2010), thus corroborating previous findings of a "subject-first preference" in European languages (e.g. Dutch (Frazier, 1987), German (e.g. Hemforth et al., 1993; Schriefers et al., 1995; Bader and Meng, 1999; Schlesewsky et al., 2000; Bornkessel et al., 2004), Italian (de Vincenzi, 1991; Penolazzi et al., 2005). Beyond these earlier findings, however, the findings from non-European languages rule out a range of interpretations for this preference based, for example, on structural simplicity, frequency or a functional advantage for subjecthood (see Wang et al., 2009, for a summary). The finding of an actor-first preference even in a split-ergative language (Hindi) further suggests that this

---

[11] This focus should, of course, not be taken to suggest that verb-specific information is not important for incremental sentence interpretation.

interpretive preference may be able to override morphosyntactic criteria – at least under certain circumstances.

The evidence for corollary (b) of the AIS (competition for actorhood) essentially stems from the results on actor prototypicality (or atypicality) that were discussed in the previous section. In this regard, however, the question of where these atypicality effects do *not* appear may be just as informative as where they do surface. Thus, recall that actor prototypicality effects are typically not found when an argument could be the sole argument in an intransitive relation (S). In addition, non-actor (P) arguments do not appear to be subject to comparable prototypicality effects, e.g. in showing a preference for inanimate Ps (for a review of the evidence in this regard, see Bornkessel-Schlesewsky & Schlesewsky, 2009b; for additional evidence from English, see Paczynski & Kuperberg, 2011). Finally, prototypicality effects for A arguments appear to be dependent on the presence of a second argument. These observations led Bornkessel-Schlesewsky and Schlesewsky (2008b) to conclude that the full range of results in this domain is best explained in terms of *competition for the actor role*. In other words: in accordance with the AIS, all arguments encountered by the processing system (more generally, all "nouny" constituents) within a sentence compete for the actor role. The degree to which they are good competitors is defined by two points: (a) their own prototypicality in terms of the actor features in (10) and the correlating prominence features in (11), and (b) the existence and prototypicality of further competitors. These assumptions explain why actor prototypicality effects are not generally observed when the argument under consideration could still be the only argument, since there is no competitor under these circumstances (Bornkessel-Schlesewsky and Schlesewsky, 2008b). Thus, actor competition effects can be derived from well-established principles of similarity-based interference (for overviews, see McElree, 2006; Lewis et al., 2006; Jonides et al., 2008). Interference increases when several elements (arguments) have overlapping properties (e.g. both are animate), thus leading to increased effort in memory retrieval because of the absence of a unique target. This accounts for the fact that actor typicality effects appear to be confined to situations in which the actor is encountered in the context of a second argument, since interference cannot arise with only a single element. This approach also explains the fact that prototypicality effects are observed for actors but not for other arguments (e.g. undergoers), since competition is *for* the actor role only (Bornkessel-Schlesewsky and Schlesewsky, 2009b; but see Alday et al., 2014, for a more detailed discussion of similarity-based interference and actor competition).

If competition for the actor role is a possible universal of language processing, as we have suggested, this raises the question of what basis there might be for such a universal (see section 1). In this regard, we propose that the actor role

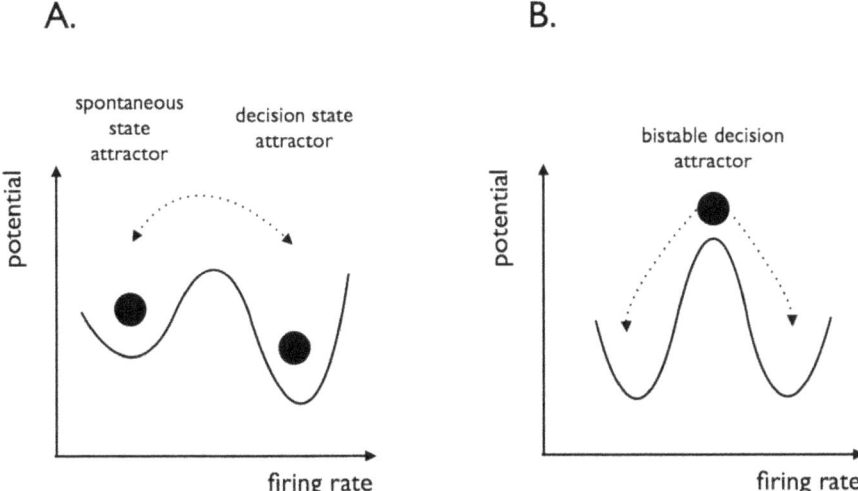

Figure 2: A. Schematic illustration of how a neural attractor network may change from a spontaneous state attractor with a low firing rate to a decision (categorisation) state attractor with a high firing rate. B. Schematic illustration of different attractor states in a neural attractor network. Crucially, the attractor state that is reached and, hence, the decision / categorisation undertaken depends both on the input and initial stochastic firing pattern of the network. Hence, the behaviour of an attractor network is non-deterministic. Both figures adapted from Deco et al. (2009), Bornkessel-Schlesewsky and Schlesewsky (2013b).

may be a candidate for a cognitive and neural *attractor category*.[12] In cognitive terms, an attractor can be envisaged as a stable, language-independent category, possibly rooted in the human ability to understand goal-directed action. The bases for this category may be related to the view of the self as an acting agent (Haggard, 2008), thus rendering the first person the basic agent prototype (Tomasello, 2003; Dahl, 2008). In neural terms, these notions could potentially be modelled by means of attractor networks (e.g. Deco et al., 2009). Attractor networks have been used in computational neuroscience to study decision making, for example. Here, decisions are modelled via attractor states in a neural network which are associated with (stable) high firing rates. Which state "wins" during decision making is determined by the current input and the initial

---

[12] This view is, in some sense, related to the perspective that Evans and Levinson (2009) present in their review of the importance of cross-linguistic diversity for cognitive science. Specifically, they propose that the "statistical distribution of typological variation suggests an evolutionary model with attractors [...], "canals," and numerous local peaks or troughs in an adaptive landscape", going on to say that "[s]ome of the attractors are cognitive" (2009, p. 446).

stochastic firing behaviour of the network. This is illustrated schematically in Figure 2A, while Figure 2B illustrates the transition from a spontaneous stable network state with a low firing rate to a decision state with a high firing rate.

The decision states in Figure 2 can essentially also be viewed as states that allow for a categorisation, for example of an entity as an actor. We could assume, then, that an attractor network for actor categorisation exists independently of language and that, as a result of the general human ability to recognise goal-directed action and to differentiate between self and other, it is universal. The stable firing patterns inherent to this network will be based on sets of input features that co-occur in domain-general actor recognition. The linguistic actor category overlaps to a certain degree with these general features (e.g. via the features +human, +animate and +1st person), thus leading to a propensity for actor recognition via the general attractor network. With regard to more language-specific features (e.g. case marking), the system will learn that these correlate with the remaining actor features such that, in the mature system, they also push the network towards the actor recognition attractor state (for further discussion, see also Alday et al., 2014).[13]

In summary, the notion of actor as a cognitive and neural attractor category can account for the importance of this category in cross-linguistic language comprehension. It is also compatible with the variation described in the preceding section: for the purposes of producing an attractor state within the network, it appears natural that the overlap between a linguistic actor and acting agents in general will be conditioned by language-specific properties, e.g. the strength of a particular cue for determining actorhood. In addition, attractors have the advantage that they naturally allow for exceptions: they are stable, but not irreversible states in a non-deterministic system. Thus, in contrast to linguistic universals in the traditional sense, they provide a possible explanation for why some patterns occur frequently in the languages of the world while nevertheless not being exceptionless.[14]

---

[13] In this context, one might ask whether the actor category is, in fact, one that emerges as a result of the interplay between general cognitive properties and the properties of the language being learnt, as has been proposed for categorisation in other domains (e.g. Bowerman and Choi, 2001; Choi, 2006). If this were the case, one could expect to find "Whorfian" effects on actor categorisation. This has, to the best of our knowledge, not been investigated to date.

[14] In addition, the interaction of several attractors may serve to produce more complex patterns than would be expected on the basis of a single attractor.

6 Neuroanatomical evidence for a non-linguistic actor attractor network

Having proposed that the ubiquitous effects of the actor category on language comprehension in different languages could be due to an actorhood attractor based on more general cognitive properties, we would now like to underscore this proposal with some concrete evidence. Specifically, we will describe findings from functional neuroimaging which demonstrate that the brain regions involved in actor identification in language also appear to support non-linguistic processes of recognising actors. The results discussed in this section stem from experiments using functional magnetic resonance imaging (fMRI), a method which can reveal stimulus- or task-related changes in the activation of neural regions based on relative blood oxygenation. In contrast to EEG/ERP data, fMRI offers a very high spatial resolution, thereby allowing for the precise localisation of brain functions. However, its temporal resolution is relatively poor due to the delay of the haemodynamic response. For an introduction to fMRI as applied to sentence and discourse processing, see Bornkessel-Schlesewsky and Friederici (2007); for a more detailed introduction to the methodological details directed at a linguistic audience, see Bornkessel-Schlesewsky and Schlesewsky (2009a).

A region that appears to be particularly important for the processing of actor information is the posterior portion of the left superior temporal sulcus (pSTS), the location of which is depicted in Figure 3. Increased activation in the pSTS arises whenever the A-argument does not outrank the P-argument in terms of some dimension of prominence. This has been demonstrated for both animacy (Grewe et al., 2006; Grewe et al., 2007) and definiteness/specificity (Bornkessel-Schlesewsky et al., 2009). For example, sentences such as (12a), in which both the A and the P arguments are animate and definite, engender increased activation in this region in comparison to sentences such as (12b), in which the A-argument is animate and the P-argument is inanimate. Note that this activation difference is unlikely to be due to a difference of animacy at the word level (i.e. to the processing of two animate arguments as opposed to one animate and one inanimate argument) as this is known to engender activation differences in other neural regions (for a detailed discussion, see Grewe et al., 2007).

(12) Example stimuli from Grewe et al. (2007)
    a. Wahrscheinlich hat der Mann den Direktor gepflegt.
        probably has [the man]:NOM [the director]:ACC cared.for
        'The man probably took care of the director.'
    b. Wahrscheinlich hat der Mann den Garten gepflegt.
        probably has [the man]:NOM [the garden]:ACC cared.for
        'The man probably took care of the garden.'

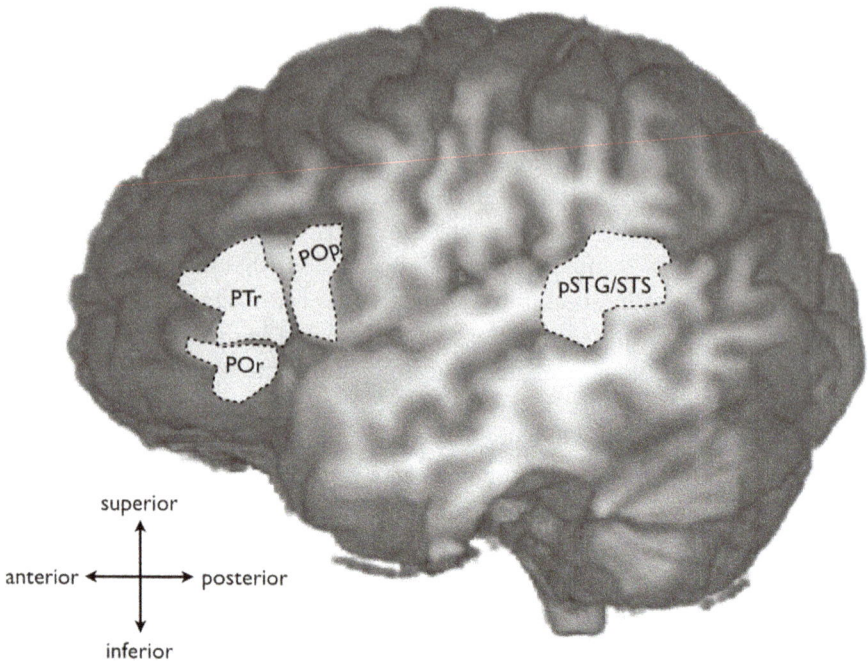

Figure 3: Lateral view of the left hemisphere of the human brain. The following regions are identified schematically: pSTG/STS – posterior superior temporal gyrus / sulcus; POp – pars opercularis of the inferior frontal gyrus (IFG); PTr – pars triangularis of the IFG; POr – pars orbitalis of the IFG.

These findings provide a first indication that the pSTS may be crucially involved in the assessment of role prototypicality during language comprehension. Importantly, this region (or its right-hemispheric homologue) has also been implicated in the inference of agency (Frith and Frith, 1999) and the processing of goal-directed action (Saxe, 2006) in non-linguistic tasks. It also shows increased activation for biological vs. non-biological motion (Grezes et al., 2001; Saygin et al., 2004) and when autonomous, goal-directed movements of geometrical shapes gives rise to the percept of animacy (Schultz et al., 2005). Thus, the pSTS appears to provide an interface between the comprehension of (linguistically expressed) transitive events and more general cognitive mechanisms for the processing of actor features (e.g. autonomous movement, goal-directedness, sentience) in the understanding of actions and events.

Effects of prominence information have also been observed in a cortical region distinct from the pSTS, namely within the pars opercularis (POp) of the left inferior frontal gyrus (lIFG). This region (see Figure 3 for its location) forms part of one of the most well-known classical language "centres", namely Broca's area. Sensitivity to prominence scales within the POp has been most readily apparent in studies examining the processing of word order variations. Thus, the POp shows increased activation whenever, in a transitive sentence, the first argument (in terms of linear order) is outranked by the second argument on one of the prominence scales in (11). This has been demonstrated for case marking (e.g. Röder et al., 2002; Friederici et al., 2006; Kinno et al., 2008), animacy (Grewe et al., 2006), definiteness/specificity (Bornkessel-Schlesewsky et al., 2009) and pronominality (Grewe et al., 2005) as two aspects of referentiality, as well as for generalised semantic roles (Bornkessel et al., 2005). Strikingly, all of these information sources modulate activation within the same neural region – the POp – thus suggesting that semantic prominence scales such as animacy and referentiality affect the neural processing of word order in a qualitatively similar manner to morphosyntactic prominence scales such as case marking.

In summary, functional imaging results have revealed that the processing of prominence information in sentence comprehension draws upon a left-lateralised fronto-temporal neural network comprising the pars opercularis of the inferior frontal gyrus and the posterior superior temporal sulcus. This assumption is further supported by data from English, which has shown that animacy information serves to modulate (or even neutralise) the activation of Broca's region in the processing of object relative clauses, in addition to influencing activation in left posterior superior temporal regions (Chen, West, Waters, & Caplan, 2006). Existing findings thus suggest that the pars opercularis is particularly involved in mapping prominence information onto linear order, with a general preference for more prominent arguments to precede less prominent arguments. The pSTS, by contrast, engages in the relational construction of an argument hierarchy, with a preference for natural transitivity (i.e. for the A-argument to outrank the P-argument on all available dimensions of prominence).

7 Conclusions

To conclude, there is a good deal of empirical evidence to suggest that prominence scales play a central role in real-time language comprehension, particularly in allowing for online role assignments and the assessment of role prototypicality. Moreover, rather than being dissociated from "classic" morphosyntactic features, semantic scales such as animacy fulfil qualitatively similar functions to these in the comprehension process and show activation in similar neural networks. They also engender highly comparable neurophysiological responses across typologically different languages and this is independent of their language specific weighting (importance for the comprehension process). We have argued that the ubiquity of scales in language processing can be traced back to their origin as characteristics of the actor attractor category, via which language neurally interfaces with the human ability to understand goal-directed action. Hence, in spite of their centrality in comprehension, scales are nevertheless an epiphenomenon of the actor concept.

Appendix A: A brief introduction to event-related brain potentials (ERPs) in language research

Event-related brain potentials (ERPs) are small changes in the spontaneous electrical activity of the brain, which occur in response to sensory or cognitive stimuli and which may be measured non-invasively by means of electrodes applied to the scalp. ERPs provide a very high temporal resolution, which is particularly useful as a means of tracking real time language processing. Furthermore, ERP patterns ('components') can be characterised along a number of different dimensions, thus providing a qualitative measure of the different processes involved in language comprehension. These dimensions are: polarity (negative vs. positive), topography (at which electrode sites an effect is visible), latency (the time at which the effect is visible relative to the onset of a critical stimulus), and amplitude (the "strength" of an effect). While a number of language-related ERP components have been identified (cf., for example, Kutas et al., 2006), we will not introduce these here for the sake of brevity. For a more detailed description of the ERP methodology and how it has been applied to psycholinguistic domains of investigation, the reader is referred to the overviews presented in Coles and Rugg (1995), Garnsey (1993), and Kutas and Van Petten (1994).

The ERP methodology only provides relative measures, i.e. an effect always results from the comparison of a critical condition with a minimally differing control condition. For example, at the position of *socks* in He spread the warm bread with *socks* in comparison to the position of *butter* in He spread the warm bread with *butter*, a negativity with a central distribution and a maximum at 400 ms post critical word onset (N400) is observable (Kutas and Hillyard, 1980). Thus, in the experiments discussed here, we always compare the response to a critical condition with that to a control condition at a particular (critical) position in the sentence.

A schematic illustration of the ERP methodology is shown in Figure 4.

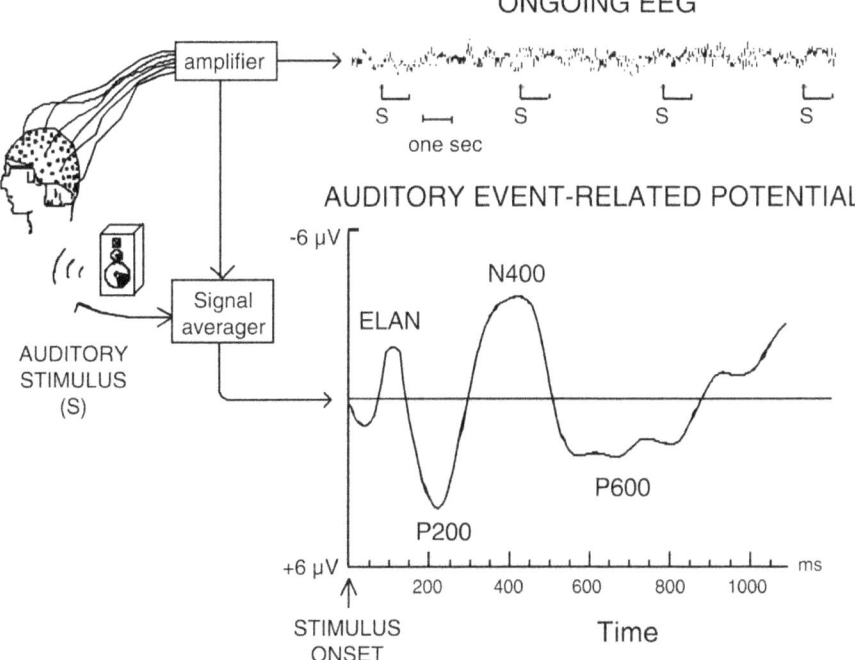

Figure 4: Schematic depiction of the setup of an ERP experiment on language processing (adapted from Coles & Rugg 1995). The ongoing EEG is recorded while participants read or listen to linguistic stimuli. Critical stimulus-related activity is isolated from the background electrical activity of the brain by means of an averaging procedure, which applies to a set of stimuli (typically 30–40) of the same type. The resulting event-related brain potential, which is shown in the bottom right-hand corner of the figure, consists of a series of negative and positive potential changes. Note that, by convention, negativity is plotted upwards. The x-axis depicts time (in miliseconds or seconds) from critical stimulus onset (which occurs at the vertical bar), while the y-axis depicts voltage in microvolts. ERP components are typically named according to their polarity (N for negativity vs. P for positivity) and latency (an N400, for example, is a negativity with a peak latency of approximately 400 ms relative to critical stimulus onset). ERP comparisons are always relative, meaning that negativities or positivities in a critical condition can only be interpreted relative to a control condition and not in absolute terms (i.e. relative to the zero-line).

References

Alday, Phillip, Matthias Schlesewsky & Ina Bornkessel-Schlesewsky. 2014. Towards a computational model of actor-based language comprehension. *Neuroinformatics* 12. 143–179.
Bader, Markus & Michael Meng. 1999. Subject-object ambiguities in German embedded clauses: An across-the-board comparison. *Journal of Psycholinguistic Research* 28. 121–143.

Bates, Elizabeth et al. 1982. Functional constraints on sentence processing: A cross-linguistic study. *Cognition* 11. 245–299.
beim Graben, Peter et al. 2000. Symbolic dynamics of event-related brain potentials. *Physical Review E* 62. 5518–5541.
Bever, Thomas G. 1970. The cognitive basis for linguistic structures. In J.R. Hayes (ed.) *Cognition and the development of language*, 279–362. New York: Wiley.
Bickel, Balthasar. 2010. Grammatical relations typology. In Jae Jung Song (ed.) *The Oxford Handbook of Language Typology*, 399–444. Oxford: Oxford University Press.
Bisang, Walter. 2006. From meaning to syntax: semantic roles and beyond. In Ina Bornkessel, Matthias Schlesewsky, Bernard Comrie & Angela D. Friederici (eds.) *Semantic role universals and argument linking: theoretical, typological and psycholinguistic perspectives*, Berlin: Mouton de Gruyter.
Bornkessel-Schlesewsky, Ina & Matthias Schlesewsky. 2008a. An alternative perspective on "semantic P600" effects in language comprehension. *Brain Research Reviews* 59. 55–73.
Bornkessel-Schlesewsky, Ina & Matthias Schlesewsky. 2008b. Unmarked transitivity: A processing constraint on linking. In Robert D. Van Valin, Jr. (ed.) *Investigations of the syntax-semantics-pragmatics interface*, 413–434. Amsterdam: John Benjamins.
Bornkessel-Schlesewsky, Ina & Matthias Schlesewsky. 2009a. *Processing syntax and morphology: A neurocognitive perspective*. Oxford: Oxford University Press.
Bornkessel-Schlesewsky, Ina & Matthias Schlesewsky. 2009b. The role of prominence information in the real time comprehension of transitive constructions: A cross-linguistic approach. *Language and Linguistics Compass* 3. 19–58.
Bornkessel-Schlesewsky, Ina & Matthias Schlesewsky. 2013a. Reconciling time, space and function: A new dorsal-ventral stream model of sentence comprehension. *Brain and Language* 125. 60–76.
Bornkessel-Schlesewsky, Ina & Matthias Schlesewsky. 2013b. Neurotypology: Modelling cross-linguistic similarities and differences in the neurocognition of language comprehension. In Montserrat Sanz, Itziar Laka & Michael K. Tanenhaus (eds.) *The Cognitive and Biological Basis for Linguistic Structure: New approaches and enduring Themes*, 241–252. Oxford: Oxford University Press.
Bornkessel-Schlesewsky, Ina, Matthias Schlesewsky & D. Yves von Cramon. 2009. Word order and Broca's region: Evidence for a supra-syntactic perspective. *Brain and Language* 111. 125–139.
Bornkessel-Schlesewsky, Ina D. & Angela D. Friederici. 2007. Neuroimaging studies of sentence and discourse comprehension. In M. Gareth Gaskell (ed.) *The Oxford handbook of psycholinguistics*, 407–424. Oxford: Oxford University Press.
Bornkessel, Ina et al. 2004. Multi-dimensional contributions to garden path strength: Dissociating phrase structure from case marking. *Journal of Memory and Language* 51. 495–522.
Bornkessel, Ina & Matthias Schlesewsky. 2006. The Extended Argument Dependency Model: A neurocognitive approach to sentence comprehension across languages. *Psychological Review* 113. 787–821.
Bornkessel, Ina et al. 2005. Who did what to whom? The neural basis of argument hierarchies during language comprehension. *NeuroImage* 26. 221–233.
Bowerman, Melissa & Soonja Choi. 2001. Shaping meanings for language: Universal and language-specfifc in the acquisition of spatial semantic categories. In Melissa Bowerman & Stephen C. Levinson (eds.) *Language acquisition and conceptual development*, 475–511. Cambridge: Cambridge University Press.

Brouwer, H., H. Fitz & John C.J. Hoeks. 2012. Getting real about semantic illusions: Rethinking the functional role of the P600 in language comprehension. *Brain Research* 1446. 127–143.

Chappell, Hilary. 1986. Formal and colloquial adversity passive in standard Chinese. *Linguistics* 24. 1025–1052.

Choi, Soonja. 2006. Influence of language-specific input on spatial cognition: Categories of containment. *First Language* 26. 207–232.

Choudhary, Kamal K. et al. 2010. An Actor-preference in a split-ergative language: Electrophysiological evidence from Hindi. *23rd Annual Meeting of the CUNY Conference on Human Sentence Processing*.

Coles, Michael G. H. & Rugg, Michael D. 1995. Event-related brain potentials: An introduction. In Michael D. Rugg and Michael G. H. Coles (eds.), *Electrophysiology of mind: Event-related brain potentials and cognition*, 1–26. Oxford, UK: Oxford University Press.

Comrie, Bernard. 1978. Ergativity. In W.P. Lehmann (ed.) *Syntactic typology: Studies in the phenomenology of language*, Austin, TX: University of Texas Press.

Comrie, Bernard. 1989. *Linguistic universals and language typology*. Oxford: Blackwell.

Crocker, Matthew W. 1994. On the nature of the principle-based sentence processor. In Charles Clifton, Jr., Lyn Frazier & Keith Rayner (eds.) *Perspectives on sentence processing*, 245–266. Hillsdale: Erlbaum.

Dahl, Östen. 2008. Animacy and egophoricity: Grammar, ontology and phylogeny. *Lingua* 118. 141–150.

de Vincenzi, Marica. 1991. *Syntactic parsing strategies in Italian*. Dordrecht: Kluwer.

Deco, Gustavo, Edmund T. Rolls & Ranulfo Romo. 2009. Stochastic dynamics as a principle of brain function. *Progress in Neurobiology* 88. 1–16.

DeLancey, Scott. 1981. An interpretation of split ergativity and related patterns. *Language* 57. 626–657.

Demiral, Şükrü Barış, Matthias Schlesewsky & Ina Bornkessel-Schlesewsky. 2008. On the universality of language comprehension strategies: Evidence from Turkish. *Cognition* 106. 484–500.

Dixon, Robert M.W. 1994. *Ergativity*. Cambridge: Cambridge University Press.

Dowty, David. 1991. Thematic proto-roles and argument selection. *Language* 67. 547–619.

Evans, Nicholas & Stephen Levinson. 2009. The myth of language universals: Language diversity and its importance for cognitive science. *Behavioral and Brain Sciences* 32. 429–492.

Fanselow, Gisbert. 2000. Optimal exceptions. In Barbara Stiebels & Dieter Wunderlich (eds.) *Lexicon in Focus*, 173–209. Berlin: Akademie Verlag.

Ferreira, Fernanda. 2003. The misinterpretation of noncanonical sentences. *Cognitive Psychology* 47. 164–203.

Ferreira, Fernanda, V. Ferraro & K.G.D. Bailey. 2002. Good-enough representations in language processing. *Current Directions in Psychological Science* 11. 11–15.

Ferreira, Fernanda & Nikole D. Patson. 2007. The 'good enough' approach to language comprehension. *Language and Linguistics Compass* 1. 71–83.

Frazier, Lyn. 1978. *On comprehending sentences: Syntactic parsing strategies*. University of Connecticut dissertation.

Frazier, Lyn. 1987. Syntactic processing: Evidence from Dutch. *Natural Language and Linguistic Theory* 5. 519–559.

Frazier, Lyn & Charles Clifton, Jr. 1996. *Construal*. Cambridge, MA: MIT Press.

Frazier, Lyn & Giovanni B. Flores d'Arcais. 1989. Filler-driven parsing: A study of gap filling in Dutch. *Journal of Memory and Language* 28. 331–344.
Frazier, Lyn & Keith Rayner. 1982. Making and correcting errors during sentence comprehension: Eye movements in the analysis of structurally ambiguous sentences. *Cognitive Psychology* 14. 178–210.
Friederici, Angela D. et al. 2006. Processing linguistic complexity and grammaticality in the left frontal cortex. *Cerebral Cortex* 16. 1709–1717.
Frisch, Stefan & Matthias Schlesewsky. 2001. The N400 indicates problems of thematic hierarchizing. *Neuroreport* 12. 3391–3394.
Frith, Christopher D. & Uta Frith. 1999. Interacting minds – a biological basis. *Science* 286. 1692–1695.
Garnsey, Susan M. 1993. Event-related brain potentials in the study of language: An introduction. *Language and Cognitive Processes* 8. 337–356.
Gibson, Edward. 1998. Linguistic complexity: Locality of syntactic dependencies. *Cognition* 68. 1–76.
Grewe, Tanja et al. 2007. The role of the posterior superior temporal sulcus in the processing of unmarked transitivity. *Neuroimage* 35. 343–352.
Grewe, Tanja et al. 2006. Linguistic prominence and Broca's area: The influence of animacy as a linearization principle. *Neuroimage* 32. 1395–1402.
Grewe, Tanja et al. 2005. The emergence of the unmarked: A new perspective on the language-specific function of Broca's area. *Human Brain Mapping* 26. 178–190.
Grezes, J. et al. 2001. Does perception of biological motion rely on specific brain regions? *Neuroimage* 13. 775–785.
Haggard, Patrick. 2008. Human volition: towards a neuroscience of will. *Nature Reviews Neuroscience* 9. 934–946.
Hagoort, P. 2008. The fractionation of spoken language understanding by measuring electrical and magnetic brain signals. *Philosophical Transactions of the Royal Society B* 363. 1055–1069.
Hemforth, Barbara, Lars Konieczny & Gerhard Strube. 1993. Incremental syntax processing and parsing strategies. (eds.) *Proceedings of the 15th Annual Conference of the Cognitive Science Society*, 539–545. Hillsdale, NJ: Erlbaum.
Hoeks, John C.J., Laurie A. Stowe & G. Doedens. 2004. Seeing words in context: The interaction of lexical and sentence level information during reading. *Cognitive Brain Research* 19. 59–73.
Hopper, Paul & Sandra A. Thompson. 1980. Transitivity in grammar and discourse. *Language* 56. 251–299.
Jonides, John et al. 2008. The mind and brain of short-term memory. *Annual Review of Psychology* 59. 193–224.
Kamide, Yuki & Don C. Mitchell. 1999. Incremental pre-head attachment in Japanese parsing. *Language and Cognitive Processes* 14. 631–662.
Kim, Albert & Lee Osterhout. 2005. The independence of combinatory semantic processing: Evidence from event-related potentials. *Journal of Memory and Language* 52. 205–225.
Kinno, Ryuta et al. 2008. Neural correlates of noncanonical syntactic processing revealed by a picture sentence matching task. *Human Brain Mapping* 29. 1015–1027.
Kolk, Herman H.J. et al. 2003. Structure and limited capacity in verbal working memory: A study with event-related potentials. *Brain and Language* 85. 1–36.

Kuperberg, Gina R. et al. 2007. The role of animacy and thematic relationships in processing active English sentence: evidence from event-related potentials. *Brain and Language* 100. 223–237.
Kuperberg, Gina R. et al. 2003. Electrophysiological distinctions in processing conceptual relationships within simple sentences. *Cognitive Brain Research* 17. 117–129.
Kutas, Marta & Kara D. Federmeier. 2000. Electrophysiology reveals semantic memory use in language comprehension. *Trends in Cognitive Sciences* 4. 463–469.
Kutas, Marta & Steven A. Hillyard. 1980. Reading senseless sentences: Brain potentials reflect semantic incongruity. *Science 207.* 203–205.
Kutas, Marta & Cyma Van Petten. 1994. Psycholinguistics electrified. In Morton Ann Gernsbacher (ed.) *Handbook of Psycholinguistics*, 83–143. New York: Academic Press.
Kutas, Marta, Cyma Van Petten & Robert Kluender. 2006. Psycholinguistics electrified II (1994–2005). In Matthew Traxler & Morton Ann Gernsbacher (eds.) *Handbook of Psycholinguistics*, 659–724. London: Elsevier.
Lau, E., C. Phillips & D. Poeppel. 2008. A cortical network for semantics: (de)constructing the N400. *Nature Reviews Neuroscience* 9. 920–933.
Lewis, Richard L., Shravan Vasishth & Julie A. Van Dyke. 2006. Computational principles of working memory in sentence comprehension. *Trends in Cognitive Sciences* 10. 447–454.
Li, Ping, Elizabeth Bates & Brian MacWhinney. 1993. Processing a language without inflections: A reaction time study of sentence interpretation in Chinese. *Journal of Memory and Language* 32. 169–192.
MacWhinney, Brian & Elizabeth Bates (eds.) 1989. *The crosslinguistic study of sentence processing*. New York: Cambridge University Press.
MacWhinney, Brian, Elizabeth Bates & Reinhold Kliegl. 1984. Cue validity and sentence interpretation in English, German and Italian. *Journal of Verbal Learning and Verbal Behavior* 23.
Marslen-Wilson, William. 1973. Linguistic structure and speech shadowing at very short latencies. *Nature* 244. 522–533.
McElree, Brian. 2006. Accessing recent events. In B.H. Ross (ed.) *The psychology of learning and motivation*, 155–200. San Diego CA: Academic Press.
Miller, George A. 1962. Some psychological studies of grammar. *American Psychologist* 17. 748–762.
Mitchell, Don C. 1994. Sentence parsing. In Morton Ann Gernsbacher (ed.) *Handbook of Psycholinguistics*, 375–409. New York: Academic Press.
Muralikrishnan, R., Matthias Schlesewsky & Ina Bornkessel-Schlesewsky. 2008. Universal and cross-linguistic influences on the processing of word order and animacy: Neurophysiological evidence from Tamil. *21st Annual CUNY Conference on Human Sentence Processing*.
Ott, Melanie. 2004. Verarbeitung von variierenden Animatheitsmerkmalen: Eine Studie zum Animatheitseinfluss bei nicht ambig kasusmarkierten W-Fragen im Deutschen.
Penolazzi, Barbara et al. 2005. Processing of temporary syntactic ambiguity in Italian "who"-questions: a study with event-related potentials. *Neuroscience Letters* 377. 91–96.
Philipp, Markus et al. 2008. The role of animacy in the real time comprehension of Mandarin Chinese: Evidence from auditory event-related brain potentials. *Brain and Language* 105. 112–133.
Primus, Beatrice. 1999. *Cases and thematic roles*. Tübingen: Niemeyer.
Primus, Beatrice. 2006. Mismatches in semantic-role hierarchies and the dimensions of role semantics. In Ina Bornkessel, Matthias Schlesewsky, Bernard Comrie & Angela D. Friederici

(eds.) *Semantic role universals and argument linking: Theoretical, typological and psycholinguistic approaches*, 53–87. Berlin: Mouton de Gruyter.

Röder, Brigitte et al. 2002. Brain activation modulated by the comprehension of normal and pseudo-word sentences of different processing demands: A functional magnetic resonance imaging study. *Neuroimage* 15. 1003–1014.

Roehm, Dietmar et al. 2004. Fractionating language comprehension via frequency characteristics of the human EEG. *Neuroreport* 15. 409–412.

Saxe, Rebecca. 2006. Uniquely human social cognition. *Current Opinion in Neurobiology* 16. 235–239.

Saygin, AP et al. 2004. Point-light biological motion perception activates human premotor cortex. *The Journal of neuroscience* 24. 6181.

Schlesewsky, Matthias & Ina Bornkessel. 2004. On incremental interpretation: Degrees of meaning accessed during sentence comprehension. *Lingua* 114. 1213–1234.

Schlesewsky, Matthias et al. 2000. The subject preference in the processing of locally ambiguous wh-questions in German. In Barbara Hemforth & Lars Konieczny (eds.) *German sentence processing*, 65–93. Dordrecht: Kluwer.

Schriefers, Herbert, Angela D. Friederici & Katja Kühn. 1995. The processing of locally ambiguous relative clauses in German. *Journal of Memory and Language* 34. 499–520.

Schultz, J. et al. 2005. Activation in posterior superior temporal sulcus parallels parameter inducing the percept of animacy. *Neuron* 45. 625–635.

Slobin, Dan I. 1966. Grammatical transformations and sentence comprehension in childhood and adulthood. *Journal of Verbal Learning and Verbal Behavior* 5. 219–227.

Stabler, Edward. 1994. The finite connectivity of linguistic structure. In Charles Clifton, Jr., Lyn Frazier & Keith Rayner (eds.) *Perspectives on sentence processing*, 303–336. Hillsdale: Erlbaum.

Sturt, Patrick & Matthew W. Crocker. 1996. Monotonic syntactic processing: A cross-linguistic study of attachment and reanalysis. *Language and Cognitive Processes* 11. 449–494.

Tomasello, Michael. 2003. *Constructing a language: a usage-based theory of language acquisition*. Cambridge, Mass.: Harvard University Press.

Townsend, David J. & Thomas G. Bever. 2001. *Sentence comprehension: The integration of habits and rules*. Cambridge, MA: MIT Press.

van de Meerendonk, Nan et al. 2009. Monitoring in language perception. *Language and Linguistics Compass* 3. 1211–1224.

van Herten, Marieke, Dorothee J. Chwilla & Herman H.J. Kolk. 2006. When heuristics clash with parsing routines: ERP evidence for conflict monitoring in sentence perception. *Journal of Cognitive Neuroscience* 18. 1181–1197.

van Herten, Marieke, Herman H.J. Kolk & Dorothee J. Chwilla. 2005. An ERP study of P600 effects elicited by semantic anomalies. *Cognitive Brain Research* 22. 241–255.

Vosse, T. & Gerard A.M. Kempen. 2000. Syntactic assembly in human parsing: A computational model based on competitive inhibition and lexicalist grammar. *Cognition* 75. 105–143.

Wang, Luming et al. 2009. Exploring the nature of the 'subject'-preference: Evidence from the online comprehension of simple sentences in Mandarin Chinese. *Language and Cognitive Processes* 24. 1180–1226.

Wang, Luming, Schlesewsky, Matthias, Philipp, Markus, & Bornkessel-Schlesewsky, Ina 2012. The role of animacy in online argument interpretation in Chinese. In Peter de Swart & Monique Lamers (eds.) *Case, word order, and prominence. Interacting cues in language production and comprehension*, pp. 91–119. Berlin: Springer.

Subject index

absolutive (case) 82, 88–89, 181–82, 223, 237, 250, 257–58, 263, 266–67, 283, 292, 297–303, 306, 308–309, 311, 313–14, 317
– *see also:* ergativity, marked absolutive
accessibility hierarchy 1, 297, 319
Actor Identification Strategy (AIS) 337, 339–40
actor (prototype, role) 322, 327, 330, 337–40, 342, 343, 344, 346
Agree 4, 175, 177–80, 183, 185–7, 190–2, 205, 207, 211, 212, 213, 215, 218, 219, 224, 227, 229, 231, 244–5, 247–8, 251–60, 261–3, 266–9
– defective Agree 177–87, 192
– multiple Agree 178, 179
– specificity-driven Agree 227, 251–5
agreement 1, 3, 4, 11, 102, 131–5, 137, 141, 144, 146, 148–51, 153–4, 157, 159, 162–3, 173, 175, 177, 180–2, 186, 187, 189–92, 198, 212, 227–34, 237–45, 251, 253, 255–8, 260, 263, 265–6, 268–9, 280–3, 285–6, 302, 313, 330, 331
– Number Agreement 144–5, 163, 178–86, 231
– Person Agreement 146–51, 163, 175, 178–86, 187, 190, 233, 256, 260
agreement displacement 230, 251, 266–8
alignment 9–13, 23, 27, 36–40, 197, 200–1, 203, 208–9, 212, 215–220, 222, 280–6, 290–1, 297–303, 306–311, 313–315, 317–319
– alignment hypothesis 299, 301–03, 306, 308
– *see also:* overt marking hypothesis
– alignment sets 10–13, 15, 20, 23–24, 26–27, 32, 40
– alignment splits (split alignment; see also: split ergativity) 4, 7, 11, 20, 23, 26, 27, 32, 39–40, 131, 275, 277, 279–81, 283–85, 287–93, 297, 299–303, 307–11, 313–15, 317–19
– aspectual (perfective/imperfective) split 95–6, 279–82, 285–91, 293

– by clause type 26, 308–15, 319
– noun-based 275, 279
– split by gender 315–18
– Tense-Aspect-Mood (TAM)-based 279, 289, 291
– Tense-Aspect-Mood (TAM)-hierarchy for alignment splits 281–85, 288, 289–93
– one-dimensional 285
– two-dimensional 287–8
– *see also:* case alignment, ergativity, harmonic alignment
alternations:
– asymmetric 291
– case 173–74, 177, 183, 187–90, 277
– direct-inverse 227, 229–31, 234–35, 238, 240, 243–44, 246, 259, 268
– fluid 277, 301
– inchoative/causative 3, 61, 63, 66–67
– symmetric 291
– transitivity 277
– zero/nonzero 8, 75–77, 87, 91, 97, 102, 106, 109, 112, 124, 125, 237–38
ambiguity 246, 278, 323, 331
– ambiguity resolution 324
animacy 3–5, 33, 94, 131, 173–76, 180–82, 186–88, 190–93, 250, 276, 277, 321, 325–37, 343–45
– animacy restriction 180–182, 192
– *see also:* scale(s)
antipassives 204, 223, 281, 284
'anti-Silverstein' pattern 279
argument structure 215, 217, 222, 224, 277
attractor (neural) 5, 322, 337, 341–3, 346

blocking 121, 142, 162, 163

case, case marking 7–9, 11–12, 17, 20, 22, 30–31, 33, 35, 38–40, 50, 75–77, 80, 98, 103, 113, 164, 176–77, 187–90, 192, 204, 230, 257, 275–81, 289, 291, 297, 299–303, 305–06, 308–09, 313–15, 323, 325, 329, 331, 333–35, 342, 345
– discriminating function of 275–76, 302–03

– indexing or identifying function of 275–77, 293, 303
– *see also:* alternations: case; case alignment; differential argument encoding, differential case marking
case alignment 7–8, 15, 20, 40, 310, 315, 318
causatives 61–63, 66–72
– *see also:* alternations: inchoative/causative
clause type: *see* alignment splits
Clitic Binding Restriction 193–94
comparative concepts 16, 45, 52–55
constraint conjunction 80, 131, 162, 292
countercyclicity 228, 255, 269
crossing 197, 203–04, 208, 215, 216, 218, 220, 221
– one-way crossing 203, 208, 209, 212, 215, 216, 224
– reciprocal crossing 204, 221, 223
– two-way crossing 204, 219, 220, 221, 222, 223, 224

defective probe 183, 187, 192
definiteness 17, 101, 121, 173–76, 180, 190, 192, 250, 276, 287, 291, 325, 329, 331, 343, 345
– definiteness restriction 17, 182–87, 193
– *see also:* scale(s)
descriptive categories: *see* comparative concepts
diachronic bias(es) 7, 24, 30, 34, 36, 38–40
differential argument encoding, differential case-marking 3–4, 20, 22, 27–29, 40, 75–82, 84, 86–87, 89–91, 98, 102–03, 105, 112–13, 116–17, 119, 124–25, 164, 173, 177, 187–90, 192, 227, 276–79, 289, 291
– differential object marking 7, 13, 46, 50–52, 56, 81, 87, 91, 94, 101–02, 106–07, 110, 112, 117–19, 131, 275, 277, 293
– differential subject marking 7, 13, 87, 94, 95, 277, 293
differential displacement 189–92
direct marking 233, 263
direction marking 131–32, 160, 162–63, 193, 227–30, 232–34, 237, 256–57, 263, 269

– *see also:* alternations: direct-inverse, direct marking, inverse marking, inversion construction
dissimilarity matrix 3, 60, 64, 71–73
Distributed Morphology 3, 76–77, 83–84, 91–92, 100, 125, 133, 248
Distributed Optimality 133
Ditransitive Person-Role Constraint 46–47

Elsewhere Principle 136, 142–44
EPP (Extended Projection Principle) 189–91, 245, 256, 260, 269
ergative (case) 8–10, 12, 26, 36, 59, 87, 94–96, 220–21, 223, 237, 250, 257–58, 263, 266, 275–76, 278, 280–87, 290–93, 298, 303, 313–14, 316, 329
– ergative displacement 266–67
– split-ergative systems 305, 308, 339
– *see also:* ergativity, split ergativity
ergativity (ergative alignment) 37, 204, 263–64, 277, 279–82, 286, 291, 297–303, 306, 308, 313–14, 316–17
– *see also:* ergative (case), split ergativity
event-related brain potentials (ERPs) 328, 331–32, 334, 343, 346–47
expletives, expletive subjects 179, 191
extended-ergative system 298

faithfulness constraint 50, 82–84, 87, 93, 96, 98–102, 105–07, 109, 111–12, 116–17, 120–22, 124–25, 277–79, 290–291, 293
feature checking 245, 253–54, 258
feature decomposition 250
feature hierarchies 293
feature structures 101, 119–121, 124, 135–37, 139–43, 150, 153–54, 156–59, 164–67, 269
feature valuation 181, 186, 188, 190–91, 209, 212, 252–54, 258–59
– *see also:* Agree
filler-gap distance 324
functional magnetic resonance imaging (fMRI) 331, 343

gender 16, 85, 91, 104, 175, 192, 315, 317–19
generalised semantic roles 323, 345

genitive of negation 183–87
goal (Agree) 4, 177–83, 185–88, 190–92, 227, 229, 244–45, 251–56, 258–59, 261, 267, 269–70
– see also: Agree, feature valuation, probe
goal (theta role) 201–02, 204–06, 215

harmonic alignment 3, 4, 50, 75–82, 84, 87, 96–97, 105, 108, 111–12, 114, 116, 123, 125, 131–32, 162–163, 174, 203, 205, 212, 215–18, 222, 228, 275, 289
hierarchy: see animacy, definiteness, scale(s)
high-ranking arguments 10–14
– see also: low-ranking arguments

iconicity 77, 84–87, 95–96, 109, 111, 124–25, 131
imperatives 123, 260, 282–90, 292, 313
implicational hierarchy: see scale(s)
impoverishment 3, 75, 77, 81, 83–87, 89–96, 99–102, 105, 109, 111–12, 115, 118–19, 121–25, 137
inchoative(s) 61, 63, 66–72
– see also: alternation: inchoative/causative
incremental interpretation 1, 276, 322–26, 329–30, 339
inferior frontal gyrus (IFG) 344–45
interface (morphology-syntax) 76, 84, 125, 228
interface hypothesis of incremental argument interpretation 328–31, 337
inverse marking 77, 87, 90, 131, 151–52, 157, 162–63, 228, 233, 257, 263, 265–66
inversion construction 45–47, 53

language comprehension 5, 321–23, 325, 328–30, 332–33, 337, 339, 342–46
locality 229, 244, 251–52
low-ranking arguments 10–14
– see also: high-ranking arguments

markedness 10, 12–14, 20, 23, 36, 79, 90–91, 108, 110, 145, 162, 197, 203–04, 206, 216, 220, 276–81, 285, 290–91, 299, 304, 307–08

markedness constraint 49, 76, 80–82, 93, 96, 99–101, 105, 107, 109, 111–12, 117–22, 124–25, 162–63, 276–77, 291
markedness hierarchy/scale 59, 75, 79, 81, 84, 87, 108, 125, 189, 275, 290, 292–93
marked-S languages 297–300, 303–05, 307–10, 314–15, 317–18
– marked absolutive 298–99, 309, 311
– marked nominative 5, 11, 297–99, 301–02, 304–08, 310, 313–14, 316–18
Minimalist Program 174, 247–49, 269–70
Multi-Dimensional Scaling 31–32

negation 217–18
– see also: genitive of negation
N400 328, 332–37, 346, 347

Object Shift 189–91
one-dimensional scales (vs. multidimensional scales) 3, 31–32, 60, 62, 285, 287, 289, 293
Optimality Theory 1, 4, 49, 51–52, 79–80, 125, 136, 275, 289, 293
Output-Output Correspondences 293
overt marking hypothesis 299, 301–03, 306, 308
– see also: alignment hypothesis

participant (formal feature, speech-act) 17, 23, 174, 189, 192, 250, 270
passives 27, 114, 115, 177, 184, 200, 209, 219–21, 223, 238–42, 312, 327, 335
perfectivity 4, 95–96, 200–01, 207, 214, 216, 279–82, 285–91, 293
Person-Case Constraint (PCC) 4, 173–74, 177–83, 185–87, 190, 192–94, 227
Phase Impenetrability Condition (PIC) 211, 217–18, 248, 252
prefixation, prefixes 4, 46, 131, 132–34, 146, 152, 163, 165, 168, 197, 199–201, 214, 216–17, 222, 224, 232, 260, 264–66, 312
prepositions 198–201, 205, 207, 211–14, 216–17, 222–23, 239, 241
privileged syntactic argument 323

probe 4, 177–81, 183, 185–88, 191–93, 212, 227, 230, 247–48, 251–61, 266, 267–70
– *see also:* Agree, feature valuation, goal
prominence (features, information) 325–31, 336–40, 344–45
prominence (scale): *see* scale(s)
pronouns 8–10, 13–14, 16–18, 23–24, 33, 39–40, 56, 78, 81, 87, 89–90, 102–03, 105–06, 113–15, 117, 119, 137, 139, 178, 292, 300, 304–08, 315, 318
proto-roles (proto-agent, proto-patient) 10, 277

referential hierarchy: *see* scale(s)
resultatives 114, 199, 214, 281–82, 284–85, 287–88, 290–91

scale(s):
– animacy 46, 47, 50–54, 59–61, 78–79, 97, 173, 221, 232–33, 275, 287–89, 292–93, 301, 321
– case 4, 197, 202, 204–05, 208, 215, 224
– comparative 45, 52–57
– complex scale trees 197, 203–04, 206, 208–09, 212–13, 215–24
– definiteness 50, 78, 81, 97, 103, 105, 114–17, 176, 288
– descriptive 45, 47, 53, 55–57
– of form 60–62, 67, 69, 71–73
– of function 60, 64, 69–73
– generalized notion of 73
– implicational 1, 7, 45–46, 49, 51, 54–55, 57, 59, 140
– person/animacy 3, 173–76, 180, 221, 232
– person/definiteness 175–76
– prominence 4, 17, 78, 107–08, 132, 140–41, 145–46, 151, 173–74, 176, 192, 197, 202, 205–06, 227, 229, 231–32, 243, 245, 250, 260, 276, 297, 299–302, 314, 318–19, 321–22, 325–31, 337, 339, 345
– referential 2, 7–11, 14–16, 27, 39–40, 173, 300
– relational 45–47, 51, 54

– Silverstein 2–4, 8–11, 78, 81, 94, 101–02, 112, 124, 173, 187, 192, 227, 232, 269, 275–76, 300–02, 306–08
– specificity 251, 261
– theta-role 197, 202, 204–06, 208, 224
– universal 4, 7, 20, 22–24, 30, 37–39, 50, 54–56, 140, 293, 315
scrambling 4, 189, 218
semantic map 52, 60, 62–63, 69
Silverstein hierarchy: *see* scale(s)
specificity (quantitative notion) 4, 84–85, 92–93, 100–01, 105, 115, 124, 227, 229–30, 248–54, 261, 267, 269–70
– *see also:* Agree: specificity-driven
specificity (semantic notion) 17, 94, 173–74, 181–82, 192, 276, 287, 329, 343, 345
split ergativity 94, 187, 227, 275, 301
– Tense-Aspect-Mood (TAM)-based 4, 279
Strong Minimalist Thesis 174
Subset Principle 92–93, 95–96, 100–02, 122–23, 142, 248
superior temporal sulcus (STS) 343–45

telicity 114, 200, 214, 216
theta roles 206, 208, 215–16, 223
topicalization 211, 243–44
transitivity 277, 280–81, 290–91, 345

unaccusatives 184–5, 198, 209–13, 215, 301–02
undergoer (prototype) 338, 340
unergatives 184, 198, 207, 209, 302
universals 8–9, 24, 29, 32, 38–40, 46, 50, 52, 54–55, 59, 79, 140, 163, 174, 249, 288–89, 297–98, 303, 319, 321, 340, 342
– *see also:* scale(s): universal

Vocabulary Insertion 83, 92–93, 121, 133–36, 140–143, 150, 164

zero (Ø-) licensing 133, 137, 139–42, 145, 150–51, 156, 158–63

www.ingramcontent.com/pod-product-compliance
Lightning Source LLC
Chambersburg PA
CBHW070604170426
43200CB00012B/2587